STATES OF CRISIS AND
POST-CAPITALIST SCENARIOS

States of Crisis and Post-Capitalist Scenarios

HEIKO FELDNER
Cardiff University, UK

FABIO VIGHI
Cardiff University, UK

AND

SLAVOJ ŽIŽEK
University of Ljubljana, Slovenia

LONDON AND NEW YORK

First published 2014 by Ashgate Publishing

2 Park Square, Milton Park, Abingdon, Oxfordshire OX14 4RN
52 Vanderbilt Avenue, New York, NY 10017

Routledge is an imprint of the Taylor & Francis Group, an informa business

First issued in paperback 2020

British Library Cataloguing in Publication Data
A catalogue record for this book is available from the British Library

The Library of Congress has cataloged the printed edition as follows:

Feldner, Heiko.
States of crisis and post-capitalist scenarios / by Heiko Feldner, Fabio Vighi, and Slavoj Žižek
   pages cm
Includes bibliographical references and index.
ISBN 978-1-4094-6189-0 (hardback) 1. Financial crises. 2. Capitalism. I. Vighi, Fabio, 1969- II.
Žižek, Slavoj. III. Title.
HB3722.F452 2014
330.12'2–dc23

                                                                                    2013034175

ISBN 978-1-4094-6189-0 (hbk)
ISBN 978-0-367-60069-3 (pbk)

Contents

Notes on Contributors

Rex Butler is Associate Professor in the School of English, Media Studies and Art History. Although professionally he is an art historian, specializing in contemporary and Australian art, he has also written and edited a number of books on theorists including Jean Baudrillard, Slavoj Žižek and Gilles Deleuze. He is currently writing a book on Stanley Cavell.

Colin Cremin is Senior Lecturer in Sociology at the University of Auckland, New Zealand. He is the author of *Capitalism's New Clothes: Enterprise, Ethics and Enjoyment in Times of Crisis* (2011) and *iCommunism* (2012). He is currently working on the new book *Eros and Apocalypse: The Excessive Subject and the Excesses of Capitalism*, forthcoming with Pluto Press.

Jodi Dean is Professor of Political Science at Hobart and William Smith Colleges, Geneva, NY. Her research and writing focus on the contemporary space of politics and media theory. She has authored and edited several books; recent publications include: *The Communist Horizon* (2012); *Blog Theory* (2010); *Democracy and Other Neoliberal Fantasies* (2009); *Žižek's Politics* (2006); and *Publicity's Secret* (2002).

Heiko Feldner teaches German studies and political theory at Cardiff University. His publications include *Das Erfahrnis der Ordnung* (1999), *Writing History* (edited with Stefan Berger and Kevin Passmore, 2003/2010), *Did Somebody Say Ideology?* (edited with Fabio Vighi, 2007), *Žižek Beyond Foucault* (with Fabio Vighi, 2007) and *The Lost Decade? The 1950s in European History, Politics, Society and Culture* (edited with Claire Gorrara and Kevin Passmore, 2011).

Marco Grosoli is a British Academy Postdoctoral Fellow at the University of Kent (Canterbury), where he is completing a monograph on the "politique des auteurs" in 1950s *Cahiers du cinema*. He has co-edited (with Monica Dall'Asta) a book on Guy Debord's cinema and is working (with Jean-Baptiste Massuet) on a volume on motion/performance capture. He collaborates with several movie journals, among which *Film Comment, La furia umana, Filmidee, Fata morgana, Sentieri selvaggi*.

jan jagodzinski is a professor in the Department of Secondary Education, University of Alberta in Edmonton, Alberta, Canada. Recent book credits include *Youth Fantasies: The Perverse Landscape of the Media* (2004); *Musical Fantasies:*

A Lacanian Approach (2005); *Television and Youth: Televised Paranoia* (2008*);* *The Deconstruction of the Oral Eye: Art and Its Education in an Era of Designer Capitalism* (2010), *Misreading Postmodern Antigone: Marco Bellocchio's Devil in the Flesh* (*Diavolo in Corpo*) (2011); *Psychoanalyzing Cinema: A Productive Encounter of Lacan, Deleuze, and* Žižek (2012), and *Arts Based Research: A Critique and Proposal* (with Jason Wallin, 2013).

Yahya M. Madra has taught at the University of Massachusetts and at Skidmore and Gettysburg Colleges. He is currently an associate professor of economics at Boğaziçi University, Istanbul, and teaches political economy and history of economics. His work appeared in *Journal of Economic Issues, Rethinking Marxism, The European Journal of History of Economic Thought*, and *Subjectivity* as well as in edited volumes. He is a member of the editorial board of *Rethinking Marxism*. He is working on a new book (co-authored with his long-time collaborator Ceren Özselçuk), provisionally entitled *Sexuating Class: A Psychoanalytical Critique of Political Economy*.

Todd McGowan teaches theory and film at the University of Vermont. He is the author of *Enjoying What We Don't Have: The Political Project of Psychoanalysis* (2013), *Rupture: On the Emergence of the Political* (2012, with Paul Eisenstein), *Out of Time: Desire in Atemporal Cinema* (2011), and other works.

Benjamin Noys is Reader in English at the University of Chichester, and the author of Georges Bataille: A Critical Introduction (Pluto 2000), The Culture of Death (Berg 2005), The Persistence of the Negative: A Critique of Contemporary Continental Theory (Edinburgh University Press 2010), and editor of Communization and its Discontents (Minor Compositions 2011).

Ceren Özselçuk is Assistant Professor at the Department of Sociology, Boğaziçi University, Istanbul. Her research intersects the fields of post-Althusserian thought, Marxian political economy and Lacanian psychoanalysis. She is a member of the editorial board of *Rethinking Marxism* and has published in edited volumes and academic journals in English and Turkish such as *Rethinking Marxism, Psychoanalysis, Culture and Society, Subjectivity* and *Toplum ve Bilim*. She is currently completing a book entitled *Economic Necessity, Political Contingency and the Limits of Post-Marxism* (Routledge). She is also working on a new manuscript (co-authored with Yahya Madra) provisionally entitled *Sexuating Class: A Psychoanalytical Critique of Political Economy*.

Darrow Schecter is Reader in the School of History, Art History and Humanities at University of Sussex, UK. He has written books and articles on social and political thought, including *Beyond Hegemony* (2005); *The History of the Left from Marx to the Present: Theoretical Perspectives* (2007), and *Critique of Instrumental Reason from Weber to Habermas* (2010). He teaches history and political theory at the University of Sussex.

Paul Taylor is Senior Lecturer in Communications Theory at the University of Leeds, UK. His on-going research interests are focused upon critical theories of mass culture. Founding Editor of the International Journal of Žižek Studies and Editorial Board member of the International Journal of Baudrillard Studies, his recent and forthcoming monographs include: *Digital Matters: The Culture and Theory of the Matrix* (2005), *Critical Theories of Mass Culture: Then and Now* (2008); Žižek *and the Media* (2011) and *Heidegger and the Media* (forthcoming, with D. J. Gunkel).

Fabio Vighi teaches Italian studies, film and critical theory at Cardiff University. He has published widely on all of these subjects. His recent monographs are *Critical Theory and Film: Re-thinking Ideology through Film Noir* (2012), *On Žižek's Dialectics: Surplus, Subtraction, Sublimation* (2010), *Sexual Difference in European Cinema: the Curse of Enjoyment* (2009), *Žižek: Beyond Foucault* (2007, with Heiko Feldner) and *Traumatic Encounters in Italian Film* (2006).

Slavoj Žižek is a Professor at the European Graduate School, International Director at the Birkbeck Institute for the Humanities, University of London, and a senior researcher at the Department of Philosophy, University of Ljubljana. Amongst his recent books are *Less than Nothing: Hegel and the Shadow of dialectical Materialism* (2012), *The Year of Dreaming Dangerously* (2012), *Living in the End Times* (2010), *First as Tragedy, then as Farce* (2009), *In Defence of Lost Causes* (2008), *Violence* (2008).

Introduction

Heiko Feldner, Fabio Vighi and Slavoj Žižek

One of the most extraordinary events in recent history has been the imposition of austerity measures on societies that, only a few years back, were coercively indebted in a collective effort to rescue the financial system. In the autumn of 2008, we were reassured that bailout and stimulus packages would correct the situation and the crisis would be over soon. By the spring of 2011, 15 trillion dollars had been mobilized from the public purse worldwide to firefight the crisis, bringing up the total of sovereign debt to a colossal 39 trillion dollars. If this is the most efficient economic system we can think of, then we had better think again. While the finance bubble was turned into a sovereign debt bubble, we have now come full circle, only on a much higher level than in 2008 and with no leeway to repeat the operation. By the summer of 2012, it became clear that policy makers had "run out of policy rabbits to pull out of their hats," as crisis economist Nouriel Roubini (2012), who had predicted the crash, put it. Through debt we have been living on borrowed time; yet, without the prospect of real growth the issue of debt sustainability only foreshadows a much trickier one, for the covenant of capitalist societies itself is rendered nil and void.

Against this background, political commentators, analysts and activists across the political spectrum are increasingly questioning the fairy tale account of the crisis according to which it resulted from a distortion of an otherwise efficient system. The intellectual agenda has begun to shift from questions of crisis management to more fundamental questions about the systemic nature and long-term implications of the crisis. It is true, however, that, as the American anthropologist David Graeber pointed out, we are faced with a peculiar historical deadlock. On the one hand, we have good reasons to assume that within the life span of only one generation capitalism as a system of social reproduction might no longer be with us—not least, as we are reminded by ecologists, because the growth imperative cannot be maintained forever on a finite planet. On the other hand, when confronted with the prospect that capitalism might actually disintegrate, the ubiquitous response—even from some of the staunchest critics of capitalism—is outright fear. Since we have lost the collective ability to imagine an alternative that would not turn out to be worse than our current predicament, we feel compelled to put up with the increasingly destructive consequences of the multiple crisis of capitalism as they unfold before our eyes (Graeber 2011: 381f).

Taking into account the seemingly untranscendable deadlock that characterizes our historical moment, in this volume we tackle crisis both at the level of its specific historical configuration (the capitalist economy) and in conjunction with theoretical questions that aim to intersect the ontological resonance we assign to the term under consideration. From our perspective, the two approaches are inseparable. It is only by bringing the specific historical analysis to converge on the ontological dimension it broaches that a critique of crisis can bear fruit; *vice versa*, a philosophical inquiry alone would smack of resignation. To be sure, the present capitalist crisis is rooted in a wider context which contains many of its immediately recognizable features. In fact, one of the main traits of modern thought is its awareness that crisis is a condition immanent to human existence. It is widely agreed that such awareness originates in the waning of metaphysical certainties and attendant disorientation within being that emerged with the rise of abstract economic rationality and the notion of instrumental reason inscribed in it. While most nineteenth century theories of modernity are about the ascent of Western bourgeois civilization and its meta-narrative of unending progress, with the start of the twentieth century such optimistic outlooks—together with their Marxist counterpart, the teleology of the communist society to come—began to dwindle. The catastrophes of the first half of the twentieth century forced a reassessment of bourgeois and proletarian illusions, which is reflected in the works of some of the most representative thinkers of that century like Max Weber, the philosophers and sociologists of the Frankfurt School and Michel Foucault. Against this background, the devastating impact of the current economic crisis has particularized the above awareness and disorientation by rekindling the anxiety-laden sentiment of a deep fracture separating the social sphere from the domain of abstract economic laws, the latter being epitomized by the apparent complexity and sidereal aloofness of the financial sector. The ongoing crisis, in other words, would seem to have provided us with a concrete manifestation of that "malaise within modernity" first lamented by Charles Baudelaire and debated ever since. More than that, it has confirmed that such malaise should be framed less within existential parameters than within the ideological order imposed by the economic system responsible for the birth and development of what we call modernity, namely capitalism.

In so far as modernity reflects the vertiginous development of market society and its concomitant use of abstract regulative principles, crisis has often been discussed in relation to what Karl Polanyi (1957) famously labelled as a phenomenon of "disembedding," according to which the economy progressively detaches itself from traditional social mores and political principles to the extent of acquiring full autonomy from the needs of the human congregation. While Polanyi's term may well be appropriate to define the current hiatus between the fireworks of the finance sector and the real needs of the increasingly impoverished masses, it is also clear to us that such disembedding has always-already been re-embedded within an ideology that justifies every new phase of capitalist self-valorization with the seemingly unassailable truism that it serves precisely the "real needs of real people." Another, more pervasive way of presenting crisis as a consequence of a condition of uprooting that has plagued capitalist modernity since its inception, is the one that found considerable fortune within the tradition of the Frankfurt School. In Adorno and Horkheimer's groundbreaking critique of modernity, human alienation originates in the unstoppable march of instrumental reason away from human needs, with abstract exchange values subsuming all experience under the deadly spell of the equivalence principle (Adorno and Horkheimer 1997). One of the central themes of this book is a persistent sense of dissatisfaction with any dualistic framing of crisis which, as such, harks back, or forward, to its own positive overcoming.

Undoubtedly, the distinctive theoretical presupposition shared by all essays in this volume is the idea that modernity is overlaid, and crucially undermined, by what Jacques Lacan would have referred to as "capitalist signifiers," namely the language and ideology of capitalism. At the same time, however, we have to be aware of the danger represented by any self-condescending simplification—or ideological gentrification—of the term crisis, which, today more than ever, is at risk of slipping into a provocative cliché devoid of substance. One of the paradoxical consequences of our "being aware of crisis" is that the negative, disruptive potential of its notion is repressed, in line with what Stuart Hall, back in 1978—borrowing a definition coined by Stanley Cohen in his work *Folk Devils and Moral Panics* (1972)—called the displacement effect of the '*moral-panic cycle*' (Hall et al. 1978: 322). The argument, back then, was that systemic crises are displaced ideologically *via* moral discourses aimed at placating social anxiety while, most importantly, prescribing the cause of the crisis itself as its solution. Today, this is again the case with regard to our economic predicament, where ideology takes the form of surges of moral panic, often artfully turned into sour resentment, against usual suspects like the immigrants and the unemployed, but also crisis-specific targets like greedy financial speculators, Southern Europeans (with their atavistic laziness), their governments (with their corruption and economic ineptitude), and, last but not least, Europe itself. Furthermore, the above displacement is part of a more subtle and pervasive blackmail functioning as a "reality check": either we accept the harsh conditions imposed by the "ill-fated" economic conjuncture (this being the main rhetoric behind today's "austerity measures") or we shall all have to face much worse, apocalyptic scenarios. In the face of this barrage of muted yet all the more effective ideological injunctions, whose aim is to disable any serious debate over the causes of the crisis, representative democracy is either devilishly complicit with the status quo or, in a gesture of unheard-of resignation, it throws in the towel before any real fight has even started—accepting, indeed fully internalizing, the sobering call to "realism" behind which lurks a debilitating *Denkverbot*. The possibility of a "change of direction" must not even be remotely entertained.

To avoid falling into the quagmire of crisis management, with its positivistic blindness, this volume proposes to examine the crisis of capitalism alongside its ontological presuppositions. If there is an awareness we especially endorse, it is inscribed in the thought that the true difficulty, even within an epoch dominated by postmodern antifoundationalist scepticism, remains to conceive of crisis as rooted in ontological "lack," i.e. as constitutive of our being. However profoundly the notion of crisis might have infiltrated modernity's malaise, it has nevertheless been regularly offset by positive visions of its (always imminent, always-already here) overcoming. Inbuilt in the common use of the term crisis is the certainty of its temporariness. The obvious example comes from the logic of our economic predicament, increasingly naturalized as "fate": it is in the very nature of capitalism to "capitalize" on crises. And while capitalist expansion, "from crisis to crisis," would seem to prove that, so far, crisis has been a condition of possibility (of capital), the latter statement would seem to apply also to conceptual frameworks that, historically, have been regarded as progressive or revolutionary. Think of how, for instance, social antagonism for Marx is superseded by the vision of a future classless society; or how, in Freud, the same formal reference to a recalcitrant antagonistic substance tends to be confined to the psychic sphere, without affecting the composition of external social reality.

The point not to be missed when discussing crisis, then, is that our ability to tackle its historical determinations goes hand in hand with our ability to identify its ontological reverberations. The advantage of this approach to crisis is that it prevents us from relativizing its meaning, avoiding the danger of turning it into yet another piece of evidence for our "hermeneutic weakness." Rather, we believe that the only way to effectively confront the current predicament and its catastrophic impact is by intervening in the knot where "everything is decided" regarding our being in the world. Precisely because it is symptomatic of the epochal exhaustion of the "world-system" (Wallerstein 1974) dominated by the capitalist economy, the current crisis needs to be grasped at its roots, where the foundational categories of our historical episteme were and continue to be formed. By locating the ontological presuppositions upon which the capitalist paradigm stands, we have a chance to bring crisis to coincide with its notion, thus opening the way to the concrete reconfiguration of the antagonism it embodies within a radically changed social order.

The proposed volume aims to provide a framework where the current state of affairs is critically unravelled in connection with a utopian urge to think new social, political and economic scenarios. Throughout this collection of essays, the desire to expose the inconsistencies of the capitalist order is coterminous with the desire to propose visions of a changed social order. What is at stake in each contribution is the effort to conceive of the critique of today's crisis as inevitably bound up with a creative intervention whose goal is to theorize new social horizons.

The volume is divided into three interrelated sections, each focussing on one of the key terms of our analysis: *Crises, Events, Scenarios*. The first section opens with an essay by Heiko Feldner and Fabio Vighi. The aim of this essay is to articulate a critique of the current economic crisis from two complementary angles: a Marxian and a Lacanian critique of the value-form as the disavowed matrix of capitalist modernity. The first part of the essay develops a Marxian reading of the economic crisis which substantiates the claim that, given its vanishing capacity to generate surplus-value, capitalism as a historical form of social reproduction is in terminal decline. The second part focuses on Jacques Lacan's critique of work as developed especially in *Seminars XVI* to *XVIII*. It examines Lacan's contention that the ruse of modernity lies in transforming the unconscious roots of knowledge-at-work into countable entities. In the following essay, Jodi Dean takes up Žižek's discussion of drive to argue that, as a force of loss, the notion of drive should be seen as a central formation of communicative capitalism in so far as the latter relies on a constant state of imbalance, i.e. on the repeated suspension of narratives, patterns, identities and norms. Although Dean's discussion draws heavily on Žižek, it proposes a significantly different understanding of drive as a political category. In the third essay of the first section, Benjamin Noys assesses how the fracturing of the until recently "untrenscendable horizon" of capitalism impacts on the theoretical articulation of radical alternatives. More specifically, Noys examines the role of utopia for critical thinking. While arguing that capitalism itself, as a self-engendering productive system, relies on "default utopianism," Noys contends that the main problem with today's anti-capitalist utopian thought is its intrinsic "fear of planning." In the final essay of the opening section, Paul Taylor proposes to re-contextualize Hannah Arendt's well-known notion of the "fearsome, word-and-thought-denying banality of evil" as a morbid symptom proliferating in today's capitalist media system. Taylor constructs his critical assessment by drawing on a tradition of illustrious critics of the "narcotic function" of the modern media (Adorno, Baudrillard, Benjamin, Kracauer, etc.), as well as on the *ante-litteram* censor of the "evil banality" inherent in our contemporary society of spectacle named Fyodor Dostoevsky.

The middle section of the book (*Events*) begins with Slavoj Žižek's essay "The Undoing of an Event," which draws on an array of cultural sources and popular themes, as well as on Hegel's notion of the "spiritual kingdom of animals," to propose a critique of capitalist "pseudo-evental interpellation." Žižek argues that one of the most effective ways in which the muted ideology of today's capitalism works is by surreptitiously transforming the public space into a private one, thereby neutralizing the possibility that real events might take place. The privatization of the public space, Žižek contends, is a key ingredient of the debilitating ideology of capitalist modernity: while all communal ends are a mode of appearance of private interests, the egotistic pursuing of these interests feeds directly into the communal framework where capital thrives. In the following chapter, Todd McGowan confronts 'the imperative to be practical' affecting every theorist during a period of crisis. He does so by examining Hegel's refusal of practice, namely his contention that it is precisely by justifying the world in its irresolvable antagonistic dimension that one lays the ground for its salvation. McGowan argues that what is required now is a "critique of practical theory" which has as its object "theory's devotion to saving the world." The paradox at work in McGowan's argument is that only by endorsing Hegel's absolute refusal of praxis are we able to commit, as theorists, to a practical end. In the next piece, Yahya Madra and Ceren Özselçuk begin by endorsing Sohn-Rethel's materialist account of "real abstraction" as a warning against over-simplified notions of post-capitalist politics. Then, by looking closely at Lacan's theory of the four discourses, they pin the affective dimension of these discourses against abstraction itself. While doing so, they also provide a perspicuous reading of the so-called Occupy movements through Lacan's discourses of the Hysteric and the Analyst, claiming that only the latter would signal a move to a post-capitalist scenario. In the final essay of the section, Marco Grosoli analyzes Steven Soderbergh's film *Contagion* (2011)—the story of a mysterious epidemic disease spreading worldwide—as an allegory of the financial crisis and its global consequences. Theoretically, Grosoli relies on Fredric Jameson's notion of "positive hermeneutics," proposing that despite its ideological closure, *Contagion* hides disavowed utopian motifs. He provides evidence for this claim by discussing how the film's articulation of its central theme of "disruption" is formally tied with the thrust toward the formulation of a new spatiality.

In the third and final section of the book, Colin Cremin begins by discussing Herbert Marcuse's analysis of the libidinal compulsion that keeps consumers aggressively attached to the capitalist economy. He assesses Marcuse's theorization of the Great Refusal as reflected in the concept of subtraction embraced by contemporary thinkers who attempt to re-marry Marxism and psychoanalysis, most prominently Slavoj Žižek. The essay then develops from a theoretical plane to the critique of employability, regarded as the main ideological lure through which the contemporary subject remains tied to capitalist relations. Eventually, Cremin suggests that only a strategically invested form of subtraction, which does not shirk practical action, can hope to succeed as an attempt to stem the catastrophic tide of capital, thus opening the way for the reconfiguration of our social space. The following chapter, by Darrow Schecter, calls into question the "dogmatically quantitative notion of economic growth" that has lead to today's crisis, while exploring the potential for a transition to "qualitatively new economic, political and educational systems" that might ignite a self-steering democratic society. Whereas most of Marx's interpreters regard the transition from political to human emancipation to consist in a centralized model of political-economic planning, Schecter explores the potential for a new approach to the question of the relations between economy and polity in a post-liberal, genuinely differentiated social order. Schecter's essay is followed by jan jagodzinski's appraisal of a post-capitalist avant-garde that might be free from both the traditional leftist "paranoid" style of theorizing, and the radical yet aggressive type of activism associated mainly with anarchist movements. By endorsing the notion of an "avant-garde without authority," and drawing on Nietzsche's *Übermensch* as much as on the geo-philosophies of Deleuze and Guattari (and a vast array of examples of contemporary artistic engagement), jagodzinski develops a theory of "an artistic Oekumenal war machine," whose task is to imagine and give shape to a new form of life beyond the control of capital. The volume comes to a close with Rex Butler's piece on Russian art theorist Boris Groys and his attempts to conceive of a post-capitalist scenario in relation to art, communism, philosophy and, more generally, his conception of thought as metanoia. Butler focuses on the merits and limitations of Groys' philosophical method, where metanoia—a religious term pointing to the transcendental ground of all things—occupies a central place, in so far as it captures Groys' desire to circumscribe a genuinely self-contradictory and paradoxical dimension outside the realm of capitalist relations.

References

Adorno, Theodor W. and Horkheimer, Max (1997 [1944]) *Dialectic of Enlightenment*. London and New York: Verso.

Cohen, Stanley (1972) *Folk Devils and Moral Panics*. London: MacGibbon and Kee.

Graeber, David (2011) *Debt: The First 5000 Years*. New York: Melville House.

Hall, Stuart; Critcher, C; Jefferson, T; Clarke J and Roberts, B (1978) *Policing the Crisis*. London: Macmillan.

Polanyi, Karl (1957) *The Great Transformation*. Boston: Beacon Press.

Roubini, Nouriel (2012) "Global Economy; Reasons to be Fearful," in *The Guardian*, 18 June 2012, http://www.guardian.co.uk/business/2012/jun/18/global-economy-perfect-storm (accessed: 20 June 2012).

Wallerstein, Immanuel (1974) *The Modern World-System, vol. I.* New York and London: Academic Press.

PART I
Crises

PART I

Crises

Chapter 1

The Matrix Cannot Be Reloaded: A Lacano-Marxian Perspective on the Current Economic Crisis

Heiko Feldner and Fabio Vighi

Over the past four years, the controversy about the nature of the current economic crisis has produced a myriad of competing explanations as to what might have caused it, which include the following:

- unrestrained greed and other psychological propensities rooted in human nature (e.g. Tett 2009, Greenspan 2009, Akerlof and Shiller 2010), a rehearsal of the anthropological leitmotif of liberal thought that "out of the crooked timber of humanity, no straight thing was ever made" (Kant 1784: 211);
- blind faith in neoliberal theories about the efficiency and self-sufficiency of markets (Davidson 2009, Elliott and Atkinson 2009, Skidelsky 2009);
- institutional failure to monitor and regulate the financial sector and especially the banking system (Acharya et al. 2011, Cable 2010, Hutton 2010);
- a failure of the collective imagination to understand systemic risk (Besley and Hennessy 2009 and King 2012) as well as to heed the lessons of history: the ever recurring "this-time-is-different-syndrome" (Reinhart and Rogoff 2009 and Gamble 2009);
- severe imbalances in the international financial, monetary and trading systems and the system of global governance (Roubini and Mihm 2011, Stiglitz et al. 2010, Krugman 2012 and Wolf 2009);
- an ill-conceived Anglo-Saxon model of capitalism imposing itself on the world economy (Sinn 2011, as well as large parts of the political elites in central Europe);
- big government along with too much regulation of the wrong kind (Ferguson 2012, Butler 2012, Dowd and Hutchinson 2010 and Beck 2010);
- a long-term crisis of over-accumulation and profitability (Callinicos 2010 and Harman 2009) as well as under-consumption caused by decades of excessive exploitation (Wolff 2010 and Harvey 2011) going back to the 1970s;
- the historical tendency of the rate of profit to fall as predicted by Marx in volume three of Capital (Carchedi 2010 and Kliman 2012);

- a blockage to the new forms of capital accumulation which are thought to have emerged with the development of cognitive capitalism (Marazzi 2011, Hardt and Negri 2009 and Vercellone 2010);
- a secular stagnation tendency of monopoly-finance capital—rather than rapid growth—generating a surplus-capital absorption problem (Magdoff and Yates 2009, Bellamy, Foster and McChesney 2012)

The first seven explanations belong to a cluster which oscillates between two related extremes: one makes the crisis into a "gigantic intellectual mistake" (Hutton 2012a), the other refers us to our "animal spirits"—the received wisdom that, rather than rational choice calculation, business and consumer decisions tend to be based on gut feeling.[1] The last four explanations are part of a cluster that stresses how the contradictory nature of capitalism leads systematically and unavoidably to economic crises. What both clusters have in common is the belief, whether explicit or implicit, that the capitalist mode of production possesses the miraculous ability to renew itself eternally, unless it is opposed and overthrown.

This chapter offers a different view of the nature, causes and consequences of the current economic crisis. In the wake of Ernest Mandel (1975) and Robert Kurz (1991 and 2009) we argue that the capitalist form of social reproduction has not only entered its deepest crisis since World War II, but that it has reached its absolute historical limit and is in terminal decline. Its demise does not depend on the rise of a political force to overthrow it, as is presumed across the political spectrum; nor does it in itself usher in a new social order, far from it. Its historic disintegration is caused by its vanishing capacity to generate new surplus-value (profit)—the life blood and telos of capitalist economies—, which condemns ever-larger parts of the world to permanent unproductivity ("underdevelopment") and a surplus humanity to the fate of drowning in survival ("unemployment").

From two interrelated angles—Marxian and Lacanian—the chapter lays out what distinguishes the present crisis from its predecessors: the "Long Depression" of the final quarter of the nineteenth century, the "Great Depression" in the 1930s, and the stagflation crisis of the 1970s. It explains why the current crisis does not simply mark the end of one particular model of growth that will give rise to a new model sooner or later, provided we are smart enough—a ubiquitous expectation elegantly expressed by Anatole Kaletsky's *Capitalism 4.0* (2011) and overwhelmingly shared throughout the political landscape (see e.g. McDonough et al. 2010, Chang 2011 and Haug 2012). Would a rerun of Keynesian economic policies resolve the crisis, as Joseph Stiglitz (2010) and Paul Krugman (2012) believe? Can a new science and technology offensive succeed, as Nicholas Stern (2009b) and Will Hutton (2012b) suggest, while the gap between work to be had and work to be done is widening before our eyes? What can Marx offer in the face

---

1   The term harks back to Keynes (1936: 162), who considered as an important source of economic instability "the characteristic of human nature that a large proportion of our positive activities depend on spontaneous optimism rather than mathematical expectations."

of the momentous failure of Marxism in the twentieth century? This chapter looks at these and other questions through the lens of a Lacano-Marxian critique of the *value-form* as the unconscious matrix of modern society.

In *Capital*, Marx projects a social totality greater than the empirically verifiable world. The object of this representational strategy is an abstract concept which brings into view a *negative objectivity*, i.e. a mysterious set of forces and effects that we can neither see nor touch, but nonetheless know have a constitutive influence over our existence. The concept designed to perform this representational manoeuvre is "value." It designates the historically specific *form* our social being assumes in capitalism, which remains intangible while its presence is experienced existentially.

In *Seminars XVI* to *XVIII* (1968–1971) Lacan developed an often overlooked critique of the value-form *sui generis*. Together with the theory of the four discourses (Master, University, Hysteric and Analyst) as articulated in those seminars, Lacan introduced a fifth discourse—the *discourse of the Capitalist*—which builds on the central narrative of the seminars to denounce modernity's blindness to its own generative matrix, namely the incessant "valorisation of value" promoted by capitalism. Starting from the postulate that the ruse of modernity consists in transforming the unconscious roots of knowledge into a countable entity, Lacan shows how the invisible mastery of the capitalist discourse is more pervasive and commanding than any historically antecedent form of authority. And yet, "wildly clever" as it may be, capitalism is, in Lacan's prescient words, "headed for a blowout" (Lacan 1972: 48).

The stress on the value-form (social link, unconscious matrix) as a mode of objectivity as well as subjectivity brings together the critique of the political economy with the critique of the libidinal economy, a tradition most effectively developed over the last two and a half decades by Slavoj Žižek (1989, 2009 and 2010: 181–243). Such an approach leads us out of the disciplinary framings of the crisis in economics, business studies or behavioural psychology. It allows us, instead, to take full advantage of the insight that in order to effect change we have to have a grip on both the dull compulsion of the economic and the deep libidinal attraction of the forms of exploitation and domination that have made us who we are. This is not an exercise in economics then, even though we will deal extensively with economic issues. Rather, our approach combines the virtues of ideology critique with those of critical theory. While the former locates the blind spot of contemporary debates on the crisis, tracing the "real" of the current juncture through a symptomatic reading, the latter explores it through a conceptual register that cuts across disciplinary grids in philosophy and positive science.

The first part of the argument develops a Marxian reading of the economic crisis, the second a Lacanian critique of capitalist work. We do not attempt some kind of "shotgun marriage" here, as Peter Gay (1985: xii) dubbed the doomed endeavour of twentieth century Freudo-Marxism. The different conceptual frameworks are not eclipsed, nor are diverging implications obscured. We develop them as complementary perspectives in the parallactic sense that they illuminate two different modes of appearance of the capitalist matrix, thereby allowing its constitutive distortion and historical limit to emerge more starkly.

1   Was the Neoliberal Turn a Mistake?

Capitalism is not only a mode of production, it is also a religion. When this thought struck German philosopher Walter Benjamin some 90 years ago, he was witnessing one of the most devastating crises of the last century. The debt crisis at the heart of it was resolved two years later, in 1923, by a colossal hyperinflation which wiped out the life savings of millions and paved the way for the economic slump of 1929 and the resistible rise of the Nazis.

Capitalism was not only conditioned by a religious mentality, as Max Weber had suggested in *The Protestant Ethic and the Spirit of Capitalism* (1904–5). For Benjamin, capitalism was itself a religious phenomenon through-and-through. It had three essential features. First, it was a purely cultic religion, without theology or theoretical justification. Second, the capitalist cult was permanent in the terrifying sense that each day was a holy day demanding unrelenting devotion without exception. Such was the monstrosity of this religion that, third, it could no longer offer redemption. Instead, the capitalist cult gave rise to "*Schuld*"—debt, guilt and blame rolled into one—and self-destruction as the only path to salvation (Benjamin 1921).

One of the most extraordinary ideological manoeuvres in recent history has been the imposition of austerity rule on societies that only a few years ago were blackmailed into getting up to their ears in debt in a collective effort to rescue the banking system. The crisis would be over soon and green shoots crop up once the silver bullets of state credit (bailout and stimulus packages), money-printing and near-zero interest rates had rectified the situation and put us back on the royal road to growth. When in February 2011 the *Financial Times*' chief economics commentator, Martin Wolf, ventured a historical retrospective on the crisis (Wolf 2011), what had come to a close was the first phase of the greatest corporate looting of public coffers in living memory. Between 2008 and 2011, 15 trillion dollars had been dredged up from the public purse worldwide to combat the crisis, bringing up the total of "sovereign debt" to a whopping 39 trillion dollars (39,000,000,000,000 and counting)—[2] not a bad tally for the most efficient economic system we can think of.

Now that we brace ourselves for the second wave of the crisis to peak—a global economic contraction with drastic forms of money devaluation lying in wait—[3] is it not time we turned our backs on the fairy-tale account of the crisis,

---

2   'World Debt Comparison: the Global Debt Clock,' in *The Economist*, http://www.economist.com/content/global_debt_clock (accessed 18 April 2011).

3   With a sense of impending doom, even mainstream economists have begun to refer to the present crisis as the "Great Stagnation" (see e.g. Cowen 2010 and Denning 2011).

according to which it resulted from a distortion (human avarice, regulatory neglect, casino capitalism, Anglo-Saxon aberration, you name it) of an otherwise efficient system? Rather than pathologise the crisis, naturalise the economic system that gave rise to it, and hunt for scapegoats, we have good reasons to look at the neoliberal turn of the past three and a half decades as a rational response to the historic crisis of industrial capitalism in the 1970s. Deregulation and financialisation—the economy's shift in gravity from production to finance—were not simply "mistakes" but utilitarian responses to an irreversible profit crunch.

Let us recall the structural crisis of the 1970s. When the Fordist growth model of industrial society hit the buffers, the state-capitalist economies of the Soviet bloc tumbled into a state of collapse, while in the West the reign of Keynesianism ended in stagflation—the double bind of stagnant growth and rising inflation. In either case, the attempt by the state to subsidise the lack of real growth had proven unsustainable. The hour had come for the "neoliberal revolution."

In the event, the crusade to subordinate all aspects of life to the imperatives of the corporate bottom line did much to damage the fabric of society, but it could not bring back the growth dynamic of the post-war boom. The growth rates of the OECD economies continued to fall from a buoyant 5.3 percent per year on average in the 1960s, to 3.7 percent (1970s), 2.8 percent (1980s), and 2.5 percent during the 1990s. Furthermore, the deregulation of the labour markets aggravated the problem of declining purchase power, while anti-state fanaticism ruined the public infrastructure required for long-term profitability. Intoxicated by their own ideological trademark belief that money was simply a "veil over barter" (Say 1816: 22), the class warriors of neoliberalism had merely shifted the debt problem from the state to the financial markets. Two and a half decades of debt-financed growth ensued, based ever more on money without substance. The rest is history.[4]

When the debt-bubble burst in 2008, a nostalgic pining for a return to Keynes led to the only seemingly oxymoronic *neoliberal Keynesianism* as a last-ditch response. As the bailout and stimulus packages shifted the debt problem back to the state, the crisis of the financial markets morphed into a sovereign debt crisis, only on a much higher level than in the 1970s and with no leeway to repeat the operation of finance-driven growth. Now, in 2012, policy makers have finally "run out of policy rabbits to pull out of their hats" as economist Nouriel Roubini (2012) put it. We have been living on borrowed time and continue to do so, since the cynically disguised nationalisations of corporate debt have been paid for by state resources that have yet to be contrived. The success of the latter relies on

---

4   As Marx (and Engels) aptly put it: "The production process appears simply as an unavoidable middle term, a necessary evil for the purpose of money-making. (This explains why all nations characterised by the capitalist mode of production are periodically seized by fits of giddiness in which they try to accomplish the money-making without the mediation of the production process)" (Marx 1992: 137).

the creation of future surplus-value at a historic magnitude that is most unlikely ever to materialise. Without real growth, however, it is not only that the question of debt sustainability becomes trickier. The ideological covenant of capitalist societies itself is rendered nil and void, as the acceptance of capitalism as a social partnership is inextricably linked to the prospect of a good life.

2 What we are Facing is not Simply a Periodic, Structural or Financial Crisis

Of course, the voyeuristic obsession with the political theatre and the idiosyncrasies of its cast—from Berlusconi and Merkel to Obama and Sarkozy—only serves to fudge the nature of the relationship between national states and "the economy." The state is in no way a sovereign actor *vis-à-vis* the mode of production on which it rests. So when we call for the primacy of politics over financial markets and for political leadership in tackling the crisis, it is worth recalling that the capitalist state is not some kind of guardian angel but rather an element within the circuit of capital. In its material capacity to act (by raising taxes, for example, or borrowing money) it is not only at the mercy of rating agencies and financial markets, as we are reminded every day, but is sustained on the drip of the economy of capital valorisation (the expanded reproduction of the economy through the competitive extraction of money profit)—the basis for enduring growth as we know it.

There is another sense of *déjà vu* in that each and every mayhem in the markets provokes renewed talk about the system being ready to explode at any moment, as well as the urgent need for reform, as was the case in the wake of Lehman Brothers' demise four years ago. The word "system" stands here for the institutional framework and management of the (global) economy. To be sure, there is plenty of room to improve the architecture of the financial and monetary system, the trading system and the system of global governance, as Joseph Stiglitz and other leading Keynesians have demanded for years (e.g. Stiglitz et al. 2010). But this will do little to address the underlying crisis, which is a crisis of capital valorisation itself.

What then distinguishes the current crisis from its predecessors? To answer the question, we need to let go of the postmodern illusion of an infinitely malleable reality. By producing goods and services the way it does, capitalism creates a historical dynamic which is as material and objective as it is directional and irreversible. While we are desperate for the light at the end of the tunnel to emerge as usual, there is no reason to believe that capitalism is endowed with an enigmatic capacity for eternal self-renewal. The present crisis does not simply spell the end of one specific model of capital accumulation ("growth") that will give rise to a new one sooner or later, provided we are smart enough. Put differently, the crisis is not merely cyclical, structural or limited to finance; nor is it simply down to factors such as over-accumulation, under-consumption or global imbalances.

Building on Ernest Mandel's analysis of the "specific nature of the third technological revolution" (Mandel 1975: 184ff.), Robert Kurz has blazed the trail for a critical understanding of the historical peculiarity of the current economic crisis, which he explored in a series of incisive analyses against the background of the history of modernisation over the past 250 years (Kurz 1991, 2005 and 2009). What sets the current crisis apart is the unprecedented scale at which human labour power—the only source of new surplus-value and, by implication, growth—is made redundant by scientific rationalisation. Whenever we get cash from a cash machine rather than a teller or use the automated checkout to pay for our daily shopping, we see the evidence of technology displacing human labour. This has long been anticipated from a variety of angles by luminaries as diverse as Norbert Wiener (1948: 59ff.) and Hannah Arendt (1958: 4–5). Three decades ago, economist Wassily Leontief wrote that the "role of humans as the most important factor of production is bound to diminish in the same way that the role of horses in agricultural production was first diminished and then eliminated by the introduction of tractors" (Leontief 1983: 3–4). This has come true in the form of digital automation and jobless recoveries. The engine of the "beautiful machine"—the business corporation—cannot be fazed by this calamity. Engaged in the civil war of competition, it must obey the law of acceleration to survive. With the rise of the knowledge economy we have reached the historical tipping point: for the first time more labour is made superfluous than can be re-mobilised through market expansion strategies (Kurz 2012: 296; see also Smith 2010: 1–23).

In other words, melting away like the Greenland ice sheet, the social substance of capital—labour—cannot acquire a new lease of life. This spells doom for a society in which the great majority can only access the means of existence through wage labour. The economic policy response to this predicament was the engineering of growth without substance, i.e. the mere simulation of growth, which hit the buffers in 2008. What should have been a blessing has turned into a nightmare: the capital valorisation economy cannot return the productivity gains engendered by technological automation back to us as free disposable time we could put to good use while working fewer hours. Quite the contrary, today's much-evoked "Third Industrial Revolution" (Rifkin 2011, The Economist 2012) leads to social Darwinism 24/7 and the savage barbarisation of our public and private lives ("austerity").

Benjamin considered his 1921 fragment *Capitalism as Religion* untimely; it remained unfinished and he never published it. However, future generations staring ruin in the face would be able to recognise the self-destructive imperative of the capitalist cult. Let us hope he was right. While the economic crystal ball has yet to be invented, this much is clear: the current crisis will force us to confront the political choice that defines the twenty-first century. Either we come up with an alternative to the dynamic of the capital valorisation machine before it is too late, or the unfolding socio-ecological catastrophe will run its course. The uncanny story of the grow-or-die society is coming to an end one way or the other.

The required alternative, however, is not "prosperity without growth" (Jackson 2009) or "degrowth economics" (Latouche 2009).[5] The notion of a capitalism without surplus-value or growth imperative is a red herring. Not only is it hopelessly nostalgic. It also rests on the implicit belief that with globalised capitalism we encounter only incontrovertible *external* "limits to growth," from climate change to finite energy and freshwater resources, whereas there are in principle no insurmountable *internal* limitations to the process of capital valorisation which could continue *ad infinitum* if only it were managed properly. This belief is obsolete. In the course of the last half century, we have reached and partly crossed *both* "the boundaries of the 'planetary playing field' for humanity," as the new science of planetary boundaries forcefully demonstrates (Resilience Alliance 2009 and Cho 2011),[6] *and* the boundaries of the economic playing field, as it were, of capitalism as a historical form of social reproduction. Though the former problematic cannot be reduced to the latter, it cannot be addressed without it either. What is therefore needed at this juncture is no longer alternative capitalism, such as eco- or "natural capitalism" (Hawken et al. 2010, Heinberg 2011 and d'Humières 2010), but an alternative to capitalism itself.

3   Between Monetary Hygiene and Keynesian Hydraulics: The Value of Marx

This, of course, is not the gospel according to mainstream economics which identifies the social either with the market or with the state. Like the Newtonian clockwork-universe, wound up by the watchmaker-God, the liberal notion of the market as a self-regulating force of nature sees the market as a gigantic machine of impersonal forces which is imbued with potential energy that will be running it *ad infinitum*. Like in the Newtonian universe, the laws of the market universe require occasional intercession, notably in times of crisis. The corrective surgery is carried out by the state. The surgeon is expected to withdraw again once the transformation of the patient's potential energy into kinetic energy is resumed. What, though, if that does not happen?

---

5   The current debate on degrowth economics points to a long tradition (e.g. Georgescu-Roegen 1971 and H. E. Daly 1977 and 1996) which can be traced back to John Stuart Mill's exploration of the "stationary state" in his 1848 classic *Principles of Political Economy* (Mill 1904: 452–455). See also Kallis (2011), Eisenstein (2011) and "Degrowth Declaration Barcelona" (2010).

6   It distinguishes nine planetary boundaries which define humanity's safe operating space: climate change, changes to the global nitrogen cycle, rate for biodiversity loss, ocean acidification, stratospheric ozone, global freshwater use, land system change, chemical pollution, and atmospheric aerosol loading. It estimates that we have already transgressed the first three of these boundaries and are likely to be on our way towards crossing others (Resilience Alliance 2009 and Cho 2011).

Marx had predicted such an historical impasse where the economic expansion required to exit the state of recession and prevent permanent contraction and decline was no longer forthcoming. He anticipated the arrival of a constellation where entire regions would go out of business because the capital valorisation economy could no longer generate enough surplus-value due to its inherent compulsion to displace human labour with cost-cutting technologies. After all, within the process of capital valorisation human labour has a dual character. On the one hand, it is a pesky cost factor which has to be reduced come what may. On the other hand, human labour is the social value-substance of capital, its living state of aggregation as it were. The exploitation of the human capacity to work is the only source of surplus-value and, by implication, sustainable capital accumulation and profit. As such, labour is indispensable for a society whose material reproduction is contingent on the competitive extraction of money profit. In *Capital*, Marx considered the historical breakdown of capital accumulation as an abstract possibility, and in the *Grundrisse* as an inevitable consequence of the development of human productivity within the parameters of capitalist economies (Marx 1990, 1992 and 1993: 692ff.).

If we follow Marx's reasoning, what would happen in such a scenario? Most notably, the relative devalorisation of the value-substance of capital (a secular process that typified the history of capitalism throughout the twentieth century and manifested itself in the establishment and collapse of the Bretton Woods system) would turn into an absolute desubstantialisation of capital accumulation and the value-form of social wealth itself (ideologically reflected by the postmodern belief in "fiat money" and "finance driven growth"). With the ever-tightening noose of the value-form around their necks, capitalist societies would be confronted with the inconceivable dilemma of rampant mass impoverishment in the face of a capacity for wealth creation that has never been greater in human history.

This, however, is exactly what we are experiencing in the current crisis. Triggered historically by the microelectronic revolution since the 1970s, the current crisis is not simply an expression of a sharp increase in the relative tendency of the rate of profit to fall, as theorised by Marx in volume three of *Capital* (Marx 1991: 315–75). Rather, it is a manifestation of the momentous fall in the absolute mass of profit, as anticipated in the "machine fragment" in the *Grundrisse* (Marx 1993: 690–712). Put differently, the present crisis gives us an indication of the extent to which the compensatory mechanism of external and internal economic expansion, which in previous crises prevented the relative fall in the rate of profit from turning *irrevocably* into an absolute fall in the mass of profit, has ground to a halt (see Kurz 2009: 782ff. and 2012: 274ff.). As a result, the creation of "jobs" and by implication livelihoods, let alone the maintenance of acquired living standards, become "unaffordable"—a stark reminder that the right to exist under global capitalism hinges for the vast majority on the dubious fortune of being utilised on profitable terms.

To give an example of the practical implications of this. A large-scale study of the finances of employed households in the United Kingdom, conducted by the think tank *Experian Public Sector*, found out that in 2012 nearly "seven million working-age adults are living in extreme financial stress, one small push from penury, despite being in employment and largely independent of state support." They have only "little or no savings, nor equity in their homes, and struggle at the end of each month to feed themselves and their children adequately" (Hill 2012). Bruno Rost, head of the think tank, notes laconically: "These are the new working class—except the work they do no longer pays" (quot. in ibid.). To put some figures on this, research from the leading accountancy firm *KPMG* into the extent of sub-living wage employment shows that in October 2012 some 4.82 million UK workers were paid less than the living wage. The latter, which stood at the time at £8.30 per hour in London and at £7.20 in the rest of the United Kingdom, is a voluntary pay rate meant to allow its recipients to afford a basic standard of living. In other words, in the country with the 7th largest national economy in the world, measured by nominal GDP, and the 8th largest if measured by purchase power, almost one in five workers struggled on wages which did not allow for a basic standard of living (KPMG 2012). If we relate this figure to

- the official unemployment rate of 7.9 percent of the economically active population, as published by the *Office for National Statistics* for June to August 2012 (2.53 million people overall, which represents an increase of 883,000 since the summer of 2007), and consider both against the backdrop of
- the economic inactivity rate of 22.5 percent for those aged from 16 to 64 during the same period (i.e. 9.04 million economically inactive people in this age bracket),
- the UK employment rate from June to August 2012 of 71.3 percent, i.e. the fact that 28.7 percent of people from 16 to 64 were for one reason or another not in employment at a time when ever fewer households can choose to live on one income alone,
- and the fact that of the 29,59 million employed people (the figure includes the 4.20 million people in self-employment and other employment groups) 8,13 million were in part-time employment during the summer of 2012 (2,14 million men and 5,99 million women, with an overall increase of 724,000 compared to summer 2007), at a time when part-time employment poses not only an acute risk of redundancy but is increasingly linked to old age poverty due to inadequate pension provisions (all figures from ONS 2012: 1, 2, 5, 35), we get a rough picture of the dimension of the problem in Britain.

This is of course not a *British* problem. Rather, it is endemic to all OECD countries which, since the beginning of the crisis in 2008, have been increasingly pressurised by the historical consequences of total capitalism. Is it not remarkable that, after 200 years of unprecedented productivity gains, the immense timesaving and wealth-creating potential of modern societies cannot but register negatively in the forms of under- and unemployment? How, indeed, is it possible that in the twenty-first century we witness the return of mass poverty in the traditional centres of capitalism under the slogan that we cannot "afford" otherwise?

John Maynard Keynes, the greatest economist of the twentieth century, was acutely aware of the "new disease [...] of technological unemployment." But he considered it "only a temporary phase of maladjustment," while in the long run the "strenuous purposeful money-makers" would "carry us all along with them" into an "age of leisure and of abundance," where we would be able to "spread the bread thin on the butter—to make what work is still to be done to be as widely shared as possible," with "fifteen-hour weeks [...], for three hours a day is quite enough to satisfy the old Adam in most of us!" The only problem he could foresee was a cultural one, namely "how to use [the] freedom from pressing economic cares, how to occupy the leisure, which science and compound interest will have won for [us], to live wisely, agreeably and well" (Keynes 1930: 364 and 367ff.).[7]

Keynes could not see that at the core of capitalist societies there is an intra-civilisatory barbarism at work, a negative force field from which they derive their laws of functioning. Marx's term for this "occult quality" that has locked modern society into a self-destructive historical trajectory, while simultaneously lending it the appearance of a quasi-natural order, is *capital* or "*self-valorising value,* value that gives birth to value" (Marx 1994: 461). The concept of self-valorising value brings into focus the generative matrix of modern society constituted by what Marx describes as the system of *abstract labour*—the systemic "combustion" of direct human energy within the circuit of work, money and consumption—which forms the enigmatic (abstract but real) social substance of capital. Marx's focus on the value-form of social reproduction brings also into view what, with Foucault, we might call the *historical a priori* of capitalist societies, i.e. the network of transcendental categories constituting the social world as we know it. Contrary, then, to the legendary account of *Capital*—according to which Marx set out to defend the dignity of labour as a wealth-creating force throughout the ages and so revealed the secret of its exploitation under capitalism, which explained why labour had to be liberated and the proletariat emancipated *via* an alternative path to modernisation , *Capital* should be read today as the uncanny tale of the value-form of social reproduction, a critique of capital as well as labour, relating the story of a compulsive expansion disorder turning cancerous.[8]

---

7   "But beware!," he cautioned, "[t]he time for all this is not yet. For at least another hundred years we must pretend to ourselves and to every one that fair is foul and foul is fair; for foul is useful and fair is not. Avarice and usury and precaution must be our gods for a little longer still. For only they can lead us out of the tunnel of economic necessity into daylight" (ibid.: 372). And pretend we did.

8   To be clear, Marx was himself in two minds about which story to tell. The "legendary account of *Capital*" was not a misunderstanding but a historical reading rooted in an era when capitalism was an expanding economic system.

It is precisely this story and its leading character, the "automatic subject," as Marx (1990: 255) calls the socio-pathological dynamic of self-valorising value, which escapes the "dismal science" of economics. Mainstream economic thought reflects the current crisis in the "whodunnit" mode of the investigative journalist-detective, exposing people living beyond their means, bankers rocking the boat, and politicians failing to develop a "shared horizon-scanning capability."[9] It cannot think—other than in the mode of paranoia—an objective historical dynamic resulting from a transcendental totality which imposes itself on every nook and cranny of society. This is no coincidence.

Dominated for more than a century by marginal utility theory with its purely subjective notion of value, mainstream economic thought identifies value with price and derives the notion of price, in turn, from the subjective utility calculus of the market actors. Strictly speaking, neither Neo-Keynesianism nor Neo-Liberalism intends to explain what constitutes capitalism any longer. While the former at least retains the notion that "a country is not a company" (Krugman 2009), the latter has increasingly confined its academic business to offering mathematical representations which optimise the reasoning of market participants (including the state). It is by no means an accident, but rather a hallmark of the deepening intellectual surrender accompanying the crisis, how, over the last three decades, the dismaying inability to conceptualise the social totality has been masked by a feverish mathematisation of economic processes.

This should not come as a surprise to us. Historically, said (neo)liberal *homo economicus* saw the light of day not only as a cynical "realist" driven by perceived self-interest. From the very beginning he was also afflicted with partial blindness. The "stupid mole's eyes of selfishness," to cite Kant's (1798: 21) *bon mot*, made him into a being of partial (limited, inverse and fetishistic) rationality. More precisely, it was the worm's-eye view of the business enterprise that condemned him forever to a two-dimensional existence between profit and loss. When all was said and done, *homo economicus* did not derive direction from the distinction between virtuous and sinful, good and evil, or true and false, but rather from profit and loss. In the delightful words of a contemporary business guru: "[p]rofits aren't everything, they're the *only* thing!" (Cloutier 2009: 1). Once this purpose was installed as a trans-subjective compulsion and universally enforced through market competition, all eyes were fixed on two things: the means required to achieve it, and the ratio at which to divide the spoils. "What for" questions lost their meaning in the process and were replaced with "How" questions. Since the dying decades of the twentieth century—with his poor eyesight mystified and celebrated as a necessary condition for the invisible hand to perform its blissful miracles for the common good—there has been nothing to prevent *homo economicus* from elevating the supreme criterion of business management, the bottom line, to the status of a categorical imperative for all

---

9   As the open letter from 22 June 2009 by leading British economists to the Queen put it (Besley and Hennessy 2009).

areas of social life. The underlying reasoning is straightforward: let's all do it like ManU, and we shall all win the Premier League next year! The fetishistic blindness towards sociality as a whole has turned *homo economicus* into a veritable sociopath.

While the public debate between Neo-Liberalism and Neo-Keynesianism is in full swing, it has not gone unnoticed in either camp that the choice between "austerity" and "growth" is in reality a choice between suffocating and drowning. There is also a growing recognition that the current crisis might not be yet another Schumpeterian event of "creative destruction" in which the foundations for new thrusts of economic expansion are being laid (Schumpeter 1942: 71ff.). Is not the ubiquitous reluctance of policy makers to allow the finance and sovereign debt bubbles to burst, i.e. the destruction of "bad assets" to run its course as a prerequisite for productive investment and renewed growth, a telltale sign for the rampant premonition that the days of "creative destructions" might be numbered and that "scorched earth" could be the more apt metaphor for economic crisis in the twenty-first century?

4   Old Wine in New Bottles

But then, the store of illusions is inexhaustible when social formations fall. Jared Diamond has shown how historical societies like the Maya and Viking Greenland collapsed. What they had in common was that at the very moment when the insight arose that their conditions of existence had become precarious, they began to intensify all those strategies and practices which until then had appeared successful. They continued to operate on the basis of past experience and practical reason, while their conditions of existence had fundamentally changed (Diamond 2006). Similarly, today, while the neoliberal and neo-Keynesian cards have both been played to devastating effects, there persists the unshakable belief that a new science and technology offensive would get us out of jail, that "[g]rowth in Britain and the west will return when that combination of innovation and good capitalism is rekindled" (Hutton 2012b); in fact, that it would allow us to hit several birds with one stone.

Few have written about this as authoritatively as Nicholas Stern, the former chief economist of the World Bank, author of the influential *Stern-Report* on the economics of climate change (Stern 2007) and current chair of the Grantham Research Institute On Climate Change and the Environment at the London School of Economics. In *The Global Deal*, he offers an accessible "blueprint" of "how to manage climate change whilst creating a new era of growth and prosperity" (Stern 2009a: 7), a green new deal which, since the outbreak of the economic crisis, he has further elaborated in a series of papers explaining the link between climate change, world poverty and economic recession. While the way we act on climate change and poverty "will define our generation," Stern argues, the current recession, severe and protracted as it may be, constitutes a "short-term crisis" that has to be overcome within the parameters of a strategic response to these two defining challenges of the twenty-first century. What is more,

> the financial and economic crisis brings the critical opportunity and the requirement to find a driver of long-term sustainable economic growth to lead us out of this crisis: we do not want again to sow the seeds of the next bubble as we emerge from the crash of the last (Stern 2009b: 7–8).

With reference to the "US$2 trillion global fiscal stimulus for 2009/10," Stern emphasises how a worldwide stimulus,

> if implemented with a long-term vision, offers the chance to invest in new technologies and investments for low-carbon growth. In the next few years we can invest in new patterns of growth that can transform our economies and societies, in much the same way as the railways, electricity, the motor car and IT did in earlier eras (ibid.).

Provided the "green component of the world stimulus" would be sufficiently large, i.e. "around 20% of the global package,"

> [t]his could enable us to grow out of this recession in a way that both reduces the risks for our planet and sparks off a wave of new technologies which will create 2 or 3 decades of strong growth and a more secure, cleaner and more attractive economy for all of us" (ibid.; see also Stern 2009a: 195).

To be clear, the selected passages highlight what has been indicative of a broader debate on green capitalism; they do not do justice to the complexity of Stern's argument. In the face of unreconstructed climate change deniers like Stanley Feldman, Nigel Lawson and Ian Plimer, we could not agree more with the urgency of his call for joined-up and decisive action. However, the underlying assumption that a new generation of green technologies would enable new patterns of growth that could transform our societies in the same way as railways, electricity, the automobile and information technology did in the past, is historically unfounded. While it might be energising and politically expedient to suggest that "[l]ow-carbon technologies can open up new sources of growth and jobs" (Stern 2009b: 3)—a belief echoed by green-minded policy makers throughout the world—they cannot do either. Whereas railroading, electricity and the Fordist motor car exerted a dynamising effect on growth and employment in the nineteenth and lengthy spells of the twentieth century, this cannot be repeated historically. The impact of ICT and especially the micro-chip computer, which inaugurated the post-industrial era, has been fundamentally different. The unprecedented rationalisation potentials of the digital revolution were not only a central factor in the economic breakdown of the state-capitalist labour regimes of the Soviet bloc. They were also the technological driver of the neoliberal turn during the 1980s, the class war against the working classes and the attendant virtual escapism into simulated growth, which have lead us to where we are today.[10]

Whatever we might think of the nature and effectiveness of "good capitalism" or "sustainable growth," capitalism cannot return to a technological infrastructure with labour intensive production lines and full employment. As long as we are stuck with a regime of social reproduction based on solipsistic business enterprises producing for anonymous markets and the extraction of human labour, neither the technological blind flight nor its social (unemployment and poverty) and economic consequences (profit squeeze and economic contraction) can be stopped. With each and every technological innovation we will continue remorselessly to saw away at the branch on which we sit.

But is this not some kind of brute economic determinism which makes a mockery of human creativity and free will? Yes it is. The brutishness, however, lies not in the critique but in its object. We live in a world of globalised economic compulsions, the most insidious of which is the compulsion for human beings to turn themselves into combustion engines of human energy that can be offered for hire, a fate that can only be borne if it is elevated to a moral good and aspirational way of life.

Besides, the plausibility of the belief that technological innovation would be the driver of long-term sustainable growth that would lead us out of the current economic crisis, rests on three problematic assumptions: first, that economics would be about the production and distribution of goods and services in the face of scarcity of resources, as every economics textbook from Samuelson (1976: 3 and 18) to Krugman and Wells (2009: 6) explains. However, within the overwhelming majority of contemporary economies—if they are indeed the subject of economics—the production and distribution of utility-values like goods and services is little more than an epiphenomenon subordinated to the generation of exchange-value (money) and money profit.

This leads us to a second, related misconception according to which we would live in a market economy, with all its illusions—such as freedom, choice and equal opportunity—attached to it. In reality, the "market" is a fleeting, if crucial, episode within the economy of capital valorisation. It is the sphere in which the surplus-value extracted through the exploitation of wage labour must be turned into money profit to be available for reinvestment. While the notion of the market economy affords us the illusion of historical timelessness (circularity, eternal return), the capital valorisation process is characterised by a historical dynamic which does not "repeat" itself. The structural crises of capital valorisation are

---

10 Will Hutton, one of Britain's leading Keynesian economists, overlooks the crucial difference as well: "It is the great general purpose technologies (GPTs)—the steam engine, the aeroplane and the computer—that transformed our lives and economies. [...] In the 1930s, evolving GPTs helped drive economic recovery, aided by a capitalism that had been reformed after the excesses of the 1920s. Recovery from today's barely contained depression will require the same alchemy" (Hutton 2012b).

only superficially expressions of the ever same ("Minsky moment," "overpro duction"/"underconsumption," "market adjustment"). While historically they might well have wiped the slate clean periodically and temporarily, they did so on an ever increasing level of productivity, which, in turn, changed each time the historical conditions of capital valorisation fundamentally and irrevocably.

Third, the notion that technological innovation could be the catalyst for sustainable growth that would lead us out of the current crisis conflates the drivers of business success with the drivers of macro-economic prosperity. Indeed, from the viewpoint of the business enterprise, technological innovation and rationalisation are the drivers of profitability and economic expansion. From the viewpoint of the capital valorisation economy as a whole, however, this is not necessarily the case. Why? Because surplus-value is a social category, as Marx explains in volume three of *Capital*. Individual businesses do not "produce" it in the same way as they produce cars, computers or other goods and services. The surplus-value created by individual businesses is not a verifiable property of any single commodity they produce. Rather, it aggregates with the surplus-value created by other businesses to form the total social mass of surplus-value in existence at any given time. The individual commodities represent the "spectral," socio-symbolic materiality of this social mass of surplus-value. Just how much of this mass an individual business manages to capture ("realise"), however, depends on its competitiveness in the market place, which in turn is an expression of its technological capacity to cut labour costs—i.e. to eliminate abstract labour and thereby the only source of surplus-value—while forcing others to follow suit. Ironically, then, the more businesses harness the spirit of innovation, the more they undermine the social mass of surplus-value, and with it the general foundation for long-term sustainable growth.

Given where we stand today, a new science and technology offensive can therefore yield the desired results only for a short period and only for some, while directly or indirectly pulling the plug on all the rest. Those who manage to bolster their technological competitiveness through economic ("common" markets and currency zones) and extra-economic violence (global governance and warfare) will control the remaining isles of prosperity. We can catch a glimpse here of why the forceful plea that "the developed world must demonstrate for all, especially the developing world, that low-carbon growth is not only possible, but that it can be a productive, efficient and attractive route to overcome world poverty," that "[i]t is indeed the only sustainable route" (Stern 2009b: 8), might send shivers down the spine of many.

Though Marx did not foresee the large-scale financialisation of capitalist economies during the twentieth century and the concomitant devaluation of the money-medium, his concept of "fictitious capital" goes a long way in explaining what is happening today. It expresses very well the accumulation of capital without substance that typifies the crisis of contemporary capitalism and the remedies pursued so far. It captures the essence of all fetishistic illusions, namely that capital can be valorised without the hassle (or moral outrage—take your pick) of exploiting wage labour. In other words, that capital does have a life beyond labour. Money-begetting-money is the dream scenario of capitalist utopia. Of course, what we witness today is the practical proof of its impossibility. If, however, we live in a world where fictitious capital has come to dominate the process of capital valorisation—not temporarily and by accident but irreversibly and by necessity—, where capital accumulation is to an overwhelming extent already fictitious (i.e. by no means "imagined," but insubstantial), why should we continue to use the economic extraction of money profit as the yardstick for what we consider "efficient," "realistic" and "affordable"? To question the notions of financial affordability, economic efficiency and fiscal realism is far more than a hysterical gesture. It is a precondition for transcending the logic of mere crisis management.

5   Returning to Marx?

Like Jason Barker (2011), Terry Eagleton (2011) and many others in recent years, we make a case here for a Marxian critique of capitalism. However, a note of caution is required before we move on. Marx's work is ambiguous and Janus-faced, split as it is between liberal modernisation theory and radical critique. What is more, the political history of the Marxist movement thwarts forever any sleek return to Marx. After all, Marxism did not become an influential political force in the twentieth century because the *Communist Manifesto*, or *Capital* for that matter, was uniquely plausible and persuasive, but first and foremost because it was upheld by an indomitable political machine. Its temporary hegemony among emancipatory movements rested on its institutional anchoring within the labour movement and its political organisations, rather than on its intellectual potency.

With the decline of industrial capitalism in the East and the West, labour movement Marxism, as the most powerful political incarnation of Marxism, has ceased to exist as a historical force. While its corpse keeps battling on, this amounts to little more than last-ditch skirmishes of identity politics. This is no coincidence. Labour movement Marxism has always been a champion of identity politics. Its chief ambition was to gain due recognition for labour, which it perceived transhistorically as the "prime basic condition for all human existence" (Engels 1876: 452) without which social life would grind to a halt. The political task was to secure a position for the working classes that would adequately reflect the central wealth-creating role labour played in society. On closer inspection, however, this "society" invariably turned out to be founded on the holy trinity of work, money and consumption. As such, labour movement Marxism was always part and parcel of the dynamics of capitalism as a mode of production and socio-political arrangement. While it expressed the really existing demands of the wage-labouring masses for equality of opportunities, distributive justice and social recognition; and while this made good political sense as long as capitalism was a developing and expanding system which was absorbing more labour than it ejected, and where tomorrow's cake could be expected to be larger than today's, with the onset of the terminal crisis of capital valorisation we experience today the time of working class identity politics has come to an end. Identity politics has lost its emancipatory potential once and for all.

If, however, "labour" is no longer a marker for the axis along which emancipatory politics could be played out, "Marxism" has also ceased to be a marker for emancipatory thought *per se*. Any return to Marx has to earn its credentials anew. It cannot settle for a partial, nostalgic critique of capitalism any longer (neoliberalism, globalisation, corporate and finance capitalism, market anarchy) but must seize those uncanny aspects of Marx's work which challenge the very matrix that constitutes capitalism as a transcendental, negative totality ("labour," "money," the "market," "competition," the "state"). All attempts to "positivise" the capitalist matrix, i.e. to put it to good use, whether in part (on behalf of identity politics and distributive justice) or in total (in the name of a green-socialist market economy or "responsible capitalism"), are destined to contribute one way or another to the authoritarian crisis management regimes which are rapidly emerging—under the flag of a growth-strategy as a unifying national project for example.

"Labour" or "work," to use the contemporary term, is no doubt the most deceptive element of the capitalist matrix. As an ethical imperative, economic compulsion and the social substance of capital, it has pervaded all areas of life and, in the event, became indistinguishable from "purposeful activity," "creative effort" and acts of "production" more generally. It clearly is a false friend. As a universalised social abstraction—the expenditure of human energy that is "measureable, quantifiable and detachable" from the people who "provide" it in exchange for money (Gorz 2005: 54)—the regime of labour emerged historically from the inaugural scene of capitalism, the original accumulation by expropriation ("primitive accumulation"), which forcibly imposed it on an ever increasing number of people as the only way to make a living. However, if the history of the capital valorisation economy began with the "liberation" of countless people from their means of production and existence, thereby forcing the character mask of "worker" on them, it is now "liberating" the workers from the only activity left to them to earn their crust, leaving behind not only "a society of laborers without labor" (Arendt 1958: 5) but also of capitalists without capital.

Knowingly or unwittingly, today's champions of "work," who continue to see a work-based society as the only possible society, support the current crisis management and the apartheid regime it has in store for us. It is worth noting that, in its own distinctive way, the joint venture of Neoliberal-Keynesianism has been busy abolishing wage labour for quite some time: by abolishing wages while continuing the regime of work. If at the present historical juncture a politics of "jobs" ("jobs for all," put-people-back-to-work schemes) is already hopelessly anachronistic, it will soon become reactionary in the extreme. As Jean-Marie

Vincent (1991), Robert Kurz (1991, 2012) and Moishe Postone (1993: 4ff. and 2012) never tired to stress: as the flipside of capital, labour must be turned from a privileged standpoint into an object of the critique of capitalism. It cannot be liberated from the constraints of capital. Instead, the regime of "work" and "jobs" must be abandoned.

The final word on this, however, belongs to Marx or, more accurately, to the part of Marx that deserves to be critically reloaded:

> "Labour" by its very nature is an unfree, unhuman, unsocial activity, determined by private property and creating private property. Hence the abolition of private property will become a reality only when it is conceived as the abolition of "labour" (Marx 1975: 277).

This leads us to one of the most penetrating criticisms of modern, capitalist rationality: Lacan's critique of "work."

6   A Wildly Clever Discourse—but Headed for a Blowout

> The crisis, not of the master discourse, but of the capitalist discourse, which is its substitute, is overt (*ouverte*). I am not saying to you that the capitalist discourse is rotten, on the contrary, it is something wildly clever, eh? Wildly clever, but headed for a blowout (Lacan 1972: 48).

Lacan's theory of the four discourses (Master, University, Hysteric, Analyst), formulated mainly in *Seminar XVII*, is, among other things, an attempt to identify the principal problem with capitalism and its self-defining injunction to produce, valorise and consume. In the seminars centred on the discourses (from XVI to XVIII, covering the period 1968–1971) we find continuous references to capitalism and its structural composition. The centrality of this theme is confirmed by the fact that, in his address to the University of Milan on May 12, 1972, as well as in parts of *Seminar XVIII* (1970–71) and *Radiophonie* (1970), Lacan introduced a fifth discourse, which he aptly named the "discourse of the Capitalist." While he did not elaborate on its meaning, such an addition was aimed at complementing the socially critical content already present in the previous four discourses, and particularly in those of the Master and of the University. In fact, we argue that Master, University and Capitalist are strictly interrelated discourses whose primary aim is to capture a shift in the social link of modernity whereby mastery is not eliminated but rendered more efficient. More to the point, the discourse of the University and that of the Capitalist are two complementary ways of showing how, in modernity, mastery increases its authoritarian grip by making itself invisible and therefore unassailable. At the same time, however, the social link embodied by the new mastery of the Capitalist discourse, Lacan tells us, is "headed for a blowout."

But before tackling this question, let us briefly remind ourselves of what is at stake in Lacan's discourse theory. The four discourses were developed during the "second phase" of Lacan's teaching, which had begun with *Seminar XI* (1964) and the "push to the Real" therein articulated. By theorising these highly formalised discourses Lacan confronts his growing concern with how to circumscribe the residual Real of *jouissance* (understood as disturbingly excessive/lacking enjoyment) within the signifying structure. In this respect, these discourses represent a milestone in Lacan's turn toward the formalisation of language, in as much as they provide him with dynamic formulas to attempt to account for the ways in which the disruptive Real is subsumed in the social link. Later on, with *Seminar XX*, Lacan will inaugurate the "third (and last) phase" of his teaching (see Voruz and Wolf 2007), marked by the awareness of the inextricable and irredeemable conflation of the Symbolic and the Real (language and *jouissance* are now seen as completely bound up). For the purpose of our analysis, we will keep the focus on Lacan's dualistic approach to the Symbolic and the Real as exemplarily represented in the four discourses. This is not meant to detract from the significance of Lacan's later conceptualisation of language as "inundated with *jouissance*," but only to enable us to focus on his explicit critique of the capitalist constellation. To do precisely this, we should keep in mind that Lacan understands discourse as a signifying structure that moulds specific social bonds.[11] As an unchanging formal framework composed of four positions whose rotation illuminates different historical constellations, Lacan's discourse is meant to capture, first and foremost, the failure and paradox of signification: it is precisely because language malfunctions by generating a surplus of meaning that we continue to communicate with each other.

Each discourse has four fixed positions (agent, other, product and truth) which can be occupied by four different formalised terms (S_1, S_2, a, $\$$) representing respectively the master-signifier, knowledge, the object-cause of desire and the barred subject. These terms stand in a fixed relationship with each other and rotate anti-clockwise by a quarter turn, thus giving shape to the four different discourses. Each one of them begins with the *agent* speaking to a "passive" receiver named *other*. The result of this speech can be verified in its distorted effect or *product*. Finally, we have the position of *truth*, which gives the properly psychoanalytic inflexion to Lacan's discourse, since there we realise that the agent was only apparently in charge: the truth about his discourse was always unconscious. The position of truth, which gives a tangible form to the ontological inconsistency of any communicative logic and social bond, manifests itself in two ways: first, on the upper, or conscious, level (agent and other) we have a relationship of *impossibility*; then, in the lower, or unconscious, level (product

---

11   In his Milan talk, Lacan defines discourse as that which, "in the ordering of what can be produced by the existence of language, makes a social link function." For Lacan, there is no natural social discourse, but only the ones brought about by the intervention of language (Lacan 1972: 51).

and truth), one of *impotence*. Let us begin with what goes on in the upper level: since the agent's speech is driven by a desire that remains hidden underneath while constituting his truth, the message to the other can only exist as a distorted one. This botched communication becomes, in the lower level, a relationship of impotence, since the product of the agent's link with the other (what the other makes of the agent's speech) is necessarily incongruent with the truth of the agent. What needs to be stressed is that the social bond described by each of the discourses is coterminous with a fundamental inconsistency that manifests itself at the level of conscious speech and unconscious truth.

$$\frac{\text{agent}}{\text{truth}} \quad \longrightarrow \quad \frac{\text{other}}{\text{product}}$$
$$\big/\big/$$

As anticipated, the four terms filling in the four positions of the discourse are locked in a fixed relation with each other. The logic behind their arrangement reflects Lacan's central conviction that the subject does not pre-exist but is a consequence of language, of the interplay of signifiers ("a signifier is what represents a subject for another signifier," Lacan 1998a: 157). From the perspective of today's capitalist crisis, we are interested in two specific shifts described in Lacan's theory, namely 1) The anti-clockwise regression from the discourse of the Master to that of the University, which captures a crucial change in the role of the master-signifier, and 2) Lacan's previously mentioned hypothesis of a fifth discourse, that of the Capitalist, which does not follow the rotating logic of the other four discourses but is arrived at by way of the inversion of $\frac{S_1}{\$}$ into $\frac{\$}{S_1}$ in the discourse of the Master:

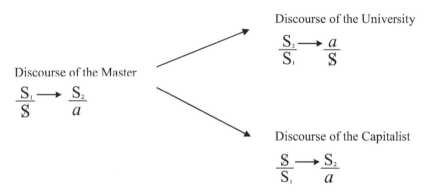

What immediately strikes the eye is that in the two discourses through which Lacan endeavours to demonstrate how our social link is in danger of imploding (University and Capitalist), the master-signifier (S_1) occupies the position of unconscious truth, while agency is taken over by knowledge (S_2) and the barred subject ($) respectively. In both cases, the truth about the agent (whether knowledge or the subject) is the disavowed master-signifier. This means that although at the helm of the social link we seem to have either an objectively neutral agent (knowledge) or the hysterical subject driven by its unquenchable desire,[12] in truth we are constantly "under orders," obeying the dictates of a harsh master whose injunctions are rendered more effective by their invisibility. Furthermore, it is precisely because mastery occupies the displaced position of truth that with the University and the Capitalist discourses we are immersed in ideology: we act *as if* we were free agents, self-determining our lives, while in fact we are at the mercy of an unconscious command. As Slavoj Žižek has demonstrated, ideology is at its most dominant when its injunctions are not experienced directly. With the University, the disavowed ideological command is "You must know!," while with Capitalism it is "You must enjoy!." In psychoanalytic terms, both are socially coercive super-ego injunctions.

Let us quickly sketch how these two discourses function. In the University discourse, which amounts to the objective discourse of modern science, knowledge somewhat outrageously attempts to directly address and control *a*, the inherently *lost* object-cause of desire, producing nothing but subjective alienation ($) and at the same time precluding any relation between master-signifier and subject ($S_1 // $). In the Capitalist discourse, which is another regression in respect of the discourse of the Master and yet one that, by not following the quarter turn of the other discourses, would seem to found a new "universe of discourse,"[13] we encounter the perverse situation whereby the barred subject, by definition powerless in its self-alienation, is empowered (as agent) to set in motion a productive knowledge. If on the one hand the outcome is formally the same as with the Master (since also the Capitalist discourse produces *a* qua lack) on the other hand we register a profound change in what takes place on the lower (unconscious) level, where S_1, the disavowed master of $, is unable to relate to the object. If we translate Lacan's mathemes into their capitalist equivalents, the meaning of this impotence will become clearer. The agent of the discourse of the Capitalist, whether the worker or the consumer (or both), is the subject of the unconscious ($) paradoxically in a position of command, believing himself to be omnipotent. The capitalist worker/consumer addresses the other as "expert knowledge" (an illusorily neutral and therefore seemingly all-powerful knowledge) and the effect of this link is the production of surplus-value, i.e. *valorized* surplus, a distortion of the surplus within *jouissance* as deadlock of any social link. Then, crucially, we arrive at the truth of the whole discourse, embodied by capitalism as master-signifier.

---

12   The discourse of the Hysteric also has the barred subject as the agent.

13   See Levi Bryant's article "Žižek's New Universe of Discourse" (Bryant 2008), where the Capitalist discourse is seen as opening up an entirely new constellation disengaged from the previous four and potentially populated by three additional discourses that are defined as those of Bio-power, Critical Theory and Immaterial Production.

Now we can see why Lacan insists that the discourse of the Capitalist is "headed for a blowout." If what plagued the discourse of the Master was the radical ambiguity of the master-signifier, expressed as $\frac{S_1}{\cancel{S}}$, the new Capitalist discourse is intimately beset by the fact that the capitalist qua disavowed commanding authority is unable to relate to what it instigates via the desiring subject, namely the accumulation of surplus-value ($S_1//a$). The paradox is that capitalism as a productive system is disconnected from the end-product of the mechanism it triggers, for the simple reason that it "forgets" how the accumulation of surplus-value is necessarily mediated by the worker/consumer's capacity not merely to produce, but especially to purchase the objects of desire. The relation between capitalism and surplus-value is therefore *explosive* in so far as it has to rely on dynamics of production/consumption that cannot be brought under full control. Put differently, while the authoritarian drive of capitalism works well to keep the consumer subjugated ("Enjoy!" being its ideological injunction), it is impotent with regard to its actual goal. Here we should consider how for Lacan the *goal* of the drive does not coincide with its *aim*, since the drive always aims at missing its explicit goal—that is to say, the object of the drive is *jouissance*, the paradoxical satisfaction brought about by lack of satisfaction. The point, then, is that there exists a gap between the capitalist drive—its *konstante Kraft* or unrelenting tension (to use Freud's words)—and what it explicitly sets out to achieve: while the explicit goal is profit, the aim is the endless, self-destructive continuation of the "pulsating" fixation that *is expected* to bring profit. Ultimately, as today's crisis is demonstrating, the production-consumption axis can be counter-productive because of the capitalist drive towards endless expansion. Lacan's theory of the discourse of the Capitalist, then, strongly disproves Adam Smith's famous metaphor about the "invisible hand" of the marketplace as the ultimate guarantee of social and economic cohesion. In *Seminar XVI* (19 March 1969) Lacan already claimed that

> capitalism reigns because it is closely connected with this rise in the function of science. Only even this power, this camouflaged power, this secret and, it must also be said, anarchic power, I mean divided against itself, and this without any doubt through its being clothed with this rise of science, it is as embarrassed as a fish on a bicycle now (see Lacan 2007a).

In relation to the crisis of the Capitalist discourse, Lacan plays exactly on the double meaning of consumption: on the one hand we must consume (enjoy) endlessly, on the other "it [capitalism] consumes itself" (Lacan 1972). With reference to this latter form of consumption, it is therefore crucial to underline how Lacan's discourses of University and Capitalism are socially critical not only because they focus on the subtly disavowed form of mastery at work in modernity (inclusive of liberal democracy as its political face); but especially because they identify the ontological inconsistency of these structural sequences, which is substantial and as such denotes the fragility and ultimate impotence of the social links they embody.

Nevertheless, Lacan regards the discourse of the Capitalist as "wildly clever." This, we argue, has to do with creating the illusion that the desiring subject is in a position of full autonomy, while at the same time secretly forcing desire to take the one-way direction of producing and consuming commodities. Through this ruse, capitalism makes sure that no desire can be stronger than the desire to work and consume. With the two faces of modernity (University as scientific discourse of objectivity and Capitalism), minus is camouflaged as plus and as such employed within the conscious signifying chain (on the upper level of the discourse). With the Capitalist discourse, this camouflaged plus is the worker/consumer himself, whose "substanceless subjectivity" is surreptitiously invested with an all-powerful command ($ in the position of agency).[14] Yet the more he enjoys his power, the emptier he becomes, since the true object-cause of desire (*a* qua lack) keeps on eluding him. The whole point, however, is that the intrinsic unruliness of the split subject is neutralised via this unheard of elevation to a position of command, as evidenced by slogans such as "consumer is king." While, as we shall see shortly, a similar operation of camouflaging is also at work in the discourse of the University, let us first go back to the specific difference between Master and Capitalist.

In *Seminar XVII* Lacan is at pains to show that in the old discourse of the Master loss was available as an indicator of the basic impotence of that social link. With the Master, the very attempt to set up a consistent connection between signifiers ($S_1 \rightarrow S_2$) can only result in the production of "lost objects," representing the short-circuit in signification as well as the impotence of the master-signifier, whose ultimate truth is $. The more effectively the master-signifier qua agent signals to the other signifiers that "il y a de l'Un" (that there is a semblance of the One, of a consistent symbolic order—in other words that there is a metalanguage), the more his actual impotence can be denounced. As Nobus and Quinn (2005: 133) have put it: "The threat posed by the subject of the unconscious to the master concerns the revelation of the master's fundamental impotence, his self-undermining dependence on the Other to establish a sense of meaning." By contrast, with the advent of modernity (scientific discourse) such impotence, in itself inerasable from the social link, is valorised and turned into surplus, to the extent that it becomes the key to capitalist accumulation. In Lacanian terms, what takes place within capitalist (but also communist) modernity is, succinctly put, the "wildly clever" distortion of loss. If, before the University discourse entered the scene, loss as related to (the slave's) production was testament to a real, substantial lack or impotence, with modernity this "roadblock" is openly endorsed as a positive feature of the system, which implies that negativity is further repressed (foreclosed). However, since the repressed does not disappear but "returns," at some point one must pay for this profound act of distortion. The specific price one

---

14   One can notice here both the similarity and the difference with the discourse of the Hysteric, where $ is also in the position of agency. While consumers can indeed be seen as hysterics on account of the gap between their status ($) and the position they occupy (agent), they nevertheless do not address the master-signifier but knowledge, thus retaining a stronger semblance of control over the signifying chain.

pays is, today, generally known with the term "crisis." And, as we have shown, the fact that today's responses to crisis are themselves nothing but attempts to positivise its impact confirms that we are still operating from within the ideological framework of capitalism, whose strongest weapon is the ability to turn any trace of ontological negativity—and thus any potential hindrance to its functioning—into an asset.

7   Enjoyment in the Name of Capital

We have argued that the discourse of the Capitalist should be read from the point of view of the worker/consumer. The agent is the barred subject inasmuch as he never stops working and consuming. The status of the barred subject is therefore completely different from the one he had in the Master's discourse. Since now he is in charge and sets knowledge to work, S is, on the one hand, typically characterised by an insatiable desire—a desire for which there is no object but lack itself—and, on the other hand, supported by the knowledge articulated in the big Other, the battery of signifiers that he (thinks) he has a hold on (S_2). What needs to be highlighted is the profound difference marking the two signifying chains, despite the fact that, in both, knowledge is articulated in the big Other; we pass from $S_1 \rightarrow S_2$ (Master) to $S \rightarrow S_2$ (Capitalist). If in the first sequence the master-signifier was in a relationship of command with regard to S_2, and remained ignorant about the knowledge therein expressed, in the second the consumer qua subject of desire is both *empty* and *filled* with the knowledge that sustains the capitalist social link, namely the knowledge about commodities. Despite remaining a barred subject, the worker/consumer qua agent is constantly deluded into believing that "he can get what he wants" (if only he pays for it); or, which amounts to the same thing, that he knows how to satisfy his desire. The fact that this never works out is, of course, the ruse upon which consumerism is based: satisfaction is forever delayed. Yet what Lacan seems to underscore is the specific historical condition of the capitalist worker/consumer as someone who is simultaneously clueless about what he wants and arrogant enough to persuade himself that he has at his disposal the necessary knowledge to satisfy all his desires (a knowledge provided, in practice, by advertising, experts, talk-shows and the media in general, and of course incarnated by money). Even though *objet a* remains fundamentally hidden on the lower right-hand side, the worker/consumer still dupes himself into believing that he can access its secret.

   With specific reference to the desire and enjoyment promoted by capitalism, the entire system thrives on the fact that we (workers/consumers) *do not* enter into a relationship with *jouissance*, i.e. that we perceive enjoyment not as lack as such, but as a fluid type of plenitude, a ubiquitous substance that, while reminding us that happiness is always a step ahead of us, nevertheless fills our life and confers meaning upon it. Here we are faced by a parallax: although enjoyment in its deepest connotation is always a painfully frustrating lack, we feed our social-symbolic order by perceiving this lack as plenitude, in the sense that it colonises every aspect of our lives. This split between lack and plenitude is indeed constitutive of enjoyment. Theoretically speaking, it makes perfect sense to assert that the enjoyment offered on the market is actually *joui-sans*, the lack of enjoyment that structures desire. It is even amusing to claim that, when we break a Kinder egg, we find a stupid plastic toy equivalent to the void at the heart of the commodity (see Žižek 2003: 145). Furthermore, this seems to be corroborated by the fact that the *plus-de-jouir* marketed by consumerism is directly connected with depressive affects, or what Freud called *Das Unbehagen in der Kultur* (discontent in civilization): by giving in to the logic of consumerism we effectively betray our desire and opt for the amassing of the "ersatz-enjoyment" prescribed by our *gourmand* superego, which can have devastating effects. The bottom line, however, is that within our social link we acquire meaning only through the anodyne *plus-de-jouir* embodied by the object-commodity in front of us (whether a real object or a life-experience). Our entire existence depends on the thrills of consuming arrays of ever-changing products, lifestyles and fashions, without which we would be deprived of the very framework in which meaning, for us, is inscribed. Here we must avoid all illusions and fully endorse Lacan's lesson on subjectivation: we form our identity via the big Other. Take our consumer identity away from us and we turn into barbarians overnight. The simple lesson to learn is that the madness of the capitalist drive, and by implication its constitutive imbalance that cuts across different historical epochs and superstructures, is not only fed but also offset by the "fetishistic common sense" of consumer demands masqueraded as desire. This is how our symbolic order registers our inclusion, gets our approval, and therefore manages to retain a degree of balance.

If, despite a crisis that is proving catastrophic, the capitalist framework retains its appeal, it is because we are happy to keep on fetishising its fruits, pretending not to notice the apocalyptic scenario looming on the horizon. And, it must be added, we enjoy its fruits because they seem to neutralise the inherent excess of our lives. The weakness of subjectivity under capitalist conditions is a guarantee of its durability. Working and consuming are compulsively therapeutic; if this is not enough, a range of other stabilising forces are ready at hand to cure any related existential turbulence, from (the return of) religion and tradition to welfarism, love of local and green economies, and of course the ever thriving pharmaceutical market! Thus, in a weird loop, existential angst is both cause and effect of consumerism: capitalism produces nothing but the very angst it promises to cure. And as angst-ridden workers/consumers, we enjoy by keeping *jouissance* at a safe distance. In fact, the injunction to enjoy is always-already kept under surveillance by market forces. It operates within the framework of a well-ordered regime of enjoyment that has been at the heart of capitalism since its Puritanical origins. Excess must be perceived as available everywhere, while it is simultaneously depoliticised, criminalised, deprived of its disturbing sting. Ultimately, the market behind consumerism, like the culture industry for Adorno and Horkheimer, is at the same time "pornographic and prudish" (Adorno and Horkheimer 1997: 140). We are egged on to experience all kinds of excessive pleasures, but only in so far as they already contain their own antibodies.

In *Seminar XVI*, Lacan had observed that although the reinvestment of profits "does not put the means of production at the service of pleasure," we nevertheless end up with a "practice of pleasure." In fact, this practice is forced on us and at the same time must be experienced as the result of our spontaneous yearning, so as to prevent "the sovereign pleasure of contemplative *far niente*." The decisive claim here is that the success of the pleasure principle must be measured against its power to intervene "in the catacombs," "in the underground *Acheronta*," namely in our unconscious. Any access to enjoyment, Lacan reminds us, takes place through the complex topology of the subject. This to say that no matter how excessive and potentially destabilising our experience of enjoyment under capitalism is, it still falls under the tempering jurisdiction of the pleasure principle, which is "careful that there is not too much heat in the wheels." Although we aim right at the heart of enjoyment, all we can hope for are "practices of recuperation." Moreover, precisely in preventing what Horace had called *otium cum dignitate*, the dignified subtraction from the imperative to work, capitalist hedonism proves all the more coercive (see Lacan 2007a, seminar of 15 March 1969). In brief, capital intervenes in the battle between the pleasure principle and its beyond by relentlessly converting the latter back into the former—which explains why, for instance, the injunction to enjoy is today primarily marketed as "enjoy wellbeing," i.e. "enjoy without enjoyment."

The political upshot of all this is that any subjective resistance from within the reigning ideology is more likely to end up being a "generalised degeneration" than a real subversion. As Lacan told the students during 1968, their "taking the floor" was more akin to "taking tobacco or coke" than "the taking of any particular Bastille" (see Lacan 2007a, seminar of 20 November 1968). Along these lines, in his "Impromptu at Vincennes" he called the Marxist-Leninist students "helots," referring to those serfs owned by the Spartan state in ancient Greece. When one of the students-agitators scornfully called Lacan a "liberal," he replied:

> I am, like everybody is, liberal only to the extent that I am antiprogressive. With the caveat that I am caught up in a movement that deserves to be called progressive, since it is progressive to see the psychoanalytic discourse founded, insofar as the latter completes the circle that could perhaps enable you to locate what it is exactly that you are rebelling against—which doesn't stop that thing from continuing extremely well. And the first to collaborate with this, right here at Vincennes, are you, for you fulfill the role of helots of this regime. You don't know what that means either? The regime is putting you on display. It says, "Look at them enjoying!" (Lacan 2007b: 208).

The University and Capitalist discourses are one and the same here. Lacan insists that the social link where students find themselves domesticates and integrates all excesses, turning even Marxist-Leninist revolutionaries into surplus-value. Hence his point that the students have failed to realise how capitalism thrives on their excitement about the (sexual) revolution in the same way as it thrives on the excitement of consumers in front of a shop window. The students, Lacan charges, are unable to see how their revolutionary enthusiasm is one of the effects of the paradigm shift determined by the onslaught of the discourse where capitalism flourishes. From this point of view, 1968 represented another chance for capital to demonstrate its ability to valorise surplus-enjoyment. In 1968, capital "enjoys" (makes a profit out of) looking at students enjoying/copulating (either enjoying playing at the revolution, or enjoying the sexual revolution). The revolutionary spirit was hijacked and turned into a valorised spectacle, a commodity whose "explosive potential" was not only constantly monitored, but also scientifically produced and regulated by the perverted master of the capitalist discourse. The explosion of political *jouissance* (extra-parliamentary splinter groups, armed struggle, etc.) was itself dexterously manoeuvred by capital (whose sole interest was to retain its hegemonic role during a period of crisis), with the kind intercession of its political ally, liberal democracy. Precisely by virtue of the background presence of the market stage-managing social upheavals, Lacan warns the leftists to "sound the depth of their commitments":

> meaning is provided by the sense each of us has of being part of this world, that is, of his little family and of everything that revolves around it. Each of you—I am speaking even for the leftists—you are more attached to it than you care to know and would do well to sound the depths of your attachment. A certain number of biases are your daily fare and limit the import of your insurrections to the shortest term, to the term, quite precisely, that gives you no discomfort—they certainly don't change your world view, for that remains perfectly spherical (Lacan 1998b: 42).

If all this is still relevant today, then the pressing question to ask is: what chances do we have to "become subjects" and take responsibility for our actions in the current condition of capitalist crisis?

8   Work as a Means of *jouissance*

If the discourse of the Capitalist tackles the problem of the positivisation of loss from the point of view of the worker/consumer (the barred subject is in the commanding position), the discourse of the University provides the same critique from a wider systemic perspective (knowledge is the agent). As anticipated, the two discourses should be read together, since, we argue, a crucial feature of modernity is that the inordinate weight associated with scientific knowledge and the type of rationality it purports is the flipside of the subject-turned-worker/consumer's arrogation of wisdom with regard to desire and enjoyment. We inhabit, in other words, a discourse where the aim of knowledge is to reduce everything to an abstract value to be produced and consumed. This is the main feature of the discourse of the University criticised by Lacan, which leads us to the often overlooked yet key Lacanian understanding of work.

Perhaps the most recurrent theme in *Seminar XVII* is the idea that knowledge and work cannot be seamlessly valorised, and glorified, without serious consequences for the human congregation. The moment "knowledge that is put to work" (Lacan repeatedly talks of "savoir-faire") begins to be valorised—i.e. the moment the capitalist buys the means of production to extract surplus-value from the workers' labour power—is also the moment a profound transformation takes place at the level of what Lacan calls surplus-*jouissance*. The latter captures precisely the lack that is consubstantial with every social link: an entropic, always-already lost dimension that accompanies the entry into play of the signifier. Everything for Lacan begins with language. Our universe of sense, the discourse in which we are immersed, depends on how the battery of signifiers is organised: "There is no natural social discourse, but only the one brought about by the intervention of language" (Lacan 1972). More crucially, while overlaying the world with "meanings," such intervention produces the effect of a loss of meaning, and that is what makes every discourse fundamentally inconsistent and vulnerable. In other words, language splits us: the signifier introduces a cut that separates the articulation of "known knowledge" from a knot of "unknown knowledge," and this frustrating division is what defines both the status of the subject and that of the symbolic order (discourse).

In *Seminar XVII* Lacan paradoxically defines knowledge as the "Other's *jouissance*" (Lacan 2007b: 14–15), by which he means the limit-dimension, the proverbial "bone in the throat," of any discourse whatsoever in so far as it is defined by the fact that it carries meaning and sustains our experience. Hence the breach between *savoir* and *connaisance*: the former stands for an obscure knowledge that overlaps with *jouissance* and, as such, brings to light the gaping hole at the heart of the "closed whole" (30) that constitutes the latter. *Savoir*, then, has to do with unconscious enjoyment, while *connaisance* is episteme. In focusing on *savoir*, and specifically *savoir-faire*, Lacan calls into question the rationality of modern science and, within it, the concept of productivity embraced by capitalist and socialist economies alike. It is a social link where "everything is merely to be counted—where energy itself is nothing other than what is counted" (80). At the same time, the goal is to demonstrate that despite its obdurate reliance on *connaisance*, the University discourse presents "an element of impossibility"—even though, as anticipated, it is much more difficult to locate.[15] Crucially, the senseless remainder of the process of signification enjoys a substantial status in Lacan, inasmuch as it

---

15   The centrality of this element of failure or negativity in Lacanian psychoanalysis allows us to clarify that, for him, structuralism itself is inseparable from the identification of the point of failure of structure (see Nobus and Quinn 2005: 116–17). His theory of the four-legged discourses (Master, University, Hysteric and Analyst) is meant to provide evidence that any structural link is inseparable from its deadlock: "In supposing the formalization of discourse and in granting oneself some rules within this formalization that are destined to put it to the test, we encounter an element of impossibility. This is what is at the base, the root, of an effect of structure" (44).

constitutes the Real, the hard kernel impervious to signification around which our being is woven:

> Sense, if I may say so, is responsible for being. It does not even have any other sense. The only thing is that it was observed some time ago that this is insufficient for carrying the weight—the weight, precisely, of existence. A curious thing that non-sense carries the weight. It grabs you by the stomach (56–7).

In pre-capitalist times, the "substantial senselessness" of the signifier that carries the weight of existence was preserved in the *savoir-faire* of those who were acting under the Master's orders, namely the slaves. With the anti-clockwise "quarter turn" of modernity, however, knowledge ceases to be in the hands of those who do not count, and instead becomes the agent, occupying the place of mastery itself. In such a position, it demands that what once was its unknown substance (the slaves' savoir-faire qua unconscious knowledge) emerge in broad daylight and is put to work under the aegis of a ubiquitous injunction to valorise. Thus, surplus-*jouissance*, this seemingly paradoxical substance shot through with negativity, is surreptitiously turned into surplus-value, a violently contradictory attempt to make loss countable—while the capitalist discourse begins to bear its fruits.

Lacan goes to the heart of the question concerning the creation of surplus-value. As we have seen, the novelty and ruse of capitalist abstraction and valorisation hinge, originally, on an operation founded upon the extraction of knowledge-at-work from the slave of pre-capitalist times. What is effectively plundered here is the surplus-*jouissance* intrinsic to the slave's work. The moment the slave's unconscious knowledge-at-work is converted into wage labour, a profound mystification takes place at the level of human activity itself: its unconscious or entropic roots are repressed, while abstract work is installed as its sole representative. The upshot is that loss—the possibility of perceiving the hole opened up by the signifier—progressively disappears from the horizon of the modern mind. The capitalist's conversion of this loss-effect into value, something to be counted and exchanged for the sole purpose of producing more value, spawns a generalised blindness with regard to the real substance of knowledge-at-work. If at the dawn of capitalism work begins to be fetishised as never before in the history of humankind, it is because its essential quality—the fact that human activity as such is rooted in the unconscious—is hijacked and transformed into a means toward the production of surplus-value. The ideological injunction to elevate work to the driving moral, cultural and economic principle of life goes hand in hand with the progressive destruction of the experience of knowledge-at-work as inseparable from a surplus (lack) of sense. Thus, science and economy become indistinguishable from morality, in a way that goes beyond even Max Weber's landmark discovery concerning the Protestant ethics of capitalism. Both the University and the Capitalist discourse originate in a logical sequence where scientific knowledge ("known knowledge") feeds into an idea of work that sustains the capitalist production of surplus-value. It is worth repeating that before the "capitalist revolution" set in, human activity was not reducible to labour power, to a valorised commodity, since, in Lacan's words, "the slave's labor is the labor that constitutes a non-revealed unconscious" (30).

Lacan's critique of the University discourse can therefore legitimately be seen as a radical critique of the specific understanding of work that characterises capitalist relations. In capitalism, the abstraction of work distorts the way humans interact with nature, precisely because it is based on the pervasive and perverse valorisation of such interaction. In its elementary function, on the contrary, the signifier brings into the equation a surplus of sense that defies quantification, thus establishing a relation to truth: "This is where work begins. It is with knowledge as a means of *jouissance* that work that has a meaning, an obscure meaning, is produced. This obscure meaning is the meaning of truth" (51). The distinctive and substantial quality of savoir-faire can only be subsumed under value via a dangerous sleight of hand which goes by the name of abstraction. With the discourse of the University, knowledge and the work it commands have been uprooted from their place in the big Other, coming instead to occupy the driving seat, ascending to the position of agency. It is owing to their "new tyranny" (32) that knowledge and work become abstract principles of human life. On the contrary, human activity *per se* defies abstraction, i.e. codification and equivalence; it is untranslatable. In Alenka Zupančič's words: "There is something in the status of work (or labor) which is identical to the status of enjoyment, namely, that it essentially appears as entropy, as loss, or as an unaccounted-for surplus (by-product) of signifying operations" (Zupančič 2006: 162). What is nestled in any signifying operation is the ontological opacity of the Real, and thus of any discourse: "everything that is produced through work—I mean this in the strict, full sense of the word "produced"—[…] is going to join company with this knowledge insofar as it is split off, *urverdrängt* [foreclosed], insofar as it is split off and nobody understands a thing about it" (Lacan 2007b: 90). The object of Lacan's scathing attacks against the University discourse is modernity's silent but fully operative belief in an abstract and therefore fully valorised universe, a universe dominated by a "knowledge-at-work" transformed into value, and where value is given to any knowledge as "knowledge that works." The modern notion of knowledge (*connaisance*), and the concept of work it intersects, "is what brings life to a halt at a certain limit on the path to *jouissance*" (Lacan 2007b: 18); in other words, it is what prevents the subject from experiencing the imp of *jouissance* via the ontological gap that qualifies experience itself in its abyssal contingency.

Against this fundamental mystification that drives modernity and its concept of work, Lacan forthrightly claims that "knowledge is a means of *jouissance*" (50). As he clarifies, there exists a logical concatenation between "knowledge-at-work," "entropy" and "*jouissance*":

> when it [knowledge] is at work, what it produces is entropy. This entropy, this point of loss, is the sole point, the sole regular point at which we have access to the nature of *jouissance*. This is what the effect the signifier has upon the fate of the speaking being translates into, culminates in, and is motivated by (50–51).

The key to grasping the critical dimension of Lacan's psychoanalytic discourse is neatly captured in the above quotation: the effect of the network of signifiers spreading over the surface of the world (discourses, knowledges, epistemes) is not only that, when set to work, they determine meanings that regulate our lives; but also, crucially, that they simultaneously create a loss, they "punch a hole" in meaning. This hole becomes a "means of *jouissance*" for as it allows us to access an untranslatable excess, a nonsense experienced as enjoyment, that in fact is what drives our subjective existence beyond the pleasure principle. It is this hole qua excess of meaning that the University discourse, and capitalism with it, attempt to convert into a countable entity. Such is the unheard-of gentrification that qualifies all ubiquitous capitalist abstractions.

From our perspective, it is vital to notice that it is "knowledge at work" (language, the signifier) that is responsible for the emergence of that surplus/loss of meaning named *jouissance*. The main novelty of Lacan's return to Freud is arguably his assertion that the signifier comes first—and, by coming first, it brings in its obscure double, which installs itself at the core of our subjective experience. Every time we try to make sense of the things around us via the signifier (since there is no other way for us) we also "produce" *jouissance* as "an obscure meaning" which is "the meaning of truth" (51). It is from this perspective that a critique of capitalist work can be articulated, in so far as the discourse of modernity tends to abolish the connection between human activity, *jouissance* and truth (in the strict Lacanian sense of *mi-dire*, half-saying, for "[w]e are *not without* a relationship with truth," 58). This claim can be expressed in simplified terms: what is capitalist valorisation if not the attempt to erase the unknowable yet substantial enjoyment at work when humans interact with the world? And, of course, by becoming themselves value, workers confirm the specific distortion operative in modern rationality: "Once a higher level has passed, surplus *jouissance* is no longer surplus *jouissance* but is inscribed simply as a value to be inscribed in or deducted from the totality of whatever it is that is accumulating [...]. The worker is merely a unit of value" (80–81).

There is, however, a significant corollary to all this. If capitalism affirms the indestructible connection of knowledge, work and value by seeking to turn the ontological limit of the social link into its productive engine, Lacan insists that the limit does not disappear, and this is why we are heading for a blowout. It is precisely because value tries to colonise every aspect of life that the price to pay for progress is deprivation.

9   Progress as Deprivation

Through their emancipation from slaves to proletarians, workers have not merely progressed. Rather, they have lost what was distinctive about their position, namely their specific knowledge, their *savoir-faire* as intimately related to surplus-*jouissance*. Pressed on the function and position of the proletariat in his theory of the four discourses, Lacan replies that it is to be found there where "knowledge no longer has any weight. The proletarian is not simply exploited, he has been stripped of his function of knowledge. The so-called liberation of the slave has had, as always, other corollaries. It's not merely progressive. It's progressive only at the price of deprivation" (149). The metaphor of the weightless worker, dispossessed of his particular knowledge, is decisive if we are to grasp the anti-capitalist potential of Lacan's stance, and more generally his critique of abstract labour. With the inception of capitalism, savoir-faire has been turned into a commodity to be bought and sold with the only purpose of creating more money. Lacan's argument is very subtle here: while the Master of pre-capitalist times knew nothing about how things were made (he simply gave orders and enjoyed the results of other people's work),[16] the new Master is an invasive knowledge about work, attempting to control everything on the strength of this link. The truth, however, is paradoxical: precisely because he knew nothing about how knowledge "produced" things, the old Master and his discourse preserved the surplus-*jouissance* attached to work, a surplus which functioned "underground," where it could be accessed, albeit illusorily, via fantasy (hence the formula $\$ \lozenge a$ in the lower part of the Master's discourse). Vice versa, the sudden and forced conversion of substantial surplus into surplus-value distorts the meaning of human activity to the extent that its entropic quality is turned into capitalism's productive engine.

In the University discourse, the link between agent and Other undergoes a crucial distortion. What gets addressed by the agency of knowledge (*connaisance*, scientific knowledge) is *objet a* filling in the position of the big Other. The key point to highlight is that the surplus of "knowledge at work" is not hidden under S_2, as with the discourse of the Master, but is instead explicitly targeted and endorsed. Thus, having emerged to the upper level (consciousness) the objects of desire (among which are workers themselves) become surplus-value, and as such are deprived of their foundational entropy. Ultimately, it is in this crucial distortion of the "substantial negativity" pertaining to *objet a* that one should locate Lacan's critique of the social link that sustains a mode of production based on the hypostatisation of an abstract principle that dominates social relations. What Lacan denounces is the universalised abstraction characterising the rapport between the hegemonic power of scientific knowledge and the valorised objects of desire forming the signifying network of the big Other. The danger, from Lacan's angle, is that within this universe saturated with countable values responding directly to knowledge and work, the possibility of locating the substantial structural inconsistency of the social link gets lost.

However, not all loss is lost, as it were, since this discourse, like all others, produces a remainder that simply does not fit (and indeed threatens to disrupt) its well-oiled mechanism. Crucially for our argument, the "objective remainder"

---

16 "A real master, as in general we used to see until a recent era, and this is seen less and less, doesn't desire to know anything at all—he desires that things work. And why would he want to know? There are more amusing things than that" (Lacan 2007b: 24).

(*objet a*) of the University discourse coincides with *the subject itself* in its radically decentred status ($). The fact that the subject appears in the bottom right-hand side, in the place of what is produced, implies that it stands for the disavowed "waste result" of the link between S₂ and *a*, namely what Lacan himself calls the sub-proletariat, masses of segregated people who are simply in excess of the University discourse. It is highly significant that in some of the most captivating passages of *Seminar XVII* Lacan refers to the production of segregation, of the lumpenproletariat, and of shame, as the precise point where the system potentially fails. For instance, in the aforementioned "Impromptu at Vincennes" Lacan rebukes the subversive students by reminding them that the process of valorisation that dominates their lives ends up producing not only exchange-values and wealth, but also a useless human surplus that contradicts the capitalist agenda. Demystifying the notion of brotherhood embraced by the leftist rhetoric of the time, Lacan comments:

> The energy that we put into all being brothers very clearly proves that we are not brothers. Even with our brother by birth nothing proves that we are his brother—we can have a completely opposite batch of chromosomes. This pursuit of brotherhood, without counting the rest, liberty and equality, is something that's pretty extraordinary, and it is appropriate to realize what it covers. I know only one single origin of brotherhood—I mean human, always humus brotherhood—segregation. We are of course in a period where segregation, ugh! There is no longer any segregation anywhere, it's unheard of when you read the newspapers. It's just that in society [...] everything that exists, and brotherhood first and foremost, is founded on segregation. No other brotherhood is even conceivable or has the slightest foundation, as I have just said, the slightest scientific foundation, unless because people are isolated together, isolated from the rest (Lacan 2007b: 114).

Later, he suggests that subversion in the University discourse is not to be found at the level of traditional class struggle but "on the other side" of his schema, where shame is produced, i.e. where "the student is not displaced in feeling a brother, as they say, not of the proletariat but of the lumpenproletariat" (190).

So here we have the final picture of the dislocation described in the University discourse: while *objet a* emerges into visibility by morphing into a commodity and losing its entropic substance, its place (the product of signification) is taken by the subject in its proper psychoanalytic status of symptom, "thing" that by not fitting the symbolic order effectively denounces that order itself. The segregated as "part of no part" define the contours of a critique levelled against a discourse where knowledge and work attempt to reduce all life to a series of abstract equivalences. Ultimately, these are the two reasons why the lower level of the University discourse provides a key to understanding the crisis of capitalism: 1) $: masses of people are increasingly rendered superfluous (jobless) by the universal valorisation of life (the "capitalist utopia" if ever there was one) and, 2) S₁: the master-signifier occupies the place of truth, pulling the strings from an invisible and seemingly inviolable position (revealing the truth about the "invisible hand of the market").

10   Surplus as Parallax, or: *quo vadis* Marx?

Lacan's insistence on the substantial status of surplus *qua* lack is of fundamental importance for a conceptualisation of capitalist crisis that aims to envision a way out of the mode of production that is at the pulsating heart of such crisis. If the left continues to struggle in its attempt to "politicize Lacan," it is because it fails to intercept the ontological presupposition of his psychoanalytic epistemology—namely, the idea that any social link is inseparable from an entropic libidinal surplus that embodies its ontological inconsistency. In this respect, the problem with the left is that, historically, it has fought its battles from within the same veneration of the ubiquitous valorisation of this entropic surplus that typifies capitalism. Lacan notices that if there is a contradiction in Marxism it relates to its concept of work as something that both transcends and is over-determined by capitalist categories. He explicitly warns that any project of radical subversion of capitalism from within the workers' perspective—whether the classic proletariat or the intellectual worker of today's information society—is destined to fail, since valorised work is an integral ingredient of capitalist ideology. In *Radiophonie*, for instance, when discussing "the ideology of class struggle," Lacan intimates that "it only induces the exploited to compete in principle in the exploitation, in order to defend their patent participation in the thirst of the lack-in-enjoyment" (Lacan 1970: 87). It is a fact that leftist categories such as progress and emancipation have mostly been deployed *within* the very productive dynamics that hinge on exploitation. Indeed, Marx himself, together with the great majority of his followers, theorised the painful passage through industrial capitalism as a necessary ordeal to reach communism.

It is undeniable that the tradition of the left, in all its historical variants, has tended to locate itself within a social and political discourse founded on the acceptance of value, abstract labour and money. Particularly striking is its cult of productive labour. This indicates that all main leftist oppositions to capitalism have been immanent to it in accepting its basic presuppositions. What they have notably tended to ignore is Marx's *critique* of abstract labour, as opposed to what Marx calls "particular labour" in the *Grundrisse* (Marx 1993: 171–73) and "concrete useful labour" ten years later in chapter 1, section 2 of *Capital* (Marx 1990: 137).[17] Although Marx invariably defines labour negatively as an alienating activity, what he has in mind is, even when not specified, the abstraction of labour under capitalist conditions. Similarly, his call for the abolition of work, which resonates in various parts of the *German Ideology*, does not imply the elimination of work as "free human activity" (see Arthur 1986). From our perspective, Marx's own insights into the dual composition of labour—abstract labour subsuming living human activity to produce value—is decisive for a critique of the modern notion of work. While abstract labour

---

17   "A thing can be useful, and a product of human labour, without being a commodity. He who satisfies his own need with the product of labour admittedly creates use-values, but not commodities. In order to produce the latter, he must not only produce use-values, but use-values for others" (Marx 1990: 131).

should not be seen as an ahistorical category coincidental with the mere expenditure of human energy (since the abstraction of labour is imposed by the value-form), it follows that work-as-such (Lacan's *savoir-faire*) should not be jettisoned as immediately functional to capitalist production. Today, despite the evidence of the failure of capitalist valorisation, the left is by and large unable to imagine a model of society that is not founded on the necessity to sell one's labour power, regardless of how difficult it has become to find "buyers." Lacan, by placing the emphasis firmly on the fundamentally value-less dimension of human activity as a residue of any signifying operation, reminds us of the risk involved in traditional Marxism's acceptance of the capitalist battlefield of positive valorisation. In fact, he was critical of "really existing socialism" as he recognised that its "scientific organisation of work" was based on the same principle of valorisation that fuels capitalism.[18]

Lacan is aware that, in a social link that has allowed itself a "relaxation" from the domineering character of the Master's discourse, the injunction to work goes hand in hand with the injunction to know: "Work has never been given such credit ever since humanity has existed. It is even out of the question that one not work. [...] I am speaking of this capitalist mutation, also, which gives the master's discourse its capitalist style" (Lacan 2007b: 168). That work, for Lacan, can attain a different status from its capitalist one can be evinced from a brief, tentative, and yet significant allusion to Maoism:

> I won't risk going into this, I would only go into it cautiously, but if there is something whose tone strikes me in the thematic called Maoist, it's the reference to the knowledge of manual labor. [...] the renewed emphasis on the knowledge of the exploited seems to me to be very profoundly motivated structurally. The question is knowing whether this is not something that is entirely dreamed up. [...] can know-how at the level of manual labor carry enough weight to be a subversive factor? This is how, for me, the question arises (149).

It is from the perspective of a critique of abstraction that Lacan also takes issue with Marx's notion of surplus-value. The problem he sees in this notion is, ultimately, that it contains two highly incompatible terms (which is why he decides to refer surplus-value back to surplus-*jouissance*): surplus as such cannot be made to coincide with a value; it over-determines value in the precise sense that it cannot be counted. Contrary to this, Marx's surplus-value is eventually caught up in the ruse of capitalist valorisation, with surplus designating the value extracted from labour power. Before elaborating on this, let us remind ourselves that, in Marx, surplus-value originates in unpaid surplus labour. Here is a familiar passage from *Capital* volume I:

---

18   In *Seminar XVII* he asserts that the University discourse is in "the driving seat" precisely "in what is commonly called the Soviet Union of Socialist Republics" (Lacan 2007b: 206). Or even more explicitly: "It's not because one nationalizes the means of production at the level of socialism in one country that one has thereby done away with surplus value, if one doesn't know what it is" (108).

> During one period, the worker produces a value that is only equal to the value of his labour-power, i.e. he produces its equivalent. Thus the capitalist receives, in return for advancing the price of the labour-power, a product of the same price. It is the same as if he had bought the product ready-made in the market. During the other period, the period of surplus-labour, the utilization of labour-power creates a value for the capitalist without costing him any value in return. He is thus able to set labour-power in motion without paying for it. It is in this sense that surplus labour can be called unpaid labour. Capital, therefore, is not only the command over labour, as Adam Smith thought. It is essentially the command over unpaid labour. All surplus-value, whatever particular form (profit, interest or rent) it may subsequently crystallize into, is in substance the materialization of unpaid labour. The secret of the self-valorization of capital resolves itself into the fact that it has at its disposal a definite quantity of the unpaid labour of other people (Marx 1990: 671–72).

Surplus-value therefore emerges from the expropriation of a quantity of labour that is in excess of the purchased labour-power. To get surplus-value, whichever its form, the capitalist transforms into value a quantity of labour he has not paid for: "Half the working day costs capital *nothing*; it thus obtains a value for which it has given no equivalent" (Marx 1993: 324). The self-valorisation of capital requires precisely this extraction of surplus-value from the worker's labour power:

> Capitalist production is not merely the production of commodities, it is, by its very essence, the production of surplus-value. The worker produces not for himself, but for capital. It is no longer sufficient, therefore, for him simply to produce. He must produce surplus-value. The only worker who is productive is one who produces surplus-value for the capitalist, or in other words contributes towards the self-valorization of capital (Marx 1990: 644).

Marx is quite explicit when, in the same passage, he claims: "To be a productive worker is therefore not a piece of luck, but a misfortune" (Marx 1990: 644).

In this respect, his crucial advance in relation to the bourgeois political economists who preceded him (Adam Smith, Ricardo, etc.) is his insight into the specific configuration of the commodity that transforms money into capital, namely labour power. It is this insight that brings us to connect Marx with Lacan. In the *Grundrisse*, echoing a theme that had emerged much earlier in his thought, and especially in the *Economic and Philosophical Manuscripts of 1844*, Marx defines labour power as something that exists "in potentiality" as the worker's "vitality," his *labouring capacity* as a living being (Marx 1993: 267). Quite explicitly, he claims that expropriation of labour power means essentially not paying for the *quality* of labour-as-such rather than for its quantity, namely for labour as a non-measurable entity, "for the fact that *labour, as labour, is labour*" (359). The recourse to this tautology is symptomatic, since it suggests that labour cannot be defined otherwise than by the signifier "labour," which underscores the contingent and unquantifiable surplus signified by the term.[19] The labour power that the worker surrenders to the capitalist, "like Esau his birthright for a mess of pottage," is thus nothing other than labour's intrinsic and non-measurable "*creative power*" (307). If, then, "[t]he great historic quality of capital is to *create* this *surplus labour*, superfluous labour from the standpoint of mere use value, mere subsistence" (325), we ought to think it alongside Lacan's surplus, namely a quality which, before being converted into value, represents an obscure entropy inseparable from human activity as such.

Capital's ability to instil in the worker the desire to produce excessively and incessantly, forcing him over the centuries to identify with a type of industriousness rooted in his own expropriated surplus-labour, needs to be connected with the psychoanalytic ontology of surplus as entropic libido. In *Seminar XVI* and *Seminar XVII* Lacan developed this decisive observation by proposing the homology between surplus-value and surplus-*jouissance*. Our contention here is that Marx's surplus-labour, which is the direct cause of surplus-value, is already in itself coterminous with Lacan's surplus-*jouissance*, for it not only refers to the worker's unpaid labour-time, but also to the incalculable quality of work-as-such. That Marx did not develop this insight is consistent with the ideological mould of his historical constellation. Instead, he focused on surplus labour-time, conceptualising it as potentially detachable from surplus-value and directly available to the workers who, in communism, would use it for the good of the whole of society. From Lacan's perspective, then, Marx's ultimate "reduction" of work-as-such to labour-time corresponds to deracinating the former from its real dimension. To an extent, it is an operation that plays in the hands of the capitalist discourse in as much as the latter is based on generalised abstraction. Lacan's suggestion, by contrast, is that the genesis of surplus-value—the invisible turbine at the heart of capitalist valorisation—should be conceived less as a supplementary lapse of non-remunerated labour-time than in relation to the non-quantifiable quality intrinsic to work. If the labour power offered by the free worker on the market, as Marx put it, "exists only as an ability, a capacity [*Vermögen*] of his bodily existence," and "has no existence apart from that" (Marx 1993: 282), it is precisely as an amorphous and intrinsically entropic power that it should be associated with the Real of *jouissance*.

The specific thesis we are advancing here is that the historical success of capitalism as an economic as well as socially synthetic system "deep down" depends on what we might describe, resorting to the fortunate image popularised by Žižek, as a *parallax shift* from surplus-*jouissance* to surplus-value.[20] What we perceive as

---

19   As Žižek puts it, far from signalling the inability to explain the exact qualities of a given object, a tautology "announces the miracle of the fragile coincidence of an ordinary object with the absolute Thing" (Žižek 2012: 775). In other words, tautology allows us to discern the presence of a surplus of meaning for which there is no adequate signifier.

20   In brief, Lacan claims that the unpaid surplus-labour turned by the capitalist into surplus-value is homologous to surplus-*jouissance*. Marx's *Mehrwert*, he avers, is actually *Mehrlust*: his point is precisely to harness surplus-value to its foundation in the Real of *jouissance*. In psychoanalytic terms, surplus-value is therefore homologous to surplus-*jouissance*, as it stands for the specious valorisation of the entropic surplus of work.

value originates in the substantial lack at the heart of being from which the little *a* emerges, this special thing that owes its precious status as object-cause of desire precisely to that lack. We must remember that in positing the homology between surplus-value (*plus-value*) and surplus-enjoyment (*plus-de-jouir*), Lacan uses the latter to debunk the former. With *plus-de-jouir*, he plays on the ambiguity of *plus* in the French language, since it stands for both a plus (something in excess) and a lack (a break in, or renunciation, of enjoyment). The capitalist valorisation of this ontological lack corresponds to an unprecedented attempt to construct a social order on what we might call an act of recycling, for capitalism achieves its goal through the invisible conversion of surplus-*jouissance* into value:

> Something changed in the master's discourse at a certain point in history. We are not going to break our backs finding out if it was because of Luther, Calvin or some unknown traffic of ships around Genoa, or in the Mediterranean Sea, or anywhere else, for the important point is that on a certain day surplus *jouissance* became calculable, could be counted, totalized. This is where what is called the accumulation of capital begins.

All of a sudden, Lacan continues, "we are in the field of values." And "from that moment on, by virtue of the fact that the clouds of impotence have been aired, the master signifier only appears even more unassailable [...]. Where is it? How can it be named? How can it be located?—other than through its murderous effects, of course. Denounce imperialism? But how can this little mechanism be stopped?" (Lacan 2007b: 177–78).

11   Crisis and Human Surplus

Far from being reducible to a value, then, surplus for Lacan is entropic in two ways: first, in a concretely historicist way, as the human surplus of capitalist dynamics, which today corresponds to the excluded masses rendered redundant by the capitalist obsession with valorisation, which has hit the buffers; secondly, at a more fundamental formal level, as surplus-*jouissance* (*plus-de-jouir*), that is to say as the ontological impasse of any discourse whatsoever. This surplus coterminous with lack is hijacked and "dressed up in sexy garments" by capitalism; as such, it becomes the engine at the heart of what Marx had aptly named commodity fetishism.

Lacan's analysis would seem to confirm Marx's well-known claim from volume 3 of *Capital* that the limit of capitalism is capital itself (since, briefly stated, developments in productiveness lead to a fall in the rate of profit). The argument is fairly straightforward: what initially gets lost (surplus-*jouissance*) through the process of valorisation, does not disappear, but returns in the shape of masses (millions) of excluded, ghostly subjects. To put it in psychoanalytic terms, the repressed substance returns with a vengeance as radically dislocated humanity, people who are symbolically dead. As we have seen, among the most critical contradictions of modernity and progress Lacan identifies segregation, namely disposable, redundant, useless human surplus. We argue that today's name for such segregation is "unredeemable unemployment." Here we should add a second crucial interpretation of what is produced (*a*) in Lacan's discourse of the Capitalist. While it is correct to speak of *a* as surplus-value, at the same time what is *effectively* generated by capitalism—as today's crisis emphatically confirms— is not just unemployment, but a condition of radical exclusion which threatens the very foundations of society. Ultimately, the disturbing "lost object" of the capitalist social link corresponds to the displaced humanity brought about by the failed connection between the capitalist drive and surplus-value.

It is important to insist that Lacan's theorisation of surplus-*jouissance* as a parallactic specification of surplus-value functions as a critique of work, an especially pressing one if read alongside today's capitalist crisis. As anticipated, our view of such crisis identifies the historical limit and explosive contradiction of capitalism in its constantly augmenting creation of surplus labour that causes a progressive fall of global capital, since the process of capitalist valorisation is systematically tied to the exploitation of the work-force. It is paradoxical, and yet all the more true, that the technological development through the centuries has been both the great engine behind capitalist accumulation and its lethal harbinger of crisis. Scientific development (the University discourse!) has allowed the capitalist to increase production and maximise profit, but simultaneously it has made the work-force replaceable by machines and therefore ever more superfluous. What today the protagonists of capitalism and liberal democracy seem to ignore, is the Marxist insight that machines by themselves cannot create new value. On the contrary, only "live" human labour creates profit and growth. The absurdly ideological situation we are experiencing is that, while wage work is less and less necessary in terms of productivity, at the same time it is regarded as the only form of social mediation available to human beings.

Historically, we see the stagflation of the 1970s, the advent of neo-liberalism and the finance industry, and today's economic crisis as a logical sequence where each passage is nothing but a consequence of the previous one: the answer to the crisis of the Fordist system of production, which determined the stagflation of the 1970s, was the financialisation of the economy, whose purpose was to hide the crisis of real growth through the creation of fictitious surplus-value generated by the finance industry. When the speculative bubble exploded in 2008, the system was again faced by the harsh crisis of valorisation, to which it is now desperately trying to respond, though no other option is available apart from, again, the prestidigitations of the finance industry. What all this highlights is that we are close—closer than ever before—to the insurmountable historical limit of capitalism, in so far as growth is hindered precisely by the perverse capitalist connection between valorisation and the creation of human surplus aptly described by Lacan more than three decades ago.

While we have proposed a reading of the current crisis that underscores the capitalist tendency to displace human labour—which has been tremendously incremented by the turn to micro-electronics and digitalisation during the so-called "third industrial revolution"—at the same time we have drawn on the Lacanian insight that the capitalist declension of work originates in the valorisation of entropic labour power. In so far as work is aimed at augmenting the mass of value, capitalism will continue generating more and more superfluous work-force, thus accelerating the process of crisis to a point of no return. What Lacan allows us to perceive is that the key capitalist contradiction concerning the creation of surplus labour, which hampers valorisation and threatens the capitalist system itself, is rooted in the capitalist's original abstraction of labour power. As we have seen, Lacan maintains that the shift from pre-capitalist to capitalist times was based on the attempt to intercept, internalise and re-invest the surplus ontologically inherent to work qua human activity, in its generalised signifying function—work as savoir-faire. Lacan tells us that this work, in its deepest connotation, is a function of surplus qua lack. If, therefore, the capitalist utopia resides in converting all surplus into value, i.e. in putting everyone to work, today we know this one thing: that it does not work. The superfluous masses at the heart of today's crisis will not find a way back in.

References

Acharya, Viral, et al., eds (2011) *Regulating Wall Street: The Dodd-Frank Act and the New Architecture of Global Finance*. Hoboken/NJ: John Wiley & Sons.

Adorno, Theodor and Horkheimer, Max (1997) *Dialectic of Enlightenment*. London and New York: Verso.

Akerlof, George and Robert Shiller (2010) *Animal Spirits: How Human Psychology Drives the Economy, and Why it Matters for Global Capitalism*. Princeton and Oxford: Princeton University Press.

Arendt, Hannah (1958) *The Human Condition*. Chicago and London: University of Chicago Press.

Arthur, Chris (1986) *Dialectics of Labour: Marx and his Relation to Hegel*. Oxford: Blackwell.

Barker, Jason (2011) *Marx Reloaded*. Films Noirs and Medea Film.

Beck, Glenn (2010) *Broke: The Plan to Restore Our Trust, Truth and Treasure*. New York: Simon and Schuster.

Bellamy Foster, John and Robert McChesney (2012) *The Endless Crisis: How Monopoly-finance Capital Produces Stagnation and Upheaval from the USA to China*. New York: Monthly Review Press.

Benjamin, Walter (1921) "Kapitalismus als Religion" (Fragment), in *Gesammelte Schriften*, ed. by Rolf Tiedemann and Hermann Schweppenhäuser, vol. 6. Frankfurt on Main: Suhrkamp, 1991, pp. 100–102.

Besley, Tim and Peter Hennessy (2009) [Open Letter to the Queen, 22 July 2009], http://www.ft.com/queenletter, accessed 27 July 2009.

Bryant, Levi R. (2008) "Žižek's New Universe of Discourse: Politics and the Discourse of the Capitalist," in *International Journal of Žižek Studies*, vol. 2, n. 4.

Butler, Eamonn (2012) *Public Choice*. London: Institute of Economic Affairs.

Cable, Vince (2010) *The Storm: The World Economic Crisis and What It Means*. London: Atlantic Books.

Callinicos, Alex (2010) *Bonfire of Illusions: The Twin Crises of the Liberal World*. Cambridge: Polity Press.

Carchedi, Guglielmo (2010) *Behind the Crisis: Marx's Dialectic of Value and Knowledge*. Leiden and Boston: Brill.

Chang, Ha-Joon (2011) *23 Things They Don't Tell You About Capitalism*. London, New York and Toronto: Penguin.

Cho, Renee (2011) "Have We Crossed the 9 Planetary Boundaries?," in *State of the Planet*, Columbia University, http://blogs.ei.columbia.edu/2011/08/05/have-we-crossed-the-9-planetary-boundaries/, accessed 5 March 2012.

Cloutier, George (2009) *Profits Aren't Everything, They're The Only Thing*. New York: Harper Business.

Cowen, Tyler (2010) *The Great Stagnation*. London, New York and Toronto: Penguin.

Daly, Herman (1977) *Steady-State Economics the Economics of Biophysical Equilibrium and Moral Growth*. New York and San Francisco: W. H. Freeman.

———— (1996) *Beyond Growth: Economics of Sustainable Development*. Boston: Beacon Press.

Davidson, Paul (2009) *The Keynes Solution: The Path to Global Economic Prosperity*. New York: Palgrave Macmillan.

"Degrowth Declaration Barcelona 2010" (2010), http://degrowth.org/wp-content/uploads/2011/05/Degrowth_Declaration_Barcelona_2010.pdf, accessed 25 May 2011.

Denning, Steve (2011) "From the Great Recession to the Great Stagnation," an interview with Glen Hutchins, in *Forbes*, 10 October 2011, http://www.forbes.com/sites/stevedenning/2011/10/10/from-the-great-recession-to-the-great-stagnation/, accessed 2 May 2012.

Diamond, Jared (2006) *Collapse: How Societies Choose to Fail or Survive*. London, New York and Toronto: Penguin.

Dowd, Kevin and Martin Hutchinson (2010) *The Alchemists of Loss: How Modern Finance and Government Intervention Crashed the Financial System*. Chichester: John Wiley & Sons.

Eagleton, Terry (2011) *Why Marx Was Right*. New Haven and London: Yale University Press.

The Economist (2012) *The Third Industrial Revolution: A Special Report*, 21 April 2012, http://www.economist.com/node/21552901, accessed 21 April 2012.

Eisenstein, Charles (2011) *Sacred Economics: Money, Gift and Society in the Age of Transition*. Berkeley/CA: Evolver Editions.

Elliott, Larry and Dan Atkinson (2009) *The Gods That Failed: How the Financial Elite Have Gambled Away Our Futures*. London: Vintage.

Engels, Friedrich (1876) "The Part Played by Labour in the Transition from Ape to Man," trans. Clemens Dutt, in *Marx-Engels Collected Works*, vol. 25, London: Lawrence & Wishart, 1987, pp. 452–65.

Ferguson, Niall (2012) "The Darwinian Economy," The Reith Lectures, no. 2, New York Historical Society, broadcast on BBC Radio 4, 26 June 2012, http://www.bbc.co.uk/programmes/b01jmxqp/features/transcript, accessed 26 June 2012.

Gamble, Andrew (2009) *The Spectre at the Feast: Capitalist Crisis and the Politics of Recession*. London and New York: Palgrave Macmillan.

Gay, Peter (1985) *Freud for Historians*. New York and Oxford: Oxford University Press.

Georgescu-Roegen, Nicholas (1971) *The Entropy Law and the Economic Process*. Cambridge/MA: Harvard University Press.

Gorz, André (2005) *Reclaiming Work: Beyond the Wage-Based Society* (trans. Chris Turner). Cambridge and Malden, MA: Polity.

Greenspan, Alan (2009) "Market Crisis 'Will Happen Again,'" BBC interview, 8 September 2009, http://news.bbc.co.uk/go/pr/fr/-/1/hi/business/8244600.stm, accessed 9 September 2009.

Hardt, Michael and Antonio Negri (2009) *Commonwealth*. Cambridge, MA: The Belknap Press of Harvard University Press.

Harman, Chris (2009) *Zombie Capitalism: Global Crisis and the Relevance of Marx*. London: Bookmarks Publications.

Harvey, David (2011) *The Enigma of Capital and the Crises of Capitalism* (updated and extended). London: Profile Books.

Haug, Wolfgang Fritz (2012) *Hightech Kapitalismus in der Großen Krise*. Hamburg: Argument Verlag.

Hawken, Paul, Amory B. Lovins and L. Hunter Lovins (2010) *Natural Capitalism: the Next Industrial Revolution* (revised edition). London and Washington: Earthscan.

Heinberg, Richard (2011) *The End of Growth: Adapting to Our New Economic Reality*. Forest Row: Clairview Books.

Hill, Amelia (2012) "Millions of Working Families One Push from Penury, Guardian Research Finds," in *The Guardian*, 18 June 2012, http://www.guardian.co.uk/society/2012/jun/18/working-britons-one-push-from-penury, accessed 18 June 2012.

d'Humières, Patrick (2010) *Le développement durable va-t-il tuer le capitalisme?: Les réponses de l'éco-capitalisme*. Paris: Editions Maxima.

Hutton, Will (2010) *Them and Us: Changing Britain—Why We Need a Fair Society*. London: Little, Brown.

——— (2012a) "Mervyn King didn't Grasp the Crisis then—and he doesn't Now," in *The Observer*, 6 May 2012, p. 34.

——— (2012b) "Britain's Future Lies in a Culture of Open and Vigorous Innovation," in *The Observer*, 14 October 2012, http://www.guardian.co.uk/commentisfree/2012/oct/14/will-hutton-britain-innovation-hub, accessed 15 October 2012.

Jackson, Jim (2009) *Prosperity without Growth: Economics for a Finite Planet*. London and Washington: Earthscan.

Kaletsky, Anatole (2011) *Capitalism 4.0: The Birth of a New Economy in the Aftermath of Crisis* (revised and updated edition). London, Berlin and New York: Bloomsbury.

Kallis, Giorgos (2011) "In Defence of Degrowth," in *Ecological Economics* 70 (2011) 873–80, http://degrowth.org/wp-content/uploads/2011/08/In-defense-of-degrowth.pdf, accessed 12 January 2012.

Kant, Immanuel (1784) "Idee zu einer allgemeinen Geschichte in weltbürgerlicher Absicht," in idem, *Von den Träumen der Vernunft*. Leipzig and Weimer: Kiepenheuer 1981, pp. 201–21.

——— (1798), *Anthropology from a Pragmatic Point of View*, trans. and ed. by Robert Louden, Cambridge, New York and Melbourne: Cambridge University Press 2006.

Keynes, John Maynard (1930) "Economic Possibilities for our Grandchildren," in idem *Essays in Persuasion*. New York: Harcourt, Brace and Company 1932, pp. 358–73.

——— (1936). *The General Theory of Employment, Interest and Money*, London: Macmillan.

King, Mervyn (2012) "The 2012 BBC Today Pogramme Lecture," 2 May 2012, http://news.bbc.co.uk/today/hi/today/newsid_9718000/9718062.stm, (accessed 3 May 2012).

Kliman, Andrew (2012) *The Failure of Capitalist Production: Underlying Courses of the Great Recession*. London: Pluto Press.

KPMG (2012) "One in Five UK Workers Paid Less than the Living Wage," available at http://www.kpmg.com/UK/en/IssuesAndInsights/ArticlesPublications/NewsReleases/Pages/One-in-five-UK-workers-paid-less-than-the-Living-Wage.aspx (accessed 29 October 2012).

Krugman, Paul (2009), *A Country is Not A Company*. Boston/MA: Harvard Business School Publishing (first published in *Harvard Business Review*, January 1996).

——— (2012) *End this Depression Now!* London and New York: W. W. Norton.

Krugman, Paul and Robin Wells (2009) *Economics* (2nd ed.). New York: Worth Publishers.

Kurz, Robert (1991) *Der Kollaps der Modernisierung: Vom Zusammenbruch des Kasernensozialismus zur Krise der Weltökonomie*. Frankfurt on Main: Eichborn.

——— (2005) *Das Weltkapital: Globalisierung und innere Schranken des modernen warenproduzierenden Systems*. Berlin: Edition Tiamat.

——— (2009) *Schwarzbuch Kapitalismus: Ein Abgesang auf die Marktwirtschaft* (2nd edition). Frankfurt on Main: Eichborn.

——— (2012) *Geld ohne Wert: Grundrisse zu einer Transformation der Kritik der politischen Ökonomie*. Berlin: Horlemann Verlag.

Lacan, Jacques (1970) *Radiophonie*, in *Scilicet 2/3* (Paris: Seuil) 1970, pp. 55–99. English translation by Jack W. Stone available online at *web.missouri.edu/~stonej/Radiophonie.pdf* (accessed 14 January 2013).

———— (1970–71) *Seminar XVIII. On a Discourse that Might not be a Semblance* (unpublished).

———— (1972) "On Psychoanalytic Discourse," in *Lacan in Italia, 1953–1978* (Milan: La Salmandra) 1978, pp. 32–55. English translation by Jack W. Stone available online at *web.missouri.edu/~stonej/Milan_Discourse2.pdf* (accessed 12 January 2013).

———— (1998a) *The Seminar, Book XI. The Four Fundamental Concepts of Psychoanalysis*. New York and London: W. W. Norton.

———— (1998b) *The Seminar, Book XX. On Feminine Sexuality. The Limits of Love and Knowledge*. New York and London: W. W. Norton.

———— (2006) *Le séminaire, Livre XVI: D'un Autre à l'autre*. Paris: Seuil (unpublished in English). English translation from unedited French manuscripts by Cormac Gallagher available online at http://www.lacaninireland.com/web/?page_id=123.

———— (2007a) *Le Séminaire. Livre XVIII D'un discours qui ne serait pas du semblant*. Paris: Seuil (unpublished in English). English translation from unedited French manuscripts by Cormac Gallagher available online at http://www.lacaninireland.com/web/?page_id=123.

———— (2007b) *The Seminar, Book XVII. The Other Side of Psychoanalysis*. New York and London: W. W. Norton.

Latouche, Serge (2009) *Farewell to Growth*. Cambridge and Malden/MA: Polity.

Leontief, Wassily (1983) "National Perspective: the Definition of Problems and Opportunities," in *The Long-Term Impact of Technology on Employment and Unemployment*. A National Academy of Engineering Symposium, 30th June 1983. Washington, DC: National Academy Press, pp. 3–7.

Magdoff, Fred and Michael Yates (2009) *The ABCs of the Economic Crisis: What Working People Need to Know*. New York: Monthly Review Press.

Mandel, Ernest (1975) *Late Capitalism* (trans. Joris De Bres). London: NLB.

Marazzi, Christian (2011) *The Violence of Financial Capitalism* (trans. Kristina Lebedeva and Jason Francis Mc Gimsey, 2nd edition). Los Angeles: Semiotext(e).

Marx, Karl (1975) "Draft of an Article on Friedrich List's book: Das Nationale System der Politischen Oekonomie" [1845], in *Marx-Engels Collected Works*, vol. 4, London: Lawrence and Wishart, pp. 265–94.

———— (1990) *Capital: A Critique of Political Economy*, vol. 1 (trans. Ben Fowkes). London, New York and Toronto: Penguin.

———— (1991) *Capital: A Critique of Political Economy*, vol. 3 (trans. David Fernbach). London, New York and Toronto: Penguin.

———— (1992) *Capital: A Critique of Political Economy*, vol. 2 (trans. David Fernbach). London, New York and Toronto: Penguin.

———— (1993), *Grundrisse: Foundations of the Critique of Political Economy* [1857–58] (trans. Ben Fowkes). London, New York and Toronto: Penguin.

———— (1994), "Results of the Direct Production Process," [1864] in *Marx-Engels Collected Works*, vol. 34 (trans. Ben Fowkes). London: Lawrence and Wishart, pp. 355–467.

McDonough, Terrence, Michael Reich and David M. Kotz, eds (2010) *Contemporary Capitalism and its Crises: Social Structure of Accumulation Theory for the 21st Century*. Cambridge, New York and Melbourne: Cambridge University Press.

Mészáros, István (2010) *The Structural Crisis of Capital*. New York: Monthly Review Press.

Mill, John Stuart (1904) *Principles of Political Economy*. New York: Longmans, Green and Co.

Nobus, D. and Quinn, M. (2005) *Knowing Nothing, Staying Stupid. Elements for a Psychoanalytic Epistemology*. London and New York: Routledge.

ONS (2012) "Labour Market Statistics, October 2012," statistical bulletin of the Office for National Statistics, available at http://www.ons.gov.uk/ons/dcp171778_279723.pdf (accessed 29 October 2012).

Postone, Moishe (1993) *Time, Labor, and Social Domination: A Reinterpretation of Marx' Critical Theory*. Cambridge: Cambridge University Press.

———— (2012) "Die Deutschen inszenieren sich am liebsten als Opfer," in Hermann Gremliza, ed., *No way out? 14 Versuche, die gegenwärtige Finanz- und Wirtschaftskrise zu verstehen*, Hamburg: Konkret Verlag, pp. 165–75.

Reinhart, Carmen M. and Kenneth S. Rogoff (2009) *This Time is Different: Eight Centuries of Financial Folly*. Princeton and Oxford: Princeton University Press.

Resilience Alliance (2009) "Planetary Boundaries: Exploring the Safe Operating Space for Humanity," in *Ecology & Society*, 14(2): 32, http://www.ecologyandsociety.org/vol14/iss2/art32/, accessed 21 November 2010.

Rifkin, Jeremy (2011) *The Third Industrial Revolution: How Lateral Power is Transforming Energy, the Economy, and the World*. New York and Basingstoke: Palgrave Macmillan.

Roubini, Nouriel (2012) "Global Economy; Reasons to be Fearful," in *The Guardian*, 18 June 2012, http://www.guardian.co.uk/business/2012/jun/18/global-economy-perfect-storm (accessed: 20 June 2012).

Roubini, Nouriel and Stephen Mihm (2011) *Crisis Economics: A Crash Course in the Future of Finance*. London, New York and Toronto: Penguin.

Samuelson, Paul (1976) *Economics* (10th ed.). New York: McGraw-Hill.

Say, Jean-Baptiste (1816) *Catechism of Political Economy* (trans. John Richter). London: Sherwood, Neely and Jones.

Schumpeter, Joseph (1942) *Capitalism, Socialism and Democracy*. London and New York: Routledge.

Sinn, Hans-Werner (2011) *Kasino-Kapitalismus: Wie es zur Finanzkrise kam, und was jetzt zu tun ist* (2nd edition). Berlin: Ullstein.

Skidelsky, Robert (2009) *Keynes: The Return of the Master*. London, New York and Toronto: Penguin.

Smith, Murray E.G. (2010) *Global Capitalism in Crisis: Karl Marx and the Decay of the Profit System*. Halifax and Winnipeg: Fernwood Publishing.

Stern, Nicholas (2007) *The Economics of Climate Change: The Stern Review*. Cambridge: Cambridge University Press.

———— (2009a) *The Global Deal: Climate Change and the Creation of a New Era of Progress and Prosperity*. New York: Public Affairs.

———— (2009b) "The Economic Crisis and the Two Great Challenges of the21stCentury," http://www.lse.ac.uk/collections/granthamInstitute/(accessed 6 September 2009)

Stiglitz, Joseph (2010) *Freefall: Free Markets and the Sinking of the Global Economy*. London, New York and Toronto: Allen Lane.

Stiglitz, Joseph et al. (2010) *The Stiglitz Report: Reforming the International Monetary and Financial Systems in the Wake of the Global Crisis*, by Joseph Stiglitz and Members of a UN Commission of Financial Experts. New York and London: The New Press.

Tett, Gillian (2009) *Fool's Gold: How Unrestrained Greed Corrupted a Dream, Shattered Global Markets and Unleashed a Catastrophe*. London: Little, Brown.

Vercellone, Carlo (2010) "The Crisis of the Law of Value and the Becoming-Rent of Profit," in Fumagalli, Andrea and Sandro Mezzadra (eds) *Crisis in the Global Economy: Financial Market, Social Struggles, and New Political Scenarios*. Los Angeles: Semiotext(e), pp. 85–118.

Vincent, Jean-Marie (1991) *Abstract Labour: a Critique*. Basingstoke: Palgrave Macmillan.

Voruz, Véronique and Wolf, Bogdan (eds.) (2007) *The Later Lacan: an Introduction*. New York: SUNY Press.

Weber, Max (1904–5) *The Protestant Ethic and the Spirit of Capitalism* (trans. Talcott Parsons, 2nd edition). London and New York: Routledge 2001.

Wiener, Norbert (1948) *Kybernetik: Regelung und Nachrichtenübermittlung im Lebewesen und in der Maschine*. Düsseldorf: Droste.

Wolf, Martin (2009) *Fixing Global Finance: How to Curb Financial Crises in the 21st Century*. New Haven and London: Yale University Press.

———— (2011) "How the Crisis Catapulted us into the Future," in *Financial Times*, 11 February 2011, http://www.ft.com/cms/s/0/5fc7e840-2e45-11e0-8733-00144feabdc0.html#axzz1CnhX3j8r (accessed 12 February 2011).

Wolff, Richard (2010) *Capitalism Hits the Fan: The Global Economic Meltdown and What to Do About It*. Northampton/MA: Olive Branch Press.

"World Debt Comparison: the Global Debt Clock," in *The Economist*, http://www.economist.com/content/global_debt_clock (accessed 18 April 2011).

Žižek, Slavoj (1989) *The Sublime Object of Ideology*. London and New York: Verso.

———— (2003) *The Puppet and the Dwarf*. Cambridge, MA and London: MIT press.

———— (2009) *First as Tragedy, Then as Farce*. London and New York: Verso.

———— (2010) *Living in the End Times*. London and New York: Verso.

———— (2012) *Less than Nothing. Hegel and the Shadow of Dialectical Materialism*. London and New York: Verso.

Zupančič, Alenka (2006) "When Surplus Enjoyment meets Surplus Value," in Clemens and Griggs (eds) *Reflections on Seminar XVII. Jacques Lacan and the Other Side of Psychoanalysis*. Durham, NC and London: Duke University Press.

Chapter 2

Still Dancing:
Drive as a Category of Political Economy

Jodi Dean

Among the remarks circulating as evidence of bankers' arrogant disregard for the destructive effects of their high risk financial strategies in 2007, the most notorious came in July from then CEO of Citigroup, Charles Prince: "as long as the music is playing, you've got to get up and dance." He added: "we're still dancing." At the time, the subprime mortgage market was in free fall. Yet over the preceding five months, Citigroup and Merrill Lynch had led Wall Street in creating and selling 50 billion dollars in new CDOs (collateralized debt obligations, a kind of derivative backed by mortgage bonds). Prince thought the "pools of liquidity" were deep enough—the amount of available capital big enough—to be virtually immunized from the collapse of subprime. That year, the total dollar amount of CDOs issued by Wall Street was 486.8 billion dollars (Schwartz and Dash 2010). In the words of one investor, "We knew the collateral for the CDOs had collapsed. And yet everything went on, as if nothing had changed" (Lewis 2010: 165).[1] The following year, the International Monetary Fund would put losses related to U.S. generated subprime mortgage assets at one trillion dollars.

The psychoanalytic term for this keeping on, this repetition, is drive. Drive is a keeping on beyond pleasure, beyond use, beyond desire. In the reflexive turn of the drive, drive's loop back round upon itself, activity becomes passivity, stuckness in a circuit: *I know that you know that I know that you know that I know ...*

One of Slavoj Žižek's most significant theoretical contributions is his activation of Lacan's teachings on drive. Žižek explores drive throughout his work, using drive to rethink subjectivity, ideology, and ontology. My interest in this essay is in the way Žižek's activation of the concept configures drive as a category for political economy. The reflexive loops, stuckness, and ruptures of drive manifest themselves in the dynamic of capitalism's booms and busts. Indeed, as Žižek writes, "Drive inheres to capitalism at a more fundamental, *systemic* level: drive is that which propels the whole capitalist machinery, it is the impersonal compulsion to engage in the endless circular movement of expanded self-reproduction" (Žižek 2006: 61). I use drive to analyze the extreme capitalism of neoliberalism, highlighting derivatives as the commodity form of drive. I begin by highlighting Žižek's account of the difference between desire and drive.

---

1   Much of my discussion is indebted to Michael Lewis.

Drive and Desire

Both desire and drive designate relations to *jouissance*, that is, the economies through which the subject structures her enjoyment. Desire is always a desire to desire, a desire that can never be filled, a desire for a *jouissance* or enjoyment that can never be attained (see Žižek 2000: 291; Dean 2010; Johnston 2005). In contrast, drive attains *jouissance* in the repetitive process of not reaching it. Enjoyment comes from the process itself, not from fulfilling an ultimate goal. Žižek writes, "In Lacanian terms, one can determine the distinction between individual greed and the striving of capital itself as the difference between desire and drive" (Žižek 2010: 132). Individual greed might be unlimited, a desire for more, more, more, a desire that ultimately can never be met. Desire alone, however, can't account for the persistence of capitalism. The fundamental structure of capitalism is a circuit; capital strives to accumulate, to reproduce itself. It circulates, ceasing to be capital if this circulation stops.

Žižek also considers the difference between desire and drive via a change in the position and function of *objet petit a*. He writes:

> Although, in both cases, the link between object and loss is crucial, in the case of the *objet a* as the object of *desire*, we have an object which was originally lost, which coincides with its own loss, which emerges as lost, while, in the case of the *objet a* as the object of drive, the 'object' *is directly the loss itself*—in the shift from desire to drive, we pass from the *lost object* to *loss itself as an object*. That is to say, the weird movement called 'drive' is not driven by the 'impossible' quest for the lost object; it is *a push to directly enact the 'loss'—the gap, cut, distance—itself* (Žižek 2008: 328).

Drive is a kind of compulsion or force. It's a force that is shaped, that takes its form and pulsion, from loss. Drive is loss as a force or the force loss exerts on the field of desire. We see this force of loss expressed in capitalism as the loss of satisfaction, completion, a capacity to be at rest. Absent an end or a limit, the process pushes on, in a relentless, nonsensical circuit.

In his compelling book on the crisis in the subprime mortgage bond market, Michael Lewis follows investor Steve Eisman to a conference on these high risk mortgages held in Las Vegas in early 2007. Seemingly unaware of the already increasing mortgage default rate, over 7000 investors turned out to gamble, play golf, and hear speeches about investing in the mortgage bond market. What had been an obscure and ill-reputable segment of the finance industry (not lease because of the exploitative lending practices involved), had become Wall Street's most powerful profit generator—even though it made no economic sense. Lewis quotes Eisman: "It was like watching an unthinking machine that could not stop itself" (Lewis 2010: 151). Individual bets and transactions in speculative finance don't have to mean anything; they don't have to be backed by something sensical (like actual assets). They just have to keep being made.

Žižek points out that drive's compulsive force captures the subject (see Žižek 2000: 297). One *has to* keep going or, in the immortal words of Margaret Thatcher, "There is no alternative." This "has to" shouldn't be confused with some kind of illusory natural law or inherent economic truth. Rather, it's the more uncanny force of drive in capitalist dynamics. During the financial crisis, drive's compulsion manifest itself in part in the absence of alternatives that pervaded official explanations for the bailout of the big banks: "they were too big to fail." Since "failure was not an option," government *had* to step in. Hands were tied. Even two years after the bailouts, Wall Street persistently spoke in the confined and compelled terms of drive. A *New York Times* article on high frequency trading, transactions that occur at a rate of something like 98 millionths of a second, quoted a research report on the *necessity* of spending hundreds of millions of dollars on faster computers and designated networks to enable higher speed trades, "Broker-dealers, hedge funds, traditional asset managers have been forced to play keep-up to stay in the game" (Bowley 2011). This high frequency trading is not confined to shadow markets. According to economist Michael Hudson, the *average time* a stock is held is 22 seconds and the *average* foreign currency investment last 30 seconds (Hudson 2011).

An additional feature of drive is its reflexivity, the inclusion of the subject in the scene she observes (see Žižek 1993). This inclusion brings with it an unavoidable (and constitutive) distortion as the presence or intervention of the subject affects the setting it encounters. Expressed in the bubble dynamics of speculative finance: if I think that you think CDOs are a good investment, then I should make and sell you some; this confirms to you that they are good investments (or else I wouldn't be selling them); consequently, you purchase more, which tells me I was right to think that you thought these were a good investment; I then share this news with others, who want to buy some, which again confirms my expectations and your savvy as an investor, etc. Rather remarkably, this reflexivity has actual market effects: deals are made (insuring payment for the brokers) and prices rise.

As Žižek emphasizes, the reflexive movement of drive is a loop. One shouldn't imagine it as a circle or oval, though, but more like a messy spiral. The loop of the drive is an uneven repetition and return that misses and errs. Stuck in the loop of drive, the subject keeps doing the same thing, trying to get the same result, but rarely really gets it. Still, the subject gets something, a bit of enjoyment, in the repeated effort of trying. And this nugget of enjoyment is enough of a payoff to keep the subject keeping on, although each moment is a little different. And why is each movement a little different? Because it comes next, it adds itself and thereby changes the setting of the next circuit.

At some point, doing the same thing over and over shifts from order into chaos. Persistent repetition can amplify patterns to the point of overload and collapse, as in the bursting of market bubbles. The reiterations that fail to respond to changes in their setting themselves change the setting. Here we encounter capitalism's creative destruction or the centrality of crises to capitalism's peculiar persistence.

In sum, Žižek's activization of drive mobilizes the category for political economy as it highlights drive as a compulsive, reflexive circuit that captures the subject and whose repetitions can intensify to points of destruction and rupture.

The Commodity Form of Drive

A significant feature of capitalism in the US and UK is the neoliberal form it has taken over the last 30 years.[2] The dismantling of the regulatory features characteristic of the Keynesian consensus unleashed a predatory financialization. One of the finance sector's primary weapons of mass destruction (to use the term applied by investor Warren Buffet) is the derivative.

Derivatives are a class of custom-made financial tools such as commodity futures, stock options, currency swaps, and collateralized debt obligations that let traders insure or bet against movements in other financial instruments (see Fox 2009; LiPuma and Lee 2004: 35). Most derivatives trade privately in the unregulated over-the-counter or OTC market. Although initially a rather obscure, specialized investment vehicle, from 1987 to 2007, the derivative market expanded from $866 billion to $454 trillion (Fox 2009: xii). As a class, derivatives have three key attributes: they are limited term contracts to exchange capital in an agreed upon description of the future on the basis of the price of the underlying asset at that time; "limited term" here means that the contract has an expiration date (LiPuma and Lee 2004: 34). Thus, the derivative instrument is reflexive: it steps back from one level of circulation (like trade in stocks or bonds) and commodifies a possible future moment of circulation (how investors will assess the asset in the future). It's not just a bet; it's a bet on how others will bet.

Consider the "synthetic CDO." This is a collateralized debt obligation comprised of credit-default swaps (insurance on tranches of bonds). Lewis explains, "The market for 'synthetics' removed any constraint on the size of risk associated with subprime mortgage lending. To make a billion-dollar bet, you no longer needed to accumulate a billion dollars worth of actual mortgage loans. All you had to do was find someone else in the market willing to take the other side of the bet" (Lewis 2010: 77–8). Derivatives don't simply profit from risk. Risk is not primarily a side effect of complex, interlinked market transactions. The securitization of risk, its bundling into a commodity to be sold, is deliberate and intentional. When a market is made for a specific designer instrument, like a credit default swap, the surplus risk shifts from being a byproduct to being the product; it occupies the place previously held by the asset.

This reflexivized, commodified bet contributes to producing the future on which it is betting. Derivatives enable enormous leveraging; small outlays of capital can have huge pay-offs or pay-outs in the future. Because the immediate

---

2   For a more detailed discussion of neoliberalism, see Dean 2009.

cost of risk is comparatively small, firms can undertake more investments than they would with regular stocks and bonds. Derivatives also contribute to the future on which they are betting insofar as they require counter-parties. Someone has to be on the other, losing, side of the deal. Complex derivatives combine, slice up, recombine, and sell bundles of assets and/or swaps (J. P. Morgan designed synthetic CDOs; there were also CDOs of CDOs and CDOs of CDOs of CDOs) (see Patterson 2010: 190). From one perspective, these recombinant financial instruments distribute risk broadly so that no one firm suffers too badly when an investment sours. From another, more firms become susceptible to investments gone wild. Because derivatives "tighten intermarket connectivities," enabling the circulation of gains and losses to cross from one market to another, no market is shielded from the effects of big events (LiPuma and Lee 2004: 105).

Derivatives are thus commodified forms of drive in that they repeat in their own structure and relations the circulatory regime of global capital. Products of the perceived need to protect investors against the risks involved in complex speculative financial transactions, derivatives make these transactions possible, thereby producing, retroactively, their own conditions of emergence. In the words of LiPuma and Lee (2004: 118) "once the speculative capital devoted to financial derivatives becomes self-reflexive and begins to feed on itself, it develops a directional dynamic toward an autonomous and self-expanding form." Since abstract financial relations are themselves treated as underlying assets, money markets can expand seemingly without limit—that is, as long as everyone involved believes that they will, as long as the circuit keeps on going on and no one tries to cash in or call.

Derivatives commodify drive in another sense as well: they presuppose, reinforce, and amplify relations of dramatic inequality. Although per capita GDP in the US nearly doubled between 1976 and 2005, about half the gains went to the top five percent of the population (see Milanovic 2009). The real median wage remained stagnant. Debt (or the extension of credit, which is the same thing) was a way of addressing the decline in purchasing power. It also had the benefit of being securitizable and thus available as an investment vehicle for the excess of capital at the top. Lewis sums the point up best when he writes, "Complicated financial stuff was being dreamed up for the sole purpose of lending money to people who could never repay it" (Lewis 2010: 179). The expansion in the number of subprime mortgages, their bundling into bonds, the bonds' dividing into tranches, the tranches' repackaging into CMOs (collateralized mortgage obligations) and CDOs (which included debts besides mortgages such as student loans and credit card debts) resulted from demand for these massive financial instruments. Working people's desire to purchase homes they could not afford did not create CDOs (which is sometimes how media accounts blaming mortgage defaults for the financial crisis make it sound). Investment banks did. Scott Patterson writes, "without the demand from the investment banks, the bad loans would never have been made" (Patterson 2010: 197). The mortgage holders "existed only so that their fate might be gambled upon" (Lewis 2010: 77).

In the years preceding the crash of 2007–2008, investment banks used CDOs to remove debt from their balance sheets, a practice part of the "shadow-banking system." The banks sold this debt to investors in the form of tranches (slices or layers) of the CDOs. Investors thought they were buying measurable risk. Those who purchased tranches with AAA ratings from Moody's or Standard & Poor's thought they were investing in something pretty secure with a very, very, low likelihood of failure, primarily because the likelihood of default on a large number of mortgages was very, very low. AAA tranches were particularly attractive for pension funds and university endowments required to keep their risk exposure low.

The problem was that the models used to figure out the correlations between the tranches assumed not only predictable, bell-curve like patterns, but also that the price information fed into the models was coming from a bubble in the housing market, inflated in part by historically low interest rates after 9/11, the rush of investors wounded in the burst of the dotcom bubble into ostensibly secure real estate, banks' enthusiasm for mortgages and other loans that generated lots of fees, and the rise of derivatives themselves. As Patterson explains, "what resulted was a vicious feedback loop—an echo chamber, one might say, in which enthusiastic investors snapped up tranches of CDOs, creating demand for more CDOs—and that created a demand for more mortgage loans" (Patterson 2010: 194).

Demand for CDOs corresponded to the rise in inequality. Prior to the subprime mortgage boom, subprime mortgage lending was a barely legitimate business. Mortgages were issued with little regard for whether they could be repaid; the money was in the fees. Lenders attached exorbitant charges to the loans made to customers at high risk of default, relying on teaser rates that would balloon up after a couple of years. Most of these early lenders went bankrupt in the mid-nineties. Less than a decade later, the subprime market was larger than before, offering even lower quality mortgages to people who, facing a decade of stagnant wages and maxed out credit cards, jumped at the chance of no money down, interest only mortgages. The debts of poor and working people were fodder for the Wall Street finance machine. So even though adjustable-rate mortgages were defaulting at epic rates in 2005, the price of houses continued to rise as people refinanced when their rates turned over. Consequently, the subprime mortgage market continued to expand. This massive financial boom required, was made possible by derivatives created out of the debts of the people seemingly furthest from Wall Street, those considered the least credit-worthy. At this interface of the extremes of profit and loss, poverty (like risk) isn't an unavoidable byproduct of capitalism but its condition and content—the increase in the number of poor people is an investment opportunity. The system turns in on itself and feeds on its own excesses. The derivative is the commodity form of this reflexive circuit.

Even in the last months of the bubble in subprime mortgage bonds (between February and June of 2007), the market in CDOs continued to generate billions. Turbulence increased as banks tried to dump the bad investments, but insofar as buyers kept purchasing them, the market remained afloat. Lewis's description suggests the trap of drive: "it was as if an entire financial market had tried to change its mind—and then realized that it could not afford to change its mind" (Lewis 2010: 165). The interconnected banks were themselves caught in a circuit beyond their control. If there were no buyers for the CDOs, and the mortgages deep in their bowels were defaulted upon as house prices continued to drop, the CDOs would be worth nothing. The credit-default swaps suggest a kind of insurance, a way to hedge against massive losses, but that hedging depends on the seller's ability to pay. If the seller couldn't pay, then the insurance wasn't worth anything either. In effect, the over-leveraged derivatives market, a substantial component of Wall Street's exorbitant profits and bonuses, led the financial system to deceive itself.

Žižek often describes Capital as Real, suggesting at times an almost ahistorical, economic force that necessarily exceeds any attempts at regulation. As he writes, "The self-propelling circulation of Capital thus remains more than the ever the ultimate Real of our lives, a beast that by definition cannot be controlled, since it itself controls our activity ..." (Žižek 2009: 37). Read empirically, Žižek's description directs attention away from the role laws and states play in enabling the paths capital takes. This would then occlude the ways neoliberal capitalism differs from welfare state capitalism, its emergence through specific monetary policies, regulatory and deregulatory practices (not the least of which was the end of the separation between commercial and investment banks, descriptively), and tax laws (on corporations and individuals). It makes more sense to understand Žižek's point in terms of drive as the Real of Capital, the persistent force compelling capital's ceaseless circuit and entrapping us within its need to accumulate. This is what cannot be controlled as long as capitalism exists, what underlies capitalism in its different guises, this perpetual push to accumulate, expand, and intensify, this endless circuit of creation and destruction, the inescapable drive to profit and grow.

Understanding Capital in terms of drive expresses Capital's compulsive force without reiterating liberal and capitalist claims for an inevitable economic logic and thereby obscuring changes in capitalism. As Foucault discusses in his 1978–1979 lectures, *The Birth of Biopolitics*, classical liberal economics emphasized free markets. If the state would refrain from interfering, fair prices and reasonable distributions of goods would result from individuals self-interested transactions—Adam Smith's famous "invisible hand." Should the state attempt to manage or regulate these transactions, however, it would inevitably distort them. In contrast, neoliberals stressed competition. Here the role of the state was to insure not free markets but free competition. At every level of society, competition—inclusive of the resulting inequalities—was alleged to unleash excellence and productivity.

Over the course of the first decade of the twenty-first century, it became clear that real-existing neoliberalism involved neither free markets nor free competition. Whether one focuses on ongoing tariffs, subsidies, and restrictions in global trade, the exclusivity of most Wall Street deals, capitalism's tendencies toward monopoly, the social and control conditions establishing many of presuppositions for what can be bought and sold, or mainstream economists' own acknowledgements that the suppositions of their models don't hold in real-life conditions, the free market is a myth—with powerful effects. Likewise, contemporary financial markets might be blood-thirsty and cut-throat, but they aren't competitive, not if by "competitive" we imagine some kind of open contest with clear, fair rules, and not if we think that competition has disciplining effects. On Wall Street, the competition is between bankers for their salaries and bonuses, a mindset that rewards short-term deal-making and the overall number of deals made, not the outcome of the deal for parties to it.

A noteworthy aspect of the new "winner-take-all" logic of transactions in the contemporary networks of communicative capitalism is the way they change the very meaning of competition. Žižek misstates the primary question here as "beyond which point does competition break down and the winner take all?" (Žižek 2010: 212). He overlooks not just the differences between popular and economic notions of competition, but the way this ambiguity informs a new configuration of work. Rather than having a right to the proceeds of our labor by virtue of a contract, ever more of us are in win/ lose situations where remuneration is treated like a prize. In academia, art, writing, architecture, entertainment, and design people feel fortunate to get work, to get hired, to get paid. In growing numbers of fields, more tasks and projects are conducted as competitions: those doing the work are not paid unless they win. People work for a *chance* at pay.

The Obama administration has given "inducement prizes" a key role in its "Strategy for American Innovation." Explicit in its goal of amplifying competition, the White House wants to use "high-risk, high-reward policy tools such as prizes and challenges to solve tough problems" (Lowrey 2010). But who is in a position to take such risks? Only those who are already "the haves." The prize as inducement does more than amplify the entrepreneurial risk presupposed in capitalist models of innovation; it alters it such that the risk is distributed downward, transferred from the capitalist to the worker. Work performed may not be work remunerated. Winners get money; losers don't. The only link between the work and the remuneration comes from the prize giver, who is now in the position of judge, charitable giver, and beneficent lord with no particular obligation to those who have worked. Work as a collective enterprise, with multiple conditions and participants, all of whom depend on the "prize" for their livelihood vanishes. Workers don't even appear as workers; they are competitors, and then the winner and the losers.

Most prizes involve an element of prestige, that "extra something" associated with a prize. Discussing the "extra something" provided by brands like Nike, Žižek notes a kind of impossible limit position: although the capitalist ideally would like to be able to sell just a brand name and "get money for nothing," this is impossible "since nobody is prepared to pay for nothing more than a name" (Žižek 2010: 211). Perhaps more radical is the shift effected by a prize-based reward structure: workers pay to work. In the instance of one competition, appropriately called the "X Prize," competitors "spent 10 to 40 times the amount" of the award. The material costs were transferred onto the ones doing the work;

they paid to do the work. For writers, bloggers, artists, and film-makers, working for less than nothing, paying for work, has become a commonplace (bringing with it the elimination of growing numbers of print newspapers in the US and cuts in numbers of paid journalists). In the form of an explicit governmental policy, prizes usher in a new and acceptable relation to work bringing with them a likely decrease in opportunities for contract based work and work for pay.

Insofar as prizes produce the one, the winner, they elaborate a form of exploitation and expropriation of the common particular to communicative capitalism—network exploitation (see Dean 2009). Complex networks are characterized by a particular distributive pattern, "power laws." As theorized by Albert-László Barabási (2003), under conditions of free choice and preferential attachment, nodes in a complex network will distribute themselves such that the top one or two get a lot and the majority get a little. Academic citations, book sales, movie tickets, blog hits, and the distributed labor of creating of apps for smart phones all follow this pattern, one described in popular media as the 80/20 rule or the "winner-take-all" or "winner-take-most" characteristic of contemporary capitalism. In these examples, the general field out of which the one emerges is the common. Without the work of the many, the one would not emerge. Exploitation consists in stimulating the creative production of the field in the interest of finding, and monetizing, the one. Expansions in the field produce the one (hubs are an immanent property of complex networks). Such exploitation contributes to the expropriation of opportunities for income and paid labor, as in the examples of print journalism and university presses. Network exploition results in a de-waging of skilled, intellectual labor.

Keep on Knowing

As markets plummeted during the financial crisis, the mainstream media repeatedly intoned that financial instruments like collateralized debt obligations and credit default swaps are beyond our comprehension. Not only are they too hard for average citizens to understand, but Alan Greenspan couldn't even understand them. In fact, as hundreds of lobbyists for the finance sector worked ceaselessly to teach US members of Congress, derivatives *can't* be regulated, precisely because *no one* understands them. Beyond comprehension, they are beyond control.

Initially, finance porn (I have in mind here mainstream media treatment of the finance sector as well as the multiple books on the subprime mortgage crisis) lauded "quants" as the ones who actually knew what was going on. These nearly magical geeks, siphoned off from academia, used their advanced mathematics and high powered computers to identify statistical anomalies and price differentials and quickly capitalize them. The economic theory at the basis of their calculations, the Efficient Market Hypothesis, cast these profiteering moves as necessary and ethical: buying up underpriced assets helped move their prices to their proper place, back to equilibrium.

Other wizards then came up with alchemical strategies for managing risk, strategies that involved lots of borrowing (leverage) and shifting (structured investment vehicles). For example, many CDOs were new combinations of slices (tranches) of other CDOs that a bank had created but had been unable to sell. Their interrelation was circular; they contained each other yet were somehow able to transform this mutual containing into gold. With regard to the CDOs built out of subprime mortgage bonds, the supposition was that real estate would nearly always rise in value, that any declines in the housing market would be local rather than national, and that mortgage backed securities distributed risk so broadly as to dissipate it almost completely. Each one of these assumptions ended up being wrong. The CDOs' opaque, exotic names—Abacus, Carina, Gemstone—heighten the sense that one is approaching the inner sanctum of finance's arcane mysteries. At the heart of finance are impossible objects that create money, objects that incarnate futures. A Goldman Sachs trader described them in an email to his lover as "a product of pure intellectual masturbation, the type of thing which you invent telling yourself: 'Well, what if we created a 'thing,' which has no purpose, which is absolutely conceptual and highly theoretical and which nobody knows how to price?'"[3]

The powers that be allegedly at the helms of the big investment firms—Bear Stearns, Lehman Brothers, Merrill Lynch, Citigroup, Goldman Sachs—claimed that they both knew and didn't know what was going on as the financial markets heated up and burned out. On the one hand, their risk management strategies necessarily involved all sorts of bets and plans on what could happen. Their justification for the creation of credit default swaps (CDSs) was protection, security, prevention of the worst. On the other hand, the bankers and regulators claimed that the crisis was the once in a century event that no one could have predicted. *Finance is simply too complicated.* Under questioning at the Congressional hearings on the financial crisis, investor Warren Buffett (chief shareholder in Moody's ratings agency) said that he didn't know what Moody's was doing; he didn't know that it was making massive mistakes in rating mortgages and bonds before the crisis. Neither he nor anyone else could be expected to know. His own business is too complex for him to understand (see Carter 2010).

Complexity displaces accountability. The big banks were not accountable because there were all sorts of things for which they couldn't account. To be sure, they can enjoy complexity, getting off on the obscure objects they create, abstracting themselves from the risks that are taken with pension funds and municipal bonds, reveling in a sense that their power puts them above it all. This is the sense at the heart of the culture of extreme bonuses, the only sense such excess makes. Outlandish bonuses inscribe the surplus inequality before which politicians and press bow down. Grossly unequal salaries would still inscribe the bankers in the same world as the politicians, an economic world based in labor, production, and commodities rather than a financial world based in fantasies, bets, risks, and will.

---

3   See   http://jdeanicite.typepad.com/i_cite/2010/05/infamous-fabrice-tourre-email-of-january-29-2007.html (see also Harper 2010).

Complexity displaces accountability onto knowledge. In documents that Goldman Sachs made available to the Senate Permanent Subcommittee on Investigations, the firm stated that it "did not have access to any special information that caused [it] to know that the US housing market would collapse" (Goldman Sachs 2010). The banks' actions were primarily reactive: "The firm's risk management processes did not, and could not, provide absolute clarity; they underscored deep uncertainty about evolving conditions in the US residential housing market. That uncertainty dictated our decision to attempt to reduce the firm's overall risk." Goldman describes its decisions as attempts to reduce its risk in conditions of uncertainty. Yet it fails to acknowledge how its decisions are part of these very conditions. It's as if Goldman only reacted to extreme conditions rather than created them. Not being able accurately to predict the future of the US housing market is not the same as not knowing that the large default rate of subprime mortgages issued after 2004 would threaten the value of the bonds for which they provided collateral and consequently of the CDOs comprised out of bundled slices of bonds. Nor is it the same as disavowing one's own role in the market, what Goldman Sachs alludes to when it mentions its decision to reduce risk. Its reduction of its own risk transfers this risk to other places, other investors, other firms. As Lewis argues, Goldman's bets against the subprime market amplified the chaos: "Goldman Sachs did not leave the house before it began to burn; it was merely the first to dash through the exit—and then it closed the door behind it" (Lewis 2010: 209).

In Seminar XVII, Lacan associates the change from the discourse of the Master to university discourse with a change in the place of knowledge. In university discourse, which Lacan also views as capitalist discourse, knowledge no longer serves the Master. It is no longer knowledge of what the Master desires. Rather, knowledge occupies the place of the Master. For Lacan, this means that university discourse affirms nothing but knowledge. University discourse is all-knowing not in the sense that it knows everything but in a sense that it is fully comprised of knowing. Only knowing counts. When knowledge is in the position of Master, knowing cannot be mastered. It is Master.

Lacan thus sees in university discourse a "new tyranny of knowledge" (Lacan 2007: 32). In its new position, knowledge isn't knowledge for a purpose, but knowledge as a command: "keep on knowing more and more" (105). Consequently, the tyranny of knowledge entails the loss of the subject or the subject as loss. Knowledge isn't something that a subject assumes; it is a command, a drive, shaped around and through loss. The more knowledge, the greater the loss, and the more extensive becomes the gap between the movement of knowing more and more and the possibility of subjectivizing this knowledge. It's too complex. Complexity displaces accountability onto knowledge, but knowledge refuses it.

The university discourse provides an apparatus for thinking about drive as a social structure (or drive in terms of a set of discursive positions). It is particularly helpful as a diagram for analyzing the problem of knowledge and accountability in contemporary capitalism. A drive for limitless information confronts persons and things, who cannot subjectivize it, who can basically do nothing other than keep on. They are caught in an endless circuit—not a closed circuit, though, but a circuit that in its movement outward and back can alter, shift, disperse, and branch.

Democratic theorists mistakenly presume that the command to know more and more is a democratic demand, a demand that enables and empowers radical politics. The formula of the university discourse makes clear how knowledge in the position of Master disables a political subject: the addressee of the all-knowing is just any old object. To treat the command to keep on knowing more and more as if it were a demand that challenges the authority of the Master fails to grasp the change in the function and place of knowledge. In the terms of the four discourses, it mistakes university discourse for the discourse of the hysteric, a discourse that does address and challenge the Master. Treating the command to keep on knowing as if challenged the Master also disavows the way this injunction entraps its poor addressee in the circuit of drive: there will never be a knowledge that itself will be cause enough to stop, get out, do something else. Stopping, doing something else, is a matter of desire, not drive.

References

Barabási, Albert-László (2003) *Linked*. New York: Plume.

Bowley, Graham (2011) "The New Speed of Money, Reshaping Markets," *New York Times*, January 1, 2011 (available at http://www.nytimes.com/2011/01/02/business/02speed.html?_r=1&pagewanted=2&ref=general&src=me).

Carter, Zach (2010) "Living Blogging the Ratings Agencies Hearing" (June 2, 2010) (available at http://www.ourfuture.org/blog-entry/2010062202/liveblogging-rating-agencies-hearing).

Dean, Jodi (2009) *Democracy and Other Neoliberal* Fantasies. Durham, NC: Duke University Press.

———— (2010) "Drive as the Structure of Biopolitics," *Krisis* vol. 2. Available at http://www.krisis.eu/content/2010-2/krisis-2010-2-01-dean.pdf.

Fox, Justin (2009) *The Myth of the Rational Market*. New York: Harper Business.

Goldman Sachs (2010) "Goldman Sachs: Risk Management and Residential Mortgage Market," in *New York Times* 24 April 2010 (available at http://documents.nytimes.com/goldman-sachs-internal-emails#document/p11).

Harper, Christine (2010) "Goldman's Tourre Email Describes 'Frankenstein' Derivatives," *Bloomberg* (April 24, 2010). Available at http://www.bloomberg.com/news/2010-04-24/-frankenstein-derivatives-described-in-e-mail-by-goldman-s-fabrice-tourre.html.

Hudson, Michael (2011) interview available at http://www.therealnews.com/t2/index.php?option=com_content&task=view&id=31&Itemid=74&jumival=6000.

Johnston, Adrian (2005) *Time Driven*. Evanston, IL: Northwestern University Press.

Lacan, Jacques (2007) *The Other Side of Psychoanalysis. The Seminar of Jacques Lacan, Book XVII*, trans. Russell Grigg. New York: W.W. Norton.

Lewis, Michael (2010) *The Big Short*. New York: W. W. Norton and Company.

LiPuma, Edward and Lee, Benjamin (2004) *Financial Derivatives and the Globalization of Risk* (Durham, NC: Duke University).

Lowrey, Annie (2010) "Prizewinning Policy," *Slate* (December 27, 2010) (available at http://www.slate.com/id/2279272?wpisrc=newsletter).

Milanovic, Branko (2009) "Two Views on the Cause of the Global Crisis," *YaleGlobal* (May 4, 2009) (available at http://yaleglobal.yale.edu/content/two-views-global-crisis).

Patterson, Scott (2010) *The Quants*. New York: Crown Business.

Schwartz, Nelson and Dash, Eric (2010) "Questions for Banks That Put Together Deals," *New York Times*, April 20, 2010 (available at http://www.nytimes.com/2010/04/21/business/21cdo.html).

Žižek, Slavoj (1993) *Tarrying with the Negative*. Durham, NC: Duke University Press.

——— (2000) *The Ticklish Subject*. London: Verso.

——— (2006) *The Parallax View*. Cambridge, MA: The MIT Press.

——— (2008) *In Defense of Lost Causes*. London: Verso.

——— (2009) *First as Tragedy, Then as Farce*. London: Verso.

——— (2010) *Living in the End Times*. London: Verso.

Chapter 3

"The Untranscendable Horizon of Our Time": Capitalist Crisis and the Ends of Utopia

Benjamin Noys

Sartre famously remarked, in *Search for a Method* (1960), that Marxism was the "untranscendable horizon of our time." In 1989, Francis Fukuyama would rework this statement to make liberal democracy, resting on its capitalist supplement (in the Derridean sense of 'necessary addition'), the new horizon to which the world would eventually conform. This was the common-sense of the 1990s and early '00s, codified as 'TINA' ('There is no alternative'). Although it certainly did not remain uncontested—from the Chiapas uprising in 1994 to Seattle and the alter-globalization movement, along with the theoretical preservation and exploration of the communist alternative—the 'horizon' remained a default. Christopher Nealon has noted that: "Then came the economic crisis of 2008, and abruptly 'capitalism' was pronounceable for the first time in decades as the name, not of an inevitability, but of a contingent economic form" (2011: 140). While capitalism had been the unsayable name, dissolved into the plurality of capitalism*s*, crisis produced an estranging effect that rendered the 'horizon' of capitalism visible in its disintegration, and in the attempts at recomposition. This fracture has, however, had intermittent effects on the attempts to provide an *actual* rupture with global capitalism as a social system. It seems that if capitalism is not working, then nothing works; hence the marked apocalyptic tone prevalent at this moment.[1]

My aim here is to take the measure of this 'moment' of crisis, which is already gaining the sense of a drawn-out process as the crisis continues to unfold across global space. In particular, I want to assess the implications of the fracturing of the global horizon of capital for the theoretical articulations of radical alternatives, most centrally communism. The dimension on which I will focus is the vexed one of the utopian. While Marx and Engels (2000) recognized utopian thinking could have a critical function they finally condemned it for its tendency to detachment from social reality, for building mere castles in the air. In light of the disasters of

---

1 In fact the apocalyptic and utopian accompany each other, as the apocalyptic provides the necessary moment of "world reduction" (Jameson 2006: 271) in order to give birth to the new. Jameson, twisting his own well-known remark (1994: xii), notes that today we "witness the attempt to imagine capitalism by way of imagining the end of the world" (2003: 76).

actually-existing socialism *and* capitalism, the explicit rehabilitation of the utopian as critical component was undertaken by figures such as Ernst Bloch and Fredric Jameson. In fact, as we will see, many contemporary invocations of communism depend on a utopian element, often implicitly, which they regard as the necessary means to break the dominance of the 'horizon' of capitalism. There is, we could say, a default utopianism at work.

The form of this default utopianism is the search for some point, or enclave, of resistance to capital that already embodies communism, or the potential of communism. In what follows I will sketch a preliminary typology of such utopian enclaves, which take multiple forms but hold in common the promise of utopia as a place already present. Hence the 'utopian' thinking of the present is not the classical utopian desire to radically re-work society as a whole and submit it *en masse* to a new order, as in Fourier. Instead it seeks to find utopia already embedded in existent social forms—utopia as *somewhere* rather than *nowhere*—and so rejects any imposition of utopia as abstract. This affirmative conception of utopia risks, I will argue, a malign convergence with the utopian horizon of capital—not least as it shares the same fundamental fantasy of self-engendering production (Žižek 2011: 297–298).

Of course the utopian is an equivocal form, regularly flipping-over into its dystopian opposite. Thomas More's *Utopia* (1516), the Ur-text, is indicative in this respect. Utopia as *Eutopiā*—the 'good' place of rational planning and organization—is unstably close to dystopia—as the nightmare of repressive observation and control. The distance from Fourier's *Phlanestères* to Foucault's Panopticon is not very far. This, I think, accounts for the anti-utopian appearance of utopia in our present moment. Our dystopian horror is of planning, transparency, 'purity,' and social control—hence the unlikely continuing appeal of Orwell's *1984* (1948). The unresolvable debates as to whether Orwell's object of satire is Stalinism, 'totalitarianism,' or even the post-war British welfare state, indicates the ideological flexibility and persistence of the Cold War tropes of anti-planning. Utopias today are 'soft utopias,' designed to resist the dangerous transformation into dystopia.

The problem here is the projection onto capital of dystopian planning, which then licenses the utopian anti-planning alternative. What is missed is the functioning of capitalism as an 'acephalic' form of power—one that itself operates through an immanent and 'open' dynamic of accumulation, coupled to forms of political and social organization. There is no tracking of how neoliberalism operates as a peculiar critique of the state, aiming to release alternative forms of value, or the modes in which capitalism separates production from reproduction and subjects us to social abandonment. This coupling of anti-planning and planning, or of what Deleuze and Guattari (1983) called deterritorialization and reterritorialization, is occluded in the tendency to split these forms apart and pose one (deterritorialization) against the other (reterritorialization). It is this one-sided valorization that fails to grasp the real utopian fantasy of capital—as self-engendering productive system—and that fails to grasp its own convergence with this dynamic.

Capitalist Utopias

One of the merits of Karl Polanyi's *The Great Transformation* (1944) was that it established that the imposition of capitalism as a 'market society' was itself a utopian project. Contrary to the usual conservative and liberal claims that communism or socialism were errant examples of abstract planning that oppressed a 'natural' human freedom, Polanyi demonstrated that capitalism was a planned and violently-implemented social form that reshaped social relations primarily through the commodification of land, labour, and money. Reversing the schema Badiou sets out in *The Century* (2005), in which communism was a utopian dream of the nineteenth century violently realized in the short twentieth-century, we can say that it was the nineteenth century that was the century of capitalism's 'passion for the Real' and the 'concrete' instantiation of its utopia. In this way the short twentieth-century was the attempt to reverse this process (in part), to uproot this social form and re-embed social relations, while the period post-1989 sees multiple 'returns' to the 'utopia' of a disembedding capitalism.

Whereas in Polanyi's hands this revelation of capitalism's own utopian reworking of social relations served the purpose of a critique of its 'spontaneity' and the instantiation of an alternative of rational social planning, this is not the case today. The ideological trope of the contemporary moment is to use the 'utopian' nature of capitalism as the means to run-together and criticize *all* utopian projects of planning. In this schema the Cold War critiques of planned societies are updated to include neoliberalism as yet another instance of the utopian. The result are some unlikely bedfellows—including John Gray, Bruno Latour, Simon Critchley, and Jacques Rancière, amongst others—each concerned to denounce the 'economic determinism' of neoliberalism. This issues in a postmodern version of the 'totalitarianism' thesis, in which it is no longer Nazism and Stalinism that are collapsed together, but Marxism, as a *critique* of capitalist economic determinism, is collapsed into capital's 'economic determinism.' The 'economic' itself, the key category of capitalism, is projected as the central core of our moment that must be displaced to discover spontaneous and excessive powers that cannot be subject to any plan or any measure.

In a signature gesture of this style of thought the novelist and poet Iain Sinclair, in his critique of the "grand project" of the London 2012 Olympics, opposes the "vertical thrust" of the planned project to "horizontal energies: which are always democratic, free-flowing, uncontained" (2011: 103). He also instances the collapsing together of all planning as the malignant sign of totalitarianism:

> The landscape, in the shadow of the Olympic park, is in the process of being brought on-stream as a virtual paradise. The model is German, old East and older West: Honecker's urban planners, the propaganda of Dr Goebbels. A surgical removal of stubborn traces of the local makes way for a mindless verticality. Statements of control. New blocks, lacking Berlin's communal courtyards, are positioned for convenient access to extended malls that will replace the free-flowing anarchy of the street market (2011: 104).

Here Nazi, Soviet, and neoliberal planning instantiate "mindless verticality," which is opposed to the "free-flowing anarchy of the street market." The potential risk in the invocation of the anti-utopian utopian horizontal energies of the 'street market' should be self-evident. While certainly, and rightly, opposed to destructive neoliberalism, the critique falls short.

This contemporary 'structure of feeling' is one of constant movement, spontaneity, and the creative potential of the 'productive forces,' which turn against the dead hand of capitalism. Capitalism, contrary to the Marxist emphasis on its irrationality, is identified, in a Weberian gesture, with rationality. The result is the valorization of the anti-rational, if not the irrational. What lies at the heart of contemporary anti-utopian utopianism is a fear of planning or, as Alberto Toscano argues (2011–12), a fear of *logistics*—the necessity to consider the organization of material needs as the means to overcome capital. It is this, as I will argue, that results in the convergence of this anti-utopian utopianism with the capitalist utopias of the market and production 'freed' of state control. While the critiques of neoliberalism correctly note that this implantation of capitalism requires constant state intervention, they do not understand the particular *form* of this intervention. Foucault had noted that "neo-liberal government intervention is no less dense, frequent, active, and continuous than in any other system" (2008: 145). This intervention is, however, directed at subtracting the role of the state by subjecting it to the market. Again, we witness a project that aims at conditioning and 'freeing' life by subjecting all is elements to the operation of the market form. What I am suggesting is that the opposition to this form of intervention replicates the logic of separation from the state and capital to discover or release previously subjected forms of freedom and capacity.

So, the irony is that the condemnation of neoliberalism as a form of capitalist rationality is cast within capitalist terms. Anti-planning is reworked to argue that capitalism, like the sorcerer's apprentice of Marx and Engels's metaphor (2000), releases forces it cannot and *should not* control. The reliance of the utopian is on those 'productive forces' of capital to do the work of the moment of escape from capital. In the moment of crisis this narrative is reworked to suggest if capitalism fails then it only reveals the potential of another social form that can do the job better. The apocalypse of capital—its unveiling—results in the revelation of forces or moments that are supposed to both exceed capital and to prefigure both its end and a communist future.

Real Concrete Utopias

The formations of 'communist' utopia today are often predicated on the need to find the real concrete instantiations of utopia secreted within contemporary capitalist life. Such utopias cannot be nowhere and certainly cannot be negative, but have to be *positive*. The result is a kind of 'enclave-thinking' that seeks out these 'utopian' points. This positivization of utopia takes a number of forms. We can trace a continuum that ranges from the explicitly political, affirming nascent communist political projects, to the economic, in which new communist relations of production are affirmed. The movement along this continuum indicates something of the tension of utopia. While the more political forms are most explicitly resistant to capitalism they often remain detached and localized sites, which seem to lack global purchase. As we pass to the affirmation of new economic forms of possible communism, what we find is the dangerous convergence of the utopian with capital's own utopias.

To begin with the political forms of enclave thinking we find real concrete utopias of forms of resistance or explicit (or even implicit) anti-capitalism. This type of thinking seeks out the remnants or new possibilities of 'communist' or 'proto-communist' prefigurations. For example, we have Alain Badiou's invocation of a range of such 'points' that have existed since 1977: the first two years of the Portuguese revolution, the beginning of the Solidarity movement in Poland, the first phase of the insurrection against the Shah in Iran, the creation of L'Organisation Politique (Badiou's own group) in France, and the Zapatista movement in Mexico. In more contemporary terms, Badiou suggests the need to analyze Hezbollah and Hamas, to pay attention to peasant uprisings in China, and to look at the actions of 'Maoists' in Nepal and India (Badiou 2008: 111 n.6).

In the case of Badiou, and in line with his politicization of Marxism and his relegation of the economic as capitalist through-and-through, this takes the form of anti-economic resistance. Communism here is the intransigent fidelity to the Idea of communism, materially incarnated, and the faith in the rebirth of history against the prophets of economic planning. We could also include in this kind of modelling Jacques Rancière's argument for a fundamental political dissensus that no amount of capitalist planning or state control can fundamentally repress (Rancière 2007: 257). This axiomatic equality takes a more general and dispersed form than Badiou's localized points of resistance, but ultimately serves a similar purpose. If we track back Rancière's claim to his earlier work, especially his *Proletarian Nights* (1981), we can see that this utopian thinking of equality and the refusal to stay in one's place is also concretely instantiated in the 'utopians' of the French workers movement. We might note here that Badiou's suggestion that our current moment is like that of the 1840s (2008: 116–117; 2010: 66–7), is suggestive of the utopian character of this kind of thinking of communism. The 'return' is to the moment of communism as an idea, of communism as the moment of the refusal of the economic, and of Marx before *Capital*.

It is this political 'utopianism' that finds itself in violent conflict with the more economically instantiated forms of proto-communism. This is evident in the virulent disputes between Badiou and Antonio Negri. It is Negri's insistence that capital releases vital forces of production that it cannot control and which instantiate communism here and now that Badiou regards as mere fantasy. Badiou's accusation is that Negri is a "Marxist without even being communist"—in the sense of his stress on the immanent powers of the multitude that celebrates capitalism as residual communism (Badiou 2012: 7). Again, Badiou makes a slightly dubious equation between the insistence on the determining role of the economy in Marxism and its determining role in contemporary capitalism, but his critical point holds when he stresses the risks of insisting that capitalism realizes communism in "a capitalism worthy of Deleuze and Guattari's desiring machines" (Badiou 2012: 10). In fact, it is Deleuze and Guattari who are often invoked by contemporary utopians, as they struggle to track 'lines of flight' immanent to capital. The desire of the present moment is the desire for desiring-production, we could say.

This is evident in those theorizations that track communism by arguing that there is no singular object 'capitalism' (Gibson-Graham 1996, 2006; Holland 2011). Drawing on the work of Michel Foucault, Bruno Latour, and Deleuze and Guattari, they use the argument that 'capital' is merely a plural network of relations to suggest it can never saturate or subsume alternative forms of counter-production. In this schema the vampire of capitalism is transformed into a 'net' that cannot cover the various human and nonhuman relations that make up the world. The interstices that form 'outside' the network of capitalism create new forms of cooperation emerging spontaneously that chart new kinds of incipient communist 'economic' relations. We witness the valorization of cooperatives, freeware, filesharing, improvization, and other social forms that incarnate, in this reading, an encrypted communism emerging from within capitalism. These give concrete form to utopias embedded within the present moment.

Something of the style of these interventions, some of which were initially formulated in the 1990s, seems to speak to that earlier moment when capitalism could not be named as a social form. The pluralization of 'capitalism' into capitalism*s*, its de-totalization, was not so much the result of the fragmentation or weakness of capitalism, however, but of its (relative) success at that moment. The seemingly successful functioning of a 'smooth' financialized capitalism, already lurching (or slouching) towards crisis, created an effect of plural productive possibilities. The moment of crisis, in which capitalism emerges as an insistent signifier requiring 'saving,' did not simply disable these network and plural conceptions. Rather the failure of capitalism, its 'compacting' under crisis, could be taken to signal that it could no longer control or handle the pluralities of production and distribution on which it depended; hence the persistence and return of such modes *after* the current crisis. This argument—which I update from Lukàcs's argument that in moments of successful functioning capitalism appears as plural, while in crisis it appears as one bloc (2007: 32)—suggest that while these plural conceptions claim *detachment* from capital they actually remain all-too firmly *integrated* in the horizon of capitalism.

In the soluble horizon of capitalism, which functions precisely through the dispersion of the law of value, the effect of crisis renders utopia in the capitalist form of saving social relations that can re-start the 'boom.' The irony is that prophets of neoliberal creative destruction and austerity come into alignment with the celebrations of the self-destruction of capital as the sign of communism. Tracking across the continuum, while Badiou and Rancière's political critiques mark themselves off as resolutely incompatible with capitalism they repeat the characterization of neoliberalism and capitalism as economically determinist. In this way they abandon the economic and so leave their utopias ungrounded. For Negri and the prophets of plural capitalism the problem lies in the grounding of their utopias in the forces of capitalist production. We face an antinomy: a communism that seeks grounding in the economic and the productive forces replicates capital, especially in its neoliberal form, while a political communism retreats into the specification of communism as receding Idea.

Productive Utopias

Perhaps the best way in which to analyze the persistence of the antinomy of the utopian is to consider a case that tries to render this antinomy dialectical. This is the work of Fredric Jameson, which has tried to figure the utopian as rupture with the horizon of capital, while attending to the necessity to instantiate communism as a form of rational economic planning. It is the tension of Jameson's attempt to hold this antinomy as real, while also trying to indicate how it might be dialectized, that indicates the problems of the present. In his work of the 1980s Jameson predicated his analysis of the postmodern on the 'sublime' immensity of nuclear and cybernetic productive forces that resisted cognitive mapping. His prescience was to shift this account, which conceded too much to the supposed 'powers' of capitalism, and to note, in the 1990s, the opaque and pseudo-dynamic world of financialized capitalism (Balakrishnan 2009: 15). In this way Jameson problematized the image of production that subtended the utopian promise of capitalism.

The difficulty is that Jameson's work still inhabits this promise in the desire to rework and recover the force of production from out of the stasis of financialization. His work tracks the utopian search for a superior moment of production against the inertia and stasis of capital. Once again, Deleuze and Guattari are called upon to instantiate this utopian productivism. Their insistence on the productiveness of desire, on multiplicity, and on the 'force' of deterritorialization, plays a useful role in Jameson's conceptualization of utopian production. In his *Fables of Aggression* (1978) Jameson deployed Deleuze and Guattari's work as an "aesthetic" (2008: 7 n.6). There it functioned to analyze Wyndham Lewis's protofascist libidinal apparatus, while recognizing the power of his "schizophrenic" textual production and the "immense mechanical energy" of his writing (2008: 25). This relatively negative valence of libidinal production would be affirmed in Jameson's diagnosis of postmodern 'schizophrenia' as characteristic of late capitalism, even as he tried to disentangle new utopian productive energies. In this way Deleuze and Guattari function as both diagnosis and cure (as did Lewis) for postmodern inertia, indicating the equivocal status of the utopian.

In his essay on Andrei Platonov's novel *Chevengur* (which Platonov wrote between 1927–1928, although it was only published in 1972), Jameson takes this disturbing statement on the violent instantiation of communism in the countryside as reliant upon "the blank slate of absolute peasant immanence" (1994: 89). The 'destructive' element of the novel generates a Deleuzian plane of immanence on which to construct the new relations of communism. We should also note how Jameson traces the ambiguity of this novel, which although explicitly pro-Bolshevik gives, in its insistence on the necessity of violence, scope for a dystopian anti-Communist reading.[2] In fact, Jameson insists that "the very violence of *Chevengur*, for some of us almost intolerable, is the very price to be paid for its Utopian impulse" (1994: xvii). Fully embracing the consequences, Jameson suggests that the anonymity of communism as an "intensely productive force" be identified with the anonymity of death (1994: 128).

Similarly, in *Brecht and Method* (1998), Jameson audaciously proposes reading Brecht's use of dialectics alongside to Deleuze to suggest the construction of productive contradictions as one of pluralization and differentiation (1998: 80). Brecht's productivism is re-read through the lens of Deleuzian virtuality and multiplicity to provide a new image of the dialectic in the moment of the 'postmodern' as a dialectic that refuses the stabilization of difference. Contrary to dialectical 'synthesis' we find a productive dialectic of difference. This work is explicitly written against the stasis of capitalism seemingly triumphant (Jameson 1998: 4), and the deployment of Brecht is aimed at the re-engagement of agency in this context. And yet, this recovery is couched in the image of a certain sense of passivity to the flux and flow of time itself as the means to break with capitalism's incessant production of the "bad new" (Jameson 1998: 4). Jameson notes the danger that "the sheerest celebration of change, change as always revolutionary" risks coinciding with the "dynamic" of capitalism (1998: 17). This is why we face the task of constantly trying to draw out and develop a true communist production from out of the false capitalist dynamism.

Jameson re-iterates this point in a recent interview:

> There is a tendency among the Left today—and I mean all varieties of the Left—of being reduced to protecting things. It is a kind of conservatism; saving all the things that capitalism destroys which range from nature to communities, cities, culture and so on. The Left is placed in a very self-defeating nostalgic position, just trying to slow down the movement of history. There is a line by Walter Benjamin that epitomizes that—though I don't know how he thought of that himself—revolutions are 'pulling the emergency cord,' stopping the onrush of the train. I don't think Marx thought about it like that at all. It seems to me that Marx thought that productivity would increase by getting rid of capitalism. On the level of organization, technology and production, Marx did not want a return to handicraft labour, but to go on into all kinds of complex forms of automation and computerization [as it would emerge] and so (Jameson in Leonard 2012).

---

2   This ideological polyvalence can be noted by T. J. Clark's use of Platonov's *Chevengur* as part of his embrace of a tragic and pessimistic analysis of the state of the contemporary left (Clark 2012: 62).

Now, certainly I would accept that communism does not imply the simplification of social relations, nor would it exclude new forms of production and a new richness of possibilities. That said, however, what concerns me is the slippage here between arguments about resisting simplification and arguments endorsing the forms of production that seem all-too consonant with capitalism. The difficulty turns, as we will see, on the ability and the necessity to split the communist utopian desire from the capitalist utopian desire.

In the moment of crisis the attraction of this kind of utopia persists in the desire to recover or restart the wasted promise of capitalist productivity. The capitalist abandonment of wage labour during the crisis leads to the embedding of the utopian promise in these detached forms of potential which no longer seem to have a direct linkage to capitalist production. The very abandonment by capitalism of a commitment to the future leads to a radicalization that aims to create the future capitalism can no longer provide. Hence the equivocation of the slogan 'No Future,' taken from the 1977 moment of UK punk, which at once indicates the inability of capitalism to 'deliver' the future it promised (at least to some, and in some countries), and the utopian possibility to recover an infinite, demand-less, and protean sense of possibility 'released' from the constraints of capitalist value-generation.

This is why the present remains a vitalist moment, in the sense of the recovery of this 'living' force against the dead hand of capitalism in crisis. The moment of 'living labour,' detached from actual work, is taken as the prefiguration of communism in the excessive powers of life. Rather than probing the separation of reproduction from production, one of the ground conditions of capitalism, instead this separation is valorized. So, while the horizon of capitalism appears to have been rendered contingent what concerns me is how it persists in its operations in the 'alternative' imaginaries of contemporary radicalisms, communist or otherwise. These 'alternatives' find the utopian in new figures of production and life as ontological categories, whilst treating capitalism as mere externality. In this way contingency risks being retranslated into necessity—the contingency of capitalism becomes the necessity to return to the powers of capitalism.

The interest of Jameson's work is that his attempt to dialectize this moment brings it into extreme tension. He wants to retain production as the signature of communism, while also retaining a sense of the violence that is, or has been, required to create an alternative. In this way, he does not simply represent the quietist vitalism of our moment, although his figuration of utopia in terms of anonymity and death suggests the difficulty of sustaining this productivist 'alternative.' The utopian becomes the unstable moment of bridging between dystopian capitalism and the promise of communist utopia, but a vanishing point rather than a vanishing mediator.

This tension reaches its highpoint when Jameson more explicitly admits the necessity and utopian potential of planning and organization. In the key essay of *Valences of the Dialectic* (2009), he suggests the utopian potential of Wal-Mart's system of distribution (Jameson 2009: 410–434). In a classic example of the Brechtian embrace of the "bad new" it would appear that Jameson runs against the current of the prophets of emergent complexity and suggests the need for a communism that can include and embrace planning, in terms of both distribution and the linkages to production. Yet, this utopian reversal of the valence of Wal-Mart—from extreme example of capitalist misery, to presaging a new socialist organization—is left as a mere thought-experiment. The 'valence' of this dialectic, which might appear more like an antinomy, is simply to reverse the value of Wal-Mart from bad to good *in thought*. So, Jameson's title—'Utopia as Replication'—starts to have an ironic ring, as it should not be replicated ... In Kyle A. Wiggins (2007) rhetorical question: "How 'utopian' is a series of toggling ideological reversals?"

Jameson's own account of the utopian explicitly admits its negative function, as a kind of therapy for disrupting the horizon of capitalism by the imperative to imagine alternatives (Jameson 2006: 416). This Kantian categorical imperative of utopian desire sits somewhat uneasily with the more Hegelian accents of Jameson's work, and with the recognition of the need to actualize utopia. Hence his work incarnates, again, the instability, or antinomy, between communism as idea or imperative and communism as 'real movement.' This is visible in the equivocation of his fictional and real examples, which seem to gesture towards actualizing utopia and then withdrawing, as if aware of the danger of becoming entangled with capital's own utopian drive. It could also be said that his valorization of utopia in terms of productive difference, drawn from Deleuze and Guattari, again courts an anti-dialectical splitting into a difference that can never be stabilized. So, either we have the risk of utopia remaining merely therapeutic, or the risk of utopia being instantiated in a form insufficiently distinguished from capital. To put it another way, the utopian is too concrete and too abstract at the same time; too concrete, in that when instantiated its replicates the capitalist forces of production, and too abstract, in that it remains a floating imperative.

Utopian Ends

My suggestion of the end of utopia—the collapse of communist utopia back into capitalism—could easily be regarded as a capitulation to 'things as they are.' The emphasis on the convergence of the search for non-capitalist moments of life with neoliberalism's emphasis on the withdrawal of the state and capitalism's separation of production from reproduction would then be another story of total recuperation. In this way I would be returning to the insistence on the absolute nature of the horizon of capital and, secretly, simply another agent of capitalist despair. My argument, unsurprisingly, is contrary to this conclusion. The very search for these non-capitalist moments as utopian invocations, I am arguing, disables the very powers of resistance it claims to invoke. In fact, I regard this way of proceeding as more likely to produce an oscillation between the elation of the utopian and the pessimism that such moments will always be sucked back into capitalist production. My critique of the utopian is that it serves as a consolatory alibi—if there is always a utopian moment, no matter how bad it gets, this may as well pacify as galvanize. Worse than that, it leaves us with a constant searching out of such moments that always fail to connect with practice. Finally, worse than even that, it repeats the mantra of capital's own dynamic of self-engendering production.

This is, in part, because the insistence on the utopian does, however, serves a real felt need. While it may be consolatory, it points to the disconnection between actuality and communism as 'real movement.' It is this disconnect that is the central strategic problem of our moment, mired as it is by the collapse of 'traditional' forms of resistance. In this sense the invocations of communism as idea or utopian moment can claim license as the means to start to solve this problem by breaking the spell of capitalist dominance. The difficulty I have indicated is their tendency to ratify this dominance, both by replicating the utopian elements of capitalism and by detaching the utopian moments from actuality. This is the 'floating' existence of the utopian, which rather than functioning as a dialectical category splits into mere reality or mere imperative.

At the heart of my critique lies my concern that this kind of utopian thinking renaturalizes capitalism as a social form. The very choice of organic and vital metaphors to describe the 'powers' of resistance is one sign of this. At the more general level the appeal to powers of disruption and production, whether internal or external to capitalism, again seems a gesture of naturalization. Although couched as an anti-capitalist gesture—capitalism is the *unnatural* parasite, drawing on this power—this invocation repeats the capitalist utopia of an endlessly productive labour power on which it can draw at will in the guise of critique. The reason for this is the lack of consideration of communism as a movement of *negation*. In light of the general tendencies of contemporary theory, our utopias are affirmative and positive. They allocate negativity to capitalism, as the negation of our powers, or allocate it to the more 'violent' forms of protest and 'resistance.' In this way negativity is reified and made subject to capital.

I want to suggest that this positive utopianism, often local and modest, is, in fact, grandiose and problematic. The grandiosity lies in the belief in eternal separate powers, which then often slides into despair as it seems these powers are always absorbed or rechanneled. While aiming to separate from capital, these utopian moments replicate the capitalist fantasy of separate and eternal 'labour-power,' which can always be drawn upon. Hence I want to argue that we end this utopian thinking, as it finally remains within the horizon of capital. Here 'negation' takes the form of positing an affirmative alternative, whereas we lack the imagination to actually disrupt and negate the forms of capital and state power here and now. It is for this reason I propose that we de-utopianize, to use a barbarous neologism, our thinking of communism. In this way, I think, we can better engage with the strategic demands of the present.

References

Badiou, Alain [2005] (2007) *The Century* (trans. with commentary and notes A. Toscano). Cambridge: Polity.
——— (2008) *The Meaning of Sarkozy* (trans. D. Fernbach). London: Verso.
——— (2010) *The Communist Hypothesis* (trans. D. Macey and S. Corcoran). London: Verso.
——— (2012) *The Rebirth of History* (trans. G. Elliott). London: Verso.
Balakrishnan, Gopal (2009) "On the Stationary State," *New Left Review*, 59: 5–26.
Clark, Timothy James (2012) "For a Left with No Future," *New Left Review*, 74: 53–75.
Deleuze, Gilles and Guattari, Felix (1983) *Anti-Oedipus* [1972] (trans. R. Hurley, M. Seem and H. R. Lane). Minneapolis, MN: University of Minnesota Press.
Foucault, Michel (2008) *The Birth of Biopolitics: Lectures at the Collège de France, 1978–79* (trans. G. Burchell). Basingstoke: Palgrave.
Gibson-Graham, J. K. (1996) *The End of Capitalism (As We Knew It)*. Oxford: Blackwell.
——— (2006) *A Postcapitalist Politics*. Minneapolis, MN: University of Minnesota Press.
Hardt, Michael and Negri, Antonio (2000) *Empire*. Cambridge, MA: Harvard.
Holland, Eugene W. (2011) *Nomad Citizenship: Free-Market Communism and the Slow-Motion General Strike*. Minneapolis, MN: University of Minnesota Press.
Jameson, Fredric (1994) *The Seeds of Time*. New York: Columbia University Press.
——— (1998) *Brecht and Method*. London: Verso.
——— (2003) "Future City," *New Left Review*, 21: 65–79.
——— (2006) *Archaeologies of the Future: The Desire Called Utopia and Other Science Fictions*. London: Verso.
——— (2008) *Fables of Aggression: Wyndham Lewis, the Modernist as Fascist* [1979]. London: Verso.
——— (2009) *Valences of the Dialectic*. London: Verso.
Leonard, Aaron (2012) "Capitalism, the Infernal Machine: An interview with Fredric Jameson," *rabble.ca*, 9 February 2012, http://rabble.ca/books/reviews/2012/02/capitalism-infernal-machine-interview-frederic-jameson.
Lukács, Georg (2007) "Realism in the Balance," Adorno et al., *Aesthetics and Politics*. London: Verso.
Marx, Karl (2009) [1859] "A Contribution to the Critique of Political Economy," *Marxists Internet Archive*, http://www.marxists.org/archive/marx/works/1859/critique-pol-economy/index.htm
Marx, Karl and Engels, Frederick (2000) "The Manifesto of the Communist Party," [1848] *Marxists Internet Archive*, http://www.marxists.org/archive/marx/works/1848/communist-manifesto/index.htm.
Nealon, Christopher (2011) *The Matter of Capital: Poetry and Crisis in the American Century*. Cambridge, MA: Harvard University Press.
Polanyi, Karl (1957) *The Great Transformation* [1944]. Boston: Beacon Press.

Rancière, Jacques (2007) "Art of the Possible: Fulvia Carnevale and John Kelsey in Conversation with Jacques Rancière," *Artforum* XLV.7: 256–9, 261–4, 266–7, 269.

Sinclair, Iain (2011) *Ghost Milk*. London: Penguin.

Toscano, Alberto (2011–12) "Logistics and Opposition," *Mute* 3.2: 30–41.

Wiggins, Kyle A. (2007) "Futures of Negation: Jameson's *Archaeologies of the Future* and Utopian Science Fiction," *Postmodern Culture* 17.3, http://muse. jhu.edu/journals/postmodern_culture/v017/17.3wiggins.html

Žižek, Slavoj (2011) "With Hegel Beyond Hegel," *Criticism* 53.2: 295–313.

Chapter 4

The Media Crisis in Capitalism: A Report on the Evil of Banality

Paul Taylor

Introduction

> In later years, Arendt agreed that some of her catchwords were erroneous or exaggerated. Most mistaken was the famous or infamous subtitle on the cover of her book. The phrase "banality of evil" entered popular dictionaries and books of familiar quotations. In retrospect, she was sorry she had used it. It had led her into an ambush ... She ... stood accused of exculpating the murderers and offending the memory of the dead (Elon 2006: 100).

> The crisis consists precisely in the fact that the old is dying and the new cannot be born; in this interregnum a great variety of morbid symptoms appear (Gramsci 1971: 276).

This chapter uses Hannah Arendt's *Eichmann in Jerusalem: a Report on the Banality of Evil* in order to explore the relevance of her analysis of banality to the ideological role played by the contemporary media as a result of its systematic promotion of the banal at the expense of the substantive. Banality is shown to be an essential feature of the capitalist media system's standard operating procedure (SOP) that, *pace* Dwight D. Eisenhower, ultimately serves to produce a crisis of public discourse that can best be described as the *Military Industrial Non-Complex*. The crisis of the media in this banality-generating form paradoxically stems from the fact that there is no apparent crisis caused by a lack of substantive meaning, instead, widespread mediated banality generates examples of Gramsci's morbid symptoms in the form of two inherently passive outcomes:

1. It is uncritically and unreflexively accepted as a now naturalized part of the society of the spectacle in which, as Guy Debord pointed out, the ubiquitous conflation of images and commodity values pervasively defines our cultural environment.
2. It is noticed—only to then be cynically disavowed in a contemporary ideological version of the psychoanalytically observed response "*Je sais bien mais quand même ...*" ("I know very well but even so ...")

Before thinking about the contours of a desirable alternative post-capitalist media scenario, it is first necessary to address these morbid symptoms that manifest themselves in the current body politic and which any post-capitalist media system would need to cure. To do this, Arendt's account of Eichmann's trial, and its subsequent reception, is examined in the light of the theoretical distinction Žižek makes between the categories of *objective, subjective* and *symbolic* violence. It is suggested that, taken together, Arendt and Žižek's analyses provide the basis from which some intellectual purchase can be gained on the otherwise profoundly destructive yet concept-retardant phenomenon of banality.

The Objective Trouble with Subjective Banality

> Adolf Eichmann ... medium-sized, slender, middle-aged, with receding hair, ill-fitting teeth, and nearsighted eyes, who throughout the trial keeps craning his scraggy neck toward the bench (Arendt 1992 [1964]: 5).

> The resultant storm broke out mainly because of Arendt's portrait of Eichmann as a diligent yet "banal" bureaucratic criminal. (The term "banality" actually appears only on the last page but is implicit throughout the entire book.) Eichmann's mediocrity and insipid character struck Arendt on her first day in court. Her initial reaction, expressed in letters to Jaspers, McCarthy, and Blücher, was impressionistic. He isn't even sinister, she wrote (Arendt used the common German term *unheimlich*, which can also be translated as "uncanny"). He was like a "ghost in a spiritualist sauce." What was more, he had a cold and was sneezing inside his bulletproof glass cage (Elon 1996: 100).

Elon described (in a subtitle of his own) Hannah Arendt's now (in)famous phrase "The banality of evil" phrase as *The Lethal Subtitle* because of the furore her book caused upon publication amongst World Jewry. Now a well-worn expression, an under-acknowledged consequence of this over-familiarity is the inattention it fosters towards the full political implications of banality produced by today's media on a globally industrial scale. There is a tautology-infused irony to be found in the fact that, in itself, the media reception of Arendt's book about banality's evil represents an illustration of the media's evilly banal effects. Arendt's original phrasing is thus reversed in this chapter's own subtitle in order to reassess more precisely the relationship between banality and evil. "The banality of evil" implies that evil may persist *despite* a banal form. "The evil of banality," helps to focus upon the nature of evil that occurs *because of* banality. In what follows, it is argued that, notwithstanding Arendt's regret at her choice of words, any sense of error and exaggeration to be associated with the phrase stems, not from Arendt's inaccurate choice of words, but rather, a self-serving defensive response from a mass media system both ill-equipped and poorly motivated to reflect upon its own innate involvement in the highly profitable business of banality.

The paradoxical contrast between Eichmann's underwhelming, wheezy appearance and the enormity of his crimes encapsulates the crucial problem encountered when we try to understand objective processes using subjective criteria—a problem greatly heightened by the fact that the media's SOP is devoted to exacerbating this conceptual incommensurability. In keeping with McLuhan's adage, "The medium is the message," the true significance of the media's SOP lies not in the nominal content being represented but the merging of form with content. Rather than risk a banal discussion of the finer points of trite and drearily predictable media content, readers are invited to draw upon their own direct daily media experiences in order to save time for a deeper discussion of the more profound political implications of the *form/content* imbrication that lie behind such banality. Just a few perennial, illustrative examples of my own would include: the uncritically naturalized accommodation of viewers to an ultimately imbecilic use of images (the *de rigeur* presence of journalists standing outside [frequently closed] significant buildings to bolster a story's gravitas); the routine reduction of structural political issues to personalities and/or personal feelings; and, the incantatory use of sound-bites and/or clichés, for example, the way in which the political relationship between the US and the UK cannot be discussed by British journalists without the ritualistically obsessive invocation of the phrase "the special relationship."

Arendt's use of the word *unheimlich* (uncanny) to describe Eichmann is significant. Freud's explanation of the term describes the close association of the phrase with its opposite root-meaning:

> we can understand why linguistic usage has extended *das Heimliche* ['homely'] into its opposite, *das Unheimliche*; for this uncanny is in reality nothing new or alien, but something which is familiar and old-established in the mind and which has become alienated from it only through the process of repression. This reference to the factor of repression enables us, furthermore, to understand Schelling's definition of the uncanny as something which ought to have remained hidden but has come to light (Freud 1919).

Thus, the uncanny is troubling not because it is shocking and unexpected, but precisely the opposite—we see something we have always known but from a disturbingly new perspective. The uncanny nature of the Holocaust stems from the fact that this most egregious episode in humankind's cruelty involved such a mind-numbing number of victims not primarily because of the blood lust of the sort of killers witnessed in other historical genocides, but rather, because personifications of calmness like Eichmann were able to oversee, with exemplary levels of bureaucratic efficiency, processes that were highly "reasonable" in so far as one is able to forget the specific tasks to which those processes were applied. The Holocaust's horror frequently acts as a sort of Medusa's face that paralyzes consideration of the the almost surreal magnitude of mass murder. The extreme obscenity of the Holocaust as a particular event tends to blind us to its status as the ultimate warning of more general, universalizable dangers. Arendt's recognition of Eichmann's essential banality forces us to consider the specific role played by general processes and the remoteness from reality and morality that they are able to engender.

For Zygmunt Bauman, we should resist the all too understandable temptation to quarantine off considered analysis of the Holocaust's roots in everyday life because of its atypically horrific nature. Dwelling solely upon its inhuman aspects risks overlooking the otherwise important, traceable links that exist to some of the deepest cultural norms of modernity:

> These pictures ... represent only an extreme manifestation of a tendency which may be discovered in all bureaucracies, however benign and innocuous the tasks in which they are currently engaged. I suggest that the discussion of the dehumanizing tendency, rather than being focused on its most sensational and vile, but fortunately uncommon, manifestations, ought to concentrate on the more universal, and for this reason potentially more dangerous, manifestations (Bauman 1989: 102).

For some, the mere use of the Holocaust for wider illustrative purposes is deeply problematic. However, this chapter is motivated by the belief that there is an intellectual duty to, as Arendt puts it, avoid "interpreting history *by* commonplaces" (Arendt 1994: viii [emphasis added]), but that this includes the duty to recognize and interpret the role *of* the commonplace in history. An unnoteworthy, bespectacled figure in the centre of one of the most uncommon events in history, Eichmann's uncanny effect upon Arendt came from his embodiment of the thoughtless disassociation from reality that is a recognizably integral part of wider modern technological society and, in particular, a media system devoted to a naturalized institutionalization of thoughtlessness.

The Media's Violent Banality—Thinking about Thoughtlessness

> "[Eichmann] is actually stupid," [Arendt] wrote Jaspers, after listening to one of Eichmann's exhortations "but then, somehow, he is not" (Er ist eigentlich dumm aber auch irgendwie nicht) ... Evil comes from a failure to think. It defies thought, for as soon as thought tries to engage itself with evil and examine the premises and principles from which it originates, it is frustrated because it finds nothing there. That is the banality of evil (Elon 2006: 96 and 97).

> ... for when I speak of the banality of evil, I do so only on the strictly factual level, pointing to a phenomenon which stared one in the face at the trial. Eichmann was not Iago and not Macbeth, and nothing would have been farther from his mind than to determine with Richard III "to prove a villain." ... It was sheer thoughtlessness—something by no means identical with stupidity—that

predisposed him to become one of the greatest criminals of that period ...
That such remoteness from reality and such thoughtlessness can wreak more
havoc than all the evil instincts taken together which, perhaps, are inherent
in man—that was, in fact, the lesson one could learn in Jerusalem. But it was
a lesson, neither an explanation of the phenomenon nor a theory about it ...
(Arendt [1963]1992: 287).

The above excerpts point to a crucial feature of the contemporary experience of
banality: the simultaneous appearance of stupidity alongside a distinctly non-
stupid ability to frustrate thought. A practical illustration of this reason-defying
process in action is provided by the reception of Arendt's book itself. Her attempt
even just to portray (not even explain) the paradox of simultaneous banality and
horror was lost in manufactured controversy as critics wilfully failed to see the
difference between a diligent attempt to understand and a reprehensible desire to
exculpate. Despite Arendt's insistence that she spoke "on the strictly factual level,"
her profoundly serious discussion of the relationship between evil and banality
was subjected to a series of misrepresentations, selective emphases and distortions
("spin") that now function as essential features of the media's basic grammar. Such
manipulations are, of course, eminently possible in such non-mass media discourse
as one-to-one face-to-face and written communication, but, within the mass media
system those manipulations are much less conscious and unreflective because they
are inherently contained within its forms. True openness to Arendt's discussion of
banality raises a series of uncomfortable questions relating to the media's role in
the systematic promulgation of sheer thoughtlessness—the systematic nature of
which, is indeed by no means identical with stupidity.

To provide at least the beginnings of the explanation and theory of banality's
ideological function that Arendt sought we turn to Žižek's conceptualization
of violence:

Subjective Violence

This is what we commonsensically understand by the notion of violence and
is defined by Žižek as that which is "performed by a clearly identifiable agent"
(Žižek 2008:1). In other words, subjective violence does not refer to any notion of
an excessively personal interpretation of what constitutes violence, it is violence
that can easily be attributed to an individual source.

Objective Violence

Žižek subdivides objective violence into two parts:

i. *Symbolic violence*: the basic form of violence "... that pertains to
language as such" (ibid.:1). The cardinal philosophical point is that all
communication has a violent element, the key political question rests in

the type of violence that results. Thus, Baudrillard finds in the agonistic, threatening challenges laid down by anthropological forms of symbolic exchange a desirable form of communicational violence. Subtle nuances are contained within traditional rituals of gift-giving that produce a culture full of seductive ambiguities—to be contrasted with the pre-ordained, pre-enscribed cultural values transmitted within commodity culture of mass media society. At one level, the transmissions of this technologically-mediated commodified order appear less symbolically violent than its more "primitive" counterparts because less is demanded from the sender and recipient, but on another level it is steeped with:

ii. *Systemic violence*—"the often catastrophic consequences of the smooth functioning of our economic and political systems" (ibid.:1). This concept refers to the predominantly unrecognized levels of force and repression that form a base level, frequently dispersed, but nevertheless effective and powerful circumscription of social activity. Žižek's concept of objective violence draws attention to those cultural elements that have profound effects but are largely invisible to the ideologically-acclimatized eye:

> Objective violence is invisible since it sustains the very zero-level standard against which we perceive something as subjectively violent. Systemic violence is thus something like the notorious "dark matter" of physics, the counterpart to an all-too visible subjective violence. It may be invisible, but it has to be taken into account if one is to make sense of what otherwise seem to be "irrational" explosions of subjective violence (ibid.: 2).

In our society of the spectacle, the invisibility of objective violence makes it media-unfriendly. Typically cursory attempts by TV News to provide historical context to its items are dominated by metronomically metonymic images. Complex cultural histories become inseparable in our mediated mind's eye with reductively familiar pictures—bombed-out downtown Beirut, emaciated African babies, Uzi-toting Israeli soldiers and *keffiyeh*-wearing Palestinian stone throwers. The media propagates a fundamental form of mediated violence through the way in which its explicit spectacles supplant sustained consideration of their primary causes—past and present. For example, the mundane day-to-day violence of life under France or Russia's pre-revolutionary Ancien/Tsarist Regimes is typically overlooked in documentaries in which the objective political causes of violence are supplanted by sustained fascination with subjective experiences of post-revolutionary Terror. The same can be said of the process of exclusion regarding the background level of global state-sponsored terror necessary for the continuation of "normal" international politics by other means—the Bush Administration's "War on Terror." In the latter case, the repetition of the banal creates the necessary conditions of thoughtlessness for war to be declared upon an abstract noun.

At her time of writing in 1963, Arendt described the 'permissive' nature of a culture premised upon exposure and repetitious exhibition as values in themselves (cultural tendencies that have only increased since) and how, even in a trial devoted to some of history's most heinous crimes, this:

> ... permits the prosecutor to give press conferences and interviews for television during the trial (the American program, sponsored by the Glickman Corporation, is constantly interrupted—business as usual—by real-estate advertising), ... it permits frequent side glances into the audience, and the theatrics characteristic of a more than ordinary vanity, which finally achieves its triumph in the White House with a compliment on "a job well done" by the President of the United States (Arendt [1963] 1992: 5).

Judging the ideological effects of the mass media has thus evolved from the yardstick of covert exploitation (the false consciousness of the proletariat) to this much more inchoate ideological ghost "in a spiritualist sauce"—a heavily mediated form of political thoughtlessness in which even the question of achieving scant justice for millions of racially-profiled victims is vulnerable to the ubiquitous and pervasive influence of sound-bites, advertising, and cheap theatrics.

The Military Industrial Non-complex

> The thing is, Schindler's List is about success, the Holocaust was about failure (Stanley Kubrick).

> I don't like the red coat; it gave me a queasy feeling the first time I saw *Schindler's List*. And I know that it was in the profound nature of Hollywood that the concentration camp story could only be told in a big, mainstream picture if someone found a story that had at least a touch of the upbeat. That was Oskar Schindler (Thomson 2013).

In their above observations about the movie *Schindler's List*, both Kubrick and Thomson highlight the symbolic violence typical of Hollywood's output. The film *industry* is designed to obfuscate the distinction to be made between subjective and objective forms of violence. The tritely optimistic nature of its output even extends to films about the Holocaust and demonstrate an innate need to privilege rare subjective sources of hope (Schindler) amidst the pervasively objective facts of continent-wide genocide. This is a general problem that persists within the media's SOP—the mismatch encountered when attempting to engage with themes of objective causality in a media system totally infused by subjective values. In Lacanian terms, the subject of the enunciation resists being separated out from the enunciated subject. It should be recognized that outside the purview of the media, rational consideration of objective processes are still not easily divorced from their grounding in subjective factors. Thus, in addition to Arendt's ill-received juxtaposition of evil and banality, Martin Heidegger's analysis of the essentially shared underlying nature of otherwise disparate objective processes (with radically different purposes and outcomes) and the censure it has generated also demonstrates the difficulty with which commentators struggle to disassociate subjective and objective considerations.

In subjective terms, Heidegger's initial membership of the Nazi party and preternaturally stubborn post-war refusal to apologize, create an obvious inducement to be biased towards any comments related to the Holocaust which he did in this much cited example:

> Agriculture is now a mechanized food industry, in essence the same as the production of corpses in the gas chambers and extermination camps, the same thing as the blockading and starving of countries, the same thing as the production of hydrogen bombs (Heidegger 1949: 27 in Mitchell 2012).

The equivalence repeatedly asserted here with 'the same thing' led to such representative criticisms as Davidson's observation that:

> When one encounters Heidegger's 1949 pronouncement, one cannot but be staggered by his inability—call it metaphysical inability—to acknowledge the everyday fate of bodies and souls, as if the bureaucratized burning of selected human beings were not all that different from the threat to humanity posed in the organization of the food industry by the forces of technology (Davidson 1989: 424).

Using the phrase "were not all that different," Davidson fundamentally misses Heidegger's central philosophical point by concentrating solely on Heidegger expression "the same thing as" to the exclusion of the crucial qualification contained in the immediately preceeding "*in essence*." It is with his use of this specific phrase that Heidegger draws attention to the fact that it is possible for activities which are vastly different in both their substantive content and the overt intentions that lie behind them to, nevertheless, still share a common underlying quality.

This is the argument succinctly conveyed in Heidegger's statement from his *The Question Concerning Technology* essay, that "the essence of technology is by no means anything technological"—in other words, once again emphasizing the notion of *essence*, there are many different forms of technological artefact, but, common across such diverse forms, there is an underlying commonality—the instrumental facilitation of an objectifying attitude towards human experience. The fact that Heidegger's reprehensible past makes him vulnerable to charges of heraldic insensitivity does not, on its own, explain away the persistence elsewhere amongst other prominent Jewish thinkers like Zygmunt Bauman and Richard Bernstein of sentiments that, like Heidegger, also insist upon the wider and more generalizable significance of the uniquely industrial nature of the Holocaust. Thus in terms reminiscent of imagery present in Heidegger's work, Bauman argues:

> Like everything else in our modern society, the Holocaust was an accomplishment
> in every respect superior if measured by the standards that this society has
> preached and institutionalized. It towers high above the past genocidal episodes
> in the same way as the modern industrial plant towers above the craftsman's
> cottage workshop, or the modern industrial farm' with its tractors, combines
> and pesticides, towers above the peasant farmstead with its horse, hoe and hand-
> weeding (Bauman 1989:89).

Similarly, Bernstein pointed out that although:

> We may find it almost impossible to image how someone could "think"(or
> rather, not think) in this manner, whereby manufacturing food, bombs, or
> corpses are "in essence the same" and where this can become "normal,"
> "ordinary" behavior. This is the mentality that Arendt believed she was facing in
> Eichmann ... (Bernstein 1996: 170).

It is understandable that in such an horrific instances as the Holocaust
subjective factors cannot always be dispassionately removed from discussions of
objective processes, and that there is a natural human tendency to seek to embody
and anchor objective causes of violence in human subjects but it still remains
true that Arendt's identification of Eichmann's striking banality raises important
questions regarding the subjective embodiment of objective violence.

Arendt's comments on Eichmann's insipidness book-end her report. In her
early description of the accused she points out how, "Half a dozen psychiatrists
had certified him as 'normal'—'More normal, at any rate, that I am after
having examined him,' one of them was said to have exclaimed ..." (Arendt
[1963]1992: 25) whilst in the Epilogue she states that:

> The trouble with Eichmann was precisely that so many were like him, and
> that the many were neither perverted nor sadistic, that they were, and still are,
> terribly and terrifyingly normal. From the viewpoint of our legal institutions and
> of our moral standards of judgment, this normality was much more terrifying
> than all the atrocities put together (Arendt [1963]1992: 276).

Our pressing need to see in Eichmann some sort of psychosis in preference to
confronting the full objective implications of his disturbing normality reflects a
conflation of the subjective/objective categories of violence that, present in such
extreme form at Eichmann's trial, occurs much more naturally and unobtrusively as
part of the media's SOP. The uncanny resonance Eichmann's terrifying normality
has with our situation today can be found in, to repeat once again, the similarities
in essence (if not necessarily equivalent outcomes) to be found between the way in
which his banality produced a barrier of thoughtlessness that protected him from
reality and the ever more sophisticated forms of mediated standards and codes that
currently screen our lives, both literally and figuratively.

The Perfect Crime of Existential Banality

> ... his cliché-ridden language produced on the stand, as it had evidently done in his official life, a kind of macabre comedy. Clichés, stock phrases, adherence to conventional, standardized codes of expression and conduct have the socially recognized function of protecting us against reality, that is, against the claim on our thinking attention that all events and facts make by virtue of their existence (Arendt 1978: 04, cited in Assy 1998).

> Sex is everywhere else to be found, but that's not what people want. What people deeply desire is a spectacle of banality. This spectacle of banality is today's true pornography and obscenity. It is the obscene spectacle of nullity (nullité), insignificance, and platitude. This stands as the complete opposite of the theater of cruelty. But perhaps there is still a form of cruelty, at least a virtual one, attached to such a banality. At a time when television and the media in general are less and less capable of accounting for (rendre compte) the world's (unbearable) events, they rediscover daily life. They discover existential banality as the deadliest event, as the most violent piece of information: the very location of the perfect crime. Existential banality is the perfect crime. And people are fascinated (but terrified at the same time) by this indifferent "nothing-to-say" or "nothing-to-do," by the indifference of their own lives. Contemplating the Perfect Crime—banality as the latest form of fatality—has become a genuine Olympic contest, the latest version of extreme sports (Baudrillard, 2001).

Baudrillard's phrase "existential banality" and Dovey's "the *pre-digested* detail of banal everyday life" (Dovey 2000: 1) describe in similarly cogent terms the excessively personalized and trivial approach, tone and content that, bad enough in the realm of entertainment programmes, are now also increasingly merging with the previously distinct category of "serious" news programming creating such neologisms as *factual entertainment* and *docu-drama*. This is a practical illustration of Baudrillard's contention that, in practice, modern communications technologies actually serve to fabricate non-communication. The dominant value they sponsor is tautology—that which is transmitted is privileged by virtue of the fact that transmission is society's defining cultural feature. The result is a crassly mediated reduction of the full ambiguity and open-ended potentiality of unmediated reality—a quality Baudrillard terms *seduction*—that has now been replaced by the pornographic excessiveness of media representations. *Ratio* is the term with which Kracauer describes the industrially standardized nature of mass media capitalism when he suggests, in presciently pre-Baudrillardian terms, that: "The desolation of Ratio is complete only when it removes its mask and hurls itself into the void of random abstractions that no longer mimic higher determinations, and when it renounces *seductive* consonances and desires itself even as a concept" (Kracauer, 1995:180).

Contemporary Ratio has evolved so that its "random abstractions" include celebrity variations upon a reality TV theme that are almost endless—celebrities compete in contexts ranging from a jungle (*I'm a Celebrity Get Me Out of Here*) to various sorts of competition, in dance (*Strictly Come Dancing, Dancing With the Stars*), ice-skating (*Strictly Ice Dancing*), circus acts (*Cirque de* Celebrite, *Celebrity Circus*), weight loss (*Celebrity Fit Club*) etc. etc.). The predictability of a format that appears to have fallen in love with itself becomes increasingly independent of any "higher determinations." Culturally grounded symbolic values are replaced by the ready-made commodified categories of a culture industry that effortlessly reaches beyond Adorno's darkest imaginings. Kracauer's argument that Ratio renounces "seductive consonances" is a direct forbearer of Adorno's emaphasis upon that industry's systemic, operationalized nature and reappears in Baudrillard's notion of a precession of simulacra closely akin to Kracauer's self-desiring concept:

> What else does the media dream of if not raising up events by its very presence? Everyone deplores it, but everyone is secretly fascinated by this eventuality. Such is the logic of simulacra: no longer divine predestination, but the precession of models, which is no less inexorable. And it is for this reason that events no longer have any meaning: not because they are insignificant in themselves but because they have been preceded by models with which their own process can only coincide (Baudrillard 1986: 22).

More critical than McLuhan's attempt to find optimism in the media's *mosaic* quality, Kracauer is scathingly unambiguous about the banal cultural consequences of a media that inexorably generates its own autonomous precession of models:

> The monotony of this hodgepodge is the just revenge for its inconsequentiality, which is heightened by the thoughtless way the individual sequences are combined into a mosaic … almost all of them avoid the most urgent human concerns, *dragging the exotic into daily life rather than searching for the exotic within the quotidian* (Kracauer 1995: 311).

The political implications of this hodgepodge of conceptually disparate material is that all cultural issues become subject to the same passive indifference to truth content that produces at worst a population progressively remote from the values of unmediated reality, or, at best, a population whose very inertial status becomes its only hope of assuming radical status as Baudrillard somewhat mischievously suggests with his notion of fatal strategies—the name he gives to the "radical inertia" of the media masses.

In authentically seductive and symbolically rich forms of communication, social meaning is derived from the interplay of unpredictable interactions. Unlike the pre-encoded nature of the culture industry's products, authentically empowering play is indeterminate and truly fascinating. In banal media, by contrast, open-ended and unpredictable outcomes are expunged from culture (just as Benjamin described aura being "pumped out like water from a sinking ship") by the combined effects of the dumb narcotic fascination of the screen and the formulaic nature of the content: "Any system that is totally complicit in its own absorption such that signs no longer make sense, will exercise a remarkable power of fascination" (Baudrillard 1990:77). The ideological effect of the *society of the spectacle* is such that essentially empty, tautological and vacuous media content can still be fascinating—but in this absorbing rather than revealing sense. The fascination it generates is a *dumb fascination* much more akin to Marshall McLuhan's notion of the media's narcotic effects than Walter Benjamin's hopes of media empowerment contained within his essay "The Work of Art in the Age of Mechanical Reproduction."

For Walter Benjamin, the media's symbolic violence promised to explode open our traditionally confined ways of seeing the world: 'Then came the film and burst this prison-world asunder by the dynamite of the tenth of a second, so that now, in the midst of its far-flung ruins and debris, we calmly and adventurously go travelling' (Benjamin 1969 [1936]: 316). In his eyes, the camera was able to find the exotic in the quotidian, 'by focusing on hidden details of familiar objects, by exploring common place milieus' (ibid.). The reality of a post-Benjamin media system fascinated by its own models of reality, however, is a generalized ideological process in which meaning is simultaneously produced and reduced. In what Bauman terms our mediated era of *liquid modernity*, the media uses the emotional shock of subjective suffering to flood the underlying objective causes so that:

> all associations of the horrid pictures of famine, as presented by the media, with
> the destruction of work and work-places (that is, with the global causes of local
> poverty) are carefully avoided. People are shown together with their hunger—but
> however the viewers strain their eyes, they will not see a single work-tool, plot of
> arable land or head of cattle in the picture—and one hears no reference to them ...
> certainly not in the lands where people on the screen starve, and the plight of
> people offered as a carnival-like, "charity fair" outlet for a pent-up moral impulse.
> The riches are global, the misery is local—but there is no causal link between the
> two; not in the spectacle of the fed and the feeding, anyway (Bauman 1998: 74).

The paradox of this situation is that our growing inability to see the objective woods for the subjective trees results from an ideological deception based upon excessive revelation: "It is precisely when it appears most truthful, most faithful and most in conformity to reality that the image is most diabolical" (Baudrillard 1986: 13)

The Devil in the Media's Detail—The Grandly Uninquisitive

> And if this is "banal" and even funny, if with the best will in the world one
> cannot extract any diabolical or demonic profundity from Eichmann, that is still
> far from calling it commonplace (Arendt [1963] 1992: 288).

> It was some gentleman, or, rather, a certain type of Russian gentleman, no longer young, *qui frisait la cinquantaine*, as the French say, with not too much gray in his dark, rather long, and still thick hair, and with a pointed beard. He was wearing a sort of brown jacket, evidently from the best of tailors, but already shabby, made approximately three years ago and already completely out of fashion, such as no well-to-do man of society had been seen in for at least two years. His linen ... was a bit dirty and the wide scarf was quite threadbare ... (Dostoevsky 2004 [1880]: 635).

Dostoevsky's depiction of the Devil in *The Brothers Karamazov* represents perhaps the most striking literary depiction of Arendt's juxtaposition of evil and banality (including even the small detail of suffering from a cold). The Devil appears to Ivan as simultaneously prosaic and hallucinatory, resonating with Arendt's conceptualization of a mundane-looking Eichmann that, nevertheless, was far from commonplace—an uncanny ghost in a spiritualist sauce:

> "Not for a single moment do I take you for the real truth," Ivan cried, somehow even furiously. "You are a lie, you are my illness, you are a ghost. Only I don't know how to destroy you, and I see I'll have to suffer through it for a while. You are my hallucination. You are the embodiment of myself, but of just one side of me ... of my thoughts and feelings, but only the most loathsome and stupid of them. From that angle you could even be interesting to me, if I had time to bother with you ..." (ibid.: 637).

Ivan Karamazov's conversation with the Devil resonates with the lived experience of today's capitalist reality crisis. The devil in the detail of capitalist media is precisely this one-sided Arnoldian inversion—the dream and news factories' heavily standardized production of the most banal that has been thought and said complete with the quality of cynical disavowal seen in both the above comment "not for a single moment do I take you for the real truth," and also in the Devil's reference elsewhere in his conversation with Ivan to religious hermits who "contemplate such abysses of belief and disbelief at one and the same moment" (ibid.: 645)

In response to a complaint Ivan makes, "You just pick out all my bad thoughts, and above all the stupid ones. You are stupid and banal" (ibid.: 638) [one that chimes with the central thrust of this chapter's charge against the media], the Devil rejects his original remoteness from reality due to his unearthly genesis as a fallen angel, and enthusiastically welcomes his wholesale immersion in earth's determinate realism:

> Here, when I move in with people from time to time, my life gets to be somewhat real, as it were, and I like that most of all. Because, like you, I myself suffer from the fantastic, and that is why I love your earthly realism. Here you have it all outlined, here you have the formula, here you have geometry, and with us it's all indeterminate equations! (ibid.: 638).

Not to mention the obvious affinity Dostoevksy's Devil has with Baudrillard's *Evil Demon of Images* (1986) his words have more than passing relevance to Kracauer's concept of *Ratio*, Baudrillard's precession of simulacra and the contemporary plethora of reality TV formats. Earlier in *The Brothers Karamazov*, as part of Ivan's poem "The Grand Inquisitor," the eponymous follower of the ethos of earthly realism uses the temptation of Christ in the desert to expound upon this diabolic doctrinal belief in the formulaic over the genuinely free and ambiguous:

> Had you accepted that third counsel of the mighty spirit, you would have furnished all that man seeks on earth, that is: someone to bow down to, someone to take over his conscience, and a means for uniting everyone at last into a common, concordant, and incontestable anthill-for the need for universal union is the third and last torment of men. Mankind in its entirety has always yearned to arrange things so that they must be universal (Dostoevsky 2004 [1880]: 257).

The Devil appears to Ivan in the form of such an inoffensively banal and unchallenging character because he acts as the embodiment of the Grand Inquisitor's rejection of freedom and its cost:

> There is nothing more seductive for man than the freedom of his conscience, but there is nothing more tormenting either. And so, instead of a firm foundation for appeasing human conscience once and for all, you chose everything that was unusual, enigmatic, and indefinite, you chose everything that was beyond men's strength, and thereby acted as if you did not love them at all … but did it not occur to you that he would eventually reject and dispute even your image and your truth if he was oppressed by so terrible a burden as freedom of choice? (ibid.: 254–5).

Although bathed in biblical terms and imagery, Dostoevsky's startlingly vivid portrayal of the ideologically committed Grand Inquisitor and a discombobulatingly affable Lucifer, serves to convey, *avant la lêttre*, the nub of the ideological problem created by the systematic generation of banality. With Ivan's poetic license, Dostoevsky expresses the otherwise inchoately experienced effects of banality—the implacable enervation of the truth that occurs when the indeterminate, the unusual, the enigmatic, and the indefinite are expunged from life. Dostoevksy's fictional characters convey what a range of modern critical theorists have disparaged in such previously cited terms as the society of the spectacle, the culture industry, and the seduction-free realm of simulacra—the realm of the grandly uninquisitive.

Conclusion: "Ah, mais c'est bête enfin"

> It was as though in those last minutes he was summing up the lesson that this long course in human wickedness had taught us—*the lesson of the fearsome, word-and-thought-denying banality of evil* (Arendt [1963]1992: 252).

As pointed out at the beginning of this chapter, even though it is an implicit theme that runs throughout her entire account of Eichmann's trial, apart from its presence in the book's sub-title, Arendt's famous phrase occurs as part of the description of Eichmann last words on the scaffold only on the book's final page. The breadth and depth of the phrase's subsequent resonance, despite its scant occurrence, speaks volumes for the adeptness with which it captures an uncanny remoteness from reality and moral disassociation that Eichmann personified but which, *in essence*, is now ubiquitously institutionalized within today's heavily mediated and bureaucratized world. The importance of the words that immediately precede "banality" is also seldom noticed but 'word-and-thought-denying' goes straight to the ideological effect of the media's banal essence. The media-facilitated fixation upon the phrase "banality of evil," in isolation from the denial of thinking that Arendt clearly identifies as the vector through which evil is enabled, is in itself an example of the key point that this chapter, reversing Arendt's phrase, makes about the evil effects of banal thought. The superficially benign realms of media news and entertainment may seem totally divorced from the actions of a mass murderer, but to repeat for a final time, *in essence*, they too partake of the "grotesque silliness" of Eichmann's last words.

We may think that incidents such as the News International phone-hacking scandal of July 2011 (and the on-going aftermath of the subsequent Leveson enquiry), the Watergate scandal, and the death of Princess Diana allow us the chance to question fundamentally the nature of thought-denying banality, but it is more likely that they represent an instance of impotent acting out, an impotence equivalent to Ivan's throwing of a glass of water at a Devil who responds with "Ah, mais c'est bête enfin" ("Ah, but how stupid, really!").[1] The more journalists self-flagellate, the more it becomes obvious that their *mea culpas* merely represent displacement activity designed to obstruct rather than enable any genuine change to a capitalist system of discourse in which news and entertainment values are frequently indistinguishable. Just as we are reassured that things will never be the same, we know that the status quo has never been more entrenched. Since one cannot reason the public out of something it didn't reason itself into—radical political discourse needs to recalibrate itself to deal more successfully with the deceptively banal forms of contemporary ideology that are perversely so misleadingly effective because of their very triteness. This chapter has modestly proposed that before attempting to produce detailed plans for what a post-capitalist mediascape might look and sound like, we need to come to full terms with the importance of the banal nature of the barriers that stand in the way.

Arendt's notion that, "Justice ... demands seclusion, it permits sorrow rather than anger, and it prescribes the most careful abstention from all the nice pleasures of putting oneself in the limelight" (Arendt [1963]1992: 5) bodes ill for a society

---

1   "Ah, but how stupid, really!" – the full quotation is "Ah, mais c'est bête enfin"...
He remembers Luther's inkstand! He considers me a dream and he throws glasses at a dream! (Dostoevsky 2004: 649).

now almost completely predicated upon the glare of the limelight. A post-capitalist mass media would recognize the political ramifications of this and thereby seek to avoid the current ideological consequences of a situation in which even events as historically and morally significant as Eichmann's trial are still liable to be trivialized. When, like Ivan, we feel reduced to throwing a glass at an evil demon of capitalist images experienced as a paradoxically real figment of our worst and most stupid imaginations, and when we struggle to envisage a feasible media forum for social justice, we should know that at least our frustration is not stupid, hopefully, there is some small consolation to be found in Herbert Marcuse's observation that: "the unrealistic sound of these propositions is indicative, not of their utopian character but of the strength of the forces which prevent their realization" (Marcuse 1991 [1964]: 4).

References

Arendt, Hannah (1978) *The Life of Mind—Thinking—Willing*. New York-London: Ed. Harvest/HJB Book.

Assy, B. Eichmann (1998) "The Banality of Evil, and Thinking in Arendt's Thought" from the Twentieth World Congress of Philosophy (Boston, Massachusetts, August 10–15, 1998, available at: http://www.bu.edu/wcp/Papers/Cont/ContAssy.htm).

Baudrillard, Jean (1986) *The Evil Demon of Images*. Sydney: Power Institute of Fine Arts.

——— (1990) *Cool Memories*. London: Verso.

——— (2001) "Dust Breeding" (available at http://www.egs.edu/faculty/jean-baudrillard/articles/dust-breeding/).

Bauman, Zygmunt (1989) *Modernity and the Holocaust*. Cambridge: Polity Press.

Bernstein, Richard (1996) "Evil, Thinking, and Judging," in *Hannah Arendt and the Jewish Question*. Cambridge: The MIT Press.

——— (1992 [1963]) *Eichmann in Jerusalem: A Report on the Banality of Evil*. New York: Penguin Books.

Benjamin, Walter (1969) *Illuminations* (trans. Harry Zorn). New York: Schocken Books.

Dostoevsky, Fyodor (2004 [1880]) The *Brothers Karamazov* (trans. R. Pevear and L. Volokhonsky). London: Vintage.

Dovey, Jon (2000) *Freakshow: First Person Media and Factual Television*. London: Pluto Press.

Elon, Amos "The Excommunication of Hannah Arendt" *World Policy Journal*, Vol. 23, No. 4 (Winter, 2006/2007), pp. 93–102.

Freud, Sigmund (1919) *The Uncanny* (available at: http://www-rohan.sdsu.edu/~amtower/uncanny.html).

Gramsci, Antonio (1971) *Selections from the Prison Notebooks*. New York: Progress Publishers.

Heidegger, Martin (2012) *Bremen and Freiburg Lectures: Insight into That Which is and Basic Principles of Thinking* (trans. A. J. Mitchell). Indiana: Indiana University Press.

Kracauer, Siegfried (1995 [1963]) *Mass Ornament: Weimar essays* (trans. T. Y. Levin). Cambridge, MA: Harvard University Press.

Marcuse, Herbert (1991 [1964]) *One Dimensional Man*. London: Routledge.

Thomson, David (2013) "Schindler's Girl in the Red Coat Speaks Out" The New Republic March 7th 2013 (available at: http://www.newrepublic.com/article/112598/schindlers-girl-red-coat-speaks-out#).

Žižek, Slavoj (2008) *Violence*. London: Profile Books.

PART II
Events

Chapter 5

The Undoing of an Event

Slavoj Žižek

The German expression *rückgängig machen*, usually translated as "annul, cancel, unhitch," has a more precise connotation: to retroactively undo something, to make it as if it did not take place. The comparison between Mozart's *Figaro* and Rossini's Figaro-operas makes this immediately clear. In Mozart, the emancipatory political potential of Beaumarchais's play survives the pressure of censorship—think only of the finale, where the Count has to kneel down and ask for forgiveness of his subjects (not to mention the explosion of the collective "Viva la libertà!" in the finale of Act 1 of *Don Giovanni*). The breathtaking achievement of Rossini's *Barber* should be measured by this standard: Rossini took a theatrical piece which was one of THE symbols of the French bourgeois revolutionary spirit, and totally de-politicized it, changing it into a pure *opera buffa*. No wonder the golden years of Rossini were 1815–1830: the years of reaction, the years in which the European powers tackled the impossible task of the *Ungeschehenmachen* (making-it-not-happen) of the previous revolutionary decades. This is what Rossini did in his great comic operas: they try to bring back to life the innocence of the pre-revolutionary world. Rossini did not actively hate and fight the new world—he simply composed *as if the years 1789–1915 did not exist*. Rossini was therefore right to (almost) stop composing after 1830 and to adopt the satisfied stance of a *bon vivant* making his *tournedos*—this was the only properly ethical thing to do, and his long silence is comparable to that of Jan Sibelius and, in literature, to those of Arthur Rimbaud and Dashiell Hammett.

Insofar as the French Revolution is THE Event of modern history, the break after which "nothing was the same," one should raise here the question: is this kind of "undoing," of dis-eventalization, one of the possible destinies of every Event? It is possible to imagine the attitude of the fetishist split towards an Event: "I know very well there was no Event, just the ordinary run of things, but, perhaps, unfortunately, nonetheless … (I believe) there WAS one"? And, an even more interesting case, is it possible for an Event to be not directly denied but denied retroactively? Imagine a society which fully integrated into its ethical substance the great modern axioms of freedom, equality, democratic rights, the duty of a society to provide for education and basic healthcare of all its members, and which rendered racism or sexism simply inacceptable and ridiculous—there is no need even to argue against, say, racism, since anyone who openly advocates racism is immediately perceived as a weird eccentric who cannot be taken seriously, etc. But then, step by step, although a society continues to pay lip service to these axioms, they are *de facto* deprived of their substance. Here is an example from the ongoing European history: in the Summer of 2012, Viktor Orban, the Hungarian Rightist PM, said that in Central Europe a new economic system must be built:

> and let us hope that God will help us and we will not have to invent a new type of political system instead of democracy that would need to be introduced for the sake of economic survival. / ... / Cooperation is a question of force, not of intention. Perhaps there are countries where things don't work that way, for example in the Scandinavian countries, but such a half-Asiatic rag-tag people as we are can unite only if there is force (in Presseurop 2012).

The irony of these lines was not lost on some old Hungarian dissidents: when the Soviet army moved into Budapest to crush the 1956 anti-Communist uprising, the message repeatedly sent by the beleaguered Hungarian leaders to the West was: "We are defending Europe here" (against the Asiatic Communists, of course). Now, after Communism collapsed, the Christian-conservative government paints as its main enemy Western multi-cultural consumerist liberal democracy for which today's Western Europe stands, and calls for a new more organic communitarian order to replace the "turbulent" liberal democracy of the last two decades. In the latest installment of the saga of designating the Enemy as the coincidence of the opposites ("plutocratic-Bolshevik plot," etc.), (ex-)Communists and liberal "bourgeois" democrats are perceived as the two faces of the same enemy. No wonder Orban and some of his allies repeatedly express their sympathies for the Chinese "capitalism with Asian values," looking to "Asian" authoritarianism as the solution against the ex-Communist threat ...

But we should approach this topic gradually, in a more systematic way, beginning with the obscene underside of a post-evental reality which undoes it from within. According to a legend, Alfred Hitchcock (himself a Catholic) was once driving through a small Swiss town; all of a sudden, he pointed his finger at something through the car window and said: "This is the most terrifying scene I've ever seen!" A friend sitting at his side looked in the direction pointed by Hitchcock with surprise: there was nothing outstanding out there, just a priest who, while talking to a young boy, put his hand onto the boy's arm. Hitchcock halted the car, rolled down the window and shouted: "Run, boy, save your life!" While this anecdote could be taken as a display of Hitchcock's eccentric showmanship, it does bring us to the "heart of darkness" of the Catholic Church.

Recall the numerous cases of pedophilia that have shattered the Catholic Church: when its representatives insist that these cases, deplorable as they are, are the Church's internal problem, and display great reluctance to collaborate with the police in their investigations,[1] they are, in a way, right—the pedophilia of

---

1   Recently, the Catholic Church has been under attack from different sides for allegedly covering up its own sex abuse scandals. In 2010, the BBC reported that the scandal had to do with how the Catholic Church systematically conceals sexual abuse and other shortcomings

Catholic priests is not something that concerns merely the persons who, because of accidental reasons of private history with no relation to the Church as an institution, happened to choose the profession of a priest; it is a phenomenon that concerns the Catholic Church as such, that is inscribed into its very functioning as a socio-symbolic institution. It does not concern the "private" unconscious of individuals, but the "unconscious" of the institution itself: it is not something that happens because the Institution has to accommodate itself to the pathological realities of libidinal life in order to survive, but something that the institution itself needs in order to reproduce itself. One can well imagine a "straight" (not pedophiliac) priest who, after years of service, gets involved in pedophilia because the very logic of the institution seduces him into it. Such an *institutional Unconscious* designates the obscene disavowed underside that, precisely as disavowed, sustains the public institution. (In the army, this underside consists of the obscene sexualized rituals of fragging etc. which, I claim, sustain group solidarity).[2] In other words, it is not simply that, for conformist reasons, the Church tries to hush up the embarrassing pedophilic scandals; in defending itself, the Church defends its innermost obscene secret. In my view, what this means is that identifying oneself with this secret side is a key constituent of the very identity of a Christian priest (though, of course, not every priest will act upon such identification): if a priest seriously (not just rhetorically) denounces these scandals, he thereby excludes himself from the ecclesiastic community, he is no longer "one of us" (in exactly the same way a citizen of a town in the South of the US in the 1920s, if he denounced Ku Klux Klan to the police, excluded himself from his community, i.e., betrayed its fundamental solidarity). Consequently, the answer to the Church's reluctance should be not only that we are dealing with criminal cases and that, if Church does not fully participate in their investigation, it is an accomplice after the fact; the Church AS SUCH, as an institution, should be investigated with regard to the way it systematically creates conditions for such crimes. That is to say, what makes these crimes so disturbing is that they did not just happen in religious surroundings—these surroundings were part of them, directly mobilized as the instrument of seduction:

(see Lewis Aidan, 'Looking behind the Catholic sex abuse scandal', broadcasted on the BBC on 4 May 2010). In the same year, many Catholics called for the resignation of Pope Benedict XVI quoting evidence regarding his previous attempts (when he was a Cardinal) at stifling attempts to investigate cases of sex abuse within the Catholic Church (see Daniel Wakin, 'Do Popes Quit?', in *The New York Times*, 10 April 2010, p. 1). In September 2010, finally, Pope Benedict himself conceded that the Catholic Church had been neither vigilant nor prompt enough in responding to the issue of sexual abuse perpetrated by its clergy (see 'Pope addresses sex abuse scandal as he starts visit to Britain', broadcast by CNN on 17.09.2010). The general lack of transparency within the Catholic Church in dealing with allegation of sex abused has been claimed by David Yallup in his biography of John Paul II (see Yallup 2009: 497). For similar allegations, see also the BBC Panorama documentary *Sex Crimes and the Vatican*, by Colm O'Gorman, broadcast on 29.09. 2006.
    2   For the practice of fragging, see Lepre (2011) and Brush (2010).

[...] the seduction technique employs religion. Almost always some sort of prayer has been used as foreplay. The very places where the molestation occurs are redolent of religion—the sacristy, the confessional, the rectory, Catholic schools and clubs with sacred pictures on the walls. [...] a conjunction of the overstrict sexual instruction of the Church (e.g., on the mortal sinfulness of masturbation, when even one occurrence of which can, if not confessed, send one to hell) and a guide who can free one of inexplicably dark teaching by inexplicably sacred exceptions. [The predator] uses religion to sanction what he is up to, when calling sex part of his priestly ministry (Willis 2002: 6).

Religion is not just invoked in order to provide a *frisson* of the forbidden, i.e. to heighten the pleasure by making sex an act of transgression; on the contrary, sex itself is presented in religious terms, as the religious cure of the sin (of masturbation). The pedophilic priests were not liberals who seduced boys by claiming that gay sexuality is healthy and permitted—in a masterful use of the reversal called by Lacan *point de capiton*, they first insisted that the confessed sin of a boy (masturbation) really is mortal, and then they offered gay acts (say, mutual masturbation)—i.e., what cannot but appear an even STRONGER sin—as a "healing" procedure. The key resides in this mysterious "transubstantiation" by means of which the prohibiting Law which makes us feel guilty apropos an ordinary sin is enacted in the guise of a much stronger sin—as if, in a kind of Hegelian coincidence of the opposites, the Law coincides with the strongest transgression. And is the present US politics, in its inherent structure, not a kind of political equivalent of the Catholic pedophilia? The problem of its new moral vigor is not just that morality is manipulatively exploited, but that it is directly mobilized; the problem with its appeal to democracy is that it is not simply hypocrisy and external manipulation, but that it directly mobilizes and relies on "sincere" democratic strivings.

In the summer of 2012, there occurred in Slovenia an almost clinically pure display of the Catholic Church's obscenity. It involved two actors, the conservative Cardinal Franc Rode, a Slovene with the highest place in the Church *nomenklatura*, and Alojz Uran, the archbishop who was first deposed by the Vatican and then even ordered to leave Slovenia immediately until accusations against him were clarified.[3] Since Uran was very popular among ordinary Catholic believers, rumors started to circulate about the reasons for this extraordinarily harsh punishment. After a week or so of embarrassing silence, the Church authorities grudgingly proclaimed that Uran was suspected of fathering an illegitimate child—an explanation which, for a series of reasons, was met with widespread disbelief. First, rumors about Uran's paternity had been circulating already for decades, so why did the Church not take measures years before when Uran was nominated the archbishop of Slovenia? Second, Uran himself publicly proclaimed that he was ready to undergo

---

3   See 'Archbishop of Ljubljana transferred for allegedly concealing fatherhood' in *Vatican Insider*, 27 July 2012. Retrieved from vaticaninsider.lastampa.it on 03.07.2013.

DNA or any other tests to prove that he has no children. Last but not least, it is well-known that, in the Slovene Church, a struggle was going on for many years between Conservatives (among them Rode) and moderates (among them Uran). But whatever the truth, the public was shocked by the double standards displayed by the Catholic *nomenklatura*: while Uran was ordered to leave Slovenia due to a mere *suspicion* of fathering a child, the reaction of the Church was infinitely more soft in the numerous cases of pedophilia among the priests—the cases were never reported to the police, the responsible priest was never punished but just moved to another part of Slovenia, there was pressure on the parents of the abused children to keep things under the carpet, etc.[4]

What made things even worse was the open cynical "realism" displayed by the Cardinal Rode: in one of his radio interviews, he said that "statistically, this is an *irrelevant* problem—one or at the utmost two out of a hundred priests had a kind of adventure." What immediately drew the attention of the public was the term "a kind of adventure" used as an euphemism for pedophilia: a brutal crime of raping children was thus presented as a normal display of adventurous "vivacity" (another term used by Rode), and, as Rode quipped in another interview: "In forty years time you would expect some small sins to occur, won't you?" This is Catholic obscenity at its purest: no solidarity with the victims (children): what we find beneath the morally upright posture is just the barely concealed solidarity with the perpetrators on behalf of cynical realism (that's how life is, we are all red under our skin, priests can also be adventurous and vivacious …), so that, in the end, the only true victims appear to be the Church and the perpetrators themselves exposed to the unfair media campaign. The lines are thus clearly drawn: pedophilia is ours, our own dirty secret, and as such normalized, the secret foundation of our normality, while fathering a child is a true violation to be ruthlessly rejected—or, as a century ago G. K. Chesterton put it in his *Orthodoxy* (unaware of the full consequences of his words, of course): "The outer ring of Christianity is a rigid guard of ethical abnegations and professional priests; but inside that inhuman guard you will find the old human life dancing like children, and drinking wine like men; for Christianity is the only frame for pagan freedom" (Chesterton 1908: 292).

The perverse conclusion is unavoidable here: you want to enjoy the pagan dream of pleasurable life without paying the price of melancholic sadness for it? Choose Christianity! We can discern the traces of this paradox up to the well-known Catholic figure of the Priest (or a Nun) as the ultimate bearer of the sexual wisdom. Recall what is arguably the most powerful scene of *The Sound of Music*: after Maria escapes from the von Trapp family back to the monastery, unable to deal with her sexual attraction towards Baron von Trapp, she cannot find peace there, since she is still longing for the Baron; in a memorable scene, the Mother Superior summons her and advises her to return to the von Trapp family and try

---

4   The controversy between Rode and Uran, and related issues, is reported in English here http://www.sloveniatimes.com/cardinal-denies-role-in-exiling-of-retired-archbishop.

to sort out her relationship with the Baron. She delivers this message in a weird song "Climb every mountain!," whose surprising motif is: Do it! Take the risk and try everything your heart wants! Do not allow petty considerations to stand in your way! The uncanny power of this scene resides in its unexpected display of the spectacle of desire, which renders the scene literally *embarrassing*: the very person whom one would expect to preach abstinence and renunciation turns out to be the agent of the fidelity to one's desire.

Significantly, when *The Sound of Music* was shown in (still Socialist) Yugoslavia in the late 1960s, THIS scene—the three minutes of this song—was the only part of the film which was censored (cut out). The anonymous Socialist censor thereby displayed his profound sense for the truly dangerous power of Catholic ideology: far from being the religion of sacrifice, of renunciation to earthly pleasures (in contrast to the pagan affirmation of the life of passions), Christianity offers a devious stratagem to indulge in our desires WITHOUT HAVING TO PAY THE PRICE FOR THEM, to enjoy life without the fear of decay and debilitating pain awaiting us at the end of the day. If we go to the end in this direction, it would even be possible to sustain that therein resides the ultimate function of Christ's sacrifice: *you can indulge in your desires and enjoy, I took the price for it upon myself!* In the perverse functioning of Christianity, religion is effectively evoked as a safeguard allowing us to enjoy life with impunity. Indeed, Lacan was right in turning around Dostoyevski's well-known dictum: If there *is* God, then everything is permitted (see Lacan 1988: 128). Today, with cases of pedophilia popping up all around in the Catholic Church, one can easily imagine a new version of the scene from *The Sound of Music*: a young priest approaches the abbot, complaining that he is still tortured by desires for young boys, and demanding further punishment; the abbot answers by singing "Climb every young boy ..."

One has to draw a further distinction here, between adult male homosexuality and pedophilia. Recent outbursts of homophobia in East European post-Communist states should give us a pause to think: in gay parades which took place in recent years in Serbia and Croatia (Belgrade, Split), the police were not able to protect participants who were ferociously attacked by thousands of violent Christian fundamentalists—how to combine this wrath with the fact that the main force behind the anti-gay movement in Croatia is the Catholic Church,[5] implicated in numerous scandals involving pedophilia? (A Croat gay activist sarcastically remarked how the error of the gays is that their partners are adult men and not children ...). A parallel with the army, the other type of organized crowd mentioned by Freud in the same series with the church, shows us the way. From my own experience of military service in 1975, I remember how the old infamous Yugoslav People's Army was homophobic to the extreme—when someone was discovered to have homosexual inclinations, he was instantly turned into a pariah,

---

5   See   http://www.gaystarnews.com/article/croatia-catholic-church-forcing-people-sign-against-gay-marriage130613   and   http://www.eubusiness.com/news-eu/croatia-gay-rights.p4k.

treated as a non-person, before being formally dismissed from the Army. Yet, at the same time, everyday army life was excessively permeated with the atmosphere of homosexual innuendos.[6] How is this weird coincidence of the opposites possible? The mechanism was described by Robert Pfaller:

> As Freud observed, the very acts that are forbidden by religion are practiced in the name of religion. In such cases—as, for instance, murder in the name of religion—religion also can do entirely without miniaturization. Those adamantly militant advocates of human life, for example, who oppose abortion, will not stop short of actually murdering clinic personnel. Radical right-wing opponents of male homosexuality in the USA act in a similar way. They organize so-called 'gay bashings' in the course of which they beat up and finally rape gays. The ultimate homicidal or homosexual gratification of drives can therefore also be attained, if it only fulfills the condition of evoking the semblance of a counter-measure. What seems to be 'opposition' then has the effect that the x to be fended off can appear itself and be taken for a non-x (Pfaller 2002).

What we encounter here is a textbook case of the Hegelian "oppositional determination": in the figure of the gay basher raping a gay, the gay encounters himself in its oppositional determination, i.e., tautology (self-identity) appears as the highest contradiction. This would appear to be the immanent contradiction at the very core of the Church's identity, making it the main anti-Christian force today. The legend says that when, in 1804, the Pope was approaching Napoleon to put the Emperor's crown on his head, Napoleon took the crown from his hands and put it on his head alone; the Pope quipped back: "I know your aim is to destroy Christianity. But believe me, Sire, you will fail—the Church is trying to do this for 2000 years and still didn't succeed ..." With people like Cardinal Rode from Slovenia, we can see how the Church continues with its efforts, and there is no reason to rejoice at this sad fact—the Christian legacy is all too precious and, today, more pertinent than ever. In his *Notes Towards a Definition of Culture*, T. S. Eliot remarked that there are moments when the only choice is the one between heresy and non-belief, when the only way to keep a religion alive is to perform a sectarian split from its corps. This is what has to be done today.

This inherent inconsistency of the ideologico-legal order is not limited to church institutions—one of its most conspicuous cases today is that of China. How do official Communist theorists react when confronted with the all too obvious

---

6   Say, while soldiers were standing in line for their meal, a common vulgar joke was to stick a finger into the ass of the person ahead of you and then to withdraw it quickly, so that when the surprised person turned around, he did not know who among the soldiers behind his back sharing a stupid obscene smile did it. A predominant form of greeting a fellow soldier in my unit, instead of simply saying "Hello!" was to say "Smoke my prick!" ("Pusi kurac!" in Serbo-Croat); this formula was so standardized that it completely lost any obscene connotation and was pronounced in a totally neutral way, as a pure act of politeness.

contradiction: a Communist Party which still legitimizes itself in Marxist terms, but renounces Marxism's basic premise, that of workers' self-organization as a revolutionary force in order to overthrow capitalism? It is difficult to avoid the impression that all the resources of the legendary form of Chinese politeness are mobilized here: it is considered impolite to directly raise (or insist on) these questions. This resort to politeness is necessary, since it is the only way to combine what cannot be combined: to enforce Marxism as official ideology while openly prohibiting its central axioms would cause the collapse of the entire ideological edifice, thereby rendering it meaningless. The result is thus that, while certain things are clearly prohibited, this prohibition cannot be publicly stated, but is itself prohibited: it is not merely prohibited to raise the question of workers' self-organization against capitalist exploitation as the central tenet of Marxism, it is also prohibited to publicly claim that it is prohibited to raise this question.[7] In this way, we violate what Kant called the "transcendental formula of public law": "All actions affecting the rights of other human beings are wrong, if their maxim is not compatible with their being made public" (Kant 2007: 58–9). A secret law, a law unknown to its subjects, would legitimize the arbitrary despotism of those who exercise it—compare with this formula the title of a recent report on China: "Even what's secret is a secret in China" (The Japan Times 2007). Troublesome intellectuals who report on political oppression, ecological catastrophies, rural poverty, etc., got years in prison for betraying a state secret. The catch is that many of the laws and regulations that make up the state-secret regime are themselves classified, making it difficult for individuals to know how and when they are in violation.

This secrecy of the prohibition itself serves two different purposes which should not be confused. Its commonly admitted role is that of universalizing guilt and fear: if you do not know what is prohibited, you cannot even know when you are violating a prohibition, which makes you potentially guilty all the time. Of course, except at the climax of the Stalinist purges when, effectively, everyone could be found guilty, people *do* know when they are doing something that will annoy those in power. The function of prohibiting prohibitions is thus not to give rise to "irrational" fear, but to let the potential dissidents (who think they can get away with their critical activity, since they are not breaking any laws, but only doing what laws guarantee them—freedom of the press, etc.) know that, if they annoy those in power too much, they can be punished at the power's will. In ex-Yugoslavia, the infamous Article 133 of the penal code could always be invoked to prosecute writers and journalists. It criminalized any text that falsely presented the achievements of the socialist revolution or that *might arouse tension and discontent among the public* for the way it dealt with political, social, or other topics. This last category is obviously not only infinitely plastic, but also

---

7   What one usually gets from theorists is a private admission that, of course, this is contradictory, but that, nonetheless, such a contradictory ideological edifice *works*, and works spectacularly: it is the only way to ensure fast economic growth and stability in China. Need we add that this is the "private use of reason" at its purest?

conveniently self-relating: doesn't the very fact that you are accused by those in power equal the fact that you *"aroused tension and discontent among the public"*? In those years, I remember asking a Slovene politician how he justified this law. He just smiled and, with a wink, told me: "Well, we have to have some tool to discipline those who annoy us without worrying about legal niceties!"

But there is another function of prohibiting prohibitions which is no less crucial: that of *maintaining the appearances*—and we all know how absolutely crucial appearances were in Stalinism: the Stalinist regime reacted with total panic whenever there was a threat that appearances will be disturbed: there were, in the Soviet media, no black chronicles, no reports on crimes and prostitution, not to mention workers or public protests. This prohibiting of prohibitions is far from being limited to Communist regimes: it is operative also in today's "permissive" capitalism. A "postmodern" boss insists that he is not a master but just a coordinator of our joint creative efforts, the first among equals; there should be no formalities among us, we should address him by his nickname, he shares a dirty joke with us ... but in all this, he *remains our master*. In such a social link, relations of domination function through their denial: we are not only obliged to obey our masters, we are also obliged to act as if we are free and equal, as if there is no domination—which, of course, makes the situation even more humiliating. Paradoxically, in such a situation, the first act of liberation is to demand from the master that he acts as one: one should reject false collegiality from the master and insist that he treats as with cold distance, as a master ... No wonder all this sounds vaguely Kafkaesque—Kafka effectively wrote that "it is an extremely painful thing to be ruled by laws that one does not know" (Kafka 1995: 437) thereby bringing out the implicit superego obscenity of the famous legal principle that "ignorance (of the law) is not an excuse."[8] Derrida is thus fully justified in emphasizing the self-reflexivity of the prohibition with regard to the Law—the Law not only prohibits, it is ITSELF prohibited:

> The law is prohibition: this does not mean that it prohibits, but that it is itself prohibited, a prohibited place / ... / one cannot reach the law, and in order to have a rapport of respect with it, one must not have a rapport with the law, one must interrupt the relation. One must enter into relation only with the law's representatives, its examples, its guardians. These are interrupters as much as messengers. One must not know who or what or where the law is (Derrida 1992: 201).

---

8   The EU pressure on Greece in 2011 and 2012 to implement them fits perfectly what psychoanalysis calls the superego. The superego is not an ethical agency proper, but a sadistic agent which bombards the subject with impossible demands, obscenely enjoying the subject's failure to comply with them; the paradox of the superego is that, as Freud saw it clearly, the more we obey its demands, the more we feel guilty. Imagine a vicious teacher who gives to his pupils impossible tasks, and then sadistically jeers when he sees their anxiety and panic. This is what is so terribly wrong with the EU demands/commands: they don't even give a chance to Greece, their failure is part of the game.

In one of his short fragments, Kafka himself pointed out how the ultimate secret of the Law is that *it does not exist*—another case of what Lacan called the inexistence of the big Other. This inexistence, of course, does not simply reduce the Law to an empty imaginary chimera; it rather makes it into an impossible Real, a void which nonetheless functions, exerts influence, causes effects, curves the symbolic space. In today's political space, the most extreme case of such a Law is found in North Korea where patriarchy is effectively undermined, but in an unexpected way. Is North Korea really the last bastion of Stalinism, mixing totalitarian control with Confucian authoritarianism? Here are the words of North Korea's most popular political song:

> Ah, Korean Workers' Party, at whose breast only
> My life begins and ends. Be I buried in the ground or strewn to the wind
> I remain your son, and again return to your breast!
> Entrusting my body to your affectionate gaze,
> Your loving outstretched hand,
> I cry out forever in the voice of a child,
> Mother! I can't live without Mother! (Myers 2004).

This is what the excessive mourning after Kim's death signals: "I can't live without Mother!" As a further proof, here are the two entries ("mother" and "father") from a North Korean *Dictionary of the Korean language* (1964):

> MOTHER: 1) The woman who has given birth to one: Father and mother; a mother's love. *A mother's benevolence is higher than a mountain, deeper than the ocean.* Also used in the sense of "a woman who has a child": *What all mothers anxiously want is for their children to grow up healthy and become magnificent red builders.* 2) A respectful term for someone of an age similar to one's own mother: *Comrade Platoon Leader called Dŏngmani's mother "mother" and always helped her in her work.* 3) A metaphor for being loving, looking after everything, and worrying about others: *Party officials must become mothers who ceaselessly love and teach the Party rank and file, and become standard-bearers at the forefront of activities.* In other words, someone in charge of lodgings has to become a mother to the boarders. This means looking carefully after everything: whether someone is cold or sick, how they are eating, and so on. 4) A metaphor for the source from which something originates: *The Party is the great mother of everything new. Necessity is the mother of invention.*
>
> FATHER: the husband of one's birth mother (Myers 2011: 6).

Maybe that's why, till the third Kim, the leader's wife was not mentioned in public: the Leader was hermaphroditic with the dominance of the feminine features. Is this in contradiction with North Korea's "military first" policy, with ruthless disciplining and drilling the soldiers? No, these are two sides of the same coin. The figure of the mother we are dealing with here is the so-called "non-castrated" omnipotent devouring mother: apropos the real mother, Jacques-Alain Miller noted that "not only is there an unsatisfied mother but also an all-powerful one. And the terrifying aspect of this figure of the Lacanian mother is that she is all-powerful and unsatisfied at the same time" (Miller 2009a: 23). Therein resides the paradox: the more "omnipotent" a mother appears, the more unsatisfied (which means: lacking) she is: "The Lacanian mother corresponds to the formula *quaerens quem devoret*: she looks for someone to devour, and so Lacan presents her then as the crocodile, the subject with the open mouth" (Miller 2009b: 19). This devouring mother does not respond (to the child's demand for a sign of love), and it is as such that she appears omnipotent: "Since the mother does not respond, [...] she is transformed into real, that is to say, into power. [...] if the Other does not respond, he is transformed into a devouring power" (28). This is why the feminized features clearly discernible in the official portraits of the two Kim's are not accidental:

> Kim /Il Sung/ was more a mother to his people than a stern Confucian patriarch: he is still shown as soft-cheeked and solicitous, holding weeping adults to his expansive bosom, bending down to tie a young soldier's bootlaces, or letting giddy children clamber over him. The tradition continues under Kim Jong Il, who has been called "more of a mother than all the mothers in the world." His military-first policy may come with the title of general, but reports of his endless tour of army bases focus squarely on his fussy concern for the troops' health and comfort. The international ridicule of his appearance is thus as unfair as it is tedious. Anyone who has seen a crowd of Korean mothers waiting outside an examination hall will have no difficulty recognizing Kim's drab parka and drooping shoulders, or the long-suffering face under the pillow-swept perm: this is a mother with no time to think of herself (Myers 2004).

Does North Korea then stand for something like the Indian Kali—the benevolent/murderous goddess—in power? One should nonetheless distinguish levels here: the superficial level of manly-military discourse with the Leader as "General," with *Juche* idea of self-reliance, of humanity as a master of itself and its destiny, is sustained by a deeper level of the Leaders as a maternal protector—here is how Myers formulates the basic axiom of North Korean ideology: "The Korean people are too pure blooded, and therefore too virtuous, to survive in this evil world without a great parental leader" (Myers 2011: 9). Is this not a nice example of Lacan's formula of paternal metaphor, of the Name-of-the-Father as a metaphoric substitute for the desire of the mother? The Name-of-the-Father (Leader/General) and, beneath it, the mother's protective/destructive desire?[9] One of the New Age commonplaces is that we in the West are too much

---

9 Are then—to put it bluntly—North Koreans incestuous psychotics who reject entering the symbolic order? The answer is no—why? Because of the distance towards the

dominated by the male/paternal principle of domination, discipline, struggle, etc., and that, to reestablish balance, we should reassert the feminine principle of loving care and protection—however, cases of "hard" feminine politicians from Indira Gandhi to Margaret Thatcher should make us think. Today the predominant form of social link is no longer sustained by a patriarchal Master. Even "totalitarianism" is not the discourse of the Master; however, the tragic experience of many revolutions in which the overthrowing of the old Master ended up in a much more murderous terror should in no way lead us to advocate a return to paternal symbolic authority as the only way out of the self-destructive deadlock of the late-capitalist narcissistic Protean Self. One should nonetheless note that this Protean Self involves its own dis-eventalization masked as progress, its own reduction of a man to human animal—here is a case of it.

In August 2012, the media reported that, from December 2012, tobacco companies in Australia will no longer be allowed to display their distinctive colors, brand designs and logos on cigarette packs: to make smoking as unglamorous as possible, the packs will come in a uniformly drab shade of olive and feature graphic health warnings and images of cancer-riddled mouths, blinded eyeballs and sickly children (see McGuirk 2012). What we are witnessing here is a kind of *Selbst-Aufhebung* of the commodity-form: no logo, no "commodity-aesthetics" which should seduce us into buying the product—on the contrary, the package of the product openly and graphically draws attention to its dangerous and harmful qualities and thus provides reasons against buying it. The anti-commodity presentation of a commodity is in itself not a novelty—it also accounts for the allure of "cultural" products like painting or music which is "not strictly a commodity; it is / ... / worth buying only when the pretence that it is not a commodity can be successfully maintained" (Rosen 1975: 77). Here, the antagonism between commodity and non-commodity functions in an inverted way with regard to the logo-less cigarettes: the superego injunction is here "You should be ready to pay an exorbitant price for this commodity precisely because it is much more than a mere commodity!" In the case of logo-less cigarettes, we get the raw use value deprived of its logo form (in a similar way, we can buy in discount stores logo-less sugar, coffee, sweets ...); in the case of a painting, the logo itself "sublates" use value, i.e., as it was already notes by Marx, here, price seems to determine value.

But does this direct "pragmatic contradiction" really take us out of the commodity-fetishism? Does it not rather provide yet another example of the

---

symbolic order proper which persists even in official ideological texts. That is to say, even North Korea's official ideological discourse ("Text," as Myers calls it) does not engage in direct divinization of the Leader; instead, the divinization is elegantly attributed to "naïve" Western visitors fascinated by the Leader's wisdom: "while the Text likes to draw bemused attention to outsiders, including Americans and South Koreans, who allegedly regard Kim Il Sung as a divine being, it never makes such claims for him itself" (Myers 2011: 111). Is this not a clear case of "subject supposed to believe," of the naïve other onto which our own belief is transposed?

fetishist split signaled by the well-known phrase *je sais tres bien, mais quand même* ...? A decade or so ago there was a German publicity poster for Marlboro cigarettes: their standard cowboy-figure was this time directly pointing with his finger down towards the obligatory note "Smoking is dangerous for your health!," with the words added: "*Jetzt erst rechts!*," which can be vaguely translated as "Now things are getting serious!" The implied meaning is clear: now that you know how dangerous it is to smoke, you have a chance to prove that you have the courage to go on smoking! In other words, the attitude solicited in the subject which is targeted is: "I know very well the dangers of smoking, but I am not a coward, I am a true man and, as such, ready to take the risk and remain faithful to my smoking commitment!" It is only in this way that smoking effectively becomes a form of consumerism: I am ready to consume cigarettes "beyond the pleasure-principle," beyond the petty utilitarian considerations about health. And is not this dimension of lethal excessive enjoyment at work in every publicity or commodity appeal? Are all utilitarian considerations (this food is healthy, it was organically grown, it was paid for under fair trade conditions, etc.) not just a deceptive surface containing a deeper superego-injunction: "Enjoy! Enjoy to the end, irrespectively of consequences!"? The Australian "negative" packaging will thus bring out the superego injunction which was here all the time—that is to say, will a smoker, when he will buy the "negatively" packed cigarettes, not hear beneath the negative message the silent, but all the more present and pressing, voice of the superego? This voice will answer his question: "If all these dangers of smoking are true—and I accept they are -, why am I then still buying the package?"

This superego pressure is not limited to consumerism: it acquires different guises, some of them with catastrophic socio-ethical consequences. The documentary *The Act of Killing* (Final Cut Film Production, Copenhagen) premiered in 2012 at the Telluride film festival and was also shown at TIFF. *The Act of Killing*, directed by Joshua Oppenheimer and Christine Cynn,[10] provides a unique and deeply disturbing insight into the ethical deadlock of global capitalism. The film—shot in Medan, Indonesia, in 2007—reports on a case of obscenity which reaches the extreme: a film, made by Anwar Congo and his friends, who are now respected politicians, but were gangsters and death squad leaders playing a key role in the 1966 killing of approximately 2.5 million alleged Communist sympathizers, mostly ethnic Chinese. As emphasized in the trailer of the film, *The Act of Killing* is about "killers who have won, and the sort of society they have built." After their victory, their terrible acts were not relegated to the status of the "dirty secret," the founding crime whose traces are to be obliterated—on the contrary, they boast openly about the details of their massacres (the way to strangle a victim with a wire, the way to cut a throat, how to rape a woman in a most pleasurable way ...). In October 2007, Indonesian state television produced a talk show celebrating Anwar and his friends; in the middle of the show, after Anwar says that their killings were

---

10   Because of the nature of what was filmed, some contributions by Indonesian collaborators to the making of the film, including co-direction, were kept anonymous.

inspired by gangster movies, the beaming moderator turns to the cameras and says: "Amazing! Let's give Anwar Congo a round of applause!" When she asks Anwar if he fears the revenge of the victim's relatives, Anwar answers: "They can't. When they raise their heads, we wipe them out!" His henchman adds: "We'll exterminate them all!," and the audience explodes into exuberant cheers ... one has to see this to believe it's possible. But what makes *The Act of Killing* extraordinary is also the level of reflexivity between documentary and fiction—the film is, in a way, a documentary about the real effects of living a fiction:

> To explore the killers' astounding boastfulness, and to test the limits of their pride, we began with documentary portraiture and simple re-enactments of the massacres. But when we realized what kind of movie Anwar and his friends really wanted to make about the genocide, the re-enactments became more elaborate. And so we offered Anwar and his friends the opportunity to dramatize the killings using film genres of their choice (western, gangster, musical). That is, we gave them the chance to script, direct and star in the scenes *they had in mind when they were killing people* (Film Cut Production 2012).

Did they reach the limits of the killers' "pride"? They barely touched it when they proposed to Anwar to play the victim of his tortures in a reenactment; when a wire is placed around his neck, he interrupts the performance and says "Forgive me for everything I've done." But this is more a temporary relapse which did not lead to any deeper crisis of conscience—his heroic pride immediately takes over again. Probably, the protective screen which prevented a deeper moral crisis was the very cinematic screen: as in their past real killings and torture, they experienced their activity as an enactment of their cinematic models, which enabled them to experience reality itself as a fiction—as great admirers of Hollywood (they started their career as organizers and controllers of the black market in peddling cinema tickets), they played a role in their massacres, imitating a Hollywood gangster, cowboy or even a musical dancer.

Here the "big Other" enters, not only with the fact that the killers modeled their crimes on the cinematic imaginary, but also and above all the much more important fact of society's moral vacuum: what kind of symbolic texture (the set of rules which draw the line between what is publicly acceptable and what is not) must a society be composed of if even a minimal level of public shame (which would compel the perpetrators to treat their acts as a "dirty secret") is suspended, and the monstrous orgy of torture and killing can be publicly celebrated even decades after it took place, not even as a extraordinary necessary crime for the public good, but as an ordinary, acceptable, pleasurable activity? The trap to be avoided here is, of course, the easy one of putting the blame either directly on Hollywood or on the "ethical primitiveness" of Indonesia. The starting point should rather be the dislocating effects of capitalist globalization which, by undermining the "symbolic efficacy" of traditional ethical structures, creates such a moral vacuum.[11]

However, the status of the "big Other" deserves here a closer analysis—let us compare *The Act of Killing* to an incident which drew a lot of attention in the US some decades ago: a woman was beaten and slowly killed by a violent perpetrator in the courtyard of a big apartment block in Queens, New York; of the 38 witnesses who clearly saw what was going on from their windows, not one called the police—why not? As the later investigation established, the most prevalent excuse by far was that each witness thought someone else already had or surely would do it.[12] This data should not be moralistically dismissed as a mere excuse for moral cowardice and egotistic indifference: what we encounter here is also the function of the big Other—this time not as Lacan's "subject supposed to know," but as what one could call "the subject supposed to call the police." The fatal mistake of the witnesses of the slow Brooklyn killing was to misread the symbolic (fictional) function of the "subject supposed to call the police" as an empirical claim of existence, wrongly concluding that there must be at least one who effectively did call the police—they overlooked the fact that the function of the "subject supposed to call the police" is operative even if there is no actual subject who enacts it.[13]

Does this mean that, through the gradual dissolution of our ethical substance, we are simply regressing to individualist egotism? Things are much more complex. We often hear that our ecological crisis is the result of our short-term egotism: obsessed with immediate pleasures and wealth, we forgot about the common Good. However, it is here that Walter Benjamin's notion of capitalism as religion becomes crucial: a true capitalist is not a hedonist egotist; he is, on the contrary,

---

11 More generally, how can (relatively) decent people do horrible things? To account for this, one should turn around the standard conservative anti-individualist view according to which social institutions control and contain our, individual, spontaneous evil tendencies to follow ruthlessly one's destructive and egotist strivings: what if, on the contrary, we as individuals are (relatively) decent, and institutions have to apply all their subterfuge to make us do horrible things? The role of institutions as agents of mediation is crucial here: there are things I would never be able to do directly, in the first person, but if I leave it to my agents to do it for me I can pretend not to know what is going on. How many humanitarians, from Angelina Jolie and Brad Pitt onwards, invest their money in housing projects in Dubai which employ modern versions of slave work—and, of course, they (can pretend that they) don't know about it, that it was done by their financial advisers, etc. (see 'Brad Pitt and Angelina buy private Dubai island', in www.arabianbusiness.com. Retrieved 03.07.2013).

12 See Martin Gansber, 'Thirty-Eight Who Saw Murder Didn't Call the Police', in The New York Times, 27 March 1964. Retrieved from www.southeastern.edu 03.07.2013.

13 One can even imagine an empirical test for this claim: if one could recreate a circumstance in which each of the witnesses were to think that he or she is alone in observing the gruesome scene, one can predict that, in their opportunist avoidance of "getting involved in something that isn't your business," a large majority of them would have called the police.

fanatically devoted to his task of multiplying his wealth, ready to neglect his health and happiness, not to mention the prosperity of his family and the well-being of the environment, for it. There is thus no need to evoke some high ground moralism and trash capitalist egotism—against capitalist perverted fanatical dedication, it is enough to evoke a good measure of simple egotist and utilitarian concern. In other words, the pursuit of what Rousseau calls the natural *amour-de-soi* requires a highly civilized level of awareness. Or, to put it in the terms of Badiou: contrary to what he implies, the subjectivity of capitalism is NOT that of the "human animal," but rather a mode of pseudo-evental interpellation, a call to subordinate egotism to the self-reproduction of the Capital. However, this does not imply that Badiou is simply wrong: the individual caught in global market capitalism necessarily perceives itself as a self-interested hedonist "human animal," this self-perception is a necessary illusion.

In other words, self-interested egotism is not the brutal fact of our societies but its ideology—the ideology philosophically articulated in Hegel's *Phenomenology of Spirit* towards the end of the chapter on Reason, under the (very Badiouian) name of "*das geistige Tierreich*"—the "spiritual kingdom of animals," Hegel's name for the modern civil society in which human animals are caught in self-interested interaction. As Hegel put it, the achievement of modernity was to allow "the principle of subjectivity to attain fulfillment in the *self-sufficient extreme* of personal particularity" (Hegel 1991: 282). This reign of this principle makes possible civil society as the domain in which autonomous human individuals associate with each other through the institutions of free-market economy in order to satisfy their private needs: all communal ends are subordinated to private interests of individuals, they are consciously posited and calculated with the goal of maximizing the satisfaction of these interests. What matters for Hegel here is the opposition of private and common perceived by those on whom Hegel relies (Mandeville, Smith) as well as by Marx: individuals perceive the common domain as something that should serve their private interests (like a liberal who thinks of the state as a protector of private freedom and safety), while individuals, in pursuing their narrow goals, effectively serve the communal interest. The properly dialectical tension emerges here when we become aware that, the more individuals act egotistically, the more they contribute to the common wealth. The paradox is that when individuals want to sacrifice their narrow private interests and directly work for the common good, the one which suffers is the common good itself—Hegel loves to tell historical anecdotes about a good king or prince whose very dedication to the common good brought his country to ruins. The properly philosophical novelty of Hegel was to further determine this "contradiction" along the lines of the tension between the "animal" and the "spiritual": the universal spiritual substance, the "work of all and everyone," emerges as the result of the "mechanical" interaction of individuals. What this means is that the very "animality" of the self-interested "human animal" (the individual participating in the complex network of civil society) is the result of the long historical process of the transformation of medieval hierarchical society into modern bourgeois society.

It is thus the very fulfillment of the principle of subjectivity—the radical opposite of animality—which brings about the reversal of subjectivity into animality.

Traces of this shift can be detected everywhere today, especially in the fast-developing Asian countries where capitalism exerts a most brutal impact. Bertolt Brecht's "The Exception and the Rule" (a learning play written in 1929–30) tells the story of a rich merchant who, with his porter ("coolie"), crosses the Yahi Desert (yet another of Brecht's fictional Chinese places) to close an oil deal. When the two get lost in the desert and their water supplies are running low, the merchant mistakenly shoots the coolie, thinking he was being attacked, when the coolie was actually offering him some water that he still had left in his bottle. Later, in a court, the merchant is acquitted: the judge concludes that the merchant had every right to fear a potential threat from the coolie, so he was justified in shooting the coolie in self-defence regardless of whether there was an actual threat. Since the merchant and his coolie belong to different classes, the merchant had all the reasons to expect hatred and aggression from him—this is the typical situation, the rule, while the coolie's kindness was an exception. Is this story yet another of Brecht's ridiculous Marxist simplifications? No, judging from the report from today's real China:

> In Nanjing, half a decade ago, an elderly woman fell while getting on a bus. Newspaper reports tell us that the 65 year old woman broke her hip. At the scene, a young man came to her aid; let us call him Peng Yu, for that is his name. Peng Yu gave the elderly woman 200RMB (at that time enough to buy three hundred bus tickets) and took her to the hospital. Then, he continued to stay with her until the family arrived. The family sued the young man for 136,419 RMB. Indeed, the Nanjing Gulou District Court found the young man to be guilty and ordered him to pay 45,876 RMB. The court reasoned, 'according to common sense,' that because Peng Yu was the first off the bus, in all probability he had knocked over the elderly woman. Further, he actually had admitted his guilt, the court reasoned, by staying with the elderly woman at the hospital. It being the case that a normal person would not be as kind as Peng Yu claimed he was (Yuen).

Is this incident not exactly parallel to Brecht's story? Peng Yu helped the old lady out of simple compassion or decency, but since such a display of goodness is not "typical," not the rule ("a normal person would not be as kind as Peng Yu claimed he was"), it was interpreted by the court as a proof of Peng Yu's guilt, and he was appropriately punished. Is this a ridiculous exception? Not so, according to the *People's Daily* (the government newspaper)[14] which, in an online opinion poll, asked a large sample of young people what they would do if they were to see a fallen elderly person: "87% of young people would not help. Peng Yu's story echoes the surveillance of the public space. People will only help when a camera

---

14   As reported in correspondence with the author.

was present." What such a reluctance to help signals is a change in the status of public space: "the street is an intensely private place and seemingly the words public and private make no sense." In short, being in a public space does not entails only being together with other unknown people—in moving among them, I am still within my private space, engaged in no interaction with or recognition of them. In order to count as public, the space of my co-existence and interaction with others (or the lack of it) has to be covered by security cameras.

Another sign of this same change can be found at the opposite end of watching people die in public and doing nothing—the recent trend of public sex in hard-core porn. There are more and more films which show a couple (or more persons) engaged in erotic games up to full copulation in some heavily frequented public space (on a public beach, inside a streetcar or train, at a bus or train station, in the open space of a shopping mall …), and the interesting feature is that a large majority of foreigners who pass by (pretend to) ignore the scene—a minority throws a discrete glance at the couple, even fewer of them make a sarcastic obscene remark. Again, it is as if the copulating couple remained in their private space, so that we should not be concerned by their intimacies.

This brings us back to Hegel's "spiritual animal kingdom"—that is to say, who effectively behaves like this, passing by dying fellows in blessed ignorance or copulating in front of others? Animals, of course. This fact in no way entails that ridiculous conclusion that we are somehow "regressing" to the animal level: the animality with which we are dealing here—the ruthless egotism of each of the individuals pursuing his or her private interest—is the paradoxical result of the most complex network of social relations (market exchange, social mediation of production), and the fact individuals themselves are blinded to this complex network points towards its ideal ("spiritual") character: in the civil society structured by the market, abstraction rules more than ever in the history of humanity. In contrast to nature, the market competition of "wolves against wolves" is thus the material reality of its opposite, of the "spiritual" public substance which provides the background and base for this struggle among private animals.

It is often said that today, with our total exposure to the media, culture of public confessions and instruments of digital control, private space is disappearing. One should counter this commonplace with the opposite claim: it is the *public* space proper which is disappearing. The person who displays on the web his/her naked images or intimate data and obscene dreams is not an exhibitionist: exhibitionists intrude into the public space, while those who post their naked images on the web remain in their private space and are just expanding it to include others. And, back to *The Act of Killing*, the same goes for Anwar and his colleagues: they are privatizing the public space in a sense which is much more threatening than economic privatization.

References

Brush, Peter (2010) "The Hard Truth about Fragging" in HistoryNet.com. Retrieved 3 July 2013.

Chesterton, Gilbert K. (1908) *Orthodoxy*. New York: John Lane Co.

Derrida, Jacques (1992) *Acts of Literature*. New York: Routledge.

Film Cut Production (2012) publicity material of *The Act of Killing* (directed by Joshua Oppenheimer).

Hegel, G.W.F. (1991) *Elements of the Philosophy of Right*. Cambridge: Cambridge University Press.

The Japan Times (2007) "Even what's secret is a secret in China," in *The Japan Times*, June 16, p. 17.

Kafka, Franz (1995) "The Problem of Our Laws," in *The Complete Stories*. New York: Schocken Books.

Kant, Immanuel (2007) *Perpetual Peace*. New York: Penguin Books.

Lacan, Jacques (1988) *The Seminar of Jacques Lacan, book II: The Ego in Freud's Theory and in the Technique of Psychoanalysis*. New York: Norton.

Lepre, George (2011) *Fragging: Why US Soldiers Assaulted their Officers in Vietnam*. Lubbock: Texas University Press.

McGuirk, Rob (2012) "Australian Court OKs logo ban on cigarette packs," Associated Press, 15 August 2012 (available in http://news.yahoo.com/ australian-court-oks-logo-ban-cigarette-packs-004107919--finance.html).

Miller, Jacques-Alain (2009a) "Phallus and Perversion," in *lacanian ink* 33.

⸻ (2009b) "The Logic of the Cure," in *lacanian ink* 33.

Myers, Brian R. (2004) "Mothers of all Mothers. The Leadership Secrets of Kim Jong Il," in *The Atlantic*, 1 September 2004 (available in http://www. theatlantic.com/magazine/archive/2004/09/mother-of-all-mothers/3403/).

⸻ (2011) *The Cleanest Race*. New York: Melville House.

Pfaller, Robert (2002) "The Potential of Thresholds to Obstruct and to Facilitate. On the Operation of Displacement in Obsessional Neurosis and Perversion" (unpublished paper).

Presseurop (2012) "Orbán considers alternative to democracy," in Presseurop 30 July 2012 (available in http://www.presseurop.eu/en/content/ news-brief/2437991-orban-considers-alternative-democracy).

Rosen, Charles (1975) *Schoenberg*. London: Fontana/Collins.

Yallup, David (2009) *The Power and the Glory: Inside the Dark Heart of Pope John Paul II's Vatican*. New York: Basic Books.

Yuen, Michael "China and the Mist of Complicated Things" (personal letter provided by the author).

Wills, Gary (2002) "Scandal," *The New York Review of Books*, May 23 2002.

Chapter 6

Theory Without Conscience: Hegel's Absolute Refusal of Practice

Todd McGowan

In times of social and economic crisis, the imperative to be practical grows ever stronger. No one experiences this imperative more vehemently than the theorist, the figure whose vocation inherently finds itself at odds with practical interventions and yet whose work often touches directly on the crisis. In this situation, theorists must have hard hearts not to feel guilty for confining themselves to thought and failing to "do something." As David Simpson notes, contemporary cultural theorists "imagine that we ... should be changing the world" (1995: 160). Whereas theory involves just the interpretation of social relations—the attempt to understand their structure and ground—practice represents an effort to transform these relations. This is why practice seems more attractive and more valuable than theory. The widespread tendency to describe an essay or paper as an "intervention" has an appeal insofar as it offers the veneer of praxis. Making an intervention, despite the climate controlled environment and comfortable seating, is infinitely more satisfying than simply attending an academic conference because it places one proximate to the demonstrators of Occupy Wall Street or the Arab Spring and distances one from solipsistic routine that predominates the everyday life of most theorists.[1] Even when making public use of one's reason, the theorist's act of thinking is fundamentally a private activity, one with no direct link to political praxis.

---

1   We can see the guilt of the theorist over the failure to be practical in Milan Kundera's *The Unbearable Lightness of Being*. One of the secondary characters in the novel, Franz, is a French intellectual and theorist who disdains his own uninvolved life. Franz feels guilty for his failure to contribute to what Kundera calls the "Grand March" of history. He envies those who go beyond mere thinking and take action in order to change the world: "How nice it was to celebrate something, demand something, protest against something; to be out in the open, to be with others. The parades filing down the Boulevard Saint-Germain or from the Place de la République to the Bastille fascinated him. He saw the marching, shouting crowd as the image of Europe and its history" (1984: 99). As a theorist, Franz sees himself as excluded from this practical struggle, and he wants desperately to be a part of it. Like so many theorists today, Franz longs for the sense of making an actual difference in the world that one finds not in theoretical speculation but in political practice. Practice presents a more compelling relation to the world than theory, and many theorists, feeling guilt akin to that of Franz, respond by explicitly orienting their theory toward practice.

Crises reveal to us that the world demands a collective act that would save it from its present course. Amid a crisis, the world requires salvation or at least transformation, not simply theoretical justification. In one of the most dazzling passages in all his work, Giorgio Agamben advances an explanation for the effectiveness of Voltaire's critique of Leibniz in *Candide*, an effectiveness that takes us by surprise because almost every observer grants the clear philosophical superiority of Leibniz. On this merit, Voltaire should not be able to get the better of Leibniz. Agamben's analysis is significant insofar as it focuses on Leibniz's overly theoretical approach to the world, on his failure to commit himself to a theoretical praxis. In short, the philosophical giant Leibniz exposes himself to an inferior's attack because he doesn't consider the imperative to change the world.

Agamben's discussion of this philosophical quarrel bears directly on how the theorist should respond to the contemporary exigencies of praxis. In the appendix to *The Kingdom and the Glory*, he writes, "*Even the most beautiful minds have zones of opacity in which they get lost to the point that a much weaker mind can ridicule them. This is what occurred to Leibniz with Voltaire's caricature of his position in* Candide" (2011: 271). The problem with Leibniz's *Theodicy*, which occasions Voltaire's mockery in *Candide*, is that it attempts to justify the world as it is rather than saving it. Agamben adds, "*The world as it is does not require justification but saving; and, if it does not require saving, it needs justifying even less*" (2011, 271). For Agamben, Leibniz does simply commit a theoretical error that creates the space for Voltaire's sardonic riposte but falls into the error of theory as such. Theory has a tendency to justify the world as it is, while praxis aims at the world's salvation.[2]

Though he never addresses directly the relationship between Leibniz and Voltaire, Hegel provides a different solution to Voltaire's critique of Leibniz and to the relation between praxis and theory. Contra Agamben's assertion that the world demands saving and not justification, Hegel, following Leibniz to an extent, insists that the task of the theorist can only be one of justification. The theorist lacks the practical saving power. But it is precisely, Hegel implies, through justifying the world that one lays the ground for its salvation. In other words, Hegel would reject Agamben's opposition between justification and saving: he would take the side of justification for the sake of saving. All that the theorist can do is to justify the world, but this justification has a political radicality that Leibniz never suspects. By exposing the antagonism of the ruling order, the justification of the world as it is opens up the possibility for transformation. But theory can only perform this function if it refuses to concern itself with saving the world. This is the Hegelian paradox that confronts theory especially in the time of the crisis. The more one retreats into the realm of pure theory and avoids turning one's theory into a form of praxis, the more one plays a role in the collective struggle that occurs outside the realm of theory. Rather than a critique of pure theory, what is required now is a critique of practical theory, a critique of theory's devotion to saving the world.

---

2   Though Agamben has played a pivotal role in the resurgence of theory in recent years, here he betrays his former connection with a praxis-oriented Italian Marxism.

Attempting to become practical strips theory of its power to produce radical transformation through the fundamental theoretical act—the act of recognition. Theory has the ability to reconcile thought to action, thereby providing a recognition of the prevailing symbolic and ideological structure. Such a recognition entails grasping the extent of our investment in the prevailing order and refusing illusory images of alternatives. For Hegel, the effort to arrive at practice in the act of thought fails because it necessarily involves an act of *representing* practice theoretically, not attaining it.

It is by rejecting the lure of trying to transform itself into action, rather than attempting to accomplish such a transformation, that theory has a concrete and practical effect. This is Hegel's fundamental lesson for the contemporary theorist confronted with burgeoning crises and seemingly infinite imperatives to act. A return to Hegel's thought—and especially his critique of Fichte—shows us why theorists should theorize without feeling guilty for their failure to act practically. But we do not live in Hegelian times. Under the weight of the ideal of practice, contemporary theory sinks under the weight of a bad conscience.

The bad conscience of theory is not a recent invention. We cannot lay the blame at the feet of Giorgio Agamben or any other current philosopher. Since Plato's desperate attempts in his later life to find a prince to realize his ideal social organization, philosophers have wanted to leave the realm of theoretical speculation and venture into the realm of practice. They have wanted to change the world. Nonetheless, with Marx, guilt about theory's failure to be practical reached an entirely new level, the level of an imperative. In the eleventh and final of his "Theses on Feuerbach," Marx famously proclaims, "The philosophers have only *interpreted* the world, in various ways; the point, however, is to change it" (1978: 145). Rather than confine themselves to the historical sidelines, philosophers and theorists, according to Marx, should be the makers of history. In the wake of Marx, even avowedly non-Marxist theorists have taken this admonition to heart, producing theories that aim at changing the world for the better. Theorists tend to feel, in other words, as if time spent theorizing is time that might better be spent organizing or protesting or boycotting, and hence theory must transform itself into a kind of practice if it is not to serve as simply an index of the theorist's own privileged position within the existing social order and as a de facto endorsement of that order.[3]

---

3   Perhaps the greatest exception to the bad conscience of theory exists within the Marxist tradition itself, in the figure of Theodor Adorno. In sticking to theory and refusing to yoke this theory to practice, Adorno earned the vilification of the student movement in the 1960s. Despite this scorn for his position, however, Adorno never wavered (though it may have, in the end, led him to the most extreme kind of retreat—his death by heart attack in 1969). In *Negative Dialectics*, he provides his most concise rationale for his refusal of practice: "The call for unity of theory and practice has irresistibly degraded theory to a servant's role, removing the very traits it should have brought to that unity. The visa stamp of practice which we demand of all theory became a censor's placet. Yet whereas theory

The key representatives of the effort to create a practical theory are Michael Hardt and Antonio Negri, for whom the practical political imperative constitutes the basis of their theoretical speculation. They insist that not only should theory lead to practice, it should go so far as making the desired future an explicit part of the theory itself. This emphasis on the role that theory can play in organizing the future comes to its ultimate fruition at the end of the third volume of their critique of contemporary capitalism. In *Commonwealth*, "What is necessary is a global initiative to provide the basic means of life for all, throughout the world, a global guaranteed income and truly universal health care, whether furnished through global institutions such as UN agencies, citizen organizations, or other bodies" (2009: 380). Here, Hardt and Negri don't merely suggest a general direction for governance or existence, but lay out a precise way of organizing society.

Hardt and Negri contrast their theoretical method oriented around practice with Hegel's system of philosophy and its clear avoidance of practice. Referring in *Empire* to Hegel's well-known statement from the preface to the *Philosophy of Right*, they claim, "Philosophy is not the owl of Minerva that takes flight after history has been realized in order to celebrate its happy ending; rather, philosophy is subjective proposition, desire, and praxis that are applied to the event" (2000: 48–9). For Hardt and Negri, philosophy or theory does not reconcile us to our contemporary situation; it takes up and mobilizes a new and alternative future (a future that lies burgeoning within the present). Theory's importance lies in its ability to see this alternative future in the midst of a ruling symbolic structure that works to obfuscate it. Hardt and Negri are exemplary figures today because they render explicit the philosophical priority of practice.

Though Hardt and Negri manifest theory's desire to become practical on the level of high theory, the most pervasive indicator of this desire is the turn away from "high theory" altogether, replacing theoretical speculation with specific, local analyses and interventions. As Judith Butler, John Guillory, and Kendall Thomas note in their preface to *What's Left of Theory?*, "theory now arrives as part of historicism, as part of new materialistic approaches to literary texts, and it often arrives in tandem with close readings of literary texts" (2000: xi). This turn toward "new materialist approaches"—and the particular analyses that result—offers the theorist an opportunity to move theory that much closer to practice. In her discussion of the theorizing of class, Cora Kaplan points out that today critics are "challenging totalizing visions, focus[ing] on the variety of cultural movements around the world that cannot be captured in the received language of class" (2000: 13). Such interventions, the thinking goes, represent a more concrete

---

succumbed in the vaunted mixture, practice became nonconceptual, a piece of the politics it was supposed to lead out of; it became the prey of power" (1973: 143). In his rejection of transforming theory into practice, however, Adorno envisions theory itself as a practice, as a mode of resisting the course of the world rather than a way of reconciling thought with the underlying social reality. This is the short distance that separates Adorno from Hegel. Though he comes very close, Adorno ultimately fails to resist the lure of a theoretical practice.

political activity than abstract theorizing because they focus on practical, local situations. According to those who have abandoned theory, the theory revolution failed, and it failed because it mirrored epistemologically—through its tendency to universalize—the violence of oppressive structures. To those who have abandoned it, theory has revealed itself as a hegemonic activity: it subsumes all particularities within a universal framework.

If we exist in a post-theoretical intellectual world, this is due in no small part to the perception that theory is guilty—guilty of failing to render itself political enough. Many critics have indicted theory for its political failure, for its inability to produce any tangible political benefits. These indictments emerge from vastly different sources—from the liberal humanist to the radical sociologist—but they target the same political deficiency in theorizing. Those who remain invested in the theoretical enterprise today tend to feel, in light of these critiques, all the more dedicated to making clear the practical dimension of their thought. This dedication places them in the spirit of theory after Marx.

But immediately before Marx—that is to say, with Hegel—it is a somewhat different story. Hegel, the figure Marx acknowledges as his philosophical progenitor, certainly does not seem a model for theory oriented toward practice. When it comes to pointing out the great ethical or political achievements of Western philosophy, it is not often that one looks to Hegel. Hegel, of course, never wrote his own *Ethics*, and his one treatise that did explicitly concern politics, *The Philosophy of Right*, included a confession of philosophy's political uselessness, its inability to help to change the world (in the final line of the preface referenced above, "The owl of Minerva spreads its wings only with the falling of dusk" [1952: 13]). Politically speaking, Hegel seems to occupy the position of a lull in the history of thought. Unable himself to articulate an ethical or an active political philosophy, he nonetheless is situated historically after Kant and prior to Marx—that is, after Kant emphasized an ethical basis for philosophy and before Marx stressed its need to be political.

In contrast to both Kant and Marx, Hegel seems to have constructed a philosophy wholly committed to accepting the world as it is—not to discovering a way of changing it. His thought, in short, appears to be the apogee of philosophical quietism. Hegel's foremost interpreters have made this quite clear. As Alexandre Kojève puts it, Hegel "definitively reconciles himself with all that is and has been, by declaring that there will never more be anything new on earth" (1969: 168).[4] Hegel's philosophical approach, Kojève adds, involves him "limit[ing] himself to describing the given—that is, revealing through discourse the given precisely as it is given" (1969: 191). If Hegel's philosophy only promotes acceptance

---

4   It is significant that a statement such as this comes not from a critic of Hegel, but from one of the foremost Hegelians of the twentieth century. Rather than indicting Hegel for his conformism, Kojève celebrates him for his realism. Unlike those of us who try to kid ourselves that history might give birth to something new, Hegel grasps its circularity, that there is nothing new under the sun.

and provides description of what is—and refuses the question of what ought to be—then it would seem that there is no way of discovering a political core in this philosophy.

It is my claim, however, that at exactly the point Hegel rules out ethical or political action, at the point of the absolute, Hegel articulates an ethical position more exacting than that of Kant and a politics more radical than that of Marx. In refusing to make his theory practical, Hegel is able to take up a far more radical position than any of those theorists following him who devoted their theory to practical ends, inclusive of Marx himself. It is, in short, precisely in rejecting a theoretical elaboration of practice that Hegel affirms in no uncertain terms his commitment to absolute privilege of practice.[5] He creates a theory that evinces its commitment to practice through the refusal of it.

As Hegel allows us to see, theory that explicitly sets out to produce political change and shape the future deprives theory of its greatest power, its power to reconcile us with the present and thereby expose the antagonism that animates this structure. It is only at the moment when theorists give up the effort to call an alternative future into being and content themselves with theorizing the prevailing symbolic structure as a *present* structure, that they can escape its tyranny and illuminate a possibility for change. For Hegel, the ethical or political danger lies in failing to theorize completely the present, not in trying to do so. But how does Hegel escape Jacques Derrida's deconstruction? How does his thought avoid presupposing the self-presence of the present?

Avant la lettre, Hegel accepts Derrida's deconstructive activity and actually pushes even further than Derrida himself does. However, he draws radically different conclusions from the deconstruction of the present. For Derrida, the non-identity of the present means that the future—the *arrivant*—haunts every present. Hegel sees the non-identity of the present as an internal rift *within the present itself*. That is to say, in Hegel's view, presence is undermined from within, not externally by an *arrivant*. We don't need the future or the *arrivant* to reveal the non-identity of the present because this non-identity resides within the present itself. There is a gap within the present that constitutes the present as such, and it is this gap that absolute knowledge apprehends when it closes thought off to the future.

To theorize the present is, in Hegel's terms, to recognize the constraints that the prevailing symbolic structure places on subjects without the illusion of openness that acts as a supplement to such structures. Hegel understands the attractiveness of insisting on the openness of the present, its lack of presence, but he also views it as the fundamental philosophical temptation to be avoided. The primary difficulty inherent in theorizing is not, contra Derrida, keeping the theoretical enunciation open but closing it off and thereby avoiding the lure of an imaginary outside. Attempts to sustain the openness of the symbolic structure, to indicate the future haunting its presence, thus blind us to the power of the symbolic structure.

---

5   For a related and extremely compelling formulation of Hegel's politics, see Gillian Rose's *Hegel Contra Sociology* (1981).

In order to avoid this problem, Derrida attempts to distinguish between the future that exists within the present symbolic structure and the unforeseen future to come. Using the distinction between two French words for the future, he contrasts the expected and predicted future (what he calls "*le future*") with the future that comes without warning (which he names "*l'avenir*").[6] According to Derrida, thought must hold open a place for *l'avenir*, for the genuine future that exists outside the present. But here we can subject Derrida's own opposition to the Derridean act of deconstruction. The distinction between *le future* and *l'avenir* cannot be absolute and must thus be deconstructable itself. No matter how far outside of the symbolic structure we imagine *l'avenir* to be, any act of thinking *l'avenir* will place it within our symbolic structure—thereby breaking down the distinction between *l'avenir* and *le future*. As Hegel always insists, we cannot simultaneously think a concept and sustain that concept outside of thought. In attempting to do so, we present ourselves with a misleading picture of our symbolic structure. We mistake the outside for the inside.

In addition, by focusing on what haunts the symbolic structure from the outside, on what is absolutely other (that is to say, on the *arrivant*), Derrida misses the internal failure of this structure—the foundational antagonism, the central impossibility, around which every symbolic structure is organized. Clinging to the image of an open present or an open symbolic structure obscures the impossibility that every system both needs and works to disavow. The impossible is the nonsensical, contradictory point within the world of symbolic meaning. In the act of grasping the symbolic structure absolutely, as an ultimate horizon for thought, theory can illuminate the antagonism that marks the point of the structure's internal vulnerability.

Hegel's entire effort in each of his texts lies in showing that the authentically new emerges from within the present, out of the antagonism that inhabits every symbolic structure. In this way, he models the kind of absolute theorizing that I am advocating here. To take perhaps the most famous example, the discussion of "Lordship and Bondage" in the *Phenomenology of Spirit* (1977) shows how the ideology of mastery inherently undermines itself. This ideology demands that the servant act as a dehumanized servant and, simultaneously, as a human source of recognition for the master. This contradiction explodes the ideology of mastery, putting it at odds with itself and leading to the emergence of something new.

---

6   The distinction between these two conceptions of the future becomes clearest in *Without Alibi*. There, Derrida insists that the genuine political event must belong to *l'avenir*, the future that comes without our presentiment that it will come. He claims, "The eventness of the event requires, if one wants to think it, this insistence on the arbitrary, fortuitous, contingent, aleatory, unforeseeable. An event that one held to be necessary and thus programmed, foreseeable, and so forth, would that be an event?" (2002: 158). In other words, thought—specifically, politicized thought—must sustain a relationship with what exceeds it without eliminating the otherness of this event, the justice to come. This is, to Derrida's mind, what Hegel utterly fails to accomplish. Hegel is in some sense the name for this failure to leave a space open for the unforeseeable.

Through his theorizing in this section of the *Phenomenology*, Hegel exposes the implicit unraveling of the ideology of mastery. He does not do this by imagining an alternative to this ideology or by suggesting that we work to subvert it. Instead, his theorizing about mastery embraces fully the ideology and follows its logic to the point at which it breaks down.

Hegel's revelation of the antagonism that undermines the ideology of mastery represents an instance of a theoretical discussion that occurs in the midst of an urgent political crisis. As Hegel composed the *Phenomenology*, the Haitians engaged in the first successful slave revolt in human history. According to the analysis provided by Susan Buck-Morss in her remarkable *Hegel, Haiti, and Universal History* (2009), Hegel followed the slave revolt closely and used the discussion of Lordship and Bondage to comment on the revolt and possible reprisals. By exposing the antagonism on which mastery runs aground, Hegel reveals the impasse that confronts would-be slaveholders. He does not argue for a world without slaves but instead makes clear the impossibility of mastery and thus the inherent failure of the slave system. Hegel takes this path because he recognizes where theory's true power resides. Theory can illuminate the contradictions that beset all ideological formations if it remains absolutely theoretical.

It is not that theory has the ability to see everything, to recognize "absolutely" the terrain of the present and the prevailing symbolic structure. But theory does have the ability to delimit itself, to avoid falling into the trap of trying to become practical by imagining alternatives. To theorize without imagining alternatives, to push the logic of the present to its breaking point, is what Hegel means by absolute knowledge. The problem is, as Judith Butler points out in *Subjects of Desire*, that the "subject constantly misidentifies the Absolute," thereby producing "the comedy of errors that mark the Hegelian subject's travels" (1999: 196). Nonetheless, it is possible to escape this "comedy of errors" and theorize without imagining an alternative, if one recognizes that the alternative is not outside the system but inside it. This is, for Hegel, the particular vocation of theory, and it is, indirectly, a practical vocation. In this sense, Hegel's insistent refusal to merge theory into practice bespeaks a recognition that theory best contributes to practice when it disregards the latter.

Given this conception of the relation between theory and practice, Hegel sees the task of philosophy as one of reconciliation. As he puts it in the final pages of the *History of Philosophy*, "The ultimate aim and business of philosophy is to reconcile thought or the Notion with reality" (1995: 545). And in the lesser *Logic*, he confesses that "philosophy … advances nothing new" (1975: 35). But this is not to say that philosophy or theory cannot effect change. In saying that philosophy "advances nothing new," Hegel is explicitly *not* saying that philosophy has no effect. Precisely because philosophy does not advance anything new but allows us to see the social antagonism, it has the ability to effect change, so that everything is not left as it is, but can be dramatically transformed. Hegel's point is simply that recognition has a transformative power insofar as it shifts the position from which we see while leaving what we see unchanged.

Such admissions concerning philosophy's secondary status vis-à-vis the symbolic determinations of the present reality populate Hegel's mature works and reach their culmination in the *Philosophy of Right*, the apparently accommodationist text par excellence. However, this sense that the task of philosophy lies in accommodating us to the existing reality is not confined to Hegel's later years. Despite the claims of theorists such as Herbert Marcuse or Georg Lukács, who see a political devolution in Hegel's intellectual career (from the radical of the *Phenomenology* to the conservative of the *Philosophy of Right*), Hegel constantly envisions philosophy or theory as confined to an accounting of the present from the very beginning of his philosophical endeavors.[7] In fact, his first significant publication, the treatise *The Difference Between Fichte's and Schelling's System of Philosophy* (1801), is a critique of Fichte's *failure* to conceive of philosophy in this role, of Fichte's insistence that philosophy can provide for us an ethical imperative. By examining Hegel's critique of Fichte, the ultimate inability of theory to offer ethical or political imperatives will become apparent.

Rather than conceiving the end of his philosophy as a reconciliation of thought and reality, Fichte concludes with an imperative: thought and reality "ought" to be identical, and it is our impossible mission to accomplish this reconciliation. The Fichtean absolute is the ought [*Sollen*], and this ought fails to be absolute enough. For Fichte, philosophy leaves us with an opening to the future; we can never realize the ought and reach the point of complete self-identity. The future, in Fichte's philosophy, always remains futural or practical.[8] Because thought is not reconciled with reality, there is something to be done—a quite explicit imperative. In this sense, then, Fichte, despite his distance on other questions, is closer to Marx than Hegel is.

Whereas Hegel depicts thought as reconciled with the present symbolic structure, Fichte sees it striving for an alternative future. Not only is Fichte's subject revolutionary, it is the subject of permanent revolution. As he himself describes it in *The Science of Knowledge*, "*in relation to a possible object*, the pure self-reverting activity of the self is a *striving*; and ... *an infinite striving* at that. This boundless striving, carried to infinity, is the *condition of the possibility of any object whatsoever*: no striving, no object" (1982: 231). Hence, for Fichte,

---

7   See Herbert Marcuse's *Reason and Revolution* (1983) and Georg Lukács' *The Young Hegel* (1976). As Paul Franco argues, this distinction between the radical politics of the *Phenomenology* and the conservatism of the *Philosophy of Right* doesn't stand up to close scrutiny. He claims, "Though the overall purposes of the *Phenomenology* and the *Philosophy of Right* are no doubt different, their overall ethico-political perspectives completely coincide. Thus it can be said that Hegel's development with respect to his moral and political philosophy, as with respect to almost everything else, comes to its conclusion in the *Phenomenology*" (1999: 119).

8   Fichte saw his philosophical project as one of clarifying the Kantian system through an emphasis on the priority of the practical subject. Kant's failure, in Fichte's eyes, lies in his inability to see fully the dependence of the subject's theoretical reason on its practical act of self-positing.

we cannot even conceive of reality at all unless we conceive of it as something we are striving to attain. Philosophy, in this conception, leaves us with something to accomplish and thereby appears to avoid the quietism that infects the philosophy of reconciliation.

Hegel's critique of Fichte makes clear, however, that Fichte has not left the opening to the future that he thinks he has, precisely because such an opening is, strictly speaking, impossible. By concluding his system with striving, rather than moving on to the identity of thought and reality, Fichte believes that he sustains freedom. The future is not closed off, but something yet to be accomplished. But this conception of freedom, according to Hegel, is only a negative freedom—and this is the problem with accepting the ought as a philosophical endpoint. In the *Difference* essay, Hegel provides a concise formulation of this critique: "the character of freedom in Fichte's system ... is not the suspension of the opposites, but the opposition to them, and in this opposition it gets fixed as negative freedom. Reason constitutes itself through reflection as a unity that is absolutely opposed by a manifold. The ought expresses this standing opposition; it expresses the non-existence of the absolute identity" (1977: 133). The freedom of absolute striving is a purely negative freedom because it is conditioned by what it is striving from. While it may seem to be open to future possibility instead of being stuck in the present actuality, it is in fact thoroughly conditioned by the present—which represents its unsurpassable limit. Fichte's striving strives against the present, but in doing so it necessarily takes all of its cues from that same present. As a negative freedom, it constitutively fails to break from that which it is attempting to negate. It is the rebellion that desperately wants to sustain the law it attacks in order to sustain itself qua rebellion.[9]

In order to see the implications for the relationship between theory and practice, we must generalize Hegel's critique of Fichte. For Hegel, all philosophy is philosophy of the present symbolic structure. Even when it conceives of steps we ought to take—or envisions a possible future that we should try to realize—it necessarily remains within the confines of this present. Whenever we are within the realm of thought, the future has always already been realized. This is why, for example, Hegel insists that Plato's ideal republic was not at all an ideal toward which Greek society might aspire, but was itself already the truth of Greek society. What we are able to conceive, even if we only conceive of it as a possibility, is always possible within the prevailing symbolic structure; if it were not, we would not be able to conceive it. Hence, rather than telling us about the possible future, the imagined alternative world tells us about our prevailing symbolic structure, albeit in a disguised form. When theorists issue practical imperatives, these imperatives may appear as critiques of the ruling system, but they cannot but express its hidden logic.

---

9 In essence, Hegel charges Fichte with hysteria, with obtaining satisfaction from his sense of dissatisfaction.

This becomes evident in the political program of Peter Singer, who theorizes a way of combating world poverty. In *The Life You Can Save: Acting Now To End World Poverty*, Singer inadvertently reveals the costs of a complete abandonment of theory for the sake of practice within a theoretical work.[10] His thesis is that with even a modest amount of charity by all moderately wealthy and wealthy individuals, we could instantly eradicate poverty everywhere. Singer puts the need to act in the starkest moral terms. He claims, "Most of us are absolutely certain that we wouldn't hesitate to save a drowning child, and that we would do it at consider cost to ourselves. Yet while thousands of children die each day, we spend money on thing we take for granted and would hardly notice if they were not there" (2009: 12). Singer's basic claim is irrefutable: it is correct that millions of relatively well-off individuals spend thousands of dollars a year on items that they could easily give up without reducing their happiness and that this money, if properly directed, could ameliorate the situation of the impoverished in the world. But what Singer does not account for is the often deleterious effect of aid and aid organizations, even those with the least corruption and the best intentions.[11] Much more importantly, he does not recognize the structural antagonism of capitalism itself that will continue to produce impoverishment. No amount of giving will overcome this antagonism, and it will likely exacerbate it (if only by disguising it). Singer's well-intentioned effort to better the world through philosophy, if put into practice, would only cement into place the capitalist structures that ensure global inequality. Realizing his theoretical elimination of poverty would undoubtedly lead to a political nightmare, a world that would make us long for the good old days of contemporary capitalism.

The problem that haunts Singer's project also besets those who target capitalism as a system when they attempt to theorize an alternative future. In the effort of *Empire* to begin the practical struggle toward a future alternative to global capitalism, Hardt and Negri define this alternative—the world toward which we should struggle—in the precise terms of global capitalism itself. For instance, they contend that one challenges the hegemony of Empire through mobility and constant migration. As they put it, "circulating is the first ethical act of a counterimperial ontology" (2000: 363). In the future utopia that they imagine, "the cities of the earth will become at once great deposits of cooperating humanity and locomotives for circulation, temporary residences and networks of the mass distribution of living humanity" (2000: 397). Hardt and Negri foresee an alternative world of border crossing, hybridity, and impermanence. What is this "alternative" future if not the present reality of global capitalism itself? The economy today demands exactly what Hardt and Negri call for as the means of contesting it: utilizing a

---

10   Singer's book is an elaboration of a much earlier essay entitled "Famine, Affluence, and Morality" (1972). This essay made the case for charity so convincing that it became perhaps the most assigned essay in university philosophy classes around the world.

11   For a devastating and disturbing account of how humanitarian aid worsens conditions in the world, see Linda Polman's *The Crisis Caravan* (2010).

large population of migrant labor and staffing businesses with large numbers of temporary employees. Permanence and stability are barriers to the functioning of global capitalism. Though they imagine that they are envisioning a future alternative to Empire, Hardt and Negri are in effect articulating this alternative in the very terms of the Empire they aim to contest.[12] Their effort to provide practice with a theoretical aid by thinking the future ends up limiting the power of their theoretical endeavor.

The turn to the future—the impossible turn—rather than helping to make an alternative future possible, actually works as a barrier to the possibility of its emergence. It does this because it has the effect of filling in the gap of the present, of occluding the present antagonism with the image of the future. When we imagine the future, we prescribe how it might be from the position of the present (thus circumscribing certain possibilities a priori). Absolute knowledge, in contrast, has the virtue of wiping the slate clean. This is exactly how Rebecca Comay describes it in *Mourning Sickness*, where she notes, "Exposing the subject to its collective emptiness, it clears the slate for a new beginning" (2011: 125). Absolute knowledge is freedom insofar as it liberates the subject for the future that it will produce.[13] But in order to create freely, we must see clearly the deadlock of the present.

The refusal to turn toward the future and, instead, an absolute focus on the present has the effect of allowing the antagonism of the present to emerge. This is precisely what we see in the philosophy of Hegel. However, the turn to the future obscures this antagonism because, through the act of envisioning or working toward its overcoming, this turn immediately transforms the antagonism into simply an empirical obstacle. That is to say, envisioning the overcoming of the antagonism or anticipating the steps necessary for transcending it relieves us from the need to confront antagonism in practice. In this way, practically oriented theory becomes a barrier to actual practice by disguising the antagonism that structures the present. The antagonism is no longer something that represents an unsurpassable limit—or a possible opening—but instead it is something that we have already moved beyond. The antagonism no longer constrains us.

---

12   To be fair, Hardt and Negri would readily acknowledge that their attempt to combat Empire relies on the very logic of Empire itself. Following Deleuze and Guattari's conception of how to challenge capitalism, they insist that pushing the logic of Empire to its extreme point will have the effect of dismantling Empire. What this line of thought misses is the antagonism within Empire itself—the fact that Empire is at odds with itself. In imagining an alternative future, Hardt and Negri's thought has the effect of obscuring this antagonism and creating the illusion that there is a single, self-identical logic of Empire.

13   Catherine Malabou arrives at a similar point when she identifies the absolute with plasticity. She notes, "It is not *stasis* but *metamorphosis* that characterizes Absolute Knowledge. Consequently it forms and transforms individuals, fashioning their ways of waiting for and expecting the future" (2005: 134). Absolute knowledge is not just another change, but the possibility of a radical transformation, a shift of one's coordinates, that would not be possible without taking the theorization of the present to its endpoint.

Antagonism is at once an impossibility—no matter what arrangement of society we come up with, we cannot overcome antagonism as such—and a possibility—an empty space within the present social organization that indicates the possibility of acting in a way that would transform society. For Alain Badiou, this empty space is the void, which contains in it the possibility of all political change. In *Being and Event*, he notes, "the void, which is the name of inconsistency in the situation (under the law of the count-as-one), cannot, in itself, be presented or fixed" (2005: 93). It is the void in the social situation that enables an event—a rupture with the prevailing structure—to occur. One cannot identify the void through prescribing a practice. Instead, one must theorize the antagonism so that the void becomes tangible.

The role of theory is not to solve crises but to make them apparent. Nonetheless, in times of crisis, the temptation for the theorist to become an activist inevitably reaches a new height. But this is a temptation that the theorist must resist. Hegel provides a philosophical model for this resistance, and his political importance for us today rests on his refusal of the turn to practice within theory. If theory is able to think the present absolutely—as Hegel himself attempts—then it can make antagonism evident not merely as something to be surpassed (as it is for Marx), but as that which inhabits and even constitutes the disavowed essence of every social order. In this way, absolute knowing can establish the groundwork for a complete transformation of how we conceive the social order. Bringing the antagonism of the present to light is the political task of theory. Rather than striving to go beyond itself into actual practice, theory can commit itself to practice only by remaining wholly within its own domain, by resisting the lure of practice and of an alternative future. We can change the world in theory only insofar as we resist the temptation to do so.

References

Adorno, Theodor (1973) *Negative Dialectics*. Trans. E.B. Ashton. New York: Continuum.

Agamben, Giorgio (2011) *The Kingdom and the Glory: For a Theological Genealogy of Economy and Government* (trans. Lorenzo Chiesa, with Matteo Mandarini). Stanford: Stanford University Press.

Badiou, Alain (2005) *Being and Event* (trans. Oliver Feltham). New York: Continuum.

Buck-Morss, Susan (2009) *Hegel, Haiti, and Universal History*. Pittsburgh: University of Pittsburgh Press.

Butler, Judith (1999) *Subjects of Desire: Hegelian Reflections in Twentieth-Century France*. New York: Columbia University Press.

Butler, Judith, John Guillory, and Kendall Thomas. Preface. *What's Left of Theory? New Work on the Politics of Literary Theory*. New York: Routledge, pp. viii-xii.

Comay, Rebecca (2011) *Mourning Sickness: Hegel and the French Revolution*. Stanford: Stanford University Press.

Derrida, Jacques (2002) *Without Alibi* (trans. Peggy Kamuf). Stanford: Stanford University Press.

Fichte, J.G. (1982) *The Science of Knowledge* (trans. Peter Heath and John Lachs). New York: Cambridge University Press.

Franco, Paul (1999) *Hegel's Philosophy of Freedom*. New Haven: Yale University Press.

Hardt, Michael, and Antonio Negri (2000) *Empire*. Cambridge: Harvard University Press.

——— (2009) *Commonwealth*. Cambridge: Harvard University Press.

Hegel, G.W.F. (1952) *Philosophy of Right* (trans. T.M. Knox). London: Oxford University Press.

——— (1975) *Logic* (trans. William Wallace). Oxford: Clarendon Press.

——— (1977) *The Difference Between Fichte's and Schelling's System of Philosophy* (trans. H.S. Harris and Walter Cerf). Albany: State University of New York Press.

——— (1977) *Phenomenology of Spirit*. (trans. A.V. Miller). Oxford: Oxford University Press.

——— (1995) *Lectures on the History of Philosophy: Medieval and Modern Philosophy*. Vol. 3 (trans. E.S. Haldane). Lincoln: University of Nebraska Press.

Kaplan, Cora (2000) "Introduction: Millenial Class." *PMLA* 115 (2000): 9–19.

Kojève, Alexandre (1969) *Introduction to the Reading of Hegel* (trans. James H. Nichols, Jr.). Ed. Allan Bloom. Ithaca: Cornell University Press.

Kundera, Milan (1984) *The Unbearable Lightness of Being* (trans. Michael Henry Heim) New York: HarperCollins.

Lukács, Georg (1976) *The Young Hegel: Studies in the Relations Between Dialectics and*

Economics (trans. Rodney Livingstone). Cambridge: MIT Press.

Malabou, Catherine (2005) *The Future of Hegel: Plasticity, Temporality, and Dialectic* (trans. Lisabeth During). New York: Routledge.

Marcuse, Herbert (1983) *Reason and Revolution: Hegel and the Rise of Social Theory*. 2nd Ed. New Jersey: Humanities Press.

Marx, Karl (1978) "Theses on Feuerbach." *The Marx-Engels Reader* (ed. Robert C. Tucker). New York: Norton, pp. 143–5.

Polman, Linda (2010) *The Crisis Caravan: What's Wrong with Humanitarian Aid?* New York: Metropolitan Books.

Rose, Gillian (1981) *Hegel Contra Sociology*. London: Humanities Press.

Simpson, David (1995) *The Academic Postmodern and the Rule of Literature: A Report on Half-Knowledge*. Chicago: University of Chicago Press.

Singer, Peter (1972) "Famine, Affluence, and Morality." *Philosophy and Public Affairs* 1.1 (1972): pp. 229–43.

——— (2009) *The Life You Can Save: Acting Now to End World Poverty*. New York: Random House.

Chapter 7

Affective Economies: Lacan's Four Discourses against the Historicism of Capitalist Abstraction

Yahya M. Madra and Ceren Özselçuk[1]

Materialism of Practice Versus Materialism of Affect

The representation of capitalism as a system of abstraction gains a widespread reception in contemporary analyses of social relations. A particular version of this representation is the account of real abstraction, where commercing subjects are said to be practicing a form of material abstraction even when they are not aware of it. This representation and its versions are usually mobilized to remind the proponents of post-capitalist politics (e.g., solidarity economies, community economies, Occupy movements) that they should not underestimate the hold of abstraction and fetishism of commodities on subjectivity. What seems to give the account of real abstraction its persuasive appeal is the way in which it posits abstraction not as a "veil" that obscures the real relations of production but rather as a "reality-effect" of markets. We welcome this sobering warning, not only because it gestures to break with an idealist model (appearance as epiphenomenon) in favour of a materialist one (appearance as constitutive), but also because it foregrounds the problem of intellectual difference and the question of the division of mental and manual labour—which is itself a primary concern for many forms of post-capitalist politics. On the other hand, we worry that it attributes to capitalist abstraction an ontological solidity and uniformity that does not exist, especially if we take seriously the matter of affect (*jouissance*) and its various modalities. This is not to suggest a false opposition between the "necessity" of real abstraction and the "contingency" of *jouissance*—for the latter is neither simply contingent (hence, the insistence of the repetitive loop of the drive) nor simply necessary (hence, the instabilities caused by the smear of *jouissance*). Our aim is rather to deploy psychoanalysis and, to be more specific, the Lacanian theory of four discourses, in order to think systematically about the *affective* tonalities associated

1 We express our gratitude to Heiko Feldner, Fabio Vighi and Slavoj Žižek for inviting us to contribute to this important volume. We thank Lara Fresko for being the fastidious reader of a previous draft of this essay. We also thank the co-editors for their patient and careful labours of composing and editing the book. The usual caveat applies.

with different forms of social links that the subject entertains in relation to both capitalist and post-capitalist forms of abstraction.

We begin by bringing into question the broadly accepted assumption that real abstraction provides the truly materialist account of capitalist abstraction. To the extent that this assumption automatically deduces subjection from a presumably uniform practice of exchange, we think it is more in the vein of materialism to explore the ways in which subjection is both sustained and disrupted by *affective experiences*. The introduction of the dimensions of the unconscious and affects enables us to provide an explanation of the resilience and solidity of capitalist abstraction by accounting for its libidinal sources which is absent in the real abstraction literature. Moreover, it enables us to foreground the fact that the traversal of this resilience cannot be enacted merely through reflexive knowledge, but rather through a dislocation in the affective attachments to our ways of being and doing. If we proceed with the psychoanalytical insight that subjection is always sustained by some libidinal enjoyment (i.e., the *Real*), that it always generates surplus enjoyment as a by-product, then the question becomes: what are the different affective experiences of submitting to economic abstractions? Is capitalist abstraction the obstacle to articulating a *post-capitalist politics*, or is what matters the way in which we relate to different regimes of abstraction?

Real Abstraction and the Real

In *The Sublime Object of Ideology*, Slavoj Žižek takes apart those conventional readings of Freudian dream analysis and Marxian commodity fetishism that portray them as seeking to uncover some hidden content behind a manifest form (respectively, latent dream content and labour-behind-value). Taking the opposite direction, he instead locates the shared object of these theoretical formations in the "secret of the form" (respectively, form of the unconscious and commodity form). In order to underscore the structural homology between the interpretive grids of these formations Žižek then turns to Alfred Sohn-Rethel's discussion of real abstraction as the analysis that "has gone furthest in unfolding the universal reach of commodity form" (Žižek 1989: 17). For Žižek, the ontology of real abstraction "as the act of abstraction at work in the very effective process of the exchange of commodities" displays a "striking" homology with "that of the unconscious, this signifying chain which persists on 'another Scene'" (17–8). Yet the homology Žižek locates between the unconscious and real abstraction has its limits. And exploring these limits will enable us to distinguish the psychoanalytical account of the affective *experiences* of capitalist abstraction from the *practice* of real abstraction.

In his influential *Intellectual and Manual Labour*, Sohn-Rethel finds the origins of abstraction in the practice of exchange, in the activity of life itself, rather than in the interiority of intellectual reflection. Indeed, real abstraction is not only Sohn-Rethel's rebuttal of the idealism which he considers to prevail in philosophical thinking, but also his answer to what he perceives to be a major lacuna in Marxist theory, namely, the absence of a historical materialist explanation of the origins of scientific and philosophical thought. By obtaining the historical origins of the "thought form" in "commodity form" (Sohn-Rethel 1978, xiii), real abstraction is argued to furnish such an overdue explanation with comprehensive implications. Commodity form is not only tied up with the origins of scientific thought, but also connected with the historical emergence of the division of intellectual and manual labour.[2] And in so far as this division conditions the phenomenon of alienation on which exploitation and domination of ruling classes depend, real abstraction stipulates a clear criterion for how a class society can be distinguished from a classless society. In short, the implication is that real abstraction is the ultimate obstacle to articulating a post-capitalist politics.

For Sohn Rethel, a defining aspect of real abstraction is that abstractness does not apply to the consciousness of the agents, but to their actions (26). In other words, real abstraction inscribes a "form of thought" within the practice of capitalist exchange without the exchanging subjects becoming cognizant of it. Or rather, we should say, without the exchanging subjects becoming cognizant of it *initially*—since Sohn-Rethel also adds that, in the end abstractness of exchange "does enter their minds, but only after the event, when they are faced with the completed result of the circulation of commodities," that is, when they encounter abstractness in the separate embodiment of money (27). Sohn-Rethel's note on consciousness eventually catching up with "exchange abstraction" is not so accidental to his argument as it might first appear. Quite on the contrary, we think it is actually revealing of the manner in which Sohn-Rethel imagines real abstraction as a spontaneous order, as a unifying condition that is supposed to eventually impose its colonizing influence on the entire social space.

This can be discerned from the way real abstraction subsumes *all* practices. It operates as their absolute condition of possibility just as it renders them as so many expressions of itself: Emanating from the action of commodity exchange, real abstraction spreads out and grafts itself not only on the mentalities of assessing individuals (e.g., legally equivalent exchanger-producer subjects, citizen-subjects); but also, on the methods of counting labour and value (e.g., the formation of intellectual

---

2   We want to distinguish "commodity-centered approaches" from "labour-centered approaches" to real abstraction (Kordela 2006; Toscano 2008a). The latter set of approaches sees real abstraction as "the properly ontological character of capitalist abstraction" (Toscano 2008a: 276). While Sohn-Rethel takes a "commodity-centered" approach, thus loosening real abstraction from the historicity of capitalism, now and then he switches to a slightly different explanation of tracing the origins of abstraction, besides commodity exchange, to the division of labour necessitated by class relations (as measurement becomes a necessary device to manage the appropriation and distribution of surplus labour produced by the direct labourers). This is why there is room in Sohn-Rethel's discourse, otherwise absent in analyses of real abstraction, for the difference between surplus labour (or product) and surplus value, thus, for the application of the separation of intellectual and manual labour not only to capitalist, but also, to other non-capitalist forms of surplus labour appropriation.

labour as different from manual labour, fulfilling the function of supervising and quantifying the production of surplus labour); and on the procedures of thought itself (e.g., philosophical and scientific abstractions and conceptual basis of cognition for which Sohn-Rethel gave examples ranging from Greek philosophy to the Kantian categories of thought). While various scholars (Arthur 1993; Toscano 2008b) have connected the resilience of capitalist social relations to the embedded character of abstraction in the "real practice" of commodity exchange, one nonetheless wonders what makes this practice so intact and far reaching, if not the ontology that it presumes which assembles social being into an "expressive whole."[3]

If one agrees with our reading that the ontology of real abstraction, in a historicist vein, presents a unifying horizon from which nothing seems to escape, one is obliged to ask: where is the unconscious in real abstraction? To this question, Žižek's response is that the *a priori* inscription of a "form of thought" in the action of commodity exchange is the correlate to the unconscious (Žižek 1989: 19). This implies that real abstraction occupies a similar position to the institution of an "alien kernel," a dimension of nonrecognition within subjectivity: Just like the unconscious, as the unrecognized effects of the signifier on the subject, does not lie in the depths of subjective interiority and is constituted in the field of the Other, real abstraction operates outside the consciousness of the subject, as a structuring albeit unacknowledged "part of its social being" (Sohn-Rethel 1978: 18). We wonder, however, how far this analogy can really be extended, especially because the "partial and plural" being of psychoanalysis (Copjec 2002: 9) and the "social being" of real abstraction are fundamentally at odds with one another. To summarize beforehand the argument we develop below: The fragmented and not firmly placed being that psychoanalysis has discovered in relation to the

---

3 Is not this presumption also what instigates the critical remarks of Louis Althusser on the topic of abstraction (of labour) in the first section of *Capital*? Althusser argues that the ambiguous formulations of Marx in these pages give way to a historicist interpretation, as a result of which Marx's new problematic is misrecognized simply as another version of Hegelian "expressive totality." Althusser finds this historicist interpretation problematic because it represents abstraction as the absolute knowledge that is directly produced by the generalization of commodity relations and given in the immediate form of consciousness (Althusser and Balibar 1997: 124–5). This suggests not only that consciousness already contains its own self-criticism, leading to the union of consciousness and science into one and the same thing, but also that all knowledge concerning a historical object is reducible to an expression of the present consciousness. Thus, there is a refusal to acknowledge the real differences separating the different practices, levels, and instances of a historical "presence." While Althusser's interlocutor is not Sohn-Rethel, his criticism can be readily extended to the former's thesis of real abstraction as a "social synthesis," and to its historicist implication that "the socially necessary forms of thinking in an epoch are those in conformity with the socially synthetic function of the epoch" (Sohn-Rethel 1978: 5). For another trenchant critique of historicism that is psychoanalytically oriented see Joan Copjec who offers one possible definition for historicism as "the reduction of society to its indwelling network of relations of power and knowledge" (Copjec 1994: 6).

formation of the drive and its disequilibrating function is radically different from the "social being" which the synthesizing order of real abstraction anticipates as *one* consistent process. There is no *Real*, thus, there is no experience of *Real* qua affect in real abstraction. Let us explicate.

For psychoanalysis, the encounter with the symbolic order (the Other as the locus of language as well as the culture a subject inherits and is submitted to), rather than providing the subject a familiar place of its own, results in the out of jointness of her being with herself. We can elaborate further on this statement with the hypothesis that the arrival of the subject in language involves a *forced choice* between being and meaning. The choice is forced, not only because choosing being is not an option, since this would amount to losing both being and meaning and entering into psychosis, but also because choosing meaning comes with a splitting within being that entails a loss (Zupancic 2000, 40). As various scholars of psychoanalysis put it, the being that is lost is not to be regarded in terms of some originally existing state of plenitude. The subject's desire for a wholeness of being is rather a retroactive effect of the splitting within being, and of the concomitant formation of partial objects of the drive, as a necessary result of the "network of signifiers overlaying the world" (Lacan 2007: 48). The lost object forever eluding the desiring subject (that is, object *a* as the object cause of desire) is suggested to us only through the bits of satisfaction (surplus *jouissance*) attained by the repetitive loops of the drive.[4] Object *a*, or *jouissance* is what refers to the split being, as both that which constitutes the alien core of subjectivity, and that part of the subject's corporeal being located outside his or her body. In fact, Lacan's concept of *extimacy* points precisely at this ambivalent status of object *a* as that which is simultaneously internal and external to the subject. Object *a* is not only what makes being out of joint with itself, but also what makes the Other itself inconsistent, thus, rendering it impossible for the subject to seamlessly unite with the Other.

We are already distancing ourselves significantly from the issue concerning the synthesizing function of real abstraction, which causes subjectivity to combine into a network and act as an extension of the social being of abstraction. Real abstraction presumes a social interface, an "actor-network" integration, through which the "whole of the subject's corporeal presence is engaged or chiasmically intertwined with the Other, 'directed in what is called [its] total intentionality'" (Copjec 2006: 97–8). Whereas object *a* disqualifies just such an ontology of being that would fit and merge smoothly with any social design. If there is a synthesizing function of object *a* (and one might argue that there is) this function is at the same time destabilizing and without a purpose or telos. Similarly the drive, which has no goal, aims at satisfaction through circling around partial objects that come to occupy the void of the lost object—it has no measure, or moderation. Singular

---

4   This is how Lacan explains this fictitious materiality of the drive: "The drives are our myths, said Freud. This must not be understood as a reference to the unreal. For it is the real that the drives mythify, as myths usually do: here it is the real which creates [*fait*] desire by reproducing therein the relationship of the subject to the lost object" (1996: 418).

and contingent to each subject's history, partial objects serve as representatives of unevenly charged zones of affective intensity. These cathected privileged partial objects have a contradictory status: On the one hand, they are the objects of an acephalic drive that knows nothing other than its own satisfaction. On the other hand, they function as screens for the projection of synthesizing fantasies of wholeness that account even for what thwarts their attainment. To put it differently, the very extimate objects that disrupt the rational and functional integration of the "actor" with the network (of real abstraction) are also, as privileged nodal points, what enable partial totalizations of a non-all social field.

It should by now be evident that the "partial and plural" being of psychoanalysis does not overlap with the totalizing ontology of social being implied in real abstraction—on the contrary, it provides a resolute critique of it. Rather than a unifying structure that imposes a comprehensive and cohesive historical present (without heterogeneity), capitalist abstraction is recast as a partial totalization that is supported by the surplus of affective investments. Moreover, when we say that capitalist abstraction is a partial ordering, this should not imply that it is part of a complete, well-defined, or eventually definable whole (of economy), but rather that it is partial, even when hegemonic, to a heterogeneous field along with other, non-capitalist, partial orderings of abstraction, obliging us, in effect, to talk about discontinuous regimes of abstraction in the plural, rather than about the consolidative practice of real abstraction in the singular. This critique of abstraction may also lend some insight on why Louis Althusser adopted an analytics of ideology and insisted on the necessity of reproduction, instead of working within the problematic of commodity fetishism. By doing so, one possible aim of his was to move the focus of analysis from the market and its narratives of spontaneous order to the state and its dispositifs, constitutive of the social order. Another aim was to displace a centered understanding of materiality based on the *practice of exchange* through an aleatory understanding of materiality based on the *plurality of practices*, which do not line up to produce some uniform Zeitgeist, in which whatever happens happens as a corresponding part of one consistent totality. Following the perspicacity of Althusser's remarks on the non-contemporaneity of history, we argue not only that one cannot explain the phenomenon of capitalist abstraction without taking account of the practices of capitalist (re-)production, but also that the practices of abstraction are irreducible to the capitalist form.[5] Yet, diverging from Althusser's materialism which—along with the break with a humanist tradition centered on the subject—attempts to dismantle any notion of the subject, we think that taking the affective dimension of practices into account is a necessary materialist step against the regeneration of totalizing logics.

---

5   To relate this insight to our discussion further down the road, we can suggest that the master signifier of the value of labour-power (for capitalist abstraction) both conditions as well as is conditioned by state ideological apparatuses (as state's various signifying practices), such as the "money minted by the state, transactions registered by state agencies, and courts capable of settling possible disputes" (Althusser 2006: 132).

Uses and Limits of Homology

The complex relationships between regimes of abstraction and the dimension of affect can be explored through Jacques Lacan's four discourses, a set of mathemes which he designated as "a four footed apparatus, with its four positions" (2007: 20), and which constitute a conceptual matrix to make sense of the four different social links through which subject's affective experiences are organized and transformed: The discourses of the Master, the University, the Analyst, and the Hysteric. In deploying the four discourses in the theoretical context of the relation between abstraction and affect, we follow Lacan who posits a structural homology between signification and abstraction, discourse and social link, signifier and value (1998: 17). Yet, working within the frame of this structural homology (or any homology as we have already observed above) requires an awareness of its limits, of what it obscures as much as what it sheds light on. This section establishes the terms as well as the limits of Lacan's homology.

The structure of these mathemes find their initial form in the Lacanian adage: a signifier (S_1) represents (constitutes) the subject for the other signifiers (S_2), "which implies that there is no signifier of the subject, so that this is a process of an always failing representation" (Dolar 2006: 143–4). Hence, the divided, barred subject under S_1.

$$\frac{S_1}{\$} \longrightarrow S_2$$

This matheme—which is yet to become the first of the four discourses as the surplus product, object *a*, is missing—is a formalization where a multiplicity of problematics can be discussed simultaneously. Indeed, *Seminar XVII* represents an important milestone in Lacan's gradual turn towards formalization. In particular, Lacan's return to Freud's metapsychological writings represents a significant level of formalization of Freud's discussions (Grigg 2008). For instance, it is in this seminar that he proposes "to analyze the Oedipus complex as being Freud's dream" (Lacan 2007: 117), and substitutes the already structuralist notion of Name-of-the-Father with the even more purely formal notion of the master signifier (S_1) (Verhaege 2006: 30). The particular accent of reading and deployment of Lacan's mathemes and the four discourses is conditioned by Lacan's distinct usage of formalism. Informed neither by the positivist tendency to find the true essence of what appears to be complex phenomena, nor simply by an attempt to get rid of Freud's turn-of-the-century Viennese morality, Lacan's turn towards formalization was an attempt to develop a conceptual framework for the analysts both to make sense of, and strategically intervene in, the discursive structures that entrap the subject.

For Lacan the above basic matheme is as much a formalization of the constitutive splitting of the subject between that of the enunciation and the enunciated in the very moment of its suturing to the signifying chain, as it is of the logic of the signifier where meaning is always produced retroactively within the chain of signifiers. Since language is the quintessential social institution, the ground zero of the social link among speaking beings, this matheme also lends itself easily to the articulation of "a strict *structural homology* between economic and semantic systems of representation" (Kordela 2006: 540). Similarly, Ernesto Laclau, when mobilizing the psychoanalytical categories in his discussion of hegemonic logics of populist reason, maintains that categories of psychoanalysis "are not regional but belong to the field of … a general ontology" (2005: 114). For Laclau, some time around early twentieth century, psychoanalysis and politics simultaneously discovered the same formal dislocation in "the very structure of objectivity" (114). We agree with the basic premise of these observations. Lacan's drive towards formalization did enable post-Marxist thought to identify the similarities between the Freudian unconscious and social systems of representation. It is now possible to add to this couple the Marxian value theory—with the proviso that we read it symptomatically. In particular, rather than treating *abstract-labour time* as an ontological given (a metaphysical presence, a transcendental signified) *represented* by the system of values, we propose to read this central Marxian category as a retroactive product, a theoretical abstraction that exists only in its effects which are visible and measurable through the *differential* signifying operations of the value-form (Roberts 1996). Just as "the unity of the object is a retroactive effect of naming it" (Laclau 2005: 108), the system of value "transforms every product of labour into a social hieroglyphic," which we then "try to decipher" (Marx 1976: 167).

Yet, some care is necessary when exploring the structural homologies between different systems of representation. For instance, Gayatri Spivak carefully problematizes the "isomorphic analogy" that Jean-Jacques Goux makes in his *Symbolic Economies: After Marx and Freud* (1988) between the phallus and gold as the universal equivalents of the subject and products respectively, finding the analogy to be a "domestication [oedipalization?] of Marx's analysis of Value" (Spivak 1988: 156).[6] The existence of "general morphological similarities between centralized sign-formations," Spivak maintains, warrants neither overlooking the specificities of the analogized sign-formations, nor excluding "the fields of force that make them heterogeneous, indeed discontinuous" (156). Identifying "in those similarities the structural essence of the formations thus analogized," she notes, courts the risk of excluding those relationships between the fields "that are attributive and supportive and not analogical" (156). And finally, forcing a very "strict structural homology" risks overlooking the dimensions of the fields that exceed the terms of the homology.

For instance, according to Spivak, because in constructing the homology between the phallus and gold Goux has limited his discussion to Marx's account

---

6   According to our reading, "isomorphic analogy" and "structural homology" refer to the same phenomena where two fields are composed of elements which are positioned in relation to one another in a similar manner.

of "the emergence of the money-form" (found in the infamous first three chapters of *Capital*), the Marxian accounts of the value of labour-power and the process of exploitation are excluded as what exceed the terms of the homology (156–7). Similarly, there will be something exceeding on the psychoanalytical side of the homology as well. Regimes of economic representation through the differential system of markets, while constitutive of economic value, are nonetheless secondary phenomena, as they presume the prior symbolic castration and the simultaneous sexuation of the subject. In other words, not all readings of the matheme are at an equal ontological level. To retain the difference between "the fields of force" of the two sign-formations is necessary not only to evade the pitfalls of a linguistic reductionism (which may entail the denial of the specificity of the economic and its internal heterogeneity) but also to remark the immanent possibility of re-organizing the economic system of representation. If one ontologically equates the "signifying operations" of economic regimes of abstraction with the constitutive processes of symbolic castration, without theoretically acknowledging that the latter is the very condition of sociality as such, and the former is merely a regional sign-formation, one will end up hypostatizing, in this case, the capitalist value-form as the only form of economic representation possible.

Value of Labour-power: A Master Signifier for Capitalist Abstraction

Given that theoretical choices made in establishing the terms of the homology have strategic and conceptual consequences, we propose to develop a Marxian reading of Lacan's matheme as a formalization of the *differential* and *retroactive* determination of the economic value of a commodity within the nexus of exchange. In this regional sign-formation, the commodity which has no value outside of the network of values is placed under S_1, in the place occupied by the barred subject, and S_2 represents the values of all the other commodities in the marketplace. Here the commodity is barred, because a *thing* can only become an *object* once it is part of a differential system of value, i.e., when it becomes a *commodity*. A *commodity* is a (useful) *thing* that is produced for exchange and thereby it is split in its very constitution between use-value (which is supposed to satisfy concrete needs and wants) and exchange-value (which represents the *socially necessary abstract-labour time* for the production of the commodity at any given moment, under given production conditions).[7]

Yet, the central contribution of Marxian political economy, as Spivak as well as many others have noted (e.g., Resnick and Wolff 1987), does not lie in the analysis of the commodity or money-form, but rather in the analysis of a very specific commodity, that of *labour-power*. To do a properly Marxian reading of

7 This is not to say that use value is the firm ground against which the differential determination of value-form unfolds. Use-value is also pervaded by the unstable economy of desire.

these mathemes, we need to read them in relation to capitalist exploitation. And to do that we take the cue from Lacan's humorous reminder that, despite the fact that the master never works, she "gives a sign, the master signifier, and everybody jumps" (2007:174). What is this sign, if not the variable capital extended by the agent of Capital in order to purchase the capacity of the worker to perform living labour, her labour-power, so that "Capital consumes the *use*-value of labour-power" (Spivak 1988: 161)? Accordingly, the split subject can now enter this regional sign-formation, the system of commodity exchange constituted by the *value of labour-power* (v_{LP}) extended by the capitalist Entrepreneur "who never works." In foregrounding the value of labour-power as the master signifier we are treating it as the privileged signifier that turns the system of market exchange, which preceded the historical emergence of capitalism, into a specifically capitalist mode of abstraction. In the place of S_2, we have once more the battery of all other exchange values that the subject gains access to in order to reproduce her capacity to perform living labour by purchasing a subset of them, given her wage rate. The value of labour-power has a very paradoxical function; on the one hand, it enables the subject to bridge the division of labour and reproduce her labour-power and, on the other hand, it enables the partitioning of the living labour performed by the worker into its necessary and surplus components, entailing her alienation from the surplus, namely, the exploitation of the subject.

$$\frac{V_{LP} \quad \rightarrow \quad V_{Other}}{\text{Exploited Subject}}$$

The institution of a regime of value requires a founding gesture of giving a sign, throwing a master signifier which would make everyone jump. The first of the four discourses, the discourse of the Master, formalizes precisely this constitutive act embodied in the organizing intervention of the master signifier in a given battery of signifiers (S_2). Yet, this network of signifiers, provisionally organized and made to do work by the master signifier (S_1), always ends up producing a remainder, an excess. This excess, an after-effect of the signification process, is nothing but a trace of a pre-supposed wholeness that is lost forever as a result of the splitting of the subject.

$$\frac{S_1 \rightarrow S_2}{\$ \; // \; a} \quad \frac{\text{agent} \quad \rightarrow \quad \text{other}}{\text{truth} \; // \; \text{product}}$$

Above the line, the relation between S_1, the dominant term occupying the position of *the agent* under the discourse of Master, and S_2, the battery of signifiers occupying the position of *the other*, is one of *impossibility*. As Lacan notes, "it is effectively impossible that there be a master who makes the entire world function" (2007: 174). Below the line, the relation between *the product* and *truth* is one of *impotence*: "Whatever the signs, whatever the master signifiers that come to be inscribed in the place of the agent, under no circumstances will production have a relationship to truth" (Lacan 2007: 174). The *impossibility* that structures the agent's relation to the other is linked with the *impotence* of conjoining the product with the truth of the agent. On the one hand, the (surplus) product qua excess marks the *impossibility* of the agent to fully master the other; on the other hand, the inadequacy of the (surplus) product to account for the truth of the agent, the barred subject, marks the relation of *impotence*.[8] Let us try to think through these relations of impossibility and impotence in the context of the capitalist mode of abstraction.

If "a fair day's wage for a fair day's labour" is an attempt to constitute a harmonious social division of labour through the authority of the master signifier (value of labour-power), it is one that is nonetheless bound to fail. On the one hand, there is an *impossible* communication between the value of labour-power and the world of commodities, where we can think of this impossibility as standing in for the irreconcilable relation of the subject to her needs. At the same time that the articulation of needs through the signifying chain S_1 and S_2 cuts the subject off from coinciding with some mythical pre-symbolic enjoyment, it also produces an unassimilable excess, a surplus product/surplus *jouissance*, i.e., *a* as product. The consequence is that needs are never that self-evident to be defined and fulfilled, and not because they are socially contingent, but rather because they are mediated through symbolic and imaginary demands which try to get at a bit of *jouissance*. Needs are in the first place derailed from any presumed course of biological survival since they are caught up in the formation of partial objects of the drive. Clearly, this impossibility that pertains to the opaqueness of needs is not unique to capitalist abstraction per se; indeed it holds for all regimes of abstraction. On the other hand, there is no conjoining of this product, the excess produced by the representational system of capitalist abstraction, with the truth of the exploited subject. A plausible translation of this statement would be the alienation of the exploited subject from the product of surplus value, the fruits of her labour. Nonetheless, to bring out the affective dimension of the psychoanalytical notion of alienation, and to distinguish it from a Marxian one, we locate in the place of product not an actual physical object, or even the quanta of (surplus) value appropriated by capitalist agents, but the uncanny presence of surplus *jouissance*. Approached this way, the consequence is not only a Marxian one which exposes the division of the total product into its necessary and surplus components, but more properly a psychoanalytical one which argues that the unification of the divided subject with the product of her labour is an idealization: There is no perfect organization of class whereby the subject masters the enjoyment, the "usufruct" (qua *jouissance*) of the property of surplus value she participates to produce (Lacan 1998: 3).

---

8   In the discourse of the Master, this inability of conjoining the product with the truth of the Master is rendered by the matheme of fantasy $S \lozenge a$. When Lacan claims that "the master's discourse excludes fantasy" (2007: 108), this is because the foundational gesture of the Master relies on the illusion of an identity of the *term* (the master signifier) with the *position* it occupies (that of the agent) (Žižek 1998: 76), the illusion that the Master is truly the agent of the discourse. Such an identity, however, is impossible.

Pushing forth the limits of the homology between Lacan's discourse of the Master and Marx's value-form brings about a result that applies more broadly than just to the institutions of capitalist abstraction: If the discourse of the Master is "the founding gesture of *every* social link" (Žižek 1998: 77; emphasis added), then the non-descriptivist, differentialist perspective of retroactive constitutivity can be deployed to make sense of *all* institutionalized practices of abstraction as regimes of signification, or, to use Karl Polanyi's (1944) term, as "forms of integration" that facilitate the distribution of "objects" at any given social scale, from a town using a (post-capitalist) local exchange trading system (LETS) to a trans-national (capitalist) economy using a common currency (e.g., euro). Given that impossibility marks the relation between the master signifier and the network of signifiers, a notion like "forms of integration" should be handled with care and with full recognition of the impossibility of instituting a "mode of distribution" that would enact a harmonious integration, a social synthesis that would cancel all the contradictory consequences of the different concrete forms of division of labour (between intellectual and manual labour, between the producers and appropriators of surplus labour, between genders, etc.).

In fact, following Marx's indications from the *Critique of the Gotha Program* (1966), we need to concede that, as long as society is organized through different forms of division of labour, there will always be a division between necessary and surplus labour; "the total social product" will always need to be "shared" by a non-all and socially negotiated list of deductions inclusive of, but not exclusive to, the remuneration of direct labourers.[9] What differentiates one social organization of division of labour from another is the nature of the institutional mechanisms and devices through which the decisions and measurements pertaining to how much to produce, what is necessary and what is surplus, how to distribute the surplus, and so on, are negotiated and struggled over. In other words, direct labourers are exploited in the Marxian sense not because abstraction forces them to produce a surplus product above and beyond what is socially deemed necessary for their reproduction, but because abstraction is organized by an exception which excludes them (as well as other stakeholders) from the appropriation of this surplus product. Therefore, given that (some forms of) abstraction are here to stay, a post-capitalist politics, rather than advocating an imaginary abolition of surplus, could strive to encircle the moment of appropriation and render visible and politicize the occluded (through political, cultural, ideological and legal discourses) social (class) antagonism. But, in and of itself, this post-capitalist agenda of "speaking truth to power" cannot be enacted without hitting the *Real*, the affective dimension of abstraction. We have turned our attention to the four discourses precisely in order to take this very dimension of affect into account. But, there too, before we proceed further, we need to identify certain historicist tendencies to grant Lacan's formalist turn the dignity it deserves.

---

9   For an extended discussion of the *Critique of the Gotha Program* in relation to Lacan's formulae of sexual difference, see Özselçuk and Madra (2005).

A Psychoanalytical Historicism of One Quarter-turn

Our reading of the discourse of the Master through the founding gesture of the commodification of labour-power is somewhat different from the more popular reading of this discourse derived from the dialectics of the Master and the Slave (or the Lord and Bondsman). According to the latter, which is rendered quite plausible by Lacan's own recurrent (albeit, on occasion sarcastic) references to Hegel, the Lord (or the Master) occupies the position of the agent, and the exploited Bondsman (or Slave), the position of the other. Here the truth of the Lord is that he too is a divided subject, a mere *träger* of the role of the master; he receives his status of master only because the slave grants him that status, "it is delivered to him by the work of the slave" (Lacan 2007: 79). While work here could be read in the sense of producing economic values, a proper psychoanalytical reading would supplement this with the sense of "doing the affective work" of reproducing the status of the Lord. Indeed Mladen Dolar, in an acute reading of the Master's discourse, argues that "the slave is enslaved by his own enjoyment, and not by the master's, he is paid off with bits of enjoyment, and the surplus enjoyment is what his work produces and what makes him work" (2006: 133). Even the puritan ethics of denouncing enjoyment in the name of work generates a surplus enjoyment as a by-product of this process of domination. This standard interpretation accounts for both the *impossibility* of a harmonious class relationship between the master and slave, the fact that we need to take into account the affective dimension to make sense of what makes the production of surplus labour to happen, and the *impotence* of the master "who, as usual, fails to understand anything about it [surplus *jouissance*] and what constitutes his truth" (Lacan 2007: 108). Nevertheless, this interpretation of the discourse of Master as a feudal relation, when combined with various passages in Lacan's text that refers to a *historical transition* from "the old masters" to "the new masters," lends itself too easily to a historicist reading of the four discourses. Let us take a closer look at this.

Lacan seems to identify early on in *Seminar XVII* a historical transition, roughly located in the late 1960s, from a society of prohibition, where "prohibition was observed, purely and simply" (Lacan 2007: 40) and a puritanistic renunciation of desire turned into a source of satisfaction (surplus *jouissance*), to a society of enjoyment, or "of permissiveness, where what can sometimes be the cause of difficulty is the prohibition on prohibiting" (Miller 2006: 12). While elsewhere Lacan speaks of "the persistence of a Master's discourse," he also indicates that "the present one does not have the structure of the old" (Lacan 2007: 31). In fact, throughout the *Seminar*, Lacan articulates a "capital mutation," a particular regressive quarter-turn from the discourse of Master, towards a University discourse, that gives it "its capitalist style" (168).

$$\frac{S_2 \rightarrow a}{S_1 \; / / \; \$}$$

In one of the more careful readings of the *Seminar*, Alenka Zupancic (2006), following the work of Todd McGowan (2004), develops a reading of the discourse of the University as a new configuration of the Master's discourse in a historical passage from a prohibitive order to that of a permissive one, where there are no impossibles, where everything is permitted and everything is possible.[10] In the old regime, repetition, necessitated by enjoyment structured around a constitutive hindrance, functioned as a symptom of "a fundamental impotence" regarding conjoining the (a) with master's truth ($\$$). In the new regime of "enjoyment without hindrance" nothing can be impossible—even *jouissance* ends up being accountable and accumulable ($S_2 \rightarrow a$). Let us explain how this regressive quarter turn towards the University discourse plays out in this reading. First, S_2 qua "complex signifying operation" (Zupancic 2006: 169) comes to occupy the position of the agent, not unlike, Zupancic notes, "value becoming the subject of the process" (170) in Marx's discussion of the self-valorization of capital. Standing for the value-form, S_2 turns living labour into an amassable and countable abstract labour, or in Zupancic's preferred terminology, "*pure* work" (through the commodification of labour-power). Hence, "surplus value [a] combines with capital [S_2]" in the "homogeneous [...] field of values" (Lacan 2007: 177–8). But this accumulation of valorized enjoyment, the rendering of every form of enjoyment into a safe-for-use commodity, into an enjoyment-without-enjoyment, is a colonizing process propelled by the fact that the plasticity of the drive always finds newer sources of satisfaction, until the subject is reduced to a pure negativity, into pure death drive (Zupancic 2006: 173).

While we do not disagree that these readings may describe certain affective economies in relation to capitalist abstraction, we question the *historicism* that structures the grand narrative of a historical passage from the society of prohibition to the society of enjoyment, as well as the *historicist usage* of the four discourses. Let us begin with our former concern. While Lacan does explicitly refer to the time of his writing as the moment when "this society called capitalist society can afford to allow itself a relaxation of the university discourse" (2007: 168), elsewhere he notes that, even in 1960, "we were a long way away—are we any closer? that's the question—from challenging authority" (40). Taken together these declarations indicate that he is speaking from within a historical conjuncture where the said transition from a prohibitive to a permissive capitalism is far from fully completed ("are we any closer?"). But, perhaps more importantly, elsewhere in the same *Seminar*, when Lacan refers to the transition from the "old" to the "new" discourse of the Master (qua the University discourse), he seems to be referring to the transition from feudalism to capitalism.

> Something changed in the master's discourse at a certain point in history. We are
> not going to break our backs finding out if it was because of Luther, or Calvin,
> or some unknown traffic of ships around Genoa, or in the Mediterranean Sea, or

---

10   See Yannis Stavrakakis (2012) for a critical extension of this argument where he argues for both "spirits" of prohibition and the commanded enjoyment to be simultaneously operative in the history of capitalism as well as in contemporary discourses on austerity and consumption-oriented credit push, in effect, "constituting a single functional system" (2305).

anywhere else, for the important point is that on a certain day surplus *jouissance* became calculable, could be counted, totalized. This is where the accumulation of capital begins (Lacan 2007: 177).

This conflation between these two different transitions (one *within* capitalism, the other *into* capitalism) is reproduced in Zupancic's discussion of the discourse of the University. When explaining the commodification of labour-power as a result of "the complex signifying operations" of the value-form $(S_2 \rightarrow a)$, she argues that "in itself and before that operation, pure work is never *pure* work, but is something closer to the slave's 'knowledge at work'" (2006: 169). In doing so, she theorizes the regressive quarter-turn from the Master's discourse (where the "concrete-labour" of the slave and the specific know-how associated with it is unattainable by the Master) to the "new" discourse of the University (where the unpaid portion of the "abstract-labour" performed by the direct labour combines with the capital) as the transition from the pre-capitalist modes of production (e.g., feudalism, slavery) to the capitalist mode of production, with labour-power as its defining commodity. So, we are tempted to ask, does the regressive quarter turn towards the University discourse refer to the transition from pre-capitalism to capitalism (i.e., the commodification of labour-power) or to the transition within capitalism (from the prohibitive to the permissive order)?

Radicalism of the Mathemes

Perhaps the problem lies in the historicist usage of the four discourses. Lacan, both in *Seminar XVII* and later on in *Seminar XX*, consistently tries to distance himself from the structural necessity of historicism associated with Hegel (Feltham 2006). At one point, he notes that his "little quadrupedal schemas [referring to four discourses] are not Ouija boards of history. It is not necessarily the case that things always happen this way, and that things rotate in the same direction" (Lacan 2007: 188). Or, elsewhere when he discusses Hegel's conception of history as "the succession of phases of dominance, of composition of the play of the mind," he notes that in Hegelian historicism the entire game is directed by "the cunning of reason" (170–71). And, in *Seminar 20*, Lacan notes that the four discourses are "not in any sense to be viewed as a series of historical emergences—the fact that one may have appeared longer ago than the others is not what is important here" (Lacan 1998: 16).

In fact, if one reads Lacan's commentary on four discourses and the rhythm with which he uses them, the anti-historicist, formalist tendency becomes even more accentuated. He likens the mathemes of the four discourses to "an apparatus ... a lever, as a pair of pliers, that can be screwed down, assembled in one way or another" (2007: 169). He insists that "these more or less little terms" of the four discourses "can be of use in a very large number of relations" if one becomes "accustomed to how to manipulate them" (188). For Lacan, the four discourses constitute a matrix, a structure that enables the analyst to make use "these manipulations of the signifier and its possible articulations" (45). Yet, this would be a very particular type of structure organized around the real: "In supposing the formalization of discourse [...] we encounter an element of impossibility" (45). In a number of places, when defining the real as the impossible, Lacan refers to the three impossible professions that Freud identified earlier: "governing, educating, and analyzing" (166). To these three impossible professions, Lacan adds "causing desire, so as to complete the series with a definition of what the hysteric's discourse might be" (173).[11]

These discourses are within history; yet none of them describes the shape of history, which is a non-all, heterogeneous field, as rich and diverse as the plasticity of the drive and the singularity of the objects of its satisfaction. In fact, the real as the impossible is the condition of possibility of historicity itself. The four discourses provide a conceptual matrix to analyze and strategically intervene into the articulated social structures that produce history through regulating and transforming relations to *jouissance*. Thus, it is possible to read them as a matrix of potential affective relations the subject can have towards the exact same signifier, the exact same "unary trait." In a brilliant reading of Hegel as the other side of psychoanalysis, Dolar (2006) does exactly this: He goes through the four different affective dispositions that Lacan entertained throughout *Seminar XVII* towards *Hegel, the unary trait*: Hegel, the Master; Hegel, the most sublime of Hysterics; Hegel, the Professor from Jena; and Hegel, the Impossible. If read in this manner, it becomes possible to conceptualize the four discourses as invariably co-existing in an articulated formation within any given institution, at any given moment in history.

With this insight, we can see the "quarter-turn regression" in the Master's discourse not necessarily as an epochal transition to the discourse of the University, but rather as the identification of a particular combination of "governing" and "educating" functions in the libidinal constitution of a capitalist social link at a given historical conjuncture. Having said this, Lacan's own dynamic deployment of "little quadrupedal schemas" gives us no reason to expect that the libidinal constitution of a capitalist social link will be exhausted by the articulation of these two discourses: at any given moment, the discourse of the hysteric may also come to entertain a dialectic tension with the other two.[12] Furthermore, the distance gained this way from the historicism of one quarter turn enables us "to authorize" not only the same

---

11   It may be useful to contrast these "professions" with Althusser's ideological state apparatuses: the Family, the School, the Church, the Army, and so on. Yet, Lacan's conceptual matrix differs from Althusser's approach in, at least, two fundamental ways. First, the four discourses, unlike the ideological dispositifs, take affect into account. Second, these "professions," because they describe the formal structures within/through which subjects relate to the signifying systems, regimes of abstractions, and so on, inhabit all institutional dispositifs, whether it is the schooling system, or the trade unions.

12   After making the point that the master/hysteric couple is "found throughout history" Collete Soler demonstrates the ways in which the discourse of the Hysteric is responsible for the "present state," that is, the state of the scientific-capitalist couple functioning as the discourse of the University (2002: 47).

historical moment with different configurations of tools, but also different historical moments with the exact same configurations of tools: Hence, Lacan's discussion of transitions to and within capitalism in relation to the discourse of the University.

As a final stab at the historicist-empiricist reading of the four discourses, let us note that the analytical discourse has a different relation to the other discourses. Lacan says in *Encore* that the analytical discourse emerges "whenever there is a movement from one discourse to another" (1998: 16). In this sense, it must be located simultaneously at the same level as the other three discourses as well as apart, since its function is to operate through dislocating them; that is, to force, through interpretation, the subject's production of new meanings (always linked to new forms of satisfaction) in place of her nonsensical *jouissance*, and, ultimately, the subject's production of a new master signifier. The analytical discourse has this dislocatory effect of the uncanny on the other discourses as much as it is able to force the split subject to take a position in relation to the real, the object cause of his desire, the void around which drive circulates ($a \rightarrow \$$). This dislocation is also the experience of love: "I am not saying anything else when I say that love is the sign that one is changing discourses" (16). But, if we do not want to fall into the trap of treating love here as a relation of complementarity between the analyst and the analysand, where the analyst gives the analysand the truth about her object *a*, we need to read Lacan's statement along with the one where he claims "to love is to give what you haven't got." The analyst is not the subject supposed to know; she cannot give the analysand *jouissance*. She is not the object cause of the subject's desire; rather, she occupies the *place* of her object cause of desire. Functioning as the screen that holds the place of the lost object, the analyst incites the analysand to produce symbolizations of her symptom and interprets them, not to proliferate them infinitely, but to reduce them in order to make the nothingness of being appear: "Interpretation is directed not so much at sense as towards reducing the signifiers to their non-sense, so that we may rediscover the determinants of the subject's entire behaviour" (Dolar 1998: 22, cf. Lacan 1986: 212; translation modified). Following this insight, it becomes even more important to read the four discourses as analytical tools that cause movement in the discursive-affective structures towards making nothingness pass into meaning. Lacan says that his "is only an appeal for you to locate yourselves in relation to what one can call radical functions, in the mathematical sense of the term" (2007: 188). When he invites us to practice a radicalism of the mathemes this way, we understand from this invitation that we need to approach his four discourses not as holding the key for the knowledge of history, but rather as strategic devices to disrupt all historical knowledge towards producing new meanings for the silently operating and overbearing affects that would transform the subject's relation to the world.

Affective Economies of Capitalist Abstraction: Anxiety, Guilt, Interpassivity

The severing of Lacan's four discourses from the grip of historicism enables us to deploy them towards delineating the different affective social links that operate in relation to capitalist abstraction—with the proviso that each social link is approached not as some stand alone unit that sits apart from others, but rather exists in a dialectical and dynamic relation to the rest, configuring the overdetermined historicity of capitalist abstraction. We have already established that the value of labour-power functions as the master signifier (S₁) given by the Master "to make everyone jump." In placing the value of labour-power in the position of the agent we have intentionally diverged from the traditional reading of the Master's discourse that carries the historical baggage of the master-slave dialectic and separate the personified master (in this case, the capitalist Entrepreneur) from the master signifier (S₁). Our aim has been to further formalize the Master discourse as a possible affective and constitutive relation to capitalist abstraction, by bringing it closer to the state of forced choice. That is, one can argue that the value of labour-power and all the other commodities for which it represents the (exploited) subject implies a forced choice—similar to the one Lacan expresses, "your money or your life"—between the "freedom" to sell one's labour-power or one's life. One might locate in this forced choice the truth of Marx's sharp criticism of bourgeois freedom that the subject is "free" in the double sense of the word: not only because she is free of her feudal obligations (so that she can sell her labour-power) but also because she is free from the means of production to procure her means of subsistence, such that she is compelled to sell her labour-power.

As much as the institution of the value of labour-power attempts to do away with *jouissance* through passing off an unambiguous communication between needs and desires, between individual and social reproduction, the discourse of the Master co-exists with the discourse of University that aims at valorizing *jouissance*. University discourse qua administrative-bureaucratic-expert apparatus is another social link to capitalist abstraction which, as Žižek (2006) reminds us, can take various guises such as (socialist) state institutions of planning, welfare state provisioning of public goods, neoliberal state's market-making devices, and so on. These apparatuses provide conditions of existence for an expanding world of lustrous commodities, or commodity-substitutes which occupy the place of the agent and address at the uncanny presence of enjoyment in order to turn it into some measurable and isolable account of what the individual needs and wants.[13] What is the nature of this uncanny presence of enjoyment that the University discourse attempts to domesticate? It is the feeling when the subject suddenly and directly encounters her *jouissance* as the object cause of her desire, manifesting

---

13   Nonetheless, it would be conferring too much agency to capitalist abstraction to reduce this attempt to transform *a* into marketable knowledge to an effect of capitalism. This attempt, we think, has always been part of what we can perhaps designate more broadly as the modern ambition, which is connected with various other social systems, including but certainly not limited to capitalism—such as the positivist scientific approach which places knowledge within the reach of our understanding, the colonial system that involves a will to unveil, affix and regulate Other's *jouissance*, or the utilitarian endeavor that attempts to make pleasure accountable and usable (Copjec 1994). The examples can indeed be multiplied.

in the paralyzing experience of anxiety. Copjec encapsulates the experience of anxiety with the concise description "riveted to being," which she explains as "[r]ather than simply and immediately being our being, coinciding with it, we are ineluctably fastened, stuck to it—or it to us" (2006: 100).[14]

Proceeding from Lacan's presentation of anxiety as the "'central affect' around which every social arrangement is organized; every social link is approachable as a response or transformation of anxiety" (Copjec 2006: 106), one can regard the organization of the network of signifiers by the plethora of capitalist commodities as a defence formation to mediate the experience of anxiety, the encounter with the alterity of the subject's *jouissance*. The signifying processes of capitalist value-form aim at anticipating and accounting for every possible mode of enjoyment by exhausting the social field with every possible choice that can be made. Even the value of labour-power, the commodity that defines capitalist exploitation, becomes something that the subject is supposed to be able to manipulate and refashion through her choices, as in the arguments of neoclassical human capital models where the subject is represented as an entrepreneur of himself, who produces her own value of labour-power, ultimately, as a means to produce her own satisfaction as a consumer (Foucault 2004: 226–7). In short, neoliberal capitalism demands that the subject "enjoys" her exploitation!

Hence, the psychoanalytical evaluation hits the mark when it points to the intensification of oppressiveness as we are increasingly called upon to perform the master, to be in control of our enjoyment. What is ironic about this intensification of oppression is that it produces what it aims to defend the subject from: the heightened feeling of anxiety experienced by the subject who is faced with an inflation of choices in the marketplace, in education, in health, in financial investments, and so on (Salecl 2011). Correcting the sociological explanation that relates the cause of anxiety to the *uncertainty* associated with the sheer abundance of choice, psychoanalytical insight instead argues that the availability of options, rather than baffling the subject regarding her true desire, puts into relief the *Real* cause of her enjoyment. The cause of anxiety in "the society of choice" is *not* not knowing how to make a choice among infinite alternatives, but the certainty of *jouissance* that becomes palpable and reins in the subject towards

---

14   Anxiety, different from fear, is "not without an object" (Lacan 2007: 147). There are two ways to think about the double negative in the "not without an object." On the one hand, it indicates that there is something that sticks out in the process of subject's integration in the socio-symbolic order, that some object *a* that cannot be fully integrated into the world of commodities always remains, something that incites anxiety crops up reminding the subject her rivetedness. On the other hand, the double negative can be interpreted as an attempt by Lacan to indicate the fact that this object *a* is not just like any object, it is at best a quasi-object which cannot be exhausted by the substitutable world of commodities. If, in the former sense, Lacan seems to be differentiating himself from the social constructivist reduction of the subject to subject positions within the social structure (underscoring an unassimilable residual that remains), in the latter sense, Lacan seems to be marking the distance between his notion of virtual object and the part objects of Kleinian object relations theory.

an inescapable choice. While anxiety is triggered neither by any random object, nor by the numerousness of objects, its precipitation is stimulated when the subject is continuously prompted to decide on the "right" enjoyment for herself. The subject's thoroughly inalienable yet alien libidinal attachment suddenly presents itself as she encounters an object among many that uncannily resembles to her object cause of desire (Salecl 2011; Copjec 2006).

If directly encountering the *Real* cause of desire is an unbearable experience, the feeling of guilt, referring to the subject's continuous inadequacy to herself in her attempts to make the "right choices," functions as a secondary formation of defence against anxiety. University discourse does not just court anxiety; as various scholars point out, it also transforms anxiety into guilt. Copjec succinctly depicts this process as the conversion of "a question of being," (i.e., the paralyzing state of being stuck to one's *jouissance* which raises a question for the subject) into a "problem of having—or, more precisely of having more" (Copjec 2006: 107). Does not this formulation precisely capture the Lacanian definition of biopolitics, not simply as the administration of life, but as the administration of enjoyment? The discourse of capitalist abstraction, through erecting ideals that argue for the malleability and perfectibility of the individual producer and consumer, bind us to attain goals that can never be attainable. It, thus, externalizes the inability to be at one with one's *jouissance*. Rather than being experienced as "being stuck to an inalienable alienness," *jouissance* is now experienced as an "inability to close the distance that separates us from something that excludes us" (Copjec 2009: 174). The contemporary problem of "having more" then does not merely refer to the capitalist interests for commodification, but rather to the paradoxical excess, the drive of guilt that pushes forth commodification. The more the subject obeys ideals, the more she is excluded from her enjoyment, and the more she tries to compensate for it through obeying. This guilt in fact can be so burdensome that it leads to a solution of *interpassivity* (Žižek 1997) where the subject delegates her enjoyment to fantasmatic others (successful entrepreneurs, financial risk-takers, celebrities of all sorts, fearless adventurers, and so on) who enjoys on her behalf, thus, releasing her to some extent not only from the anxiety of encountering her own *jouissance*, but also from the guilt of constantly facing the inadequacy of enjoyment.

Our reading of capitalist abstraction has identified an articulation of the Master's discourse with that of the University, mobilizing affects that range from the generation of anxiety to the transformation of it into guilt, potentially operating simultaneously. Yet the discussion so far has described an affective economy which appears all too subservient to the expanded reproduction of the political economy of capitalist abstraction (i.e., the accumulation of capital). If, all discourses are marked by both impossibility and impotence, how is it that these two discourses, representing respectively governing and educating, so successfully function, even in their failure, to reproduce capitalist accumulation? A short answer is that there is no necessity for this to be the case. But a longer answer has to be given on at least two levels, one of which relating to the complex and overdetermined articulation of discourse-affect analysis with that of class and value analysis, and the other relating to the other two discourses, that of the Hysteric and the Analyst within the rotational structure of four discourses.

In terms of the relation between the two fields, it is necessary to recognize that the complex articulations of the field of Marxian political economy are not reducible to the sale of labour-power and the realization of surplus value through the consumption of those who receive their so called "fair wage." Consider the 2008 financial collapse and the subsequent, on-going economic crisis. The economic collapse is the outcome of an unsustainable articulation of two distinct affective economies: on the one hand, a guilt-based consumption economy which posited a superegoic injunction to enjoy, causing subjects to consume beyond their means under the idealized notion of exceptional *jouissance*; on the other hand, another guilt-based production regime which posited the Entrepreneur (who receives something for nothing) as the unquestionable exception to the exchange of equivalents, as the fantasy frame under which exploited subjects work towards uncastrated, full *jouissance*, causing the rate of surplus appropriation and exploitation (i.e., the ratio of surplus value to the cost of labour) to reach unsustainable levels (Özselçuk and Madra 2010). A nearly three-decade-long suppression of real wages, combined with an increasing pressure on boosting mass consumption, created unsustainable levels of indebtedness, both public and private, in advanced capitalist formations. The articulation of these two particular affective economies of production and consumption ended up preparing the conditions of the most devastating economic collapse capitalist network has experienced since the Great Depression.

A Post-capitalist Turn

Nevertheless, there is yet another reason why the affective register does not smoothly reproduce capitalist abstraction, or any regime of abstraction for that manner. The two discourses and their multiple readings do not exhaust all the possible affective economies that are available in the field. In fact, the underside of the University discourse is the Hysteric's discourse where the exploited subjects question the adequacy of the value of labour-power ($\$\rightarrow S_1$), and claim that an injustice is being done.[15] Today, it is possible to read the Occupy movements all across advanced

---

15   For instance, during the Great Depression, the Roosevelt Administration moved to a more convincingly populist position only later, during the so-called "Second New Deal," as a result of increasing labour militancy demanding higher wages, better working hours, and so on (Piven 2010). Without doubt, the institutional constellation, composed of, with different configurations and balances of power, the State, the Law, the Corporation, the University, and so on, failed (and will always fail) to adequately address the truth of the exploited subject ($a//S_2$) even while producing a *battery* of public goods such as free education, health care, child care; institutional mechanisms such as wage negotiation boards, farmer subsidy and support programs, public works programs; and welfare programs such as unemployment benefits and social security.

capitalist formations in part as a performance of the Hysteric's discourse and in part as an enactment of the Analytical discourse. One of the many operations that they are undertaking is to announce the fraud at the heart of capitalist abstraction, the inconceivably unjust distribution of wealth between the top 1 percent and the overworked (higher productivity), underpaid (lower real wages), and indebted (financialization) 99 percent. They also declare that the promised world of wealth and prosperity is a fraud because the economic growth which is necessary for it has as its "externality" the destruction of Earth itself. And yet they also register that the betterment of the value of labour-power as a result of higher wages, cheaper commodities, or even wider availability of public goods and services cannot address the partitioning of the social product between what is necessary and what is surplus at a fundamental level; it can only ameliorate the imbalance between the 99 percent who either produces or helps the production of the social product the 1 percent appropriates.

However, the hysteric's exposure of the fraud of satisfaction can go one of two ways. In so far as the discourse of the Hysteric calls upon a "more masterful" master signifier that would better measure up to what it promises, it continues to reinstitute economic ideals that will only produce more dissatisfaction.[16] To the extent that the discourse of the Hysteric begins to shift from questioning the inadequacy of the authority of capitalist abstraction towards encircling the lack of any legitimate ground for satisfaction, for a harmonious organization of the production and distribution of economic values, it moves in a progressive direction (in the analytical sense). The object a begins to rotate forward from the place of the truth to the position of the agent, facing the split subject as the Analytical discourse sets about to form. This shift, this rotation describes the analytical practice of the talking cure, which begins by hystericizing the analysand, so that she starts to question—until the accumulating signifiers reach a certain critical threshold where the quantitative changes, in a manner that causes surprise in the subject, lead to a qualitative shift at the affective level. Whenever this affective shift happens, the Occupy movements will change tracks from an anti-capitalist to a post-capitalist politics.

$$\uparrow \frac{S_1 \rightarrow S_2}{\$ \; // \; a} \downarrow \quad \uparrow \frac{\$ \rightarrow S_1}{a \; // \; S_2} \downarrow \quad \uparrow \frac{a \rightarrow \$}{S_2 \; // \; S_1} \downarrow$$

These two tendencies within Occupy movements find expression in the dual meaning of the word, occupation, which Maliha Safri (2012) notes as "to take up the space and to do work." The first meaning, as embodied in the declaration "Occupy Wall Street!" and the very *physical act of taking up the space* marks the

---

16　See for instance a recent video which puts into question the present wealth inequality in US http://www.youtube.com/watch?v=QPKKQnijnsM. While the video powerfully demonstrates the dismal failure of the promise of American Dream in terms of a fair distribution of wealth by showing the extremely large gap between the existing distribution and the popular ideal of what it should be, it nonetheless erects yet another ideal of what wealth distribution should be like in capitalism. For the research underlining the video, see Norton and Ariely (2011).

fraud of capitalist abstraction in a bodily manner. We see this as the necessary moment of hystericization in the analytical rotation. The second meaning, which refers to *the creation of a space through doing work* marks, for us, the post-capitalist moment of the Occupy movements. Once engaged in an analytical rotation, the Occupy movements begin to create a (sublimated) public space where difficult questions about who is, what and how to produce and distribute values are debated and navigated. In practicing politics, economics and communication they adhere to a set of principles of conduct that emphasize horizontality, collaboration and equity at each turn of decision. The question of who is to produce attends not only the tensions and negotiations between the occupiers, the homeless, and the visitors but also the "intellectual difference" in the organization of the division of labour between the "'political' work of running meetings" and the "manual" work of providing for welfare infrastructures (Herring and Glück 2011; Dowling et al. 2012). The question of what to produce has generated the *in vivo* experiment of working committees (such as kitchen, library, education and empowerment, facilitation, press, comfort, technology, and janitorial) as self-organized institutions of welfare and care that address the immediate manifestations on the very ground of occupation of a wider crisis of social reproduction of capitalism (Safri 2012). And the question of how to produce has forced to negotiate the tensions pertaining to the politics of representation (e.g., between centralized versus de-centralized decision making structures) and the redistribution of abilities through job rotation and active participation.

Safri argues that in "doing work" the Occupy movements demonstrate "how society can and does organize partial production and distribution of goods and services outside market mechanisms." We witness that this partiality is often banalized, at best, as an insignificant localized alternative; at worst, as a misguided distraction from the real struggle against the structural power of capitalist abstraction. These views suffer from, among other things, reading the Occupy movements literally—restricting them to particular representations, particular productions, and particular places. In doing so, such views misrecognize how the Occupy movements operate metaphorically, as cathected representatives of different ways of organizing the economy, instituted at the empty place of power otherwise occupied by capitalist abstraction. In fact, if it were not for the metaphoric surplus of Occupy, how else would we make sense of the appearance of so many Occupy movements? It is this affective investment which estranges occupation from its literal coordinates and makes it move as a partial model that travels across many different scales and sites.

References

Althusser, Louis, and Balibar, Étienne (1997) [1970] *Reading Capital* (trans. B. Brewster). London and New York: Verso.

———— (2006) *Philosophy of the Encounter. Later Writings, 1978–1987* (eds. F. Matheron and O. Corpet, trans. and intro. G. M. Goshgarian). London and New York: Verso.

Arthur, Chris (1993) "Hegel's Logic and Marx's Capital," in *Marx's Method in Capital: A Reexamination*, ed. F. Moseley (Atlantic Highlands N.J.: Humanities Press) pp. 63–87.

Copjec, Joan (1994) *Read My Desire: Lacan against the Historicists*. Cambridge, MA: The MIT Press.

———— (2002) *Imagine There's No Woman. Ethics and Sublimation*. Cambridge, MA: The MIT Press.

———— (2006) "May '68, the Emotional Month," in *Lacan: The Silent Partners*, ed. S. Žižek (London and New York: Verso) pp. 90–114.

———— (2009) "The Censorship of Interiority," *Umbr(a)*, Islam pp. 165–86.

Dolar, Mladen (1998) "Cogito as the Subject of the Unconscious," in *Cogito and the Unconscious Sic 2*, ed. S. Žižek (Durham and London: Duke University Press) pp. 11–40.

———— (2006) "Hegel as the Other Side of Psychoanalysis," in *Reflections on Seminar XVII. Jacques Lacan and the Other Side of Psychoanalysis Sic 6*, eds. J. Clemens and R. Grigg (Durham and London: Duke University Press) pp. 129–54.

Dowling, Emma; Feigenbaum, Anna; Pell, Susan; and Stanley, Katherine (2012) "Occupy London" *SAQ* 111 (3), pp. 608–15.

Feltham, Oliver (2006) "Enjoy Your Stay: Structural Change in *Seminar XVII*," in *Reflections on Seminar XVII. Jacques Lacan and the Other Side of Psychoanalysis Sic 6* (eds. J. Clemens and R. Grigg). Durham and London: Duke University Press), pp. 179–94.

Foucault, Michel (2008) *The Birth of Biopolitics. Lectures at the College de France, 1978–79* (ed. M. Senellart, trans. G. Burchell). Basingstoke: Palgrave Macmillan.

Grigg, Russell (2008) *Lacan, Language, and Philosophy*. Albany: State University of New York Press.

Goux, Jean-Joseph (1990) *Symbolic Economies: After Marx and Freud* (trans. J. C. Gage). Ithaca, NY: Cornell University Press.

Herring, Christopher and Glück, Zoltan (2011) "The Homeless Question," in *Occupy! Scenes From Occupied America*, eds. A. Taylor, K. Gessen, and editors from *n+1, Dissent, Triple Canopy* and *The New Inquiry* (London and New York: Verso).

Kordela, Kiarina (2006) "Capital: At Least It Kills Time," *Rethinking Marxism* 18 (4), pp. 539–63.

Lacan, Jacques (1986) *The Four Fundamental Concepts of Psycho-analysis* (ed. J. A. Miller; trans. A. Sheridan). London: Penguin.

——— (1996) "On Freud's '*Trieb*' and the Psychoanalyst's Desire," in *Reading Seminars I and II. Lacan's Return to Freud*, eds. R. Feldstein, B. Fink, and M. Jaanus (Albany: State University of New York).

——— (1998) *On Feminine Sexuality, the Limits of Love and Knowledge: The Seminar of Jacques Lacan Book xx, Encore 1972–1973* (ed. J. A. Miller; trans. (with notes by) B. Fink). New York and London: W. W. Norton & Company.

——— (2007) *The Other Side of Psychoanalysis Book: The Seminar of Jacques Lacan xvii* (ed. J. A. Miller; trans (with notes by) R. Grigg). New York and London: W. W. Norton & Company.

Laclau, Ernesto (2005) *On Populist Reason*. London and New York: Verso.

Marx, Karl (1966) [1875] *Critique of the Gotha Programme*. New York: International Publishers.

——— (1990) [1976] *Capital. A Critique of Political Economy. Vol. 1* (trans. B. Fowkes) London: Penguin Books.

McGowan, Todd (2004) *The End of Dissatisfaction? Jacques Lacan and the Emerging Society of Enjoyment*. Albany: SUNY Press.

Miller, Jacques-Alain (2006) "On Shame," in *Reflections on Seminar XVII. Jacques Lacan and the Other Side of Psychoanalysis Sic 6*, eds. J. Clemens and R. Grigg (Durham and London: Duke University Press), pp. 11–28.

Norton, Michael I. and Ariely, Dan (2011) "Building a Better America–One Wealth Quintile at a Time," in *Perspectives on Psychological Science* 6 (9), pp. 9–12.

Özselçuk, Ceren and Madra, Yahya M. (2005) "Psychoanalysis and Marxism. From Capitalist-All to Communist Non-All," *Psychoanalysis, Culture & Society* 10, pp. 79–97.

——— (2010) "Enjoyment as An Economic Factor: Reading Marx with Lacan" *Subjectivity* 3 (3), pp. 323–47.

Piven, Frances Fox (2010) "An Era of Crisis and Struggle," *Socialist Worker* Website, July 29. http://socialistworker.org/2010/07/29/era-of-crisis-and-struggle.

Polanyi, Karl (2001 [1944]). *The Great Transformation: The Political and Economic Origins of Our Time* (foreword by J. Stiglitz and introduction by F. Block). Boston: Beacon Press.

Resnick, Stephen A. and Wolff, Richard D. (1987) *Knowledge and Class. A Marxian Critique of Political Economy*. Chicago and London: The University of Chicago Press.

Roberts, Bruce (1996) "The Visible and the Measurable: Althusser and the Marxian Theory of Value," in *Postmodern Materialism and the Future of Marxist Theory. Essays in the Althusserian Tradition*, eds. A. Callari and D. F. Ruccio (Hanover and London: Wesleyan University Press) pp. 193–211.

Safri, Maliha (2012) "The Economics of Occupation," *The Economists' Voice* http://www.degruyter.com/view/j/ev.

Salecl, Renata (2011) *The Tyranny of Choice*. London: Profile Books.

Sohn-Rethel, Alfred (1983) [1978] *Intellectual and Manual Labor. A Critique of Epistemology*. Atlantic Highlands, NJ: Humanities Press.

Soler, Colette (2002) "Hysteria in Scientific Discourse," in *Reading Seminar XX. Lacan's Major Work on Love, Knowledge, and Feminine Sexuality*, eds. S. Bernard and B. Fink (Albany: State University of New York Press) pp. 47–55.

Spivak, Gayatri C. (1988) [1985] "Scattered Speculations on the Question of Value," in *In Other Worlds. Essays in Cultural Politics* (New York and London: Routledge) pp. 154–75.

Stavrakakis, Yannis (2012) "Beyond the Spirits of Capitalism? Prohibition, Enjoyment, and Social Change," *Cordozo Law Review* 33 (6), pp. 2289–2306.

Toscano, Alberto (2008a) "The Open Secret of Real Abstraction," *Rethinking Marxism* 20 (2), pp. 273–87.

——— (2008b) "The Culture of Abstraction," *Theory, Culture & Society* 25 (4), pp. 57–75.

Verhaeghe, Paul (2006) "Enjoyment and Impossibility: Lacan's Revision of the Oedipus Complex," in *Reflections on Seminar XVII. Jacques Lacan and the Other Side of Psychoanalysis Sic 6*, eds. J. Clemens and R. Grigg (Durham and London: Duke University Press) pp. 29–68.

Žižek, Slavoj (1989) *The Sublime Object of Ideology*. London and New York: Verso.

——— (1997) "The Supposed Subjects of Ideology," *Critical Quarterly* 39 (2), pp. 39–59.

——— (1998) "Four Discourses, Four Subjects," in *Cogito and the Unconscious Sic 2*, ed. S. Žižek (Durham and London: Duke University Press) pp. 74–116.

——— (2006) *"Objet a* in Social Links," in *Reflections on Seminar XVII. Jacques Lacan and the Other Side of Psychoanalysis Sic 6*, eds. J. Clemens and R. Grigg (Durham and London: Duke University Press) pp. 107–28.

Zupancic, Alenka (2000) *Ethics of the Real. Kant, Lacan*. London and New York: Verso.

——— (2006) "When Surplus Enjoyment Meets Surplus Value," in *Reflections on Seminar XVII. Jacques Lacan and the Other Side of Psychoanalysis Sic 6*, eds. J. Clemens and R. Grigg (Durham and London: Duke University Press) pp. 155–78.

Chapter 8

Ocean Doesn't Live Here Anymore: Steven Soderbergh's *Contagion* and the Stock Market Crash

Marco Grosoli

Albeit no longer occupying a central place in terms of cultural hegemony, as a mass industry cinema still manages to capture significant reverberations of social events. The 2008 stock market crash has already left abundant traces in mainstream Hollywood and televisual productions—to name but a few: *Up in the Air* (Jason Reitman, 2009), *Capitalism: A Love Story* (Michael Moore, 2009), *Too Big to Fail* (Curtis Hanson, 2011).

It is by no means surprising that Steven Soderbergh has dedicated considerable efforts lately to this topic. His third film (*King of the Hill*, 1993) was already a rather crude depiction of the post-1929 crisis; many of the works by the director of *Che* (2008), while remaining unproblematic pieces of mainstream entertainment, underline their economic contexts very explicitly (for instance, the marginality of industrial production in recent times was, in quite different senses, at the core of both *Out of Sight*, 1998, and *Bubble*, 2005). *The Girlfriend Experience* (2009), *The Informant!* (2009) and especially *Contagion* (2011) all directly relate to 2008 economic crisis and its consequences.

This chapter closely analyzes *Contagion* (2011) as an allegory of the crisis of finance capital, and of the global consequences thereof. My approach substantially relies on the "positive hermeneutic" famously developed by Fredric Jameson; in other words, my aim is to spot through formal analysis the implicit utopian inputs lying under the ideological dystopia in the narrative—hopefully as a token of what can still be detected in mainstream movies in terms of "political unconscious," even in today's relatively marginalized Hollywood.

The Casino Metaphor

Although this will not be an auteurist reading, a brief summary of Soderbergh's *Traffic* (2000) and *Ocean's Eleven, Twelve* and *Thirteen* (2001, 2004, 2007) will prove indispensable as my argument goes on.

The former is a drama composed of four intersecting stories that variously revolve around drug trade between the United States and Mexico: a patent allegory for globalization and the new dynamics it sets in place (Baker 2011: 18–19). The common theme uniting all four stories is arguably the necessity to question, rethink and ultimately blur the borders between the public and the private, especially in the cases of the two "heroes": Ohio State Supreme Court Justice Robert Wakefield, appointed by the president as the anti-drug czar, neglecting his own addicted daughter but eventually getting back in touch with her, and the Mexican cop, who asks for the construction of a well-lit baseball field to keep Mexican children out of the streets as the reward for his dangerous work as an infiltrator to reveal the large-scale complicity between dealers and local police—a task that demanded the difficult sacrifice of his own best friend and colleague. What is most interesting is that *Traffic* is (in his own words) Soderbergh's "45 million dollar Dogme movie": (Baker 2011: 74)[1] he used "handheld camera, available light, and the appearance of improvisational performance" (19) to enhance a shaky, ultra-realist appeal. But the film is also peculiarly marked by yellowish and bluish tints violently characterizing the Mexican (the former) and Ohio (the latter) sequences. The symbolic implications of this choice are clear: the seemingly shapeless camera work suggests that under globalization, laws and rules increasingly lose their relevance in favor of the immoral almightiness of Exchange. Yet the geographical use of color suggests an *abstract spatiality* as the ultimate Law of globalization—an abstract principle somehow opening up the space even for moral distinctions and ethical choices, as in the case of the judge and of the Mexican cop.

As for the *Ocean's* heist trilogy, the reader should refer to "Competing Modes of Capital in *Ocean's Eleven*" (Tait 2010), a very convincing analysis of the first episode (as well as, somewhat marginally, of the other two) by R. Colin Tait. Two aspects will be considered here. The first is that the gang Danny Ocean pulls together each time in order to rob Las Vegas casinos allegorizes the utopian impulse to counter inhuman present-day corporate global capital with another form of capitalism belonging to the past. Indeed, the fact that this band is made of a dozen or so males, each bound to his own professional specialty, and whose collective cooperation depends on a strict organization and coordination of time, unmistakably reminds us of the notion of *Fordism*. The point is that Jameson's "positive hermeneutic" as applied by Tait in his essay, the analytic detection of the utopian underside of ideology, matches the film so closely that it would not be so preposterous to assume Soderbergh's explicit intention in this respect. The second aspect is that, corporate global capital being the enemy, and in particular its late vertiginous financial turn sweeping the last vestiges of Fordism away (see Baker 2011: 21–2), it is easy to infer that casino gambling essentially stands for stock market speculation, although Tait never directly states so. The trilogy achieves its end in 2007; one year later, the stock market crash would eventually compel any allegorical account of financial speculation to drastically change its scope—as *Contagion* effectively does.

---

1   In 1995, director Lars von Trier and a few others signed "Dogme 95," a manifesto advocating a series of shooting rules and procedures supposedly guaranteeing an effect of flagrancy and authenticity to the filmed images.

Conspiracy? No, Thanks

Contagion tells of an epidemic disease suddenly spreading worldwide, and killing millions of people, as reflected through various individual narratives. Among the main characters are: Beth Emhoff (the patient zero, who caught the disease during a business trip in Hong Kong) and his husband Mitch, trying to protect himself and his daughter after the death of both his wife and son; Dr. Cheever and Dr. Mears at the US Center for Disease Control (CDC) trying to limit the diffusion; Alan Krumwiede, a blogger sensitizing the public awareness of the fact that health institutions are concealing important issues (namely a working vaccine, named Forsythia, which Alan successfully tests on himself); Dr. Orantes of the World Health Organization, who is sent to China to inspect the origins of the disease and is abducted by some villagers who want the vaccine straight away.

There can be very little doubt about whether the epidemic stands for the stock market crash—notoriously triggering a chain reaction potentially dragging the whole world into a very deep economic crisis. A number of signs point at that. Zero-patient Beth contracts the illness in a *casino*, already an allegory for stock market speculation in the *Ocean's* trilogy. She got it while playing a game she could not handle properly ("I have no idea what's going on, but it's fun!"), very much pointing at the way detached-housed middle class members like Beth and Mitch have "played with fire" with credit (that is, with subprime loans) without being aware of the size of its danger, but being the first to receive the negative effect of economic chain reaction. The first form of contagion in the very first scene takes place when she passes a *credit card* to a casino worker. Another man is infected by her blowing on a chip. The virus has been engendered when a pig ate a piece of food infected by a bat, consequently tainting pig meat, invoking two of the most widespread insulting metaphorical epithets designating generic capitalists, the "vampire" and the "pig." State authorities are initially reluctant to spread the news since they are afraid this might affect the forthcoming shopping weekend; and when later in the film a character lists the places that will get assaulted in the wake of general paranoia, the first he mentions are banks.[2]

Indeed, this issue is particularly relevant, in that it indicates that the epidemic is directly influenced by the general perception thereof. The more the panic concerning the disease, the easier it will spread—pretty much like the basic dynamic of financial speculation according to common sense: the more it looks like getting worse, the more it will, while the more trust is given to the stock

---

2   A brief dialogue utterly devoid of narrative relevance provides a kind of "negative proof" of the fact that the immediate symbolic referent of the epidemic has to be economic. Dr. Cheever firmly rejects the hypothesis that terrorists might be behind it all: the main reason for paranoiac mass mobilization in the decade prior to 2008 being discarded, the one coming *after* that is then indirectly but rather safely assumed. In other words, the film overtly tells us that it is *not* a matter of terrorism: thus, it *has* to be the economy, the other great worry having followed terrorism in the U. S. agenda lately.

markets, the more they are likely to rise again. Hence *Contagion*'s recurrent visual leitmotif, an out of focus master shot with a fully focused small camera on one side recording what we barely see in the background: the crisis and its perception are mutually connected.

This is why *Contagion* extensively deals with the fight over the extent to which information should be rendered public: the CDC versus Alan, the blogger who accuses drug companies of spreading the virus, to ration and delay the already-known vaccine in order to make profit out of it, with the complicity of governmental organizations. Arguably the most ambiguous figure of the film, Alan is almost always wrong. The vaccine the government spreads, which Alan supposes to be just an experiment, proves to be ultimately effective. Forsythia, his own supposed actual vaccine, proves to be a fraud. Governmental organizations have truly no role in the spreading of the virus. Yet, he is *once* right, when he accuses Dr. Cheever on a live television debate of having let his own relatives know about the secure places to go before the official public announcement. The pressure on CDC will prove crucial, since the resolving vaccine is *not* discovered within the organization, but rather by an unofficially outsourced maverick doctor (Dr. Sussmann), and by Dr. Ally Hextall, who is the "bridge" connecting the organization and Sussmann even when the former orders (in vain) the latter to stop his research. So while Alan is wrong on any other side, he is right in pressuring the CDC, because only when the former lowers its defenses is the vaccine discovered.

Alan is thus neither a positive nor a negative character. The point is elsewhere. Alan is the spot where *the film's allegory is inscribed into the film itself.* In *The Geopolitical Aesthetic*, Jameson (1992) has shown that the conspiracy plot is inherently allegorical, in that it strives for a totalization that can never be achieved. Allegory stands precisely for a structurally failed totalization of meaning (Jameson 1991: 167–8). Alan is a self-proclaimed conspiracy theorist who sees drug companies at the very top of a conspiracy haunting the world. But the place that guarantees the closure of the effort to totalize *must remain empty*: drug companies are ultimately not guilty, they are not responsible for what is happening, so it is useless to make them into the ultimate scapegoat. He is very right though as *an instigator of tension*. In other words, as Jameson might put it, the allegory fails when it posits the closure of its totalization as a definite *content*: it just falls into ideology. On the contrary, this striving for totalization is actually utopian when it is a matter of *form*—that is, when it is no more than a formal antagonism (Jameson 1981: 71–89). Similarly, the film itself can be understood as an allegory of economic world crisis precisely insofar as the virus is *not* a *symbol* of the stock market crash. Although it inescapably stands for the chain effect of economic collapse, it is not *simply* that. Later on, my paper will explain why the attribution of the meaning of the virus is ambiguous and not one-way, as such implying the ambiguity pertaining to allegory proper instead of symbol (see Jameson 1991: 167–8). For the moment, it is enough to point out that the film discards the approach of the films by Michael Moore, or of the documentaries regarding the crisis (like *Inside Job*, Charles Ferguson, 2010). It is not a matter of explaining a mechanism people ignore, of individuating the ones responsible and of blaming them publicly. It is not a matter of pointing at banks' greed, who handle world debt in order to make profits from it, just as the drug companies accused by Alan do with diseases. The issue is *structural*, and we should resist the populist temptation to personify it. The properly utopian/allegorical approach would rather consist of establishing a *tension* between the (structurally unattainable) revelation of truth and its own ideological mask. What is the place for this "ideological mask" in *Contagion*? To answer this question, first of all one must bear in mind that in representation, "never more so than in the present age of a multinational global corporate network," it is a question "of social totality itself"; in our global world, narrative more often than not "conflates ontology with geography" (Jameson 1992: 4). The main topic of *Contagion* is very much a world reunited under the aegis of the same crisis burning everywhere, so it inevitably involves the representation of social totality. Jameson repeatedly stresses the eminently *spatial* or geographical nature of conspiracy plots, as a direct emanation of our global asset (see Jameson 1992: 9–85). If one accepts to regard this world epidemic as the ultimate conspiracy, for it is faceless, acephalous, unintentional and viral, unlike the simply anthropomorphic conspiratorial plots imagined by Alan, then the film's attempt to represent social totality must inevitably be a spatial/geographical one. Narration constantly, rapidly shifts from one place to the other; it "endlessly processes images of the unmappable system" (Jameson 1992: 4) much more so than in *Traffic*. Indeed, in that other Soderbergh tale about globalization, the narrative alternation between the four stories was rather traditional, whereas here the collective, dispersed, fragmented and manifold nature of narrative structure is much more uneven and irregular: a number of characters are abandoned in the way (Sussmann) or introduced very late (Cheever's wife), or die unexpectedly in the middle of their narrative arc (Mears). It thus looks like globalization is even less mappable than before, entering a terminal phase where totality is even farther from representability than in the times of *Traffic*.

This "impossible mapping" of a geographic kind is what the film declares to pursue from the very beginning: the second scene shows the first symptoms of contagion in Hong Kong, London, Tokyo, Minnesota. However, the point is that this promise of a global kind of representation will *not* be maintained. The action basically takes place entirely in the US—and although it is the World Health Organization that spots the origin of the virus, it is the US alone that finds the vaccine.

A Utopian Rethinking of the Public and the Private

Shall we conclude that *Contagion* is a blatant ideological nostalgia for the centrality of the United States in a time where its geopolitical supremacy is increasingly questioned, first of all because of economic uncertainties? In a way, this is certainly true: the vaccine injected in the end all over the world so that everything could be restored exactly the way it used to be, without any structural change, cannot but recall the hundreds of billions of dollars the Federal Reserve has injected into the credit system after 2008 to convince everyone that the old financial game could go on exactly like before the crash—an ideological claim if ever there was one. However, like for the *Ocean's* trilogy, it is certainly possible to "argue the proposition that the effectively ideological is also, at the same time, necessarily Utopian" (Jameson 1981: 276): not only must one detect ideological impulses, but "also seek, through and beyond this demonstration of the instrumental function of a given cultural object, to project its simultaneously Utopian power as the symbolic affirmation of a specific historical and class form of collective unity" (281). In order to do so, one must typically rely on the inconsistencies of a given text. There is one single story sticking out of *Contagion*'s "US hegemony." It is the story of Dr. Orantes, who flies to China and is eventually kidnapped by some Chinese villagers. Once she gets freed, and as soon as she learns that her WHO bosses have delivered placebos instead of the actual vaccine to the villagers, she chooses to come back to the village to make sure the local population get it instead of going back to WHO headquarters in Geneva. As such, she is a sort of linking figure between the local and the global, between the reality of "Main Street" and the abstraction of "Wall Street" finance capital. The palpable implausibility and irresoluteness of this isolated and quite pointless episode indicate that the resolution of these binary oppositions, the stabilization of these polar tensions, can only occur elsewhere in the text, namely through something that does not oppose these two poles in such a naively frontal way as "Dr. Orantes's choice" does. In other words, this part is a symptom of contradictions whose resolution is precisely the task of the larger US-based part of *Contagion*. In this respect, the centrality of the US here is not only an ideological burden, but also an active utopian plea for a mediation between the local and the global, and between "Wall Street" and "Main Street," *of a State kind*—what evidently lacked in the Chinese segment. The utopian point would thus be less the US than *State as such*; in effect, the discovery and the widespread distribution of the cure wholly revolve around the CDC. Some kind of State regulation is decidedly wished for: no wonder the Dogme-like shapelessness of *Traffic*, dating back to earlier and less critical stage of globalization, is replaced by a much stiffer visual asset.

After all, Jameson himself considered the State the ultimate example of a Janus-faced ideological/utopian entity (see Jameson 1981: 287–8). He gets back to the ideological/utopian couple some years later in *Archaeologies of the Future*, a study on literary science fiction and the utopian impulses therein—and once again the State is at the core of a possible new utopian concept of collectivity. More precisely, Jameson argues that the point is not so much the utopian content of some narrative, which is as such viable to fall into ideology, but rather the utopian imagination one can detect in its form, most notably in "their [that is, of the themes of the utopian content] function to demystify their opposite numbers" (Jameson 2005: 211). In other words, the utopian imagination of a new collectivity can be formulated "not by spurious syntheses or the ironic superposition of our opposites, but rather by going all the way through that contradictory content and emerging on the other side" (179). In our film, the Chinese episode stands precisely for such a false conflation of the opposites claiming for a form of collectivity that escapes it: something neither local nor global, neither sustaining "Main Street" nor "Wall Street." Such entity is again the State: Jameson (2005: 218–25) explicitly mentions *federalism* as a possible utopian way to come to terms with centralization and dispersion, obviously the main binary couple of our globalized times. Quite tellingly, the United States depicted in the film, while bearing absolutely no trace of nationalism whatsoever, are much less the site for heroic governmental centralized decisions than *a federation*, a set of states (Minnesota, Georgia, California, Illinois and a few others) that the film ceaselessly jumps between. So what is stressed is not so much the US as such, but rather the genuine federation they (according to Jameson [2005: 224]) have never really been: their utopian potential more than any ideological affirmation.

Nevertheless, Jameson (2005: 231–2) admits that the federalist model as such is far from enough to imagine a new utopian collective entity: what is first of all needed is the disruption of our seemingly eternal present.

> For it is the very principle of the radical break as such, its possibility, which is reinforced by the Utopian form, which insists that its radical difference is possible and that a break is necessary. The Utopian form itself is the answer to the universal ideological conviction that no alternative is possible, that there is no alternative to the system. But it asserts this by forcing us to think the break itself, and not by offering a more traditional picture of what things would be like after the break.

Contagion is evidently a dystopian narrative; since dystopia is "a negative cousin of the Utopia proper" (Jameson 2005: 198), its content is equally ideological, and expresses the faith that a little help (the Federal Reserve injection) can restore a pre-crisis state with regard to which no real alternatives are really needed. However, *within* this content lies a disruptive potential that must be detected and acknowledged as what specifies the otherwise too generic notion of State-as-regulator that the film also seems to suggest. In other words, *Contagion* "unconsciously" imagines underneath its ideological content a different collectivity—not by overtly illustrating it (which would fall again into ideology) but rather by forcing us to think a collective entity being able to keep together the State and *a radical rethinking of the relationship between the Public and the Private.*

CDC is here the (capitalist) State-as-we-know-it. It is first of all the guardian of individual freedom, at the price of keeping separated the Public and the Private. "Our best defense is social distance," says Dr. Cheever. According to this approach, the contagion is avoided simply by keeping people separated. This scheme is however highly insufficient, as epitomized by the one who is effectively in charge of this, that is Dr. Mears, who rapidly gets infected and dies. Significantly, Dr. Mears refused all along the friendly care of a recently-met Minnesota colleague. Isolation is thus not the answer. It is easy to spot the related post-2008 analogies here. The current crisis in Europe has primarily to do with the disparities between the low-rated debt of richer countries (such as Germany, Finland, the Netherlands, Austria) and the worryingly high one of Greece, Italy, Spain and a few others: the lack of any concrete will to break the countries' isolation has so far only rendered the crisis worse and worse.

Secondly, CDC embodies the tendency of the contemporary State to passively adhere to the perpetual "homeopathic" self-change of late capitalism, its capacity to engulf in itself any possible radical change or heterogeneity. In the film, CDC manages to get the vaccine only by breaking its own rules, that is, by collecting research results that it officially *prevented* the outsourced maverick Dr. Sussmann from conducting. However, this flexibility is not the final answer either. Procedures internal to the organization are too slow and risk letting innumerable people die worldwide before the vaccine is fully disposable. What solves this impasse is Dr. Hextall's decision to *test the vaccine on herself*, allowing the processes to decisively speed up. Her gesture *radically questions the borders between Private and Public*—it is no less than a transgression of CDC rules and of the distinction it presupposes. On the contrary, the opposition Sussmann-CDC she was equally called to mediate fully remained within the standard frontal opposition between the Public on one side and the Private on the other. A few words should also be spent about Hextall's casting. *Contagion*'s cast is an all-star one: Matt Damon, Jude Law, Marion Cotillard, Gwyneth Paltrow, Laurence Fishburne, Kate Winslet, Elliott Gould. Dr. Hextall is played by Jennifer Ehle, a much less famous actress: her own casting choice thus signals a shift from that peculiar way to triumphantly intertwine the Public and the Private we call "Stardom."[3] A few moments after her daring self-injection, as a further confirmation of the necessity to blur this line, she says while giving the medicine to her father that he has been her major inspiration all along since "he was the one who went to work and saved lives when the others stayed at home." What is crucial is that Dr. Hextall explicitly *refuses* to step into the spotlight when Cheever asks her to. Such a gesture would have reconciled the Private and the Public, presenting the State as the guarantor of the actions of "remarkable few" (in the words of a CDC officer publicly praising them during a conference); in doing so, Dr. Hextall maintains instead a certain tension between the two, while remaining within the horizon of the State.

This point is perhaps clearer in the light of another antagonism set in place by *Contagion*. On the one hand, there is the State (the CDC), whose isolationism misses the point, but proves nonetheless useful to beat the epidemic. On the other hand, there is Alan with his grassroots informational demagogy, excessively blaming the State and willing to rhetorically confer the power to the people through

---

3   "Questions raised at the level of the plot can be resolved at the level of performance, as the audience's attention is displaced away from the issues at stake in the fiction onto the way in which stars exhibit themselves under the pressure of those issues" (Maltby 2003: 387).

democracy as new media participation. *None* of them defeats the other in the end, but their tension, as mentioned in an earlier section of this chapter, positively affects the overall situation since it pushes the CDC to overcome its limits. The fact that a parallel montage right before the end shows them both doing what they have always been doing (the lab work, Alan goes on filming things on the streets and putting them on the Internet) suggests that their antagonism is maintained as such, and is not to be solved in either way, since they are but two sides of the same coin—no wonder people start to accuse Alan of making money out of his campaign, which is exactly what Alan accused drug companies and CDC of. It is not a matter of being for or against the State, for the mediation of an institution or for the people's free self-determination. It is a matter of deeply reconfiguring the relationship between the Public and the Private and *hence* re-inventing the State without getting rid of it as such. The scene immediately after that parallel montage, the penultimate one, is a striking confirmation. It takes place in Mitch's house, who so far repeatedly and almost violently prevented his teen daughter Jory to see her boyfriend Andrew. Here is what happens according to an anonymous Internet Movie Database synopsis:

> Jory finds a box in her room from her father telling her to be ready at 8:00 pm. Inside there is a dress. Jory goes downstairs and sees her father has made up the living room for a makeshift prom night since she is unable to leave the house yet. There is a knock on the door. It is Andrew, who got the vaccine and is now sporting his vaccination bracelet proudly—they can finally be near each other. He is going to be her date for the night. The two of them begin to dance. Upstairs, Mitch is in the bedroom, looking for his camera, when he turns it on and sees pictures of Beth during that final business trip that cost her her life. He breaks down crying. Mitch goes downstairs to take pictures of Jory and Andrew. Mitch watches them dance.[4]

According to the anthropological cliché, the prohibition of incest, or "handing" one's son/daughter to someone else, has generally been considered the original gesture of whatever one might call "society." This is clearly a new beginning—as Mitch crying at Beth's pictures emphasizes that the old situation is gone forever. But this new beginning cannot be separated from a radical redefinition of the relationship between the Public and the Private: hosting a prom night in one's living room suggests first of all an unprecedented interpenetration between private spaces and public ones.[5] Whatever global mapping the narration seeks to achieve with its reconstruction of a social totality united by world crisis, it has to take into account first of all *this* basic spatial coordinate.

---

4   http://www.imdb.com/title/tt1598778/synopsis (last seen on August 10th, 2012).

5   An earlier sequence provides another symptom of this need for another public/private dimension, all the more significant as this scene has absolutely no narrative end at all, and as such sticks definitely out of the action's texture: Mitch trying unsuccessfully (for strict safety reasons) to have his wife buried in the family grave.

The Origin is the Goal

Blurring the private and the public comes dangerously close to what recent political theory has usually called the *commons*: sharing property, goods, services et cetera as the concrete basis for an alternative to present-day crisis. Following especially Alain Badiou, Slavoj Žižek often insists on the necessity for the State to manage the effective establishment of the commons horizon. But he also insists that the key element of this establishment must be none other than the *dictatorship of the proletariat*: the key function of the State must be granting the coincidence between the Universal and what is excluded from the social tissue—the latter being the definition itself of proletariat (see Žižek 2009: 125–31). It would be too much to ask a Hollywood movie to bear traces of this, even if it comes from the director who dedicated a four-hour, two-part epic to Ernesto "Che" Guevara. Yet there are some timid indications thereof. The second scene is a dialogue between a janitor at CDC and Dr. Cheever. The two briefly talk about football, and then the former asks the latter to have a look at his son, who apparently suffers from attention deficit disorder. Most likely, the janitor cannot afford medical insurance. Cheever politely refuses and unconvincingly promises to find him another doctor. Next time the viewer sees this janitor is when he accidentally hears Cheever telling his wife to reach a secure place before the general alarm is publicly announced; the janitor triggers a rumour that ultimately undermines Cheever's credibility. Thus, he is depicted rather overtly as the excluded whose inclusion is a matter ultimately raised by the global crisis. In effect, when the distribution of the vaccine takes place, on the basis of lotteries using birthdays, as soon as Cheever gets one for himself and his wife he gives his own to the janitor's child. This is followed by a New Deal-ish handshake between the doctor and the janitor, very emphasized by Soderbergh's direction, which one would have rather expected in a social drama from the 1930s. By all means, we are very far from any hypothesis of dictatorship of the proletariat: here the janitor is simply included in, without any trace of the conflation between the excluded and the Universal. Yet, if this inter-class resolution might seem an ideological easy way out, the utopian is on the side of the dialogue: Cheever explains that shaking hands used to be "a way for showing a stranger that you weren't carrying a weapon, in the old days. [...] You offered your empty right hand to show that you meant no harm. [...] I wonder if the virus knows it." This is the crucial point: *sociality is ambiguously compared to the virus*, for it is fundamentally ambivalent, in that it cannot be made of a mere principle of inclusion, but rather *of a strictly dialectical and inherently problematic reversibility between inclusion and exclusion*—which, in a way, is also at the core of the dialectic of the proletariat, although this is not specifically the case. Earlier in the movie, the virus was erroneously reputed to have been incubated in some fish species—much later on, Dr. Orantes learns that the Chinese word for "fish" sounds exactly like the English "you." Elsewhere, there is a very explicit 180° shot-and-reverse-shot editing together two men both staring at the camera: a sick one and a sound one next to whom, in the background, Dr. Mears is running to apply a mask to the former. Such a staging emphasizes that connectivity, as underlined by the editing trick, can be venomous as well as it can be saving. The inherent ambivalence of sociality also belongs to media: in *Contagion*, they can separate (as the official TV announcements do) as well as they can bring together, as with the cell phones allowing Andrew and Jory to keep in touch.

At any rate, *this* is the reason why the epidemic is not a symbol of the stock market crash, but an allegory: there is a structural ambiguity pertaining to what the epidemic designates, in that it can stand for society itself *as well as* for the economic crash. This also implies that the utopian claims the film implicitly formulates regarding a collectivity able to get past the crisis have to lay their own foundations paradoxically on the economic crisis's own presuppositions themselves.

This is what *Contagion* suggests in its very final scene. The film began with "Day 2" but ends with "Day 1," that is, with the depiction of how the virus was born in the first place. This visualization of the virus only in the moment it has been finally defeated unmistakably recalls Jean-Pierre Dupuy's reversed teleology of catastrophe: in order to avoid catastrophe, we have to posit it as something which already happened (Dupuy 2005). Thus, the end of catastrophe overlaps with the beginning. The solution of a catastrophic event is strictly and paradoxically retroactive: it posits its own presuppositions.

This also means that the way out of catastrophe is inscribed into the catastrophic event itself. Hence the necessity to closely watch the images of this final scene. The IMDB synopsis again:

> A construction crew from Beth's company AIMM was cutting down trees in a forest in China. That caused some bats to fly out. One bat was infected with the virus. It grabbed a piece of banana and perched above a pig's pen. It dropped the banana piece which we are to assume had the virus on it. A pig eats it and is eventually slaughtered at market for food. A chef handles the dead pig, touching the inside of the infected pig's mouth with his bare hands. He goes out to dining room and poses in a picture with Beth holding hands, transferring the virus to her and starting the chain of events.[6]

The first thing to be noticed is that the primordial origin of it all lies in capitalist exploitation—here: the ravaging of nature for construction purposes. But even more than this unnecessary confirmation of our allegorical hypothesis, what matters is the form of this bit. On the screen, the sequence does seem as unadorned, dry and essential as this synopsis put it. Thanks to a very tight editing, and to camera movements mostly drawing limpid lines clearly connecting one object to the other through semi-pans, this sequence appears as nothing but a mute series of relations, a bare chain of connections. This is very important, because here the film points to its own form, all the more since from the content's standpoint it tells the viewer nothing s/he does not already know—the shift from content to form being the very key of the shift from ideology to utopia.

---

6   See http://www.imdb.com/title/tt1598778/synopsis.

Effectively, *Contagion*'s overall visual style is aptly resumed by these few shots. Soderbergh uses digital camera against its ordinary presuppositions: he keeps it generally very still, and when he moves it, the movements are very straight and clear; he chooses ultra-traditional angles one would rather expect from classical 1930s or 1940s Hollywood, daringly playing with focus in order to design square, elementary geometries within the frame which are integrally continuity-oriented. As Aaron Baker (2011: 62) brilliantly put it, Soderbergh's films "function 'beneath' and 'beyond' Hollywood continuity." This means that whereas Hollywood typically conceives continuity editing as engendering the effect of an invisible flow of images, Soderbergh's visual stylization builds up continuity as if *emphasizing* the way every carefully constructed single shot relates to the following. In other words, spatiality is vehemently stressed—as it is by making montage ceaselessly jump from one location to the other. Simultaneity is repeatedly stressed. Time, on the other hand, is severely compressed, as epitomized by the highly discontinuous plot's timeline, passing from Day 2 to 3 to 4, 5, 6, 7, 8, 12, 14, 18, 21, 26, 29, 131, 133, 135. Unsurprisingly, at a certain moment Jory exclaims: "Why can't they make a shot that keeps time from passing?" Moreover, the very tight concatenation of events leaves little to no room for emotional depth—that is, of course, *temporal*/subjective depth; violence and pathos themselves are considerably understated, albeit such a burning topic would have easily prescribed to overemphasize them. Violent events (say, fights over food and medicines) are often left to the background of the frame, behind the imperturbably unfolding main action.

The film thus strongly privileges space over time. Indeed, in *Contagion*, the fluid passing of time belongs to the ideological level of the narrative, the one smoothly flowing from dystopia to the ideological utopia of coming back to the pre-crisis situation with just one injection without changing anything really. However, we have already repeatedly spotted a utopian counter-movement which conceives instead the end and the beginning as one and the same. According to this counter-movement, as synthesized in the very final "Day 1" scene, *disruption and the formulation of spatiality ultimately coincide*: the illustration of the disruptive virus is nothing but a spatial articulation. This is exactly Jameson's view on what contemporary Utopia should be: a disruption of current modes of spatiality as dictated by globalization in order to reinvent a new and alternative kind of spatialization (see Jameson 2005: 211–33). *Interconnectedness* is what the epidemic, the global economic crisis and sociality as such ultimately share. By emphasizing spatiality through its own form, *Contagion* seemingly suggests that the interconnectedness the global crisis has traumatically thrown at us is the lesson society should learn to go past it and re-invent itself.

Conclusion

An explicit allegory of the global economic crisis following 2008 crash, at a surface level *Contagion* seems to praise the Federal Reserve's injection of capital, its ideological agenda to restore the situation like it used to be, without any systemic change. On the other hand, the film bears several traces of a sort of utopian counter-hypothesis. It suggests that the crisis, and even the ultimately insufficient FR move, contain precious indications as to the way we might be able to get past it. It is the global finance predicament that has showed once and for all our global interconnectedness—something we cannot pretend any longer not to see, even more than in the earlier stages of globalization. It also showed that the strong presence of the State is indispensable. More generally, *Contagion* forces us to think of a new society which will have to keep together a strong State able to come to terms with the geopolitical contradictions of globalization's inevitable universal interconnectedness, including strictly financial ones; a radical rethinking of the relationship between public and private dimensions; the structural dialectic link between inclusion and exclusion—a kind of reversibility any new hypothesis of society cannot neglect any longer, nor mask behind an indiscriminate general inclusion. The film does not describe this society, but provides its basic structural elements for *us* to think of a collective form that might combine them together.

More than ever, the political unconscious of our societies is faced with the necessity to find out imaginary solutions for contradictions that are more and more burning. This analysis hopefully demonstrates that several utopian impulses are still waiting to be detected, even in contemporary mass cultural products.

References

Baker, Aaron (2011) *The Films of Steven Soderbergh*. Urbana: University of Illinois Press.

Dupuy, Jean-Pierre (2005) *Petite métaphysique des tsunamis*. Paris: Seuil.

Jameson, Fredric (1981) *The Political Unconscious*. Ithaca: Cornell University Press.

——— (1991) *Postmodernism, or, The Cultural Logic of Late Capitalism*. Durham: Duke University Press.

——— (1992) *The Geopolitical Aesthetic: Cinema and Space in the World System*. Bloomington: Indiana University Press.

——— (2005) *Archaeologies of the Future*. London and New York: Verso.

Maltby, Richard (2003) *Hollywood Cinema*. Malden: Wiley-Blackwell.

Tait, R. Colin (2010) "Competing Modes of Capital in *Ocean's Eleven*," in R. Barton Palmer and—Steven M. Sanders (eds.), *The Philosophy of Steven Soderbergh* (Lexington: University of Kentucky Press), pp. 231–45.

Žižek, Slavoj (2009) *First as Tragedy, Then as Farce*. London and New York: Verso.

PART III
Scenarios

Chapter 9

Getting Its Act Together: What Chance Subtraction Under Conditions of Scarcity?

Colin Cremin

The excuse of scarcity, which has justified institutionalised repression since its inception, weakens as man's knowledge and control over nature enhances the means for fulfilling human needs with a minimum of toil (Marcuse 2006: 92).

From the condition of scarcity arises the need for repression, self-sacrifice and sublimation of libidinal energies in socially necessary tasks (work, cultural production and so forth), or so Freud (2006) argued. Moreover, the more we submit to the superego law by internalising and sublimating aggressive instincts, the greater are its demands and through this process civilisations evolve. Herbert Marcuse's objection is an obvious one. Repression has become a function of capitalism rather than a necessity of life. The reality principle we submit to is the historically specific performance principle of instrumental reason and exchange. As Marcuse points out, the productive forces are adequately developed that if utilised for our social needs rather than in the interests of capital, scarcity could be overcome and erotic energies liberated from mundane and alienating labour. An empirically defendable proposition, Marcuse's work is a rejoinder to the now prevalent view that the human population has exceeded the planet's carrying capacity. However, it is not just the ecological argument that strengthens the ideological justification for libidinal restraint and austerity; more pertinent to this chapter is the scarcity of jobs that commands a continual sacrifice to the logic of employability. It is this reality that binds erotic energy to capital in the hope that a job will eventually materialise. As rising numbers join the dole queue and those fortunate enough to be exploited by capital fear for their futures, there is an added impetus to develop the credentials and train ourselves in the art of becoming marketable commodities for capital to use. The reality principle of capitalism today, the injunction to improve employability intensifies on diminishing job opportunities, insecurity and unfulfilling labour. "Employability" is a master signifier that connects us all to capital: materially, ideologically and libidinally.

As Marcuse (1969: 11) put it, "the so- called consumer economy and the politics of corporate capitalism have created a second nature of man which ties him libidinally and aggressively to the commodity form." A victim of the current political and economic crisis, the subject remains largely wedded to capital and it is upon such shoulders that our future, at least in Europe, depends. This is the reality that critical theory and movements against capital have to grapple with. Shifting from what Marcuse called a Great Refusal to play by the rules of the capitalist game to the more contemporary notion of subtraction most prominent in its Marxist-Lacanian inflection in Slavoj Žižek's work, this chapter charts out a map for political transformation. Questioning the value of placing libidinal subtraction (Lacan) before material subtraction (Marx), and the consequences of this for how struggle is conceived, a number of propositions are made as to how a Great, as opposed to small, Refusal or generalised *act* in the Žižekian sense can be achieved. The chapter linearly progresses from abstract theory to its deployment in an analysis and critique of employability—regarded here as the principal ideological device through which the subject remains invested in capitalist social relations—through to a discussion of the concrete possibilities of a Great Refusal or generalised subtraction. The critique focuses on productive relations as the moment which begins the cycle of accumulation, exchange and expansion, and which is thereby central to a politics of subtraction from the Capitalist State matrix.

Subtraction Without the Act

> It begins with a tickle and ends in a blaze of petrol. That's always what *jouissance* is (Lacan 1991: 72).

Signifiers dance in the gap between the bodily itch and its satisfaction, coordinated within a movement called subjectivity. *Jouissance* confirms and reveals itself through entropy, a dance of dissatisfaction in which each movement opens up a space for the next. This "spoliation" of *jouissance*, Lacan argues, is what Marx condemned in surplus value: "surplus value is surplus *jouissance*." (Lacan, 1991: 108) Thus capital and subjectivity are set in motion by a constitutive gap, a gap for making profit/signification, the closure of which brings about crises. And here, like pauses in the beat, crises anticipate new rhythms that as they kick in revitalise the dance and guarantee our hopelessly entwined future.

Writes Lacan (1991: 80), "Once a higher level has been passed, surplus *jouissance* is no longer surplus *jouissance* but is inscribed simply as a value to be inscribed in or deducted from the totality of whatever it is that is accumulating." Surplus *jouissance* tied to the commodity form creates value in the act of labour, realises it in the act of exchange and destroys it in the act of consumption. Beginning with a tickle, ending with bombs, it is the fuel that enables capital to circulate, expand and ultimately destroy everything that human life depends on. Through the Marxist and Lacanian concepts of surplus value / *jouissance* we can see that the worker is exploited twice over: in the first "materialist" instance by creating value in excess of remuneration in wage, and in the second libidinal sense through an excessive attachment to the Lacanian *objet a* operationalised for capital. Corresponding forms of alienation, one historical relating to the abstraction of labour power and the other ahistorical relating to the fundamental split between subject and signifier, are the wound for which commodified bandages in the form of DVD box-sets, new dresses, iProducts and so on are sought. As Marx (1993: 99) explains, "a definite production determines a definite consumption, distribution and exchange as well as *definite relations between these different moments.*" We can either suffer or enjoy its symptoms or else become organised into a movement that subtracts itself from the bind of surplus value/ surplus *jouissance.* And here the worker is at an advantage. Capital cannot subtract itself from the worker without undermining its own drive for profit but the worker, identifying as belonging on the side of a proletarian struggle, can end its material alienation. It can subtract its libidinal energy from the (disavowed) enjoyments of capital and "resublimate" it through a positive identification with, and excessive attachment to, the object of global emancipation, however signified. Subtraction is an *act* that reconfigures the symbolic order, placing the subject within a new linguistic constellation from which a new idea of itself and its relation to others is realised. When people strike, they establish forms of solidarity based on a common interest that negates the abstract universality of the work team or presupposition of a shared humanitarian interest. But these subtractions are often mere hiccups in the accumulative process, aimed at getting a better deal rather than constituting a subjective break. Likewise when people take part in mass demonstrations, those demonstrations are often fragile in composition and limited in duration, even when impressive in numbers. While at certain moments surplus *jouissance* is de facto subtracted from the accumulative process, it does not mean that we are any less bound to our fetishistic enjoyments of capital, that we are any less animated by the prospect of acquiring a new product or developing a career.

By withdrawing its labour, the class upon which capital depends reveals itself and therefore the antagonism that until then was disavowed. "The point of subtraction," as Žižek (2012: 33) succinctly explains, "is to reduce the overall complex structure to its antagonistic minimal difference." If we approach subtraction in a strictly Marxist sense of exploitation of waged labour, those actively contributing energies to the accumulative process are the only ones with the capacity to subtract. This would exclude surplus labour and as Fabio Vighi (2012: 154) puts it, "subtraction is already immanent to our experience of social life." Consequently, the only effective weapons against capital would be those Žižek pejoratively calls the "salaried bourgeoisie": they create value in their labour and destroy it through their capacity to consume thereby ensuring capitalist circulation and expansion. Advancing on this, it will be argued that subtraction matters irrespective of whether a person has traversed the fantasy of their enjoyment of capital. It can be "performed" materially or libidinally but in the final instance of a contingent (revolutionary) event, the two combine in the body of the exception that underpins or is excluded from capital though nevertheless intervenes against it.

According to Žižek, subtraction operates at the level of phantasy. Vighi (2012: 137) again: "subtraction is always at least minimally traumatic because I

subtract first and foremost from my fetishistic enjoyment of what I profess to hate."
Traumas are not something that can be self-induced. The Act as Žižek (2000: 374)
puts it, differs from activity in so far that the phantasmal background by which life
acquires meaning is contingently disturbed. In terms of employability, we could
think of this as the moment when everything we do to improve our job prospects
no longer has any meaning. Not only do we recognise the enjoyment derived by
filling in the lack in the Other—imagining ourselves in the place of surplus value
(the job vacancy)—but derive no satisfaction in improving our employability
because it would have no symbolic value. When the fantasy of our enjoyment of
employability is traversed, the career itself is sacrificed. A measure of the strength
of the movements against capital can be discerned when to the question *Can the
career be sacrificed?* it is possible to answer in the affirmative. We have not
reached this decisive phase, not in Europe where unemployment is chronic and
where movements, such as in Greece and Spain, are numerically significant.

A contingent change in the situation forces the decision. The 1984–5 Miners
Strike and 1989 Hillsborough Stadium Disaster can be thought of as British
instances of this: trauma necessitating a decision that reconstitutes the subject
caught up in the moment. In both examples, an abstract possibility / opposition
became a concrete reality / opposition when the police revealed itself as a brutal
weapon of state oppression, the mass media, particularly the BBC in its coverage
of the Battle of Orgreave, an apparatus of ideological distortion and the state in
general of class violence. With the fundamental antagonism thus revealed and the
symbolic fiction shattered, those involved are forced to take sides and reckon in
their very sense of being with a new symbolic reality. Events such as these, however,
are rare, and often only affect a relatively small number of people. If the political
act is necessarily traumatic and only occurs through a chance sequence of events,
the theory of subtraction has no political value. But by separating subtraction into
two different forms, corresponding to Marx's and Lacan's different concepts of
exploitation, the limitations of a theory that presupposes contingent traumatic
breaks can be overcome. Contingencies can be planned for.

The change in the biological constitution of the individual, or rather the libidinal
economy, as a result of the commodification of desire, presupposes the need for a
traumatic event but it is the political activities of such a subject that, ineluctably
entwined in the commodity form, will prove decisive in the current context of
struggle. We must contend with the thing in us more than ourselves—the *objet
a*—but can only do so if there has already been a change in the situation in which
those biologically constituted needs are organised. Political action must in the
meantime happen in spite of us, or rather in spite of our libidinal attachments to
surplus value. In contrast to Žižek, trauma, I want to argue, is not the *a priori* of
the political act of sorts. Put another way, enjoyment of capital—the *jouissance*
knotted into the creation and destruction of value—is not necessarily antithetical
to political action if that enjoyment is identified as symptomatic of a system
that itself must change in order for there to be a libidinal subtraction from the
commodity form.

Consider the role of the student in current struggles against austerity and finance capital. Here we have the archetypal subject of the university discourse invested in capital from the privileged position of being able to develop credentials that improve employability while, at the same time, campaigning against capitalism. Lacan's (1991: 201) retort to heckling students at Vincennes in 1969 is relevant in today's context of struggle:

> You are the product of the university, and you prove that you are the surplus value, even if only in this respect— which you not only consent to, but which you also applaud—and I see no reason to object—which is that you leave here, yourselves equivalent to more or fewer credit points. You come here to gain credit points for yourselves. You leave here stamped, "credit points."

Scarcity of jobs and grants is a powerful material and ideological device for justifying repressive submission to the university discourse irrespective of what we know or politically (self-consciously) desire. In this context it is difficult to deny the fleeting though ultimately dissatisfying *jouissance* spent and stained on the CV. Refusal is not an option until a political struggle reaches a decisive stage when sacrifice would not simply guarantee unemployment and political marginality.

Our relation to politics prior to a traumatic separation can be thought of in terms of Žižek's (1989) classic critique of ideology: that we know full well the "secret" beneath the commodity—that, for example, goods do not magically appear on supermarket shelves but arrive there by way of exploited labour through the plundering of natural resources, imperialist violence and so forth—yet still in our social activity we act as if such things do not happen: that the commodity is indeed a magical thing. The fetishistic illusion in this respect enables us to go on living with such knowledge, critiquing the "system" while disavowing our contributions to it. Yet, inverting the point, if only dimly aware of how enjoyment is knotted into the operation they protest against, those who nonetheless do protest are doing it: students blockade shopping centres and prise open spaces for critical dialogue, the salaried bourgeoisie go on strike and entrepreneurial slum dwellers disrupt production and prop up leftist regimes. The danger for critical theory is that it gets caught up in the abstract ideas of subtraction and ceases to be of political relevance in times when ideas do matter and strategies can be decisive. Under current conditions—a situation far from excellent—by day we engage in the proletarian struggle and by night work for the bourgeoisie. If the left, then, is to avoid staking its future on a contingent event, it needs to develop over a period of time the organisational capacity for a generalised subtraction from the circuit of capital—strikes, boycotts, and intervention—sabotage, blockades—strategies that everyone irrespective of their status within the division of labour or, up to a point, libidinal investments can partake in. Our fetishistic enjoyments of capital are an obstacle to emancipation only insofar that at the level of ideology they prevent us from doing the mundane job of taking action and developing the capacity for a generalised properly political act in the sense referred to by Žižek. In short, critical theory is essential for the ideological task of separation and strategy, articulating the problem by explaining how capitalism operates materially, ideologically and libidinally, showing what is at stake and advancing a dialogue on what can be done rather than individualising the problem which is arguably what happens when everything hinges on traversing the fantasy.

While much has been written about the pacifying effects of consumption, it is our relation to production that has greatest ideological and political significance. Through the lens of psychoanalytic theory, this relation, understood as a libidinal one, illustrates the extent to which the subject is bound to capital and what a revolutionary struggle must ultimately entail. The master signifier that draws surplus value and surplus *jouissance* into a societal wide compact is employability, an object without substance, an aim without outcome and, as it shall be argued, the material, ideological and libidinal stumbling block to a generalised subtraction or Great Refusal.

Enjoying Employability

> The most succinct definition of the reversal constitutive of drive is the moment when, in our engagement in our purposeful activity (activity towards some goal), the way towards this goal, the gestures we make to achieve it, start to function as the goal in itself, as its own aim, as something that brings its own satisfaction (Žižek 2000: 304).

The shift from desire to drive was fully systemised in respect to labour the moment that work became "precarious" through the systematic dismantling of labour regulations, the passing of anti-trade union legislation and so forth, combined with attacks on the industrial base and privileging of finance capital via the ideology of neoliberalism and the entrepreneurial self. Surplus labour is a structural element of capitalism; what changes is that the emphasis shifts from simply competing for a job to improving employability regardless of whether there are jobs available or whether a person is actually employed.[1] Employability operates at the level of drive in that satisfaction lies in the aim (there is no object to attain) rather than the outcome (an actual job). We cannot get rid of it and we cannot get enough it; there is no end to employability because there is no job that can end dissatisfaction or be materially secure in duration and arguably no movement that can currently force a more stable compact between capital and labour. The lack in capital symbolised by the job vacancy can be filled, it is the void that determines constant circulation and expansion in which drive is located.

Employability is sustained by three parties, the subject, the boss and the phantasmal "big Boss," the big Other; a symbolic refraction of capital and the

---

1   A variation of the critique of employability with more empirical examples is in the chapter *Naked Enterprise* in *Capitalism's New Clothes*.

State in the entirety of social relations. The process of becoming employable involves a gathering up of signifiers orbiting the master signifier of employability. "It is language that uses us. Language employs us, and that is how it [the big Other] enjoys." (Lacan, 1991: 66)

> Question:
> How can I keep busy while I'm unemployed?
>
> Answer:
> If you can demonstrate to employers that you have been doing everything you can to find work and to keep your skills and knowledge up to date, most will overlook the fact that you are currently unemployed.
> Always remain positive—rejections are part of life. Each 'no' that you get moves you closer to that all-important 'yes.'[2]

Oedipus is very much "alive": the more the subject responds to the injunction to develop new skills, gain "relevant" experience and so on, the more obscene are the demands of capital and the further away is that all important yes. Scarcity of jobs operationalises the performance principle that Marcuse spoke of. Capital relies here on the excess of knowledge that it has already calculated as necessary for generating profit, the increase of which dovetails with the subject's own desire to exceed what it already knows by chasing the surplus valorised by the master signifier. Idiosyncrasies, even resistance to "corporate diktat," are calculated into the operation through the perverse superego injunction to enjoy, with the typical refrain that employers want "humans" not robots, for staff to "have a life outside of work" or not take work "too seriously." Psychometric testing, personal statements, interviews and evidence of hobbies and interests and activities outside of work and in the "non-profit" sector ensure the injunction in all its ambiguities is understood. Becoming employable is an unending repetition in the failure to be the equivalent of what capital wants through the question *what does capital want from me*? At the vacant heart of both parties is the *objet a*—the perfect job in the case of the worker—that ends dissatisfaction. A communistic impulse for non-alienated labour, the end of employability is the utopian object that politically short-circuits the hostility we might feel towards the actual boss or company we work for. The relation to the actual work that is done is decentred as the struggle shifts from better working conditions onto an individualistic enterprise of getting a (better) job or simply maintaining one. Never sure what the Other wants from us, advice columns and career sites provide the clues on how to become a use value for capital. LoveMoney.com is typical in its advice on how to "survive" unemployment:

---

2 'Talent List Education Group' website (available at http://talentlist.co.nz/files/ trainings/KEEP%20YOUSELF%20BUSY%20WHILE%20UNEMPLOYED.pdf).

> If you feel yourself sinking into despair/apathy/complete inactivity, you need to drag yourself out of it as soon as possible. That could just mean getting out of the house, even if you don't feel like it ...
>
> Or, to help motivate your job hunt, you could set yourself inexpensive rewards for getting things done. So three solid job applications = ice cream and a DVD—or something along those lines ...
>
> Finally, try to keep yourself groomed and in reasonable physical shape. When you're out of work, it's all too easy to live in your pyjamas. Look good and you'll feel good (Cowdy 2009).

Unemployment = applications = ice cream, employability enters the metonymic daisy chain of desire powered by surplus *jouissance* anchored to the commodity form in an unending process of becoming employable regardless of whether we have a job. The commodity becomes the mirror double, here from the appropriately named Monster.com:

> When a company is determining how to advertise their products to consumers, they focus on its [sic] unique selling points—the things which make the product different from any other. It may be that it is smaller, lasts longer or tastes better than its competitors. The same principle applies to you when you are applying for a new job.[3]

In sum, employability decentres employment, shifting the signifier from the actual job to a phantom job that has no material location in the economy, does not exploit us in a Marxist sense nor demand anything from us. In and out of the accumulative circuit the subject's libido is oriented to the creation of value that capital may or may not want. The phantom job stands in for the capitalist laws of motion: no longer a particular capitalist that exploits us but rather the more abstract and ephemeral Capital. It is a phantom that the student imagines as he develops his CV and chooses courses according to whether they provide the skills employers can make use of. Capital overcodes the spatial and temporal totality of life: in the job, at the dole office, at home, in leisure, retroactively signifying the past, now and for the foreseeable future: the void in capital is writ large at the job centre, with "transferable" skills acting as the generic suture of the imponderables in each vacancy. The striving for further employability of those already employed guarantees that, if for no other reason, public sector workers will do the additional tasks required to ensure that, despite the cutbacks, hospitals, schools, bureaucracies and so on still function. Refusing such work, or simply "working to rule" by performing tasks according to the stated aims of the bureaucracy—police

---

3   'What are my unique selling points?' (available at http://career-advice.monster.ie/cvs-applications/cv-advice/what-are-my-unique-selling-points-ie/article.aspx).

catching criminals rather than simply fixing the "stats" (see Žižek 2012: 95)—has to be weighed against the demands of the big Boss / big Other which haunt us when there are job cuts or if we desire another job or promotion. In becoming employable, one is simultaneously becoming unemployable, creating a gap for "innovation" because, as we all know, even in the best of occupations one must continually strive to fill the void of capital in order to avoid redundancy. The crises upon which capital innovates are thereby homologous to the crises of subjective stagnation that require us, especially the unemployed, to get out of bed and become what the Other wants.

While it is impossible to subtract from employability without jeopardising future employment, there is a common interest nonetheless in such subtraction. The first step is recognition that we are the cause of employability, the recognition that our libidinal investments in improving employability as a necessity to life are in fact what guarantees submission to capital. To reiterate, the act in its traumatic dimension entails the sacrifice of the career. Dialectically, employability needs to be resignified as a collective aim to be liberated from capital by having determination over the productive forces and thereby signification. The advice from Monster to "spring clean your CV" can be interpreted in this way:

> Your CV is one of the most powerful weapons in your job-seeking armoury and is often the first point of contact with a potential boss, so it's vital to make this document as powerful as possible. … the key to developing a knock-out CV lies in actively seeking opportunities to broaden your appeal and demonstrate why employers should consider you over other candidates. In a competitive job market it's those job seekers who invest the most in their personal development who will reap the rewards.[4]

The CV counts life as use value and also illustrates the capacity in each of us to change our condition and become fit for the purpose of class struggle. The ultimate CV is the collective one that "knocks out" the big Other as Capital through a process that involves broadening the appeal of new master signifiers to demonstrate that the employer is no longer required because we already have what it takes to organise society in our common interests. Only by investing surplus *jouissance* in a generalised class struggle will we have a chance of reaping the rewards for our efforts to become employable. For this to happen the lesser refusals of isolated actions against capital, refusals in the workplace, boycotts of consumer products and so forth, need to become Great ones.

---

4 'Spring clean your cv' (available at http://career-advice.monster.co.uk/cvs-applications/cv-advice/spring-clean-your-cv/article.aspx).

Refusals Great and Small

If Facebook is a barometer of the popularity of sentiments that are frequently exposed within critical theory such as pseudo-activity (Adorno and Horkheimer), left-liberalism (Žižek) or democratic materialism (Badiou), then the many "thumbs up" on Facebook for posters such as "Top Ten Ways to Fuck the System" should be a cause for concern. The "anti-capitalist" programme is symptomatic of a narcissistic culture of enjoyment that has prevailed for the past 30 or more years:

1. Shop Local—Boycott Corporations & Vote with your Money
2. Grow a Garden—Eat Organic & Build your Community around Food
3. Become Self-Sustainable—Be Independent in Food, Water & Energy
4. Protect the Children—Don't Vaccinate, Medicate or Mutilate Kids
5. Go Homeopathic—Use Cannabis & Refuse Prescription Medication
6. Self-Educate—Homeschool & Always Teach & Speak Truth to Power
7. Make Family Priority # 1—Families that Eat Together, Stay Together
8. Turn Off the TV—Tune Out the Fear, Propaganda & Disinformation
9. Return to Nature—Abandon the City Life & Quit the Rat Race
10. Love One Another Unconditionally—Realise that We Are All One.

Anticipating the so-called cultural turn, Marcuse (1972: 48) wrote in his post-1960s essay *Counter-revolution and Revolt*: "the bourgeois individual is not overcome by simply refusing social performance, by dropping out and living one's own style of life. To be sure, no revolution without individual liberation, but also no individual liberation without the liberation of society." When capitalism becomes an empty signifier of everything that is wrong with society, anti-capitalism also becomes an empty signifier of a radicalism decoupled from the labour relation. If capitalism has as is said entered the vocabulary of mainstream politics as a pejorative term, it is no guarantee that its laws of motion are understood or, relatedly, that there is any desire to replace it with a mode of production that could satisfy our material needs and liberate us from alienated labour. "When the images of power overshadow the reality," Christopher Lasch (1991: 81) wrote, "those without power find themselves fighting phantoms." The phantoms acquire many forms, none of which serve as "the metaphoric condensation of the global restructuring of the entire social space" that for Žižek (2000: 208) is a necessary component of politics proper. The pretenders that critical theory is apt to shred are worth alighting on, global warming being perhaps the most prominent master signifier around which left-liberals rally. Badiou (in Feltham, O. ed., 2005: 139) writes:

> Let's start by saying that after 'the rights of man,' the rise of the 'the rights of Nature' is a contemporary form of the opium of the people. It is an only slightly camouflaged religion: the millenarian terror, concern for everything save the properly political destiny of peoples, new instruments for control of everyday

life, the obsession with hygiene, the fear of death and catastrophes … It is a
gigantic operation in the depoliticisation of subjects.

Global warming is the fillip to the affluent classes who in their "eco" lifestyles
assume a moral high ground which energises Oedipus as a regulator of our (the
working class) consumerist excesses and which provides business with another
means of extracting profit through surplus-*jouissance*. It begets a perverse kind of
utopianism with echoes of fascism, the eco-primitivism that Derrick Jensen (2006)
has helped to popularise being a very contemporary final solution. The argument
here is that global warming will have serendipitous consequences by reducing
the global population to 10 percent of current levels and usher a sustainable pre-
industrial age. A politics that presupposes scarcity as the natural condition of
social development is evident here and in the more subtle examples of left-liberal
environmentalism. "Industrialisation" is another phantom, a related master signifier
that condenses and obscures capitalist relations as if the forces of production are
themselves an abstract machine that is inherently destructive. The same can be said
for "anti-consumerism." While Frankfurt School critics were particularly vocal in
their hostility to mass consumption, their concern centred on the ideological role it
plays through the culture industry in pacifying the working class and manufacturing
false needs. Their opposition was not to consumption per se, nor was it a moralistic
argument to berate those who today are termed "excessive" consumers.

"No Impact Man," Colin Beavan, who spent a year in New York living a "carbon
neutral" life (see noimpactproject.org website) is the archetypal embodiment of
"anti-consumerism" with none of the insights of critical theory: a reified activity
with no political impact. By refusing certain goods and engaging in practices
deemed to be ethical or ecologically sustainable, it appears that the relations
mystified by commodity fetishism are accounted for. The opposite obtains. People
it seems really do believe the commodity is a magical thing: that the bikes they
cycle, the roads they traverse and the bricks and mortar from which their homes
are built have appeared from nowhere because nowhere can they factor in the
complex relations of production without revealing the absurdity of their actions.
They must act as if their choices have meaning because they are bound in their
libidinal enjoyment to the commodity form and the pseudo-activities to which
their identity is anchored.

Žižek (2000: 262) writes, "when a new *point de capiton* emerges, the socio-
symbolic field is not only displaced, its very structuring principle changes."
Entering the vocabulary of resistance post 2008 is the master signifier of finance.
Scapegoating financiers, CEOS and speculators, politicians such as Obama earn
their radical credentials through this populist rhetoric. While having the initial
beneficial effect of providing a useful focus for protest movements, it displaces
the problem and individualises it, in effect legitimising capitalism as a system that
can be reformed if only finance is better regulated. Crises, to be clear, have roots in
diminishing rates of profit, overproduction and relatedly underconsumption that are
themselves symptomatic of class struggle. The signifiers of resistance help make

"crisis" an ideological tool for justifying austerity as a means by which to further embed the neoliberal project in some quarters and, in others, provide politicians who set their stall against unsustainable development, consumerist excess, "dirty" industry and global finance with a reformist veneer. The materiality of crisis acquires symbolic value that can embolden the left, but the left, by embracing this rhetoric parade of a kaleidoscope of half-truths, is in essence fighting phantoms.

The master signifier of employability gets to the core of the problem. "Equality," writes Badiou (2009: 26), "means that everyone is referred back to their choice, and not to their position. That is what links a political truth to the instance of a decision, which always establishes itself in concrete situations, point by point." The decision to sacrifice one's career, the refusal of employability, is consistent with the four determinations of what Badiou (2009: 27) calls the truths of politics: "will (against socio-economic necessity), equality (against the established hierarchies of power or wealth), confidence (against anti-popular suspicion or the fear of the masses), authority or terror (against the 'natural' free play of competition)." The inexistent, the indivisible remainder, the surplus as concrete exception, is what presents itself, point by point, in a truth procedure that refuses employability, in short, to be counted as use value. A blank essay on "turnitin" (the preferred online system in academia for ensuring against plagiarism) that nonetheless was written, a blank CV to a prospective employer by a worker who nonetheless fits the job descriptor—"include me, out!," refusals such as these are a long way from becoming generalised. But what are the prospects in these current circumstances for a generalised refusal or subtraction: a collective act that thereby has political consequences rather than consequences on the individual's job prospects?

As Žižek (2012), among many others, points out, there is no going back to the Keynesian "golden age" compact between capital and labour which anyhow benefited only a few and did nothing to address the broader symptoms of capitalism including those that critical theorists wrote about at the time. Yet this is precisely why "full employment"—and related policies to realise it—as opposed to the more abstract "employability" is politically effective. If signified by and with accompanying propositions from the left (as opposed to the right as is sometimes the case), "full employment" and job security becomes a "minimal" demand—the positive content of struggle—that if instituted would bring about significant improvements to many people's lives and also reinvigorate capital. Rational from this perspective and reasonable in terms of what should be expected under 'healthy' economic conditions, yet antithetical to neoliberal ideology, the demand for full employment operates as a vanishing mediator around which all elements of the workforce can unite. It establishes a position of initial engagement—a war of position—that indirectly draws focus on the social relations of production embedded in every sphere of activity and symbolised in the ubiquitous struggle for employability. The demand for full employment gives way to the more precise articulation of those relations within a broad constellation of movements. This would be the result of an ongoing dialogue, not least on the centrality of work in our lives, and contingent possibilities would unfold as political and economic crises intensify.

Rather than disengage from the state, I want to argue that in this moment at least strategic alignments with leftist parties vying for power are crucial. The vote brought Chavez to power and has transformed the political landscape in Latin America after 500 years of extreme violence, exploitation and plunder. While there are important socio-economic and historical differences between Latin America and Europe, reforms in the former can point to possibilities in the latter. Reformist governments can themselves provoke unintended revolutionary consequences. It is unlikely, for example, that Gorbachev envisaged the dissolution of the Soviet Empire when introducing the policies of *Glasnost* and *Perestroika*. In respect to this and points made below, two positions on the left exemplify the problem in stances that put themselves at a distance from state power. The first, of which *The Invisible Committee* is typical, is the strategy of disengagement from the capitalist state and the view that an autonomous space can be created outside of it. The second, underlined by Badiou's stance towards elections (see below), is that by voting in elections the "inexistent" capitulate to the bourgeois politics of democratic materialism. Nicos Poulantzas (2000: 153) is worth quoting at length on this issue of utmost strategic importance:

> Now, (a) We know that political strategy must be grounded on the autonomy of the organisations of the popular masses. But the attainment of such autonomy does not involve the political organisations in leaving the strategic field of the relationship of forces that is the power-State, any more than it involves other organisations such as the trade unions in taking up a position outside the corresponding power mechanisms. To believe that this is even possible is an old illusion of anarchism (in the best sense of the term). Moreover, in neither case does self-organisation on the terrain of power imply that these organisations must directly insert themselves in the physical space of the respective institutions (this will depend on the conjuncture), nor *a fortiori* that they must embrace the materiality of these institutions (quite the contrary). (b) We also know that, alongside their possible presence in the physical space of the state apparatuses, the popular masses must constantly maintain and deploy centres and networks at a distance from these apparatuses: I am referring, of course, to movements for direct, rank-and-file democracy and to self-management networks. But although these take up political objectives, they are not located outside the State or, in any case, outside power—contrary to the illusions of anti-institutional purity. What is more, to place oneself at any cost outside the State in the thought that one is thereby situated outside power (which is impossible) can often be the best means of *leaving the field open for statism*: in short, it often involves a retreat in the face of the enemy precisely on this strategically crucial terrain.

Badiou (2008: 17) argues:

> The government, which would not be very different if it were chosen by lottery, declares that it has been mandated by the choice of the citizens and can act in the

name of this choice. Voting thus produces a singular illusion, which passes this disorientation through the fallacious filter of a choice.

Or, with reference to the "unknown elector,"

> Throughout the bourgeois centuries has she too not been instrumentalized and deceived, and had her voice sacrificed on the alter of a 'democracy' where she is in fact stripped, by her very vote, of any iota of power? (Badiou, 2012: 83).

While there are nuances to Badiou's politics, such repeated assertions invite a one-sided perspective on power that cannot account for the particulars of and possibilities inherent in the socio-economic, political and historical circumstances of a given nation state formation. Poulantzas does not fetishise the vote either in terms of what can be gained from it or what can be achieved by refusing it. Given the materially embedded nature of the capitalist state—that, as Poulantzas points out, condenses the broader social relations and ideologies that emanate from different spheres of influence, and essentially the class struggle itself—the capitalist state is a crucial terrain of contestation. It can neither be left alone nor can it be seized as if it exists separately from the relations that it embeds within itself and importantly, in terms of class struggle, the relations by which it is characterised. While the language has changed, what Poulantzas (2000: 257) said in the 1970s has contemporary relevance:

> ... the current road to socialism, the current situation in Europe, presents a number of peculiarities: these concern at one and the same time the new social relations, the state form that has been established, and the precise character of the crisis of the State. For certain European countries, these particularities constitute so many chances—probably unique in world history—for the success of a democratic socialist experience, articulating transformed representative democracy and direct, rank-and-file democracy. This entails the elaboration of a new strategy with respect both to the capture of state power by the popular masses and their organisations, and to the transformations of the State designated by the term 'democratic road to socialism.'

Syriza is in many respects a mirror of the movements on the ground in Greece, an alliance of disparate groupings each with their own specific agendas. Its taking of power while seeming more unlikely at the time of writing could have real political consequences though, especially if, like Chavez in Venezuela, it supported those movements which enable it to assume power. Just as it is mistaken to dismiss revolutionary politics on the basis that every revolution has ended in failure so, as Venezuela has proven, it is mistaken to dismiss engagement in parliamentary politics because, for example, of what happened to "democratic socialism" in Chile in 1973. The important difference in Venezuela is that movements that brought Chavez to power remain an active determinant in the political struggle for social transformation, attested to by the decisive role they played in bringing Chavez back to power after the homologous (to Chile) US backed coup of 2002. Contrasting the democratic discourse of inclusion to that of Chavez, Žižek's (2009: 102) point here has broader significance:

> Chavez is not including the excluded in a pre-existing liberal-democratic framework; he is, on the contrary, taking the "excluded" dwellers of favelas as his *base* and then reorganising political space and political forms of organisation so that the latter will "fit" the excluded. Pedantic and abstract as it may appear, this difference—between "bourgeois democracy" and "dictatorship of the proletariat"—is crucial.

It is pointless to talk of slum dwellers in the context of Europe. The excluded here are the swelling numbers of surplus labour and the "precariat" inclusive of the "salaried bourgeoisie" protesting because they know their futures are vulnerable. Unemployment, the threat thereof and the likely prospect that, for all our efforts, potential use values will not be realised as exchange for a job, or at least one in which any satisfaction, however small, can be drawn, is what connects us all. The possibility of a genuine act that occurs as part of a coordinated strategy of politically numerical significance depends on what happens over the coming years with regard to tactical decisions on the terrain of state power. As Poulantzas (2000: 258) emphasises:

> At any event, to shift the relationship of forces within the State does not mean to win successive reforms in an unbroken chain, to conquer the state machinery piece by piece, or simply to occupy the positions of government. It denotes nothing other than a *stage of real breaks*, the climax of which—and there has to be one—is reached when the relationship of forces on the strategic terrain of the State swings over to the side of the popular masses.

Those currently "traversing the fantasy" of their disavowed fetishistic enjoyment of capital are too small in number or marginalised from the accumulation process to effect change. Their presence becomes more significant as those still invested in capital (not only wage labourers) get politically involved through their actions and current sense of outrage at the injustices of austerity programmes, global finance and so on. In short, "anti-capitalists" can present a critical mass that establishes the grounds for a dialogue expanding the capacity of movements to force shifts in policy that in turn strengthen the possibility of popular struggle. We might call this a strategic subtraction short of a contingent traumatising one that comes not so much with an economic crisis as an unresolvable political one. That said, revolution must remain the aim towards which libido is in the final analysis sublimated. Demanding full employment should be seen simply as an initial (leftist) populist strategy, a vanishing mediator that those "with more to lose than their chains," and largely sublimating libido in parliamentary politics, employability and consumption, can identify with. A coordinated general subtraction-cum-strike-cum-intervention that the chapter title alludes to is what is ultimately required.

In sum, then, the focus of struggle must, as has always been the case in the most advanced capitalist states whatever the regulatory regime, focus on production, the moment in the circuit in which surplus value and surplus *jouissance* are materially entwined. This does not in any way suggest that subtraction, as could logically be supposed, involves only those actively selling their labour power. The subjective drive to create use-values in a vain attempt under pressure from the State to "improve" employability also matters. This is the principal object of libidinal enjoyment, the *objet a* in which drive is sublimated and which also defines the subject in its own efforts as commodity. The refusal of employability is an empty gesture or pointless sacrifice in isolation but plausible, necessary even, at a certain stage in the class struggle. Rather than fetishising the more abstract conditions for a genuine, as in libidinal, subtraction or placing emphasis on a self-defeating stance towards the State (if only so as to appear uncompromising), everyone on the underside of the capitalist relation has a role to play including by forming temporary alliances with leftist parties vying for state power. Chavez in Venezuela underlines the point that power can be contested on the terrain of the capitalist state, in the institutions, including the university where ideas are sometimes formulated and disperse. In this process of contestation, full employment via demands for new regulatory practices against capital can operate as the positive content of struggle especially given that so many young people in Europe are currently unemployed and experiencing the egregious effect of this.

It is easy for those in tenured positions enjoying the relative comforts of university life to insist on the purity of struggle while working hard to develop those all-important research profiles. The same can be said for the more affluent students that increasingly make up the numbers of those we teach and who regularly submit impressive though entirely abstract essays on fashionable theories. Nevertheless, a self-conscious strategic *partial*—as in short of libidinal—subtraction involving strikes, agitation and so forth, is an important prelude of a contingent subtraction that even those in a position of relative security can be part of. An intellectual and cultural war of position (Gramsci) can help ensure that the void opening up by the political crisis does not get filled with the ideology of fascism or indeed a "puny" left-liberalism. Is this how we "fuck the system"? There is the chance at least if we are all prepared at some point, hopefully sooner rather than later, to sacrifice our often non-existent careers by dirtying our hands with a properly political leftist violence.

References

Badiou, Alain (2008) *The Meaning of Sarkosy*. London: Verso.
——— (2009) *Logics of Worlds: Being and Event 2*. London: Continuum.
———(2012) *The Rebirth of History: Times of Riots and Uprisings*. London: Verso.

Cremin, Colin (2011) *Capitalism's New Clothes: Enterprise, Ethics and Enjoyment in Times of Crisis*. London: Pluto Press.

Feltham, Oliver ed., (2005) *Alain Badiou: Live Theory*. London: Continuum.

Freud, Sigmund (1994) *Civilisation and its Discontents*. New York: Dover Publications.

Jensen, Derrick (2006) *Endgame: The Problem of Civilisation volume 1*. New York: Seven Stories Press.

Lacan, Jacques (1991) *The Other Side of Psychoanalysis: Book XVII*. New York: WW Norton & Company.

Lasch, Christopher (1991) *The Culture of Narcissism: American Life in an Age of Diminishing Expectations*. New York: WW Norton & Company.

Cowdy, Serena (2009) "How to Survive Unemployment," in *Lovemoney*, 8 May 2009 (available at http://www.lovemoney.com/news/the-economy-politics-and-your-job/your-job/3430/how-to-survive-unemployment).

Marcuse, Herbert (1969) *An Essay on Liberation*. Boston: Beacon Press.

———— (1972) *Counter-Revolution and Revolt*. Boston: Beacon Press.

———— (2006) *Eros and Civilisation*. London: Routledge.

Marx, Karl (1993) *Gundrisse: Foundations of the Critique of Political Economy*. London: Routledge.

Poulantzas, Nicos (2000) *State, Power, Socialism*. London: Verso.

Vighi, Fabio (2012) *On Žižek's Dialectics: Surplus, Subtraction, Sublimation*. London: Continuum.

Žižek, Slavoj (1989) *The Sublime Object of Ideology*. London: Verso.

———— (2000) *The Ticklish Subject: The Absent Centre of Political Ontology*. London: Verso.

———— (2009) *First as Tragedy, Then as Farce*. London: Verso.

———— (2012) *The Year of Dreaming Dangerously*. London: Verso.

Chapter 10

Class Equality and Political Justice, or Differentiation and Mediated Non-Identity? Yes, Please!

Darrow Schecter

1

There are many possible conclusions to be drawn from the ongoing financial crisis in Greece, Spain and well beyond. Depending on individual and national perspective, highly contrasting remedies to alleviate the situation are imaginable. Regardless of one's position on the political spectrum, however, and irrespective of geographical location, there seem to be seven related points that are of pressing interest to all concerned. First, it is not an exaggeration to say that there is a crisis of the economic and political systems in Europe and North America. Second, late modern societies are too complex to organise from a political centre such as the state. Although this became abundantly clear during the rule of one-party states in Italy, Germany, the former USSR and elsewhere, it is equally apparent from numerous episodes in twentieth and twenty-first century history, thirdly, that these societies are need of steering of some kind, if not from the centre—the current crisis of political and economic systems highlights this need. Fourthly, the societies in question do not seem to be able, for the time being, to produce enough knowledge, or enough of the right kind of knowledge, at any rate, that would enable them to guide themselves to the greatest possible extent. So immediately one is confronted with the fifth point: crises usually require a planned intervention on the part of economic, political, cultural and technocratic experts who are capable of addressing the problems at hand. Sixthly, however, almost every known historical example of this kind of political-technical reorganisation suggests that these interventions tend to be authoritarian and difficult to subject to democratic accountability and control. To this extent, seventh, such interventions are politically illegitimate in democracies, where authority, in principle, *should* stem from the majority of citizens, or, at the very least, from the political parties representing the majority of the citizenry, and certainly *should not* issue from a managerial-bureaucratic elite.

These points will be returned to below at various stages in the argument developed here. One notes at the outset, however, that there is much at stake in terms of locating the specific issues where a dispassionate analysis of the current situation points to the need to reform constitutional stipulations on general rights and the rules regulating the aggregation of interests normally associated with citizenship, and where, on the contrary, the notion of a general interest in the sense of overarching, inclusive political citizenship conflicts with the discrete dynamics of economic, juridical, cultural and other processes. These dynamics distinguish late modern societies from those reliant on naturalised notions of belonging and exclusion, such as, typically, caste, rank and status, and offer the possibility of institutionalising a differentiated set of rights and organising multiple points of inclusion (including the option not to participate, where desired). De-centred, plural mediation of this kind is likely to be more appropriate for complex ensembles than generic practices of inclusion/omission, citizen/foreigner, private/public, etc. The latter implicitly rely on a non-negotiable third term such as the state, for example, in order to provide a conceptual and institutional foundation for the relevant dichotomy at hand (see section 2 below). One notes too, in relation to the aforementioned seven points and the clash between democratic ideals and technocratic realities, that the relation between facts and norms once again needs re-thinking. Whilst this re-evaluation was necessary after WWII and the establishment of the welfare state in accordance with the history of distinct national trajectories, it was required again in the wake of the transition from Fordism to post-Fordist flexible specialisation. The subsequent transition from flexible specialisation to globalisation demands another re-examination of the relationship between facts and norms (see section 4 below). One major challenge involves thinking about a form of steering that relies neither on stopgap elite interventions nor on a naturalised political foundation based on presumed popular homogeneity that is somehow fragmented and thereby undermined by foreign or subversive elements. The populist manipulation of such foundations has a long history that need not be commented upon here. In any event, serious thought about these subjects will not be able to avoid consideration of the discrete dynamics of differentiation just alluded to. The implication is that all appeals to underlying unity will have to be treated with scepticism, especially where it can be shown that suppositions of underlying unity work in tandem with techniques of coerced integration and authoritarian steering. Notions of underlying unity and strictures of non-negotiability can thus be seen to reinforce instrumental legitimacy, i.e., legitimation rather than legitimacy.

It is far from self-evidently clear what the distinction between instrumental legitimacy or legitimation, in the first instance, and legitimacy, in the second, might mean. For the moment, one can heighten the contrast by signalling that whereas modern legality is often associated with reason and individual liberty institutionalised in private property, contract, rights of assembly, and freedom of expression in the media and throughout the public sphere, legitimacy continues to retain many of its pre-modern significations, in that it is still usually linked with authority, security, welfare needs and collective identity. Today, however, legality and legitimacy each have an individual as well as collective dimensions. It will be suggested here that it is time to stop neglecting the individual aspect of legitimacy, and also time to stop thinking about the collective dimension of legitimacy in predominantly national, statist, or even blandly democratic terms. Moreover, it is misleading categorically to separate supposedly rational legality with an epistemological valence from ostensibly functional legitimacy with a security/welfare valence. The tendency to do so impedes social scientists and normative theorists from understanding the specific modalities of power in late modern societies. This may well seem counter-intuitive to those who assume that whatever rational and epistemological qualities one may wish to ascribe to legality, political legitimacy has *always* been a functionalist concept devoid of epistemological content, and that the term is by definition only relevant in terms of justifications for order. Yet to separate them into normative-rational and non-normative pragmatist components amounts to a major concession to the idea that the egoistic individual citizen is a rational, juridical subject, whilst the unified nation is a potentially irrational, collective subject, the requirements of whose non-negotiable safety can be arbitrarily defined by leadership cliques according to what they deem to be the realities of any given situation, such as perceived internal and external threats. Hence the instrumentalisation of legitimacy is typically accomplished through governance techniques organised to provide a stable framework for what are taken to be the inviolable liberties codified in private property and negative liberty. The more recognisable version of this project is well-known: mainstream politicians and journalists incessantly declare that without private investment and capital speculation there is no growth, without growth there are no jobs, and without jobs there is social unrest and political instability. It is possible, however, that discourses of legitimacy more or less had to serve this buttressing function in the past, under conditions of acute economic scarcity. There will be more to say about this possibility below in relation to post-scarcity and qualitatively increased complexity in the social structure of late modern societies.

For the moment it will suffice to note that in the absence of the right kind of knowledge, it is not entirely surprising that governments have been called upon to use the limited capacity at their disposal to try to stabilise banks and other failing financial institutions that have been deemed 'too big to fail,' with all that these measures entail in terms of imposed sacrifices and extra-legal manoeuvres. Yet very few of these temporary interventions address the epistemological problem concerning societal self-government just alluded to. Indeed, it sometimes seems that many informational resources and much organisational energy are wasted on trying to avoid any such discussion, especially, that is, if managers in the media, economy, government, etc., reckon that this displacement of attention away from fundamental issues will eventually somehow create the conditions necessary to restore economic growth. Not too long ago it was perhaps possible to be sanguine about the public sphere or civil society, in more general terms, to foment an incisive debate on such questions. In this regard, there seems to have been a second structural transformation of the public sphere.[1] How else can one explain the

---

1 The concept of structural transformations was initially developed by a number of the first generation Frankfurt School critical legal theorists. See Otto Kirchheimer (1941)

ongoing pretence, for example, that the fiscal nation state that eventually emerged (albeit at very different historical junctures depending on the state in question) from the struggle for post-feudal political form in Europe will now be able, after two world wars and a protracted period of de-colonialisation, to solve the problems posed by the cost of domestic labour in the face of globalised competition, and the continuing prospect of far cheaper labour costs elsewhere in the world? Is it really plausible that the development of new technologies in the so-called advanced economies of Western nation states will suffice indefinitely to postpone an open discussion on the human sacrifices and potential environmental damages involved in remaining blindly committed to an undifferentiated, and dogmatically quantitative notion of economic growth? These dysfunctions will not disappear or solve themselves through spontaneous adjustments. Some kind of knowledgeable planning, or, what is more likely, a transition or structural transformation to qualitatively new economic, political, and educational systems will be needed. In other words, a structural transformation need not be synonymous with a re-jigging of institutions with the aim of maintaining prevailing power relations of the kind Gramsci sometimes has in mind when referring to passive revolutions in the *Prison Notebooks* (see Gerratana 2007: 962–3; 1088–9; 1227–9; 1238).

But it is certainly not obvious which kind of thinking will be most effective in initiating a move in the direction toward a self-steering society approximating the democratic ideal of legitimate self-government. Though Marx may seem outdated and discredited in several respects, a Marxist perspective on the matter is likely to be relevant in at least one: deciding on the appropriate steps toward the implementation of new systems is going to be very difficult in view of the conflicting knowledge and interests of the affected parties and classes, not to mention the divergent perspectives of 'expert' opinion and informed popular opinion. It is highly uncertain if the public sphere, life-world, civil society or some similarly conceived mediating instance is really operative under contemporary socio-economic conditions. They effectively facilitated communication between individual citizens and government during the period accompanying the consolidation of the fiscal nation state, but the latter is now clearly in a process of substantial metamorphosis. The implication is that the structure of mediations is changing, and along with it, forms of conflict, conditions of inequality, and norms of integration. What is more, there is considerable doubt if parties are still in a position to help perform some of the co-ordinating and planning functions that they have done since they took over from the political clubs and civic associations of the early modern public sphere. There will be more to say below about the particular challenges posed by the decline of parties in this regard. Strange as it may sound,

---

and Franz Neumann, 'The Change in the Function of Law in Modern Society' (1937). These essays mark important signposts in a trajectory that runs from Max Horkheimer's 'Critical and Traditional Theory' (1937) to Habermas' *Structural Transformation of the Public Sphere* (1962), and beyond. For a more recent development in this line of theorising and historical research, see Oskar Negt and Alexander Kluge (1973).

the political authority of a post-capitalist society is likely to be post-democratic and dispersed, in that it is likely to be post-fiscal state democracy. The current economic and political crises suggest that the kind of social unity and political consensus required to stabilise the fiscal nation state can no longer be taken for granted or easily re-produced through strategic corporatist compromises between employers' associations, trade union confederations and governments in the way this was secured during the Fordist and post-Fordist periods of growth after 1945. Typically, compromises of this sort tended to be enacted within the confines of a territorial political state regarding itself as a national community generously tolerating the presence of people born elsewhere as long as they worked, paid their taxes, and respected the relevant national traditions. It is rightly a matter of some doubt if the reconstruction of that particular kind of folk-communal cohesion is feasible today, let alone desirable. Hence it is worth inquiring into the unitary premises and assumptions underpinning the workings of the fiscal state, and the modern nation state more generally. After this it will be possible to enquire into the possible contours of potential successor political forms. In anticipation of later stages of the argument, however, it is already worth signalling the parallels between post-democratic and dispersed authority, on the one hand, and contemporary relations between individuals and social systems, on the other. It will be suggested that the gradual demise of the public sphere, life-world, civil society and political parties is part of larger set of processes that are currently transforming patterns of stratification and forms of state. The most appropriate integrative norms corresponding to these transformations have yet fully to emerge. There is nonetheless clear historical and sociological evidence in support of the claim that whilst mediation and communication will persist and continue to fulfil a vital role in decision-making and the formulation of norms, they will be forms thereof that can no longer make unity the fundamental condition of difference.

2

According to the understanding of the relation between freedom and authority implicit in the ideas of many modern political thinkers, there exists a mediated unity between individual citizens, the laws they collectively make—which in turn govern them as individuals—and a state empowered to adjudicate eventual conflicts between private interests and the public good or General Will. This politically and juridically mediated unity can be compared to the mediated unity of subject and object. The comparative analogy can be illustrated as follows: if there was no unity at all between subject and object, i.e., if subject and object were hermetically separated, there would be no mediating instance to establish an epistemological point of contact making subjective knowledge of the objective world possible, and solipsism on the part of isolated subjects would reign. If, on the contrary, subject and object were fused, subjective knowledge of objective reality would be superfluous. In the first case, there is no way for subject to reach object, and knowledge becomes impossible; in the second, there is nothing outside of the subject to know, such that knowledge becomes redundant. Stating the matter in this way highlights the crucial role played by mediation, and the importance of mediation is also clear in the juridical-political analogy. If there was no way to bridge the metaphorical distance between citizens and the state via government, civil society, and law, then rational representation would be impossible. If fusion best described the relation between citizens and the state, then representation, like mediation, would be superfluous. Put another way, identity between citizens and the state would make representative institutions unnecessary, as there would be nothing outside of the citizenry to re-present. Hence just as mediation of some sort is indispensable in both epistemology and politics, it would seem that some kind of unity is as well. The question is, what kind of mediation and what kind of unity, or, to be more precise, what kind of *mediated unity* is one talking about? Is unity best conceived of in terms of a political centre, sovereign foundation, or non-negotiable, fictitious or natural origin? In short, when inquiring into the premises and assumptions informing prevalent understandings of the authority of the modern state, one notes a conceptual constellation featuring mediation, unity, representation and dialectics. Hence the pertinent question, from the perspective of immanent critique, does not really concern the alternatives to mediation, unity, representation, reason, and dialectics; immanent criticism enquires into the qualitative question concerning *which form* of mediation, unity, etc., is most conducive to rational legitimacy as opposed to different types of populist legitimation guided by technocratic-managerial elitism and clientelism.

A dialectical approach to these questions is often attributed to Hegel, Marx, certain negative idealists, or some critical theorists, such as Adorno. But if one is prepared to accept the main lines of the argument invoked thus far, one is for the most part in broad agreement that dialectics informs any vision of epistemology, law and politics that is inclined to regard knowledge and representation in terms of a relationship between various elements that are mediated rather than fused or separated. Wherever there is evidence of social complexity, one observes mediation rather than un-mediated unity or hermetic separation; where there is mediation one observes dialectical relations in operation. Like the questions about mediation and unity, however, the question is: what form of dialectics? Is it likely to be the dialectics of mediated unity (Hegel), mediated disunity (Marx), or the rather un-dialectical notion of non-mediated non-identity, as in Heidegger's conception (must imply mediation) of being? Or do the dialectics of mediated non-identity offer a fuller account of modern complexity, as Adorno seems to argue? If liberals, functionalists, ontological thinkers, post-structuralists and others may style themselves as non-dialectical or post-dialectical thinkers, they still need some conception of mediation if, that is, their respective explanations of law and politics are to have some measure of political relevance, and in order to do this, they will have at some point to resort to a dialectical argument of one kind or another in order to account for the dynamics structuring the exchanges, interactions and communications between governors and governed, lest they construe the latter as fused/separated, or as arbitrary, inexplicable and ultimately mysterious. This study contends that although de-centred and plural, they are certainly not random. If they were, explanation would not be possible anyway, and theory would be both impossible and superfluous. As such, the questions concerning the specific kind of unity one has in mind and the particular type of dialectics producing the unity in question are closely related. Here a note on traditional theory and critical theory, on the one hand, and the unifying dimension of conceptual form and political form, on the other, is indispensable for the further elaboration of the argument sketched here.

Whether one is examining the stipulations governing what can be known to be true or false, subject or object, private or public, etc., one is usually investigating the ways in which two terms are mediated by a third term. Depending on the phenomenon under consideration, the third term serves as the condition for the possibility of the relevant difference between the two terms, and lays the foundation for that distinction. The third term thus lends conceptual form to the relation encompassing all three terms, and confers a provisional unity upon them. In what may be characterised for the moment as traditional theory and positive dialectics, underlying unity acts as the basis of subsequent difference and, in a related vein, notions of natural origins, juridical mediation and monolithic political foundations are loosely articulated together to define the parameters of legitimate authority and tolerable dissent. During the years roughly spanning post-feudalism to incipient globalisation, the modern state is often credited, in traditional theory, with the capacity of providing the overarching unity of citizens and states by reconciling the legal form and legitimate content of a national political community. On this account legality furnishes an overarching form to substantive political essence, where overarching is more or less synonymous with 'perfect' in terms of form, and with 'positive' in terms of dialectics.[2] Immanent critical theory intervenes with the reminder that the apparent unity provided by idealist dialectics (mediated unity) and metaphysical notions of form that frame supposedly deeper, more fundamental content, can tend toward coerced syntheses and forced integration in social practice, i.e., they can help shape institutions in ways that demonstrably harm individuals. This is likely to occur whenever an underlying mediating unity is posited, assumed, or demanded. In sum, it has been shown thus far that where

---

2   Although objectionable in a number of ways, Schmitt is one of the first to follow Marx (perhaps somewhat ironically, given their respective political allegiances) in attempting to explain why the constant adjustment of juridical form to mutations in political essence can never exclude the possibility of extra-legal violence. Remarkable, in this context, is that Schmitt also intuits that the Weimar state, entrusted by the constitution with the task of distilling the political essence of the German people after WWI, was irrevocably losing its capacity to impose this adjustment on society's increasingly protean forms, i.e., was manifestly ill-suited to managing qualitatively enhanced social complexity. See Schmitt (1992 part 2, chapter 2). The Weimar state's incapacity in this regard, which is not unrelated to the crisis of the contemporary state in more general terms, would have come as no surprise to Georg Simmel, the most sophisticated theorist of constellational social form. See Simmel (1992: 695–708).

there is social complexity there is mediation, and, further, that where there is mediation, dialectical operations are at work. It remains to show in more detail that conceptual rigour in these matters is forfeited if underlying, mediated unity is posited as the basis of subsequent difference.[3] Some liberals may be inclined to argue that since *planned unity* is likely to be authoritarian, complex societies composed of autonomous individuals should really rely on the *spontaneous unity* engendered by minimal states and self-regulating, or so-called 'free' markets (as if society and markets are somehow synonymous).[4] Needless to say, the notion of spontaneous unity assumes the availability of a series of economic, political, administrative and cultural resources that would seem to be difficult to presuppose

---

3 For a more detailed exposition focused specifically on Hegel and Adorno see Schecter (2012).

4 It could be plausibly argued that in virtually all social formations antecedent to capitalist forms of production, labour power is always exchanged against other labour power, i.e., that it is a defining characteristic of capitalist production that labour is not directly exchanged against labour, but is bought and sold as a commodity through the abstract mediating instances of contract, money and labour markets. On this account, abstract time and abstract labour make their phenomenological appearance with this qualitative transition in the nature of exchange, i.e., with the commodification of labour power and the largely instrumental mediation of humanity and nature. The rejoinder might be that labour continues to be exchanged against labour in capitalism. But the price *humanity* pays for market-legal universality (formal equality) is abstraction in the institutionalisation of labour power and the fragmented experience of time. At that point it is no longer possible to speak of humanity—one must concede that humanity has been divided into social classes (and along other lines), such that the validity of legal-universal legitimacy becomes contingent upon some kind of mediated re-unification of humanity and nature—not their separation or identity/fusion. It is worth considering if (1) abstraction is intrinsically inimical to the project of non-antagonistic autonomy, and if (2) antagonistic autonomy, which is really more and less 'successful' adaptation to coerced integration, is the inevitable price to pay for formally abstract, juridical equality. This is a pressing issue, given that *existing* formal equality is usually inconsistently formal, in that it often perpetuates various kinds of personal dependence and residually naturalised hierarchy. It will be suggested in what follows that antagonistic autonomy is not the inevitable price to pay for formal abstraction and qualified systemic autonomy. Just as the immanently critical question does not really concern the alternatives to mediation, unity, representation, reason and dialectics, it is not so much a question of alternatives to labour and exchange, as much as it is a question of what kind of exchange, or, the institutional conditions under which labour is carried out. The argument sketched here defends the thesis that in functionally differentiated societies, where the possibility of post-scarcity is real rather than speculative, it is possible to envisage a non-oppressive synthesis of humanity and nature in and through which mediated non-identity gradually becomes institutionalised as a series of plural processes facilitating research into the real conditions of non-antagonistic autonomy. One of the tasks of critical theory today is to re-articulate the reasons why autonomy in practice is unlikely to mean anything other than defensive reaction as long as it is characterised by an unstated denial of the mediated character of all things real. Unmediated autonomy would involve self-causation, and thus imply a kind of divine or metaphysical independence from all external conditions.

in view of the current crises alluded to at the outset of this chapter. There is a history concerning the reasons why such assumptions are problematic; it is one meriting a very brief digression.

3

For many decades, and most notably since 1929, part of what one would perhaps now refer to as governance entails a certain amount of economic planning. But we have recently reached a planning impasse in which neither the Keynesian techniques of the centre-left nor the austerity budgets of the centre-right seem to be able to restore growth. What is more, the political parties and trade unions representing social democratic positions on these questions are gradually losing their capacity credibly to mediate between systemic functions and life-world contexts in the ways that they once could.[5] Hence it is worth investigating the differences between the forms of knowledge that would endeavour to enable late modern societies to be self-steering, in the first instance, and the forms of knowledge that propose to shore up the mediated unity of citizens and the state that for a long time has been the organisational task variously assigned to the nation, state, parties, unions, law, constitutions, welfare, the life-world, or any number of combinations thereof, in the second (this epistemological investigation will eventually lead back to the questions concerning mediation, unity, form, dialectics and representation, as will be seen). Schmitt and Arendt number among the many voices to have raised protest against the conspicuous absence of a distinctly political or republican dimension to this largely technical-administrative task.[6] One may conjecture that the first type of learning entails new ways of thinking about reflexivity and contingency, whereas the second, by definition, is more concerned with techniques of integration. Any persuasive explanation of modern social process that is not over reliant on the simplifications of liberalism, Marxism, elite theory or traditional notions of the state as a political centre, cannot abstract from social differentiation, and as such, must

5   This is the first of two claims requiring much more historical evidence than the scattered references made in this chapter can provide. But the evolution of social democratic parties toward centrist positions that would have been inconceivable in previous decades, and the continuing decline in trade union influence on policy in the same period, suggest that the mediation functions once performed by key institutions in civil society are to an increasing extent performed by individuals and social systems. One can analyse this development in terms of a new kind of polarisation that has relatively little to do with the standard left/right spectrum. Assessing the different possible modalities for organising the co-ordination of individual autonomy and systemic function has therefore become an urgent theoretical and institutional issue.

6   It might therefore be said that politics, in Arendt's vision of non-instrumental political action, is only detectable, excluding rare exceptions, as a trace of its manifest absence in actual institutions. See Arendt (1958 part III).

engage with the discrete dynamics of qualitatively distinct processes.[7] Whether one is attempting to guide the mediation of distinct social systems, and thereby enable them to communicate with one another without unduly infringing on their respective boundaries, or trying somehow to patch up the mediated unity of citizens and the state, important questions arise concerning unity, identity, difference, and the best ways of conceptualising their interrelations. To repeat, the matter has once again become urgent in view of the evident reality that if the one-party states of the last century were woefully inadequate at mediating between private and public concerns, today's multi-party parliamentary political systems are increasingly overburdened by societal demands for flexible and responsive mediation. Stating the matter in these terms will strike many as inadequate due to a lack of terminological clarity. There seems to be some confusion concerning *states* that are empowered to mediate between public and private, and which enjoy a monopoly on the legitimate use of force within a given national territory, on the one hand, and *systemic functions* (religious, political, economic, aesthetic, legal and others) that tend to become differentiated, across national boundaries, in the course of the evolution of modern and late modern societies toward increasing complexity, on the other. It will be seen below that there are reasons for this terminological ambiguity. The uncertainty in question corresponds to a number of sociological realities that have important implications for potential post-capitalist scenarios in an increasing globalised world in which the future role of the nation state is a matter of some debate. Straightaway, however, one notes the incongruities and incommensurable differences between the boundaries that systems have with one another, and which extend beyond national territories, and the boundaries national states have with one another, which impede inter-systemic communication across national lines.

4

One of the ambiguities to be touched upon here is bound up with the methodological difficulties involved in trying to examine the changing relations between autonomy, normativity, facticity and legitimacy. In the wake of Hegel's critique of Kantian formalism and abstraction, substantial agreement has been registered in support of the claim that history and society provide the real grounds for deciding upon the normative components of socio-political order. That is, once the epistemological superiority of historical and sociological explanation over

---

7   For the sake of brevity it might be mentioned in passing that with some exceptions, depending on the intellectual tradition in question, liberalism often simplifies public/private relations, Marxism tends to simply class relations, elite theory has a crude vision of power, and traditional political theory often relies on the a-historical fiction of a state of nature. However flawed, systems theory does attempt to engage with the discrete dynamics of qualitatively distinct social processes. There will be more to say about this below in relation to mediated non-identity.

metaphysical notions of 'the good' has been established, and autonomy as auto-causality has been relinquished as divine, there is little point in debating the merits of abstract criteria of justice, or devising ideal normative standards that would seem to condemn institutional practice in all actual historical contexts as inevitably immoral, illegitimate, or insufficiently rational. Historical perspective thus provides a juridical corrective to static notions of human rights as God-given, whilst also providing a sociological corrective to timeless conceptions of legitimacy as inherently coercive in the Weberian sense of a monopoly on the acceptable use of force. One of the prevailing normative concepts invoked mainly but not exclusively on the left during the period associated with the consolidation of the post-feudal nation state is the idea of equality of formal political inclusion (voting rights, equal rights of assembly, etc.) and socio-economic parity (equality of opportunity, redistributive equality, labour market reform, etc.). In many national contexts the norm of equality was and is still intended to serve as a partial remedy to the realities of class, race and gender stratification. It is nonetheless far from obvious how stratification is best conceived within functionally differentiated societies. The framing of the phenomenon of social class within a larger paradigm of imputed national interest and competitive unity, centred on notions of integration, affordable levels of redistribution, and guaranteed secure borders, for example, illustrates some of the problems raised by many models of stratification, and points toward the path of investigation to be followed in the rest of this chapter.

Class is frequently explained with reference to upper, middle, lower middle, and lower positions. If one invokes a spatial metaphor featuring higher and lower locations in order to explain class dynamics, however, one can easily deduce somewhat crude stratification models of inequality and power. One caricature that comes to mind is the model of society imagined as a pyramid with a small number of upper class people situated approximately three quarters of the way towards the steadily narrowing top, culminating in a pinnacle where there is room for a single person. This person can be regarded as someone who takes over from the regent, albeit with the dubious distinction of having earned his or her position. According to what one might for the moment call pyramidal logic, this tiny *number* of undemocratically inclined elites are separated by a larger number of state officials beneath them, who protect the elites above them from the far larger number of middle and lower class people who in their turn can be found beneath the state officials, and who fill out the lower echelons of the pyramid, which becomes increasingly numerous and, by extension, increasingly democratic, the further down one proceeds. Staying with the same logic, the people at the very bottom can be regarded as the most democratic of the demos, that is, they incarnate the essence of the people by being the most numerous and, in several senses, the most popular. Within the paradigm of traditionally conceived democratic politics, they are the authority in absence, or, stated differently, they re-present the trace of truly popular sovereignty. The manifest inadequacy of this model of society is not invoked to deny the ongoing reality of class, or to dismiss the persistence of gender, race or other forms of inequality—hence the 'yes, please!' in the title of this chapter. It is intended to raise questions about all accounts of action and political authority that implicitly suppose that any intricately structured society could conform to the model of a pyramid or some similar top-down, hierarchical structure crowned by an elite pinnacle that is both challenged and stabilised by a firm, popular foundation. However exaggerated this particular example may be, it is not entirely preposterous, in that lay and expert sociological opinion alike are in the habit of discussing upward mobility as a vertical journey toward spaces that become less numerous, and more to difficult to attain as one heads toward the steadily narrowing summit.[8]

Moreover, by misconstruing society in this way, there is also a tendency to view the state as something that manages to stand outside of and above society and is, somehow, nonetheless responsible for adjudicating the diverse conflicts and malfunctions within it. Alternatively, the state can be posited as the foundation that distributes homogenous *units* of power unequally, so that some people have more power than others, and thus can be grouped accordingly in classes, which, in their turn, have power over other classes, so that justice consists in a more equal sharing of the units by the central distributor. The notion of homogeneous power units is invoked to emphasise that the suitability of vertical spatial metaphors depends on the premise that the individuals involved in intra-class solidarity and inter-class conflict are struggling over the same thing. This premise is difficult to corroborate under conditions of contingency and complexity. The more general point is that equality may well be the best integrative norm for a society that is hierarchically stratified; this is likely to remain the case to a considerable extent as long as society continues to be characterised by non-egalitarian life-chances and discriminatory access to education, housing, health and information. What is clear, however, is that the debates pitting justice as redistributive fairness against individual liberty and economic efficiency, i.e., debates about the role of the state in the administration of units that are supposedly desired by all in the same way and in the same measure, rely on static ideas about human nature and a-historical

---

8   The second of the two claims requiring much more historical evidence than the scattered references made in this chapter can provide is that relatively un-differentiated societies may have actually functioned roughly in this way. Where political, military, religious, and aesthetic authority are closely bound up together, caste-like forms of legitimation tend to endow social facts and norms with a rigidly natural sense of stasis and inevitable hierarchy that is captured by the term tradition. It is not accidental that in the course of social evolution from caste to class, one witnesses increased differentiation of function and the ongoing, if somewhat faltering disaggregation, depending on context, of religious and political authority, political authority and economic power, religious ritual and aesthetic expression, etc. The fiscal state may well have offered stable institutional parameters for the parallel processes in question, but it has certainly ceased to do so in its national instantiation after 1989. These processes are now pushing for a further de-naturalised evolution from caste to class and beyond. But the coexistence of internationally differentiated systems and nationally grounded states, which in the present situation seems to make Greece and Spain seem like default nations, is impeding this possibility from unfolding. The likely consequences and possible conflicts can only be touched upon here.

conceptions of the legitimate state. Is it not time to discard a normative paradigm based on the juxtaposition of the fair, social democratic welfare state, and the efficient, individual liberty-enhancing liberal state? According to the political epistemology implied by this paradigm, fairness will inevitably appear to be a luxury, whilst efficiency will seem more realistic, if not more rational. Fairness and rationality are therefore disadvantaged vis-à-vis this particular reality principle, which reduces reason to distorted individualist realism, whilst also transposing an atomised struggle over the same thing into an imaginary collective experience akin to a spontaneous and unanimous decision to leave the state of nature.

The notion of incommensurable reality principles raises a number of hypotheses. Some of the methodological and political problems bound up with an excessive focus on vertical stratification come into focus when one considers that modern societies are not merely stratified, but also functionally differentiated, so that attempts to correct stratification that do not take differentiation into account are very likely to privilege quantitative solutions to problems that have become qualitative at distinct junctures in social evolution. Such privileging can lead to delayed reforms, missed transitions and postponed structural transformations. These phenomena can in turn appear to affect people in random, haphazard ways akin to bad luck or individual incompetence, when in fact they are really instances of inadequate societal learning and inflexible collective adaptation to socio-historical change. This is relevant to the problem of dogmatic commitment to an undifferentiated notion of economic growth, i.e. a form of growth that, at precise historical moments, needs to become educational and communicative rather than merely monetary or technical. Qualitative growth is thus not always synonymous with expansion, and may well entail reducing the scale of environmentally unsafe production and unnecessarily repetitive patterns of consumption that are simply wasteful according to several democratic criteria, such that *growth* may demand *decreased* subjection to routine and artificially accelerated temporality in and outside of the workplace. One of the many implications is that research into the dynamics of capitalism and class is not primarily about 'human interest' or the pathos of what can appear to be cases of individual or group destiny. It is really research about the interrelations between societal resource allocation, collective learning processes, and evaluating choices when adapting to contingency and complexity. To repeat, the aim here is not to deny the persistence of stratification or privileged classes. It is, on the contrary, to promote a shift in emphasis in the understanding of such phenomena. In keeping with previous observations about alternative mediations, dialectics, unity, representation, instead of alternatives to mediation, dialectics, etc., the hope is to shed light on what already exits, however provisionally at present, on a post-class basis, so that a post-class society can better become a lived reality. Similarly, there are more and less promising ways of challenging the ostensible incompatibility of sociological and normative approaches to autonomy and qualitative innovation. In the longer term it will be normatively and sociologically more beneficial and efficient to dismantle the class character of production than it will be to entrench the division of labour still further in the name of efficiency/competitive necessity, or to substitute wage labour with industrial redundancy and palliative welfare. The reason why it may be possible to re-orient production, politics, law, education, housing, medicine, and energy allocation, is that late modern societies are simultaneously caste stratified, class stratified, as well as post-class, mass societies. Class thus co-exists with the remnants of caste, its historical antecedent, as well as with its historical successor, whose sociological profile has yet clearly to emerge, and is not adequately captured by the term 'mass.' Notions of homogeneous power units and linear time cannot adequately theorise this simultaneity.

The impulse to relativise the significance of class through the valorisation of feminist, ecological, gay rights and a host of other struggles and movements goes some of the way toward addressing this theoretical problem. But relativising class can also distort the relativity of stratification within a broader sociology of power still further, especially if the conclusion is simply that we must democratise and broaden our conceptions of conflict and exclusion to include hitherto neglected groups. This can easily serve to strengthen a narrowly meritocratic view of society that exalts competition and hierarchy as the fairest and most efficient way to allocate natural, political, economic, constitutional and aesthetic resources whilst simultaneously integrating people according to a zero-sum logic that blunts particularity in the name of individual success. In other words, there is manifest evidence of the existence of vertically-structured, stratified social spaces that one can still analyse in terms of class, and there are continued indices of horizontally-structured social spaces that can be studied in terms of gender, race, generation, and a number of other indicators. There is, however, also clear evidence of the emergence of constellational social spaces that are inter-systemic and mediated according to the de-centred dynamics of proximity-distance, intimacy-formality, conservatism-innovation, competition-cooperation, communication-silence, contingency-causality, and a wide range of other interactive reciprocal exchanges (in Simmel's sense) that are asymmetrical with regard to vertical and horizontal configurations. Whilst vertically and horizontally structured fields (in Bourdieu's sense) continue to pre-form and overdetermine subjectivity in palpable ways, this is markedly less true of constellational spaces. The proliferation of the latter in late modernity indicates that differences in individual values and aspirations no longer need directly to translate into socio-economic and political inequality. Figuratively poor translation of this kind can be interpreted as symptomatic of insufficient differentiation, which, in turn, is likely to result in limited and inadequate forms of inclusion that remain wedded to dichotomous mediations carried out along a fictitious central axis (a state deciding on what is public/private, etc.). Such mediations isolate people and phenomena that might otherwise co-exist and communicate without hierarchical distinction, such as the workforce, whilst also forcing non-identical phenomena together into unities that are coerced and contrived, such as the nation-state. In this context one thinks of the separation of citizens as a juridical condition of their competitive fungibility on labour markets, misleadingly termed autonomy, and analogous to the prying apart of subject and object deemed necessary for post-metaphysical epistemology, on the one hand, and the presupposed 'democratic' unity of citizens needed constantly to reproduce post-traditional and nonetheless legally binding political legitimation, analogous to the makeshift reconciliation of subject and object required in order for there to be something like knowledge of some sort, however instrumental, following the demise of metaphysical unity, on the other. Here the parallel between instrumental knowledge and instrumental legitimacy comes into focus, thus highlighting Marx's continuing relevance as well as the limitations to his approach to these questions.

Marx may have been correct to suggest that at distinct historical stages in the evolution of the mediations of humanity and nature, class conflict promotes the development of industry as well as new forms of compromise characterised by reason and codified compromise and agreement (natural and positive law), rather than by naturally assigned roles of privilege, such as rank and status. At a later moment in that process, which may now be actual or gradually becoming actual, rigidly demarcated social classes become an impediment to the proliferation of genuinely efficient ways of analysing problems and deploying resources in search of solutions to those problems. In this context the intensification of de-naturalisation can be interpreted in conjunction with a possible transition from quantitative notions of growth and production, to more subtle and nuanced ideas and institutions fostering creativity, choice, and diversity that are incompatible not only with class rigidity, but with institutionalised gender discrimination, racial prejudice, and other forms of ossified traditional practice that make for waste in this extended sense of dysfunctional deployment of accrued learning. Marx is perhaps less visionary in his assessment that the ruling classes eventually become an impediment to the further development of the forces of production. He does not place enough emphasis on the possibility that it is humanity's conception of production and productivity that has to evolve in ways that entail reversing, differentiating, and, in the language of systems theory, de-coupling and re-coupling. This is somewhat different than saying that the forces of production must be liberated to the point where they can continually expand, and universal abundance may reign over scarcity. The alleged scarcity invoked by 'the troika' in the recent bank bailouts is certainly an attack on those who can least afford to subsidise banks. But it is also real, socially and cognitively generated scarcity, and, in an extended sense, dialectical scarcity that can be analysed and addressed. Like productivity, scarcity must be redefined, just as, for example, explanations of power will have to move away from an imputed will to exploitation and domination on the part of the tiny number at the top of a pyramid, toward an account of deficient mediations between humanity and nature, and other more epistemologically focused explanations guided by the insight that the critique of epistemology is also social critique and vice versa (see Adorno 1969: 157–8 [1982: 503]). The capability or incapability of a given society to initiate a transition from quantitative to qualitative reform, as well as a structural transformation from instrumental legitimacy to genuinely individual legitimacy, has much to do with the outcomes of collective learning processes and what is referred to above in relation to the related theses that 1) modern societies are too complex to organise from a political centre such as the state, and 2) these societies need the kind of knowledge that would enable them to steer themselves toward transitions to qualitative reform at key moments in their evolution toward increased complexity. One tentative conclusion is that the tendency of late modern societies across national boundaries to evolve toward differentiated function, if given the appropriate institutional framework, could liberate humanity from the coercive forms of normativity and integration that seem to characterise relatively undifferentiated social formations, where it may have been plausible to think that the ascension of one group was coterminous with the decline of another. Under these conditions, subaltern groups are more or less compelled to aspire to take the place of the people 'above' them, so that challenges to the existing hierarchies—even or especially in the name of equality—must also affirm the necessity of hierarchy. As Tocqueville and many others have observed, equality in practice can turn out to be one such coercive norm, especially when it helps foster a culture of passivity, conformism and specious meritocracy. But one might well ask: what are the realistic alternatives to equality and meritocracy, if not privilege and corruption? A tentative response comes in the final section below.

5

The class pyramid alluded to in overdrawn terms for the sake of argument can be compared to a barely differentiated society in which most artistic expression is related to religious worship, law and political authority are shaped by scripture, the economy is organised around sowing and harvesting rituals, and military considerations are guided by faith. The point of the comparison is to illustrate how enduring stratification and insufficient differentiation mutually condition one another, and to show, further, why it may be time to re-think the rather formulaic notion according to which 'more' freedom/liberalism/capitalism leads to 'less' solidarity/equality/democracy and vice versa, as if (1) there was a sliding scale or continuum between the most popular, democratic classes of the people, and the minuscule, anti-democratic minority ensconced at the people's summit, and (2) the state can adjudicate the claims of freedom and equality along some foundational axis that might yield a universally valid 'solution' doing 'justice' to all points, via representation through parties, along that continuum. There are two central objections to the continuum paradigm. First, if one begins thinking in terms of the most popular classes of the people, then one is very likely to pose the tautological question asking who *the most popular* of the people are. From here it is a short step to the identification of kulaks, race enemies, gender subversives and other internal foes of the people; it is a step likely to produce heroes and personality and leadership cults around those vying for the top spot of most popular/electorally successful. Otherwise stated, a political minefield opens up if politics becomes a *'who question,'* as it often does in the vertical, and to a lesser extent horizontal social space-frameworks. The problem is not that this kind of politics is personalised. On the contrary, a 'who question' can generally be administered with a 'how much' (money, status, officially assigned recognition) answer that actually marginalises what is really individual about the person identified by the who category, i.e., by the concept of the 'who' in question. Second, there are far too many constellational social spaces interrupting and rupturing this hopelessly simple vision of a tug of war, which is why terns like 'capitalism,' 'the state,' and 'democracy' need to be deconstructed into their systemic constituents, bearing in mind that there will be disagreements about how many significant systems there are, and where their boundaries lie. But extensive and creatively implemented systemic differentiation may be far more effective than what too often passes for democratisation (if, say, it is enacted as state ownership or nationalisation) in challenging the prerogatives of capital to dictate what is produced, and to subordinate all social systems to the aesthetic, legal, political, and religious commands that are still embedded in economic systems geared toward growth at all costs, where growth is typically assessed in undifferentiated terms that are usually almost exclusively quantitative. There are good grounds to believe that dis-embedding those commands from the economic system will make the decision-making processes in each system more transparent and subject to juridically-mediated criteria of accountability, if, that is, the inter-systemic mediations can be organised in such a way as to enhance the communication between them whilst also reflexively respecting—not fetishising—their particular logics. Decision-making will be needed, however, as systems are considerably less self-steering (*autopoietic*) than Niklas Luhmann and others systems theorists seem to be willing to admit.

Social systems operate according to a mode of speechless communication that couples, de-couples and re-couples them to other social systems without organically uniting them to one another. Hence the final questions raised here are: *how* does this happen, and, why are 'how questions' sociologically more reliable and normatively more promising than 'who questions'? The argument elaborated here indicates that social systems do not gravitate around a central axis in the manner of a legal form of legitimacy or a *mediated unity* of individual, law, and state. Mediated unity is as suspect as a supposed continuum between people, nation and state, or a sliding scale between 'more' liberalism and 'less' democracy or vice versa. The concept of mediated unity, like the concept of a legal form of legitimacy, invokes the idea perfect form, or, stated otherwise, it conjures up the idea of symmetrical, though dichotomous harmonisation of particular/universal, public/private, individual/state. In this context perfect form is akin to consensual rather than antagonistic integration. Given that the dialogue and communication needed to produce consensus or perfect form is manifestly absent, might it not be salutary to reconsider the dialectics of speech and speechless communication, and the mediated non-identity of social systems? In so doing it may be possible to re-think 'the how' of mediations without a central mediator, whilst re-thinking the dynamics of plural mediation in late modern societies.

The social democratic and more resolutely socialist project to fill (and eventually subvert by exceeding) abstract liberal political form with concrete social content, in the name of substantive as opposed to merely formal democracy, has ceased to command attention as a feasible solution to the current crises. Instead, it may now be possible to envisage a suitably de-centred and legitimate form of law capable of synthesising humanity and nature without damaging individual human natures. This enhanced synthetic capacity does not arise in order to realise an apparently friendly human essence against formal essence, which too often turns out to be passive, populist, mechanically assimilated, coercively integrated or, on the contrary, marginalised and even silenced. The capacity arises as an abstract and reflexive response to the reality that the synthetic mediation of humanity and nature affects the socialisation and integration of individuals according to criteria that can range in quality from arbitrary and instrumental to uniquely suited to individual ability and need, where the term 'uniquely suited' broadly corresponds to non-ideological reconciliation, i.e., non-antagonistic autonomy.

References

Adorno, Theodor W. (1969) 'Zu Objekt und Objekt,' in *Stichworte: Kritische Modelle 2* (Frankfurt: Suhrkamp), reprinted as 'Subject and Object' in Andrew Arato and Eike Gebhardt (eds), *The Essential Frankfurt School Reader* (New York: Continuum), 1982.

Arendt, Hannah (1958) *The Human Condition*. Chicago: University of Chicago Press.

Gerratana, Valentino (ed.) (2007) *Antonio Gramsci, Quaderni del carcere*. Turin: Einaudi.

Kirchheimer, Otto (1941) 'Changes in the Structure of Political Compromise,' in Andrew Arato and Eike Gebhardt (eds), *The Essential Frankfurt School Reader* (New York: Continuum) 1982, pp. 49–70.

Negt, Oskar and Kluge, Alexander (1973) Öffentlichkeit und Erfahrung [*The Public Sphere and Experience*]. Frankfurt: Suhrkamp.

Neumann, Franz (1937) 'The Change in the Function of Law in Modern Society,' in William Scheuerman (ed.), *The Rule of Law under Siege: Selected Essays of Franz L. Neumann and Otto Kirchheimer* (Berkeley: University of California Press), 1996 pp. 101–41.

Schecter, Darrow (2012) 'Unity, Identity and Difference: Reflections on Hegel's Dialectics and Negative Dialectics,' in the *History of Political Thought*, 33, pp. 258–79.

Schmitt, Carl (1992) *Legalität und Legitimität* [*Legality and Legitimacy*]. Berlin: Duncker & Humblot (fifth edition, 1993).

Simmel, Georg (1992) *Soziologie* [1908]. Frankfurt: Suhrkamp.

Chapter 11

An Avant-garde 'without Authority': Towards a Future Oekoumene—if there is a Future?

jan jagodzinski

'this fragile, broken time of transition (Übergangszeit)': the ice that supports people today becomes thinner with each passing day, so that 'we ourselves who are homeless constitute a force that breaks open ice and other all too thin 'realities' (Nietzsche, *The Gay Science*: section 377).

The pessimism that surrounds critical thought today is more than just an image of a perpetual eclipse of the sun that keeps everything cold, dark—pervaded by imperceptible movement—frozen, immobile, sluggish; it's as if the noosphere has a cancer, which has spread around the world, turning thought so inside itself as to make it cannibalistic, feeding on its own negativity. The conditions for its remission seem impossible—the patient is already dead from exhaustion and bombardment from the heavy doses of chemotherapy; all the seasons are becoming winter.

This chapter concerns itself with the intersection of two concepts—the Anthropocene and an 'avant-garde without authority'—to develop what Deleuze and Guattari called a 'new earth,' which I call a future 'Oekoumenal' (from the Greek root Oikúméne, meaning the inhabited world or better, inhabited universe).[1] The trajectory of this chapter struggles with the pervasive question of capitalist economic expansion as it continues to destroy the earth and eventually 'bury' us as a species. The Anthropocene, coined by Paul Crutzen, a Nobel Prize winning atmospheric chemist, marks a new geological epoch wherein human activity has begun to tip the planet's geological and biological levels that sustain us. Humans have become a 'geological agent' on the planet, and they are now able to affect the balance of life on Earth. It is the first time that a global awareness of what we are doing to ourselves as a species has emerged—like fish in water who finally 'get it' that they are in 'hot water' about to boil. They better figure out a way to cool themselves down as the oxygen begins to escape and they suffocate, floating belly up.

---

1 This essay is dedicated to my teacher Harry Garfinkle who first introduced the concept of Oekoumene to me many, many years ago, which has subsequently sparked this chapter.

The separation between nature and culture that forms the gap of anthropocentric thought is more and more problematic to maintain. 'Natural history' and 'human history' have now merged together. We become one species amongst many. Although we remain the dominant species, we are intimately involved in the parametric condition of our own existence with the 'rest' of them. We have reached a historical point where we are not free to do whatever we like; yet we are like the proverbial Coyote chasing the Roadrunner who has run over the cliff and has not yet realized he is ready for a long fall to his death. We have yet to look 'down,' for our species is already without any planetary ground to stand on. The 'ground' has been gradually clearing away. Hurricane Katrina ravaged New Orleans on August 29, 2005; earthquakes shook the interior of China—the suspicion was that they were caused by the building of the gargantuan Three Georges dams, which resulted in a huge artificial lake that changed the balance of the surrounding landscape; floods and fires in Australia in 2012 and 2013 seem cyclical, as they are in states like California, as well the 'superstorm,' named hurricane Sandy that hit the eastern seaboard of the United States on October 30, 2012. When New York, New Jersey and Staten Island are devastated, even the disbelievers begin to question under their breadth. Typhoon Haiyan that devastated the Republic of the Philippines led Yeb Sano, their chief negotiator, to address the 19th United Nations summit in Warsaw on November 13, 2013 to no avail. The summit ended with little to no agreement amongst the participating nations.

The Capitalist 'Climate'

Climate change has become the iconic signifier for the 'impending Apocalypse,' however this is a very small part of the story. Leading climatologists at the Stockholm Resilience Center like James Hansen have identified no less than nine 'planetary boundaries' that are crucial to sustain an environment where our species can continue to exist (Foster, Clark and York 2010). Besides climate change, they keep abreast of ocean acidification, nitrogen and phosphorous cycles, atmospheric aerosol loading, chemical pollution, stratospheric ozone depletion, global fresh water use, change in land use and the loss of biodiversity. By comparing the statistics of these nine indicators with pre-industrial levels and current industrial outputs, it seems that three of the nine processes have already crossed their planetary boundaries: climate change, the nitrogen cycle and biodiversity loss. The earth's 'carrying capacity,' its global footprint, has surpassed the ability of the planet to regenerate already by a whopping 30 percent (WWF 2008: 2). To this can be added population growth, increased consumption of natural resources as well as the potential of a global epidemic. The survival of our species doesn't appear that likely. It also highlights and makes starkly evident that our species has enjoyed its continuous expansion, and use of 'free' natural resources at the expense of other species—not to mention the extraordinary global inequalities between the affluent core industrialized nations with capitalist world economies who use up more of the planet's natural resources and emit more green-house gas emissions than the 'rest' of the globe.[2]

Capitalism's system of exploitation works on commodity production where everything is treated as if it had a price. Yet, much of what enters the capitalist system is *not produced* as commodities. Labor-power is a purchased commodity, but it is reproduced within the family and through the educational institutions. This is also true of natural resources such as water and air, which cannot be assigned a market price since they are not strictly 'produced' as commodities. Human and natural resources are wild cards in relation to commodity calculation. They are necessary preconditions for production, but their 'value' is open-ended. The old-fashioned Oedipal family that was sufficient for industrial capital has gone through modification to include both women's labor and increasingly more McJobs for the growing children who can't quite support themselves. Add to this progression the contemporary development of flexible time where work and play no longer are separate categories, and we have capitalist expansion via an increase in labor power. Consumption is calculated in two different ways: the first makes all producers consumers where production *is* consumption; the entire processes from the extraction of natural resources to their end use are 'counted.' There is an investment by producers involved in this process. In contrast, economic consumption refers only to the purchases of consumers. This economic calculation is based on the demand of consumers and not the investors. The capacity to produce in a capitalist economy requires investment, which is not factored in when consumers are asked to 'cut' consumption and 'save,' thereby also 'saving' the planet. Such rhetoric covers up the obvious claim that capital always converts savings into investment to generate new forms of capital that expand the scale of the economy. Capitalist expansion is therefore the chief worry of environmental health.

Deleuze and Guattari maintain that capitalist commodity-production system has no intrinsic limit. Any limits are continually displaced in the processes of expanding and intensifying global production and profit taking. Regardless of the catastrophe—war, natural disasters, political crisis—not to mention any form of health issue or human folly, there is some company that will manage to exploit it for profit dollars, or some reality television show that will turn it into entertainment dollars. Even a Marxist intellectual like Ivan Mészáros (2008), who still believes that only a radical mass movement can flip the course of events, is not optimistic when it comes to the ecological limits of capitalism: "The uncomfortable truth of the matter is that if there is no future for a radical mass movement in our time, there will be no future for humanity" (149) [because] "*the extermination of humanity* is the ultimate concomitant of capitalism's destructive course of development" (252, original emphasis).

---

2   "Overall the richest 20% of the world's population is responsible for over 60% of its current emissions of greenhouse gases. That figure surpasses 80% if our past contributions to the problem are considered" (Roberts 2001: 502).

The capitalist exploitation of the environment has now settled into an ecological modernization where a managerial approach spreads over technology, consumption and market-based solutions under the master signifier of 'sustainability.' Green capitalism moves into 'sustainable capitalism,' sadly a position promoted by Al Gore (2009). Multinational companies and multilateral financial institutions are charged with a new developmental role to initiate sustainable development initiatives in developing countries. The writings of Adrian Parr (2009, 2011), from a Deleuze-Guattarian perspective, captures this newly found fervor extremely well. She shows how the sustainability 'movement,' which promotes principles of equality, stewardship, compassion, renewal and sustenance is hijacked by corporate and state interests through ecobranding tactics (her examples are Wal-Mart and British Petroleum). Hollywood gets a 'piece of this green action' by supporting animal rights and reducing its ecological footprint by spending part of a film's production budget on partnering with 'green industries' that plant trees and recycle material through waste management. On a broader scale, there have been more clever ways of promoting the postmodern 'Nobel Savage' as tied to issues of environmentalism,[3] and producing apocalyptic scenarios via the movies. The spectacle and fantasies of our species destruction and environmental catastrophes through this steady stream of films end up, paradoxically 'naturalizing' our extinction. The worst scenarios (be they a global epidemic, a nuclear winter, meteoric impacts, and so on) enable audiences to take in these 'final days' as domesticated fantasies. There is a normative sense about our destruction, as if humans are still around to tell the tales of our own obliteration, making it seem as though the future anterior is still operable by assuring us that 'we' will not be forgotten as a species.[4]

The commodification of Nature within capitalist expansion is presented in such a way that it avoids all Nature's sublimity; it's as though there will be a

---

3   This trope has to be continually rethought by Hollywood to appease the growing Indigenous crisis that persists throughout the world, whether it is in Canada with the recent 'Idle no More' Movement, and other Northern countries like Finland's Sámi people, or be it New Zealand Maori, Australian Aboriginal populations and so on. In the mid-80s, the Noble Savage trope was high on the Hollywood film list because of the 500-year celebrations that marked Columbus's landing. But this has now died down. Yet, the outreach to Indigenous peoples as being ecological stewards is more to appease tensions than to take seriously their life-styles and economic ways. Many ecological groups see hunting and fishing as a bye-gone economy that does more harm than good.

4   Two excellent examples are mentioned by Tim Matta and Aidan Tynan (2012): *Wall-E* presents a robot that acts as a proxy for humanity; having developed a glitch, he rummages through the trash of human history on the deserted planet Earth assuring us that the human archive will persist. In *The Age of Stupid*, a similar scenario repeats itself. A lone archivist presides over the entire digitalized memory of humanity in a future world of 2055 that has suffered environmental collapse via climate change. Through a series of narratives of actual news and documentary footage, he reconstructs just how our species destruction came about. In both cases the future anterior is operable to teach us the 'lessons' we need.

technological 'fix' to any forms of disaster that may come our way. The call for the technological increase in energy and carbon 'efficiency' is particularly insidious, as indicated by the rhetoric over fuel-efficient cars. The gains made through fuel-efficient cars are simply lost by the increase of consumption of more such cars. Efficiency and scale are related to economic gains.[5] Speculation is now underway regarding how it will be possible and probable to secure new energy resources in the Arctic, which will be available once the ice cap melts away. It is estimated that up to one quarter of the world's oil and gas reserves are just waiting to be harnessed. Territorial borders between Canada, Russia, United States, Norway, and Denmark are already simmering. Capitalism has always disdained 'nature.' Gone are the days where Nature was to be either venerated or conquered in good-old Enlightenment or Romantic fashion.

To sell it, Nature has to become domesticated as much as possible, presented within the fantasies of healthy living and a social life-style though various ecovillage schemes, on the one hand, and gated communities on the other. Both are reactions to a growing deep-seated paranoia that one has to look after oneself in relation to the steady withdrawal of the State (various governmental agencies) for providing the populace police protection, on the one hand, and social welfare programs, on the other. The State's dwindling power in relation to capitalist corporations that privatize health, control the costs of food and housing materials, and so on is yet another source of paranoia and uncertainty. As alternatives to these social and economic contradictions, the ecovillage mentality (forms of New Age communes, religious communities, squatter settlements) presents semi-sufficient, privatized, closed environments where 'small-is-beautiful' rules to sustain human-scale cooperation, housing, organic food production and so on; whereas the gated communities (in stark distinction) privatize and 'protect' life-styles via an internalization of the broader social paranoia that is indicative via a surveillance mentality (video technologies, security guards, intercoms) that already pervades the urban landscape. Both negate urban life as having fallen to the dictates of 'lawlessness,' whether this be the inability of the State to stop crime or 'regulate' the price of sustainable living (food and housing) and life style. The extreme example is Masdar City that is being built in Abu Dhabi, billed as an eco city totally controlled for entrepreneurial living. Perhaps more alarming is the 'gated' mentality that is extended to a nation via militarism. The most extreme example is, of course, Israel with its wall that keeps it 'protected' from its enemies so as to 'sustain' and develop its internal resources and attempt to control its economy. Geopolitical military policies and environmentalism are pervasive in every country, making any attempt to grapple with the global reality of environmental degradation (clean

---

5   In economics this is known as the Jevons paradox or effect. In the nineteenth century William Stanley Jevons noted that every increase of efficiency in steam engine design led only to expanding their numbers. The amount of coal burnt increased, not decreased! Efficiency in resource translates as increase in the rate of consumption of that resource.

water, ozone depletion, pollution of the ocean, and so on) fall into a continual stalemate as prioritization and the public commons cannot be reconciled.[6]

Climate change, as can be seen, has been widely discussed, debated, and while it is a 'no brainer' for scientists who have made the necessary calculations and projections, the gap between knowledge and belief persists. Ecological disaster is inevitable but the symptoms as to its inevitability appear in various paranoid forms. Deleuze and Guattari maintain that under capitalism there are two poles of *social psychic* libidinal investment: paranoia and schizophrenia. Schizophrenia is a free-form of desire in the psyche and refers to deterritorialization as well as decoding. Paranoia, on the other hand, refers to those obstacles that prevent the free-form potential desire. Reterritorialization and artificial recording are imposed by private capital to ensure profit accumulation. Capitalism is basically a system of unsustainable development, a crisis-ridden mode of cyclical economic growth and collapse. We have, in this regard, Slavoj Žižek's (2010) constant championing of Hegel as a theorist of this very dynamic. "[F]or Hegel, every social reconciliation is doomed to fail, [...] *no organic social order can effectively contain the force of abstract-universal negativity* [...]. This is why social life is condemned to the 'spurious infinity' of the eternal oscillation between stable civic life and wartime perturbation" (336, original italic).[7] In contrast, Deleuze and Guattari's 'Marx' is Nietzschean, which calls on affirmation rather than Hegelian negation. This does not sit very well for the prophets of negativity.[8] In relation to the concept of 'an avant-garde without authority' as it impacts the Anthropocene/capitalism problematic that will be discussed in the next section, the tension between these

---

6   So the ironic example is that of the United Nations Climate Change conference in Copenhagen in 2009, which cost the Danes $122 million to secure the nation's capital so that it would go on. The self-interest amongst the well-off countries, especially China given its economic boom in Shanghai, kept weakening the accord that was 'finally' struck. In contrast the financial meltdown of 2008 was met by 'saving' the planet through government bailouts.

7   I think another irony emerges when it comes to these speculations: the double negative Žižek theorizes as the negativity of Nature as a radical Other which always threatens humanities annihilation, and the negativity of human subjectivity as destructive of Nature itself. This double-negative is, however, a positive, as it is precisely this heterogeneous symbiosis that both harnesses Nature (e.g., nuclear energy) and contains its potentially excessive threat (nuclear explosion). The symbiosis is machinic and not anthropomorphic; it implies that somehow humanity confronts its own 'essence,' as Žižek (2010: 336) maintains, the 'negative core of its being,' because of the threat of Nature that has then to be negated. The machinic symbiosis does not indicate an essence, but experimentation with it. Where such experimentation leads is never a foregone conclusion but is more in keeping with the Nietzschean (1998) caveat: "there is a world of difference between the reason for something coming into existence in the first place and the ultimate use to which it is put" (12).

8   For a thorough examination of this development see "Marx Through Deleuze " (Choat 2010: 125–154).

two positions needs some articulation since I come down on the side of Deleuze and Guattari rather than Žižek.

Žižek's Hegelianism[9] works on the topography of 'abstract universality,' which is subverted by a 'concrete exception' or singularity amongst the multiplicity of particulars that the Universal claims to 'cover.' Such an exceptional particular is both part of the Universal set and beyond the set. It is that 'exceptional' element that produces 'concrete universality' (or 'singular Universality'). Within abstract Universality there is an immediate struggle or negation as this 'singular' element—basically the abstract Universal's opposite—is engaged with other particulars within the set for hegemony. We have here essentially an open system whose dynamic is forwarded by the negentropy of the 'exceptional element,' which is absent, but then 'negated' via the struggle for inclusion (as lack) or exclusion (as excess), depending on the context. This forms the concrete Universal. Such a perpetual struggle is between the abstract Universal and its own exception (or 'remainder') where the absence of the singular exception is understood as the presence of the Real. The Real is being constantly confronted by the Symbolic in Lacanian terms. In this typology the Real is only a void by proxy since it can be 'symbolically' identified, yet it is the constant source of traumatic antagonism, which returns again and again as all attempts to 'symbolize' it fail. The Universal is thus paradoxical—it is both necessary and impossible.

The Real remains a paradoxical concept as well—and here's why: if the concrete Universal emerges at the point of exception (as embodied in those who are part of the situation but do not belong to it), we have the ironic situation, in relation to the Anthropocene, that it is 'we' who are hegemonic, and that the 'rest' of Nature—the Planet, whom we are destroying—is doing precisely what is expected: it is about to 'do' us in, not intentionally of course, but through its own machinic existence. It is humanity who is 'out of joint,' a failed experiment of the same machinic process. The Real is not absent. It is very much the 'presence' of machinic Nature as such in the way it functions through creation and destruction.[10] Hegel is simply stood on his head for the anthropomorphism inherent in this line of logic. It is not 'human' Universality that is at question, it is the Planet's Universality. We should call what the Real 'is': machinic Nature as such where there is no distinction

---

9 Žižek is never consistent in his Universal/Particular/Singular relationships as extracted from Hegel. They change throughout his many books. For various explications on this see Kisner's (2008) "The Concrete Universal in Žižek and Hegel" and McMillan's (2012) clarifying attempt to articulate Žižek's political position based on the 'concrete universal.' Žižek's (1999) defense of Hegel is introduced in a rigorous manner in the second chapter of *The Ticklish Subject* and his most recent 1000 page Magnus Opus on Hegel, *Less than Nothing* (2002). Nothing short of impressive! But misguided.

10 So when Žižek says, "Nature doesn't exist," he is referring to the 'domesticated' Nature of neoliberalism. An 'ecology without Nature' follows in the footsteps of Timothy Morton (2007), who exposes this 'Romantic' myth of Nature that capitalism exploits through its fantasy ideologies.

between it and the human. Žižek's concrete Universal recognizes anthropocentric inequalities within global capitalism via the lumpenproletariat, but offers neither a vision of the future nor a political practice of politics beyond capitalism.[11] One is tempted to claim that the 'concrete universal' that is characterized by a fundamental antagonism (or 'minimal distance') is precisely the logic of capitalism as it fluctuates between paranoia (the structure of (false) universalism—the Symbolic Order as a system for 'all,' as Lacan seemed to maintain)[12] to schizophrenia (the recognition of the exception) so that it promotes the illusions of freedom and equality by exposing the lack or excess thereby freeing up desire when new profit dollars are needed.

Deleuze and Guattari offer another alternative. Universal history is a history of contingency, not a history of necessity. The past, which includes the inhuman (inorganic) and the non-human (AI), is examined to free up the present, which itself is made up of accidents and encounters of the past. Like Marx's claim that the key to the ape's anatomy is contained in the anatomy of the human, capitalism is given 'universal' status in the way that it is in a privileged position to present a retrospective reading of history. Its coding and overcoding strategies can be found in previous societies, hence there is no definitive separation of social stages that 'progress' as a teleological trajectory. The rhizome of fortuitous connections is more the case. There is no 'one' way that the capitalist formation is established, as is evident with the case of China, where an authoritarian system helped paved the road to establish a modified 'neo-liberal' model of economic growth. The Real in this view of history certainly recognizes ruptures and limits; however, these are not explored antagonistically. From out of the gap or void we have a virtual Real where new forms of creativity emerge that are actualized as well as destroyed via catastrophes. Lives remain fated through accident.

In relation to the Anthropocene, this 'universal history' that Deleuze and Guattari develop, which in machinic terms extends to the geological span of the planet, and to the cosmic time of the universe[13] (the Big bang 13,720 billion years ago) via univocity, means that the primary ontological question is whether we, as a species, have the *right* to survive at the expense of the rest of the Planet,

---

11   I attempt to make this stick in jagodzinski (forthcoming), Jesters, Saints, Nomads: The Public pedagogies of Lacan, Žižek, Deleuze; Between Mathemes and War Machines," In *Žižek and Education*. Antonio Garcia (editor) (chapter 4). Sense Publishers.

12   As is well known, for Lacan all knowledge is imbued with paranoia: the Imaginary is paranoiac in that knowledge is acquired in relation to the other through primordial *misrecognition*, hence the illusion of self-mastery, autonomy and self-recognition can lead to anxiety and self-alienation; in relation to the Symbolic structures of languages and speech, paranoia emerges through the demand that is fostered on us by the big Other to conform so we may be at odds with our unique inner subjective experiences; finally the process of knowing is paranoiac through the confrontation with the Real (as the unknown and uncanny).

13   We are all made of cosmic stardust. Neil Shubin (2012) shows how this machinic universe can be understood as it composes our species as part of the cosmos who are but a sliver of time comparatively to the Earth in chronological terms.

which is the 'part that has no say' (to stand Jacques Rancière's anthropocentric claim on its head).[14] It is a question of extinction—[15] our death, rather than the sovereignty of our being—the biopower and biopolitics of life[16] that pervades the discourses of social and human sciences. Technological-digital-instrumental reason hegemonically defines the post-human where death is to be eliminated and life becomes something created in the lab, manipulated genetically, and extended perhaps indefinitely through the development of synthetic genomics to custom design behavior on the part of a life form. Neuropharmacology, AI, cybernetics, and nanotechnologies are the way of the future, as is risk-management, and the 'sustainable' management of resources as discussed above. Technology in this scientific sense is understood as a 'human' product made possible through reason and human capacity to make scientific 'progress' in relation to life/death, the cycle of survival. Techno-science, capital, and biopolitics, as Ziarek (2010), calling on Heidegger, has pointed out, are the 'technics' of enframing (Heidegger's *Ge-stell*), which reduce life as the exploitable reserve of capital. Added to such exploitation is the 'expediency of culture,' as developed by George Yúdice (2003), where culture becomes yet another resource for both sociopolitical and economic amelioration. By this he means a way of increasing participation in an era of waning political involvement, the rise of symbolic cultural capitalism as ways to smooth out cultural differences via pluralized democracy, and the immaterialization of labor through the creative industries where intellectual property rights are defined by the General Agreement on Tariffs and Trade [GATT] and the World Trade Organization (WTO). The packaging of intellectual property has increased the incidents of spying via Internet and outright espionage.

Ziarek (2012) has further pointed out that the term Anthropocene is poorly named. It remains based on the traditional anthropological conception of the human being. From the perspective of Planet Earth there is no climate change, biosphere, or environment. To follow Colebrook's (2010) analysis of Deleuze's vitalism, there is a 'passive vitalism' of Nature that is machinc contra to the anthropocentric vitalism of life promoted by bio/power and politics that retains the distinction between the non-living and the living most often thought through as the difference between zoë and bios. This needs to be questioned if our species is to come to terms

---

14   This is the ontological question raised by Derrida in the last writings before he died: *Aporias, The Animal That Therefore I Am* and *The Beast and the Sovereign*. Derrida shifts from interhuman to inter-living-beings but does not venture into non-living being.

15   The Deleuzian philosopher Claire Colebrook (2012) has taken up this line of inquiry.

16   Paul Rabinow and Nikolas Rose (2006) extend Foucault's initial developments of biopower and biopolitics in *La Volonté du Savoir* to examine the three elements that bring together the concept of biopower into the twenty-first century: knowledge of vital life processes, power relations that take humans as living beings as their objects, and the modes of subjectification or the 'technologies of the self' whereby subjects work on themselves as living beings.

with its own existence. Not the essence of "who we are as a species," but whether we will "exist" or not. The non-living or the inhuman has received a great deal of attention of late, from Janet Bennett's particular explorations of the vitalism of things, to the philosophical movement loosely known as 'object relations theory,' to the 'feminist materialism' of Karen Barad.[17] These are perhaps the beginnings of the creation of new concepts that may begin to break-up, disturb and fragment the deep-seated anthropocentrism that pervades the capitalist agenda.

With this backdrop in mind I would like to develop what an *avant-garde without authority* is doing to bring about a transvaluation of values (*Umwertung aller Werte*) in Nietzschean terms,[18] where the shift towards intensive rather than extensive differences in the way Deleuze[19] uses these terms is being developed: rather than the calculations that are extensive in relation to the environment, measuring the future of our existence in more or less time, the shift to intensive differences marks speeds and thresholds that initiate a qualitative change or 'phase transition.' Intensive differences have a transcendental status in relation to extensive differences; they are their genetic conditions, which are themselves structured by Ideas that are transcendent and immanent—a different understanding of a concrete Universal than the one Žižek develops.[20] It is the Idea of art—the necessary differential elements that attempts to de-anthropomorphize man in relation to the Anthropocene so as to transvalue the currency of what I call 'designer capitalism' (jagodzinski 2010)—that I would like to develop in the next section when it comes to an avant-garde without authority.

Avant-garde without Authority: Towards an Oekoumene

> The overman shall be the meaning of the earth! I entreat you, my brethren, remain true to the earth, and do not believe those who speak to you of supra-terrestrial hopes! (Nietzsche, *Thus Spoke Zarathustra*, Prologue section 3).

---

17   An array of positions can be read in the edited collections of Stacy Alaimo and Susan Hekmen (2008) as well as Diana Coole and Samantha Frost (2010).

18   Deleuze uses the term "transmutation of values." I am also thinking of historical analysis by Karl Jaspers (1953) of the Axial Age (800 to 200 BC) where such a transvaluative shift took place via Confucianism, Taoism (China), Hinduism, Buddhism, Jainism (India), Zoroaster (Persia), Judaism (Canaan) and sophism (Greece). So there is a historical precedent.

19   As developed in chapter 4 and 5 in his *Difference and Repetition* (1994). See also the 'difficult' writings of Roland Faber (2010, 2011) who attempts to think intensity through both Whitehead and Deleuze when it comes to ecology.

20   Here the paradigmatic example (taken from Bergson) is white light where the Idea of color 'perplexes' (or folds in itself) the generic relations and elements of all the colors. White light is the virtual and multiple state of the Idea of color. It is a concrete universal not a genus or a generality.

The avant-garde is dead, wouldn't you know it, yet the concept is continually brought up.[21] In a special issue *of New Literary History*, Jonathan P. Eburne and Rita Felski present a cadre of 13 authors who query the concept. Renato Poggioli's (1968) and Peter Bürger's (1974) feature as the two most often cited thesis regarding the 'historical' avant-garde, as is the neo-avant-garde developed by Hal Foster (1996) in his influential Lacanian reading. The question of decentering the concept of its Eurocentric bias via postcolonial critiques, which introduce non-Western avant-garde movements, is also discussed. The question of the "avant-garde without authority" that I wish to explore obviously dismisses the vanguardism and universalism that has plagued its past resurrections, as if someone is 'ahead of their time' and are the carriers of 'truth.' This is only the 'half' of the problematic. Rather, following Deleuze (1988) in his book on Foucault, the best way to put it is that an avant-garde (without authority) is *folded* over the 'historical avant-garde' of the twentieth century to generate a new subjectification that addresses the Capitalism/Anthropocene problematic of today. This folding takes into account the historical avant-garde's attempt to critique capitalism, and their program of bringing "art into life," thereby asserting a 'utopian' transvaluation of the social order;[22] introducing a new sensibility by a pursuit of 'new' forms of life for a life to come, as Jacques Ranciére (2004) is willing to admit, the 'historical' avant-garde "in accordance with Schiller's model, is rooted in the aesthetic anticipation of the future (29)."[23] The qualifications of such folding is that 'life' is no longer an anthropocentric vitalism but recognizes the 'passive' vitalism that affirms the mutual immanence of environments and organisms in their striving toward the intensity of Life; this is an affirmative gesture of desire rather than the negation and transgression that pervaded the historical avant-garde. Their negation has, as many have commented, been successfully absorbed by market-forces.[24]

---

21   The very fine essay by Evan Mauro (2013) provides much insight. Geralk Keaney (2011) offers yet another revival.

22   Utopian not in any idealist future sense but as the striving for transcendent values, virtues and virtuals as a symbolic transfer as actions, hopes, sympathies, purposes and enjoyments. These are the intensities that help to reconcile and affirm the mutual immanence of all environments and organisms by changing our concepts, percepts and affects toward a new sensibility to non-human differences (Faber 2011).

23   I have explored the 'aesthetic regime' of modernity that Ranciére develops in jagodzinski (2010). This regime is beset by a central antinomy whereby the self-destruction of aesthetic autonomy presents itself as freedom from political determination, and at the same time, the ability to effect political change as the demand for heteronomy is hampered. My argument in the book is that this tension is evident today between art&design, the ampersand standing for the antinomy of 'art into life' and 'life into art.'

24   The standard lament is that art is a commodity, the more spectacular or confrontational it is, the more it amasses an affect that can be packaged and sold. The view is that the inheritors of the historical avant-garde of the late 60s and early 70s, who critiqued industrial capitalism eventually sold out to the popular cultural market place—the culture industry that does away with the spaces of critique and now finds itself utilizing

'Without authority' reconfirms the Nietzschean 'will-to-power' which does away with agency: there is no separation between a will and what is willed. They are one and the same. An act (what is willed) and the subject who wills it are constituted simultaneously. So there is no pre-constituted subject who wills this or that act. A subject is constituted in the act of thinking. Deleuze says a *subject is immanent to its expression*. An artwork is not an expression of the artist's will. There is no such thing as an 'artist' who then wills an artwork into existence. The activity of 'arting' itself is an expression of a will to power that produces the art and the artist concurrently. The body of work that is produced over the years 'is' the artist. The artistic oeuvre and the artist are the expression of the same force—a will-to-power. The historical avant-garde's 'failed' gesture of 'art into life' (life here meaning the 'everyday') from this perspective, is no longer a contradiction since the 'autonomy of the artist' never existed in the first place; or rather the very notion of 'autonomy' is overturned to mean something quite different.

Added to these clarifications is the close-proximity of Deleuze's appropriation of the Nietzsche's Übermensch to the notion of an avant-garde without authority when it comes to the transvaluation through art at the minoritarian or micropolitical level that will be developed below. Once more, returning to his book on Foucault (1988), Deleuze follows him by developing resistance as an aesthetics of existence where the *fold*—taken as the outside drawn (folded) inside—forms a new subjectivation redefining what it means to be autonomous, for it is in the fold that life is created.[25] Such a gesture reaches out to the Übermensch that Deleuze addresses in the 'Appendix: On the Death of Man and Superman' to his book on Foucault. It addresses Nietzsche's concern over the 'sick becoming' of our species, as we 'do' ourselves in: "the overman as the vision of a non-anthropocentric future of the human. This would be to conceive of the 'human/transhuman'[/inhuman] as neither as predicate nor a property that belong uniquely to a ready-made subject (such as 'man')" [...] The transhuman condition is not about the transcendence of the human being, but concerns its non-teleological becoming in an immanent process of 'anthropological deregulation'" (Ansell Pearson 1997: 161–2, 163). Such a subject, Deleuze says (1990), is a "free anonymous, and nomadic singularity which traverses men as well as plants and animals independently of the matter of their individuation and forms of their personality" (107).

In the Appendix, Deleuze presents the *Übermensch* as something that can come after the passing of the "God-form" and the "Man-form" as read through

---

the complaints generated during the Student Revolts to develop 'flexible' or designer capitalism of liberation management based on planning for personal creative self-fulfillment. Situationism, Minimalism and Fluxus were the 'true' inheritors of the historical avant-garde.

25 I take this development as having parallels with Lacan's notion of the 'extimate' and his development of the *sinthome* late in his career as an answer to Deleuze/Guattarian developments. The *sinthome* drives the artist to establish a 'world' that no longer answers to the demand of the Other, which is another way of confirming the qualifier 'without authority.'

Foucault's oeuvre. The God-form of the 'classical historical formation' opens up life to infinity. It represents the idea of the *unfold* to the infinite outside that is in constant need of explaining.[26] Given that man is limited, any encounter with 'his' infinitesimal forces inside with the infinite forces outside only end in producing variations of the God-form. The nineteenth century introduces the Man-form through new finite forces of labour, language and the life science of biology. God becomes hidden or like in deistic thought, God creates the world and then leaves, so man must now discover the laws that are in operation. In Foucault's oeuvre, these forces of finitude are characterized by a *fold*. The fold is a typology of surface and depth as man's internal forces enter into the relations with outside forces that are themselves finite, yet can never be completely understood, so they are subject to an infinite deferral.

The 'birth' of man spells the 'death' of God, but Nietzsche is interested in the 'death' of man. The Übermensch ends the trilogy by presenting a new relation of inside/outside forces termed the *Superfold*, which is characterized by a 'unlimited finity.' Unlimited finity is another name for Nietzsche's 'eternal return,' and designates future 'folds': the fold of molecular biology and microbiology (the DNA genetic code), the fold of silicon and carbon (third-generation cybernetic machines), and the fold of language, where the affect of 'strange language' within language itself explores the 'limits' of grammar. Unlimited finity refers to pure differences in the way "a finite number of components yields a practically unlimited diversity of combinations" (1988, 131). Deleuze is referring to the codings of serializations and the subtle changes that they undergo through their decoding and recoding.

Deleuze is ambivalent about the future in relation to the Übermensch. Earlier he writes, "Nietzsche said that man imprisoned life, but the superman is what frees life *within man himself*, to the benefit of another form, and so on" (130, original emphasis). Here there is optimism that continues: "Man tends to free life, labor and language *within himself*" (132, original emphasis). But then an ambivalence regarding this creative capacity is heard for it opens up forms of domination. "The superman [...] is the man who is even in charge of the animals (a code that can capture the fragments from other codes [...]. It is man in charge of the very rocks, or inorganic matter (the domain of silicon). It is man in charge of the being of language. [...] it is the advent of a new form that is neither God nor man, and which, it is hoped, will not prove worse than its two previous forms" (132). It has proven worse. Given that climate change is a 'hyperobject' as Timothy Morton (2010) puts it, the forces of the outside are just too overwhelming for a technological fix alone.

Given the state of the planet and the proposed technological possibilities (the first two folds of the Superfold), it seems humanity is not faring any better ... only

---

26   The 'outside' is a complicated concept in Deleuze that first emerges with Blanchot. The outside is more of a force that causes us to think. It is difficult not to think of the fold as another way of expressing an encounter with the virtual Real, with the way that it disorientates and produces the unthought.

worse. It is the third fold that might 'stammer' the other two, if we see this as the fold of art (visual, literature, music and so on ... the realm of affects and percepts). This is the closest to what an avant-garde without authority would mean today. Adrian Parr (2009) sees this necessity as a transversal between 'science and art' (162), what she refers to an injection of *unimaginableness*. "*Unimaginableness* differs from *unimaginable* because as an immanent condition it does not aspire to realize what is otherwise impossible—the unimaginable—which would seem to suggest that it merely indulges in the production of imaginary worlds. Rather the operative mode of the unimaginableness is onto-aesthetic" (165 original emphasis). It is the onto-aesthetic that can 'stammer' us into a new subjectivation by identifying the Idea of such an art as a form of 'war machine.'

So, 'without authority' should also be qualified as it refers to an agent that must be resisted, as well as the subjective agent of humanism. The qualifier 'without authority' vigorously applies to the concept of Übermensch. Nietzsche ceaselessly maintained that this term has nothing to do with a higher kind of man, a half saint or half genius, or someone who is 'emancipated' and/or a 'master of a free will.' Übermensch in no way designates an ontological state that can be instantiated. What is required is an experimental approach to find the 'way' and the 'way' does not exist. The way has to be created.[27] It is closer, I would argue, to becoming imperceptible in Deleuze/Guattarian terms via a line of flight.

Oekoumene: Into the Future Back

Oikuménë, meaning the inhabited world or universe, has the advantage of referring to the whole inhabited planet and avoids the anthropocentrism of 'oikos' (home). Perhaps not as elegant as the 'Gaia hypothesis,' it attempts to convey the paradox of w(holism), emergence from chaos. To develop such a 'utopian' transvaluation—an art that opens up the universe to becoming-other, I come to a place where an 'affirmative nomadology' (Holland, 2011) might be developed with a particular Idea of art that acts in the capacity as a war machine to further a minoritarian molecular politics in relation to climate change and capitalist commodity culture. Deleuze/Guattari develop no less than six types or levels of war-machines, but war and war machine do not necessarily coincide; the war-machine only has the object of war under certain conditions. It was, indeed the invention of the nomad. In its essence the war machine constitutes 'smooth space' within 'striated space;' it occupies and displaces it and affirmatively establishes alternative social relations within it. An avant-garde (without authority) follow the roadmap of an affirmative nomadology as a positive utopian force that has three aspects as developed by Eugene Holland: "(1) its capacity to intervene in and transform our habitual modes of thinking, desiring, and acting; (2) its capacity to detect and draw attention to viable and actually existing alternatives to State and

---

27 For an account of this see Schrift (2000).

capitalist norms; and (3) its capacity to give expression to alternative becomings and social movements in order to strengthen them, broaden them, and even extend them to other social fields and to connect them with other movements to promote widespread social change" (28).

As I see it, the Idea of an artistic oekoumenal war machine has at least four differentiated components that make up its 'unlimited finity' at the virtual level: the necessity of smooth space, durational time (chronos and Aion), posthuman relations (with inhuman (inorganic or anorganic) and nonhuman (AI)), and the creation of a performative event to further 'anonymity' by 'becoming imperceptible'—autonomously anonymous. This, in a nutshell, is the abstract machine (or processes) that forms the new *Kunstwollen* for the as yet unthought Oekoumenal.

Smooth Space: by this I mean an intervention into the public/private/common boundaries to occupy space so as to stage an event and form a temporary Outside to capital and state space so as to forward the 'virtue' of imaging a new form of life, and to organize social reproduction differently. This means playing with the reversals of public/private/common boundaries and making them ambivalent, ambiguous, and paradoxical so as to reterritorialize and deterritorize the space. This seems straight forward enough. How can public and/or private spaces be used to affirmative ways that open up the commons for affective interaction when it comes to climate change via such art? What can such an art affectively do? Answering such a question is to maintain that every art expression that fulfills the virtual differentiations listed above is an actualization (a differentiation) of the Oekoumenal war machine. Each artistic event is therefore singular in its affects as to what it can do.

Adrian Parr calls on the artist Spencer Tunick's (along with Greenpeace Switzerland) installation of a living sculpture (hundreds of naked men and women) positioned in the Aletsch Glacier, Switzerland on August 18, 2007 that he photographed. This mass of bodies, all huddled together, symbolize the vulnerability of the glaciers under climate change. The photograph forms the cover of her book, which is then disseminated globally to those who take an interest in sustainability, which her work critiques. Here all the differentiated elements are in play. The site of the smooth space is in the public domain, a domain that is rapidly changing so attention is brought to its state. The element of duration is also brought forth: the disappearing speed of the glacier and the time it takes to take the photo forms a comparison. The element of duration is necessary to illustrate the speeds and intensities of the ecological processes that are being explored. It is one attempt to avoid the commodity structure of capitalism and the forces of its capture. Such art cannot be 'hung' on a wall, easily sold and traded and so forth. It tries its hardest not to be a commodity by 'disappearing,' becoming anonymous and imperceptible once its 'forcework' has been done (see Ziarek 2004). The relations affirmatively change here as well; the relation is with the inhuman in this case (glacier), and the relations between the huddling mass of cold and shivering naked bodies are also affected. One can imagine the exchanges amongst this 'living sculptural mass' in relation to themselves and the 'will' of the project that takes on its own 'will.' The stark contrast of 'exposure' raises many questions. It is therefore an *event* that can be *counter-actualized*, in Deleuze's (1990) terms, whereby it can be revisited for its tranvaluational affects on those who wish to engage with it.

There is a multitude of further actualizations to be explored. Niele Azevedo's series called *Minimum Monuments* is an exemplary Oekoumenal war machine. One such installation, "Melting Men," seems like an inspiration from Tunick's work. Teamed with World Wildlife Fund, "Melting Men" is also a sculptural installation, an urban intervention where the 'smooth space' is created in various cities around the globe in sites that are near city monuments and parks, theatres, and plazas. A 1,000 small ice figures, 20 cm. tall, of men and women are cast in molds, wrapped separately in plastic, and then transported to the site via a refrigerated container. The local populace (men, women, children, virtually anyone interested) can take a modular sculpture and place it on the monument or in the designated site. In this way these figurines 'occupy' the site. One of the most effective events was the placing of the ice figures on the steps in Berlin's Gendarmenmarket Square to show the effects of climate change. As these figures melted away, it was timed with the release of the World Wildlife's report on Arctic warming (mentioned earlier in footnote 2). Again, all the differential elements are in play. The video of the event shows the buzz that took place by the multitude of people who participated in placing the figures where they wished. The series of Minimum Monuments installations of these ice figures plays with the small and the micropolitics of the anonymous. They 'occupy' space without leadership, like a swarm. As interventions into monuments, they are anti-monuments that subvert or question the state's official history that establishes its official record. Yet, this is not graffiti of destruction. It is an affirmation to further *counter-actualizations*. The relations are once again reorganized and affirmed as the political strength of the small, yet the very solitude of the 'ice men' point to the nihilism that is spreading. It is (after Nietzsche) a way to resist structures only through the structures themselves, through nihilism itself.

Ziarek (2011) attempts to make a case that Heidegger's *Dasein* can still teach us something about the shift from anthropocentricism to world and event (*das Ereignis*). The site (*Da*) of the relation to being (*Sein*) refers to the clearing or lighting (*Lichtung*) as the 'opening out,' which human being can span. There would be nothing to offer humans "if it were not for *things* and the *bearing of things and world*, lighting [*Lichtung*] as the site (Da) of relation to being, that is, as Da-sein" (28, added emphasis). I interpret this as being the smooth space of the event. It offers yet another wager of the Oekoumenal war machine to isolate for us *das Ding*, the "thing's mode of being is its way of 'thinging' the world. [...] What makes things is not simply their materiality, their being a non-living being, but rather their ability to stay, to maintain and to shelter the world" (28). While this discussion can lead us to the recesses and the fine-points of OOO (object-orientated ontology) that relies heavily on Heideggerian foundations as spear-headed by Graham Harman, here I wish only to maintain that an oekumental war machine can stage the event where an attempt is made to hold our attention to the 'thing' (*das Ding*) as an event so that we get how "things thing the world" (28). The relationship between the human and inhuman is amplified as the notion of things as "human resources" that block the experience of a 'thing' undergo radical change. The 'thing' has to be lifted 'out of its world' and starkly recontextualized.

I make brief mention of a number of actualizations of Thingness, the last actualization identifies insects as 'inhuman' things. There are of course many artists that can be called on. Mark Dion's "Neukom Vivarium" begun in 2004 and completed in 2006, housed in the Seattle Art Museum has received wide attention and shows the irony of how to maintain a 'dying' oak tree by putting it on artificial life support systems within the confines of an art gallery. Once again a smooth space is created within a gallery setting and a pedagogical element is also a part of this installation to explore the developing ecosystems. The tree becomes a *das Ding*. The isolation of a particular tree species, Australia's Goolengook to regions where we see its devastation, has been the passion of Mark Hansen (2004, 2006). Hansen marshals in the Deleuze/Guattari paradigm to show how the space of nature is named, traversed and experienced. There are many artists who attempt to 'isolate' the non-human elements of earth, air, water, fire and so on, so us to bring out their 'Thingness' within an event, and thus change our relationships with it. This applies to microbes of all sorts, insects and animals.

One last example as a further actualization of this Thingness is exemplified by the Canadian artist Aganetha Dyck, who works with bees, which are disappearing species in some sectors of the world; she works with all aspects of them, especially their ability to make honeycombs where (again) science and art are traversed via an onto-aisthetics.[28] It is the swarming power of the 'small' that interests her, where questions of interspecies relations and interkingdoms turn into questions of relationships that 'becoming bee' might bring. Her symbiosis with bees shows aspects of mending and detail that bees can 'teach' us. An exchange takes place between her and the honeybee hives via 'broken' or damaged objects that she strategically manipulates by adding wax, honey, propolis or hand-made honeycomb patters. She then puts these objects back into the hives and allows the bees to swarm and 'respond.' The dialogue then begins as the bees tend to these objects. She then responds to the bees by taking the objects out and changing them, and then replacing them in the hives once again. Durational time of the work, the slow process that this takes, and the capacity to gain more insight into a swarming mentality in the way that bees are sculptors and architects, affirms a relationship that seems unimaginable.[29] A similar extraordinary symbiotic exploration with

---

28   I have made the subtle change to aisthetics rather than aesthetics to acknowledge the affective dimension, rather than the spectacularity that is associated with the aesthetic.

29   This dimension of art and the natural world is developed by Deleuze/Guattari in *What is Philosophy?*, which is their last book together written mostly by Deleuze as Guattari was ill. Elizabeth Grosz (2008) has developed has explored this aspect of their work.

caribou is explored by the Canadian wildlife biologist Karsten Heuer and the film maker/environmentalist Leanne (see Chisholm, 2013).

One can continue on by describing other artistic singularities that form this plateau of a minoritarian politics that taps into the onto-aisthetic levels with the inhuman and the anoganic, but I must bring this chapter to an end by simply mentioning Lars van Trier's remarkable film *Melancholia*, which has been equally remarkably explored by Steven Shaviro (2012) as yet another actualization of an artistic Oekoumenal war machine. The impending disaster of an asteroid, called Melancholia, is about to destroy the earth. How are we to take such an 'end' of our species? The dinosaurs did not fare well. It is the 'universal history' in the Deleuzian sense of our future: the future anterior of the change that will have occurred—from the future that has already past, which is impossible to report. I take this to be an example of the nonhuman relation utilizing the machinic technology of cinema, as an intervention into the Hollywood disaster films. Melancholia, metonymic for the fate of the earth and the psychic state of Justine, one of two sisters featured as the protagonists in the narrative, is precisely the mood, at times, that seemed to overwhelm me when I read the state of the Anthropocene. Justine is also nihilistic in a liberatory way. She does not grieve for the Planet. She tells her sister, Claire "the Earth is evil, we don't need to grieve for it. Nobody will miss it." Of course, it is not the Earth that is 'evil,' the deflection is to the species that populates it. She 'bathes' in the light of the asteroid, naked, welcoming its arrival and our destruction. Morton (2007) in his chapter "Imagining Ecology without Nature," suggests that is the ethically appropriate response to the current ecological situation. The destruction of the earth ends with a scene that might be called a 'becoming child.' Justine, Claire and her son Leo are huddled in a makeshift symbolic shelter as the asteroid hits, perhaps an allusion to Kubrick's floating fetus at the end of 2001? But, if there is 'melancholia' there is also the Nietzschean laughter. Here I think of Richard Kelly's film, *Southland Tales* (2007) where 'The End of Times' is near. Many quotes from the Book of Revelation are heard throughout the narrative. Through the raptures of media immersion, Hollywood quotes and ironies, and the nightmare of 'capitalist realism' (Fisher 2009), the audience is swept in a delirium towards an entropic end via nihilistic purification into a blissful transcendence—schizoanalysis at its best. There you have it: two bookends to the saying 'farewell' to our existence.

Can the Oekoumenal artistic war machine 'stop' climate change? I doubt it. Can it start an infectious transvaluation? Well, maybe. It is not a 'utopian' dream (as long as one feels, politics is possible), it also addresses the growing nihilism and melancholia as the world decays, where the rich become richer, and a point is reached where money cannot buy you an escape from the dying Planet. Even if you are Richard Branson, and you can circle the earth in your private spacecraft, eventually you too, like the Coyote have run over the cliff and are about to plummet back down.

References

Alaimo, Stacy and Hekmen, Susan (eds.) (2008). *Material Feminisms*. Bloomington & Indianapolis.

Ansell Pearson, Keith (1997). *Viroid Life: Perspectives on Nietzsche and the Transhuman Condition*. London and New York: Routledge.

Bürger, Peter (1984). *Theory of the Avant-Garde*. Trans. Michael Shaw. Minneapolis: University of Minnesota Press.

Choat, Simon (2010). *Marx Through Post-Structuralism: Lyotard, Derrida, Foucault, Deleuze*. London and New York: Continuum Books.

Colebrook, Claire (2010). *Deleuze and the Meaning of Life*. London and New York: Continuum Books.

——— (2011). The Sustainability of Concepts: Knowledge and Human Interests. In Adrian Parr and Michael Zaretsky (eds.), *New Directions in Sustainable Design* (221–8). London and New York: Routledge.

——— (2012). 'Introduction: Framing the End of the Species.' In Claire Colebrook (ed.), *Extinction*. Open Humanities Press. Available at http://www.livingbooksaboutlife.org/books/Extinction/Introduction.

Chisholm, Dianne (2012). 'The Becoming-Animal of *Being Caribou*: Art, Ethics, Politics.' *Rhizomes* 24. Available at http://www.rhizomes.net/issue24/chisholm.html

Coole, Diana and Frost, Samantha (2010). *New Materialism: Ontology, Agency, and Politics*. London and Durham: Duke University Press.

Deleuze, Gilles (1988). *Foucault*. Trans. Paul Bové. Minneapolis: University of Minnesota Press.

——— (1990). *The Logic of Sense*. Trans. M. Lester with C. Stivale. London: Athlone Press.

——— (1994). *Difference and Repetition*. Trans. Paul Patton. New York: Columbia University Press.

Faber, Roland (2010). 'Introduction: Negotiating Becoming.' In Roland Faber and Andrea Stephenson (eds.), *Secrets of Becoming: Negotiating Whitehead, Deleuze, and Butler* (1–49). New York: Fordham University Press.

——— (2011). 'Cultural Symbolizations of a Sustainable Future.' In Adrian Parr and Michael Zaretsky (eds.), *New Directions in Sustainable Design* (242–55). London and New York: Routledge.

Fisher, Mark (2009). *Capitalist Realism: Is there No Alternative?* Ropley, England; Washington, DC: O Books.

Foster, Bellamy John, Clark, Brett and Richard York (2010). *The Ecological Rift: Capitalism's War on Earth*. New York: Monthly Review of Books.

Foster, Hal (1996). *The Return of the Real: The Avant-Garde at the End of the Century*. Cambridge, MA: MIT Press.

Gore, Al (2009). *Our Choice: A Plan to Solve the Climate Crisis*. Emmaus, PA. : Rodale.

Grosz, Elizabeth (2008). *Chaos, Territory, Art: Deleuze and the Framing of the Earth*. New York: Columbia University Press.

Hansen, Mark (2004). 'Environmental Visions: Deleuze and the Modalities of Nature,' *Ethics & the Environment* 9 (2): 33–64.

——— (2006). *Environmental Damage: Violence of the Text*. Hampshire, England and Burlington, VT: Ashgate Publishing Company.

Holland, Eugene (2011). *Nomad Citizenship: Free-Market Communism and the Slow-Motion General Strike*. London and Mineapolis: University of Minnesota Press.

jagodzinski, jan (2010). *Visual Art and Education in an Era of Designer Capitalism*. London and New York: Palgrave Mcmillan.

——— (forthcoming). 'Jesters, Saints, Nomads: The Public Pedagogies of Lacan, Žižek … Deleuze; Between Mathemes and War Machines,' in Žižek and Pedagogy, Antonio Garcia (ed.). Rotterdam and Taipei: Sense Publishers.

Jasper, Karl (1953). *The Origin and Goal of History*. Trans. Michael Bullocki. London: Routledge & K. Paul.

Keaney, Gerald (2011). 'A New Avant Garde?' *Rethinking Marxism: A Journal of Economics, Culture & Society* 23 (4): 556–64.

Kisner, Wendell (2008). 'The Concrete Universal in Žižek and Hegel,' *International Journal of Žižek Studies* 2(2): available at http://zizekstudies.org/index.php/ijzs/article/view/72.

Matts, Tim and Tynan, Aidan (2012). The Melancholy of Extinction: Lars con Trier's 'Melancholia' as an Environmental Film, *M/C Journal* 15 (3). Available at http://journal.media-culture.org.au/index.php/mcjournal/article/viewArticle/491.

Mauro, Evan (2012–2013). 'The Death and Life of the Avant-Garde: Or, Modernism and Biopolitics,' *Mediations* 26 (1–2): 119–42.

Mészáros, Ivan (2008). *The Challenge and Burden of Historical Times*. New York: Monthly Review Press.

Morton, Timothy (2007). *Ecology without Nature: Rethinking Environmental Aesthetics*. Cambridge, Mass. : Harvard University Press.

——— (2010) *The Ecological Thought*. Cambridge, Mass.: Harvard University Press.

Nietzsche, Friedrich (1998). *On the Genealogy of Morality: A Polemic*. Trans. Douglas Smith. Oxford: Oxford University of Press.

——— (2001). *The Gay Science*. Trans. Josefine Nauckoff. Cambridge: Cambridge University Press.

Parr, Adrian (2009). *Hijacking Sustainability*. London, England; Cambridge, Mass.: MIT Press

——— (2011), 'Art, Politics, and Climate Change.' In Adrian Parr and Michael Zaretsky (eds.), *New Directions in Sustainable Design* (6–12). London and New York: Routledge.

Poggioli, Renato (1968). *The Theory of the Avant-Garde*. Trans. Gerald Fitzgeld. Cambridge, MA: Harvard University Press.

Rabinow, Paul and Rose, Nikolas (2006). 'Biopwer Today,' *BioSocieties* 1(2): 195–217.

Roberts, Timmons (2001). 'Global Inequality and Climate Change,' *Society & Natural Resources* 14: 501–9.

Schrift, Alan D. (2000). 'Nietzsche, Foucault, Deleuze, and the Subject of Radical Democracy,' *Angelaki: Journal of the Theoretical Humanities* 5(2): 151–61.

Shaviro, Steven (2012). 'Melancholia or the Romantic Anti-Sublime,' *Sequence* 1(1) (available at http://reframe.sussex.ac.uk/sequence1/1-1-melancholia-or-the-romantic-anti-sublime/).

Shubin, Neil (2012). *The Universe Within: Discovering the Common History of Rocks, Planets and People.* New York: Pantheon books.

WWF (2008). World Wildlife Fund, *Living Planet Report*: available at http://wwf.panda.org/about_our_earth/all_publications/?169242/Living-Planet-Report-2008.

Yúdice, George (2003). *The Expediency of Culture: Uses of Culture in the Global Era.* Durham and London: Duke University Press.

Ziarek, Krzysztof (2004). *The Force of Art.* Stanford, Calif.: Stanford University Press.

——— (2010). 'A Disposable Globe: Heidegger on Bio-politics, Capital, and Technoscience,' *theory@buffalo* 14: 17–35.

——— (2012). 'The Limits of Life,' *Angelaki: Journal of the Theoretical Humanities* 16(4): 19–30.

Žižek, Slavoj (1999). *The Ticklish Subject: The Absent Centre of Political Ontology* London & New York: Verso.

——— (2010). *Living in the End Times.* London & New York: Verso.

——— (2012). *Less than Nothing: Hegel and the Shadow of Dialectical Materialism.* London & New York: Verso.

Chapter 12

Boris Groys' Post-Capitalist Scenario

Rex Butler

Undoubtedly, of all the attempts to think a post-capitalist scenario, that of the Russian art theorist Boris Groys is amongst the most interesting. Born in 1947 in East Berlin and originally studying mathematical logic at Leningrad University, Groys became interested in the Soviet dissident art of the 1960s and '70s, for which he soon became one of the chief theoreticians and spokespeople. And, although emigrating in 1981 to West Germany, where he undertook a doctorate in philosophy at the University of Münster and later became a Professor of Aesthetics at the Karlsruhe Centre for Art and Media, he remained interested also in Communist art, both before and after the fall of the Berlin Wall in 1989 and the final dissolution of the Soviet Socialist Republic in 1991. But, for all of his real-life experience of life under Communism, at no point in his work is Groys simply opposed to it. The book that first made his name (at least in the West) was *Gesamtkunstwerk Stalin* or *The Total Art of Stalinism*, published in Germany in 1988, which against all of the usual understandings of the period argues that Stalinism does not at all come to repress or do away with the great experiments of the Russian Contructivists of the teens and '20s, but in fact arrives to realise them. That total renovation of society the first generation of the Russian avant-gardists dreamt of actually comes to pass under the dictatorship of Stalin. And in Groys' much later *The Communist Postscript* (2006), he insists that Communism has not ended as though defeated by capitalism, but rather ends itself—ends itself in the very form of capitalism. In other words, that triumphant Francis Fukuyama-style universal capitalism of post-1989 (and, in a way, the same thing goes for capitalism from the beginning) is only the effect of a prior Communism. Or, to invert for a moment the premise of this collection, it is a question not of a Communism that comes after capitalism, but of a capitalism that comes after Communism, a post-Communist capitalism.

In '... Our Fate as a Living Corpse ...,' an extended interview with Hannah Abdullah and Matthias Benzer for the journal *Theory, Culture and Society*, Groys says three important things for our purposes here. One: that Communism is in effect the precondition for capitalism, which it allows us to think and make clear to ourselves. So long as there is capitalism, then, there must also be Communism. Historically existing Communism is the only form in which this idea of Communism has ever appeared on earth, and it is therefore always open to be revived in the future. Communism is a "living corpse"—Groys' analogy is that it is like an Egyptian Pharaoh who is potentially able to be dug up after many years and come back to life: "I would not be surprised if the socialist or even the communist projects also came back to life in 800 or 1000 years—and maybe very successfully too. What I do not believe in at all is the end of communism, because I think that this dream of withdrawing from time and living in eternity is an everlasting dream" (Abdullah and Benzer 2011: 84). Two: in our culture, the only object that is currently like this mummy that comes back to life is art, which similarly, in the form in which it is kept in our museums and art galleries, is preserved against time and is always able to take on a new meaning or relevance. The work of art, that is, is able to break with all exigency, all sense of capitalist emergency, the shortness of time that capitalism (and, according to Groys, some theory) imposes, and occupy another time: a time of eternity or looking back from the end of things that Groys will call metanoia: "Every work of art indicates the transience of the conditions in which this artwork emerges. What the ancients understood very well was *ars longa, vita brevis*. But the point here is that not only *vita* is *brevis*, but also capitalism is ultimately *brevis*. Capitalism, too, can be outlived" (83). And three: artworks in the museum are exactly one of those objects that exist outside of capitalism and are unable to be exchanged for anything else except other works of art. The space of the museum, properly considered, is a kind of common space, and thus thinking about art in relation to the museum is always to think a certain post-capitalist scenario: "Communism is a Louvre, a British Museum. The circulation of commodities, money, the entire exchange no longer existed. Capitalism was divested of a part of its territory for the purpose of creating something that was meant for eternity and not for time" (84).

We follow Groys' argument here, first through a outlining of his position with regard to the relationship between Plato and the Sophists, which we will see is ultimately that between philosophy and capitalism. We will see Groys defend Plato against the Sophists, which defence he will conceive—along with a number of other thinkers working today—as necessarily involving a break with that otherness and difference associated with post-structuralism and other forms of "weak" thought. Then, we will attempt to elaborate Groys' conception of thought as metanoia, which we might understand as a kind of doubling of what is—and which is the truth not only of Communism, but of all authentic thought (including that of several of the post-structuralists). Finally, we will conclude with a consideration of Groys' extraordinary *The Communist Postscript*, which precisely grasps capitalism (for a moment) as the postscript to Communism, before another Communism.

The Sophists and Paradox

The revolution that marks contemporary philosophy—and the distance that separates it from the long-running hegemony of post-structuralism—is seen nowhere more clearly than in the recent defence of Plato against the Sophists. Of course, it is found in its most high-profile instance in Alain Badiou's advocacy of Plato in his *Being and Event* against—for all of his admiration of him—Gilles Deleuze's championing of the Sophists in his *The Logic of Sense* (see Badiou 2005: 31–7). And Badiou's position has been justified and elaborated at great—indeed, almost inordinate—length by Slavoj Žižek (2012: 52–78) in his recent *Less than Nothing: Hegel and the Shadow of Dialectical Materialism*. But it is a defence that art historian Boris Groys also participates in. In some very important pages in his *The Communist Postscript*, Groys takes as well the side of Plato against the Sophists, arguing that Socrates' "questions break through the smooth, glittering surfaces of sophistical speech and uncover its contradictory, paradoxical core" (Groys 2009: 4).

In an inversion of the commonly held view, that is, it is for Groys the Sophists who do not adequately grasp the paradoxical nature of reason, but rather seek to hide it. While they know that reason is essentially self-contradictory, they attempt in their oratory to construct logical, consistent argumentative positions, which take only one side (the one that is paying them), although they admit the point of view of the other to be equally valid. As a result, the true nature of reason remains obscure, and this leads to the suspicion in their listeners that there is something hidden beneath what they say, a suspicion that the Sophists, for their part, are happy to play on. In fact, for all of the Sophists' denial of the merits of the other side's case, ultimately they are prepared to compromise. However, this compromise is brought about not logically, but through money, involving the compensation of both sides for accepting the arguments of the other. The Sophists—and Groys undoubtedly means to speak here of such figures as politicians and the official representatives of justice in our society—win either way, which leads to Groys' definition of a commodity (for example, the money the Sophists are paid with). A commodity, says Groys, is a paradox that has lost its paradoxical quality.

As opposed to this, it is Plato who exposes paradox in his dialogues, both through his analysis of the speech of others and in his own (unanalysed) speech. As a result of such self-exposure, Plato is able to win the trust of his listeners, so much so that, as Groys suggests, "for lengthy periods of time" (Groys 2009: 5)—although this is complicated and we will have to come back to it in what follows—they are spellbound and unable to tear themselves away from him. Here precisely—and this is the basis of the paradoxical and self-contradictory nature of philosophy for Groys—the philosopher is not a "wise man," but merely a "seeker after wisdom" (6). They do not stand anywhere outside of the paradoxes they are remarking on, as with the "dark spaces" (11) of the Sophists. On the contrary, the Platonic philosopher operates entirely within the realm of the paradoxes they speak of, in the "bright light" or "effulgence" (17) of an exposure that would leave no room for "darkness"

We might see more clearly the distinction between Plato and the Sophists in some subtle passages Groys writes concerning the relation of each to *doxa* or common opinion. Of course, it is often suggested that philosophy begins in Ancient Greece because we had there for the first time with its commercial markets and trade with other countries the free exchange of ideas. And yet—and Deleuze and Guattari argue this also in their *What is Philosophy?*—it is the *breaking with* this opinion that constitutes philosophy's defining task (see Deleuze and Guattari 1994: 99–100). And, in many ways, Groys retraces the same trajectory. He begins by noting the situation of our own modern democracies, crossed as they are by rumours, paranoias, conspiracies, characterised we might say by the collapse of the symbolic order. Within this democratic space, each person is entitled to their own opinion, regardless of its truth or coherence. No opinion rules out any other; no opinion understands itself as ruling out any other. (When Groys speaks of the "dark spaces" behind the pseudo-logical surfaces of the Sophists, into which their listeners can enter, he means to speak of the way both that these Sophists'—think here of someone like radio shock jocks—arguments are constructed so that we see ourselves reflected in them and that there is a fundamental lack of curiosity about others' arguments.) And, as Groys (2010: 137–8) goes on to argue in his essay 'Religion in the Age of Digital Reproduction,' even the famous religious freedom of the West works like this. Not only do the various religions have to tolerate each other, but the atheist has to tolerate the religious, as the religious has to tolerate the atheist. There can be no attempt to refute another's belief by reference to any "fact" or "truth," or to persuade them that one is right. (Indeed, Groys sees much post-structuralist theory working in this manner: its emphasis on "otherness" or "difference" does not truly confront the capitalist marketplace, but merely adds another voice, another opinion, to the chorus).

What, then, is the proper philosophical response to this? Certainly, in one way, the philosopher is only able to add another opinion to all of the others. But, in another way, they must seek to formulate the rule of these conflicting opinions. In a first step, they must note that there are a number of conflicting opinions and that, moreover, each opinion—although it would deny this—clearly acknowledges that there are other opinions, and that it would make no sense outside of them. This insight is essential, but it is ultimately no more than that of the market itself: each opinion is only one of a number of conflicting opinions, without a common measure, but with these differences able to be reconciled via the medium of money. It is the market in the end that judges which opinions are best and by how much. No, the real philosophical insight is not that opinions are contradictory, but that each opinion is *self-contradictory*, divided from itself, in a way it cannot master or subsume. As Groys (2009: 8–9) writes: "Every speaker says what he intends to mean, but he also says the opposite of this ... For this reason, the philosopher can conceive of what is common to all discourses, the totality of discourses, and can transcend mere opinion in this way without thereby asserting a claim to the truth of his own opinion."

Groys' argument here, however, is complex. As he suggests, it is not a matter of the philosopher simply formulating the truth of the plurality of opinion. This is not only because the philosopher does not offer their own truth but only their own paradox, but also because it is only this paradox that allows us to see this plurality of opinion for the first time. It is what Groys (2009: 16) calls the "icon" that allows us to see for an instant—again, the temporality is very complex—the whole of language. In other words, this totality does not exist before its paradox. (Groys is using the word "icon" here in its Christian meaning of an image that does not refer to a pre-existing original or referent.) It is in this sense that we would say that the contemporary marketplace of ideas is both a falling short of the paradox of philosophy—a not-yet—and a forgetting or covering-over of the paradox of philosophy—an already-past (which is why Groys speaks of the icon holding for only a certain time). It is for this reason that Groys (2009: 25) argues both that philosophy must appropriate the "diabolical reason" of the market—which would otherwise remain hidden and undeveloped—and that the sophism of the market will come to cover over this paradox in order to enclose or "privatise" it again. (At this point, Groys comes close to Hardt and Negri's arguments (2000: 301–3) concerning the way that capitalism draws on or parasitises the previously liberated or deterritorialised state of paradoxical opinion or "commons"—and, indeed, Groys has an essay entitled 'Privatizations, or the Artificial Paradises of Post-Communism' in his 2008 collection *Art Power* that speaks of just this.) Although formal logic has its own interest in doing away with the third or *tertium*, following the law of the excluded middle, this compromise is nevertheless always actually brought about by money. This is the inevitable compromising—selling out—of the paradox by both the Sophists and the market. Capitalism does, in fact, get close to self-contradiction. It involves a constant overturning or transgression, but like the Sophist it is assured of a profit no matter what the outcome. As Groys (2009: 24) writes in *The Communist Postscript*: "If the worker receives higher wages, they can buy more and profits grow. If the worker receives lower wages, savings can be made on labour power and profits continue to grow." It is for this reason that capitalism, like the Sophist, can give the impression that it is not entirely caught up in its own self-contradiction, that somehow behind it there is a "diabolical subject" manipulating these contradictions for its own unknown ends.

Philosophy and Metanoia

How, then, does the philosopher expose the *self-contradiction* of opinion and the marketplace? How do they actually produce or bring about paradox? Groys provides several examples of this philosophical paradox in action. He begins, of course, with Plato's Socrates, who does not merely uncover the paradoxes of others, but also makes (unremarked) paradox the basis of his method. Groys then suggests Descartes, whose decision to suspend all opinion while living through a moment of doubt is just as paradoxical or self-contradictory as the decision to negate or affirm all opinion. And Husserl and the *epoché* or bracketing of his transcendental reduction is another form of this. The post-structuralists too, like Bataille, Foucault, Lacan, Deleuze and Derrida, are understood—whatever else their limitations—as striving for an ever more radical and self-contradictory paradox. And Stalin himself, like every Communist leader a proper philosopher, was also a great proponent of paradox. As Groys (2009: 29) writes in *The*

Communist Postscript, casting Communism as precisely the fulfilment of the original Platonic inspiration: "The [Communist] exposure, production and appropriation of paradox are genuine philosophical achievements, which empower the philosophers to rule." (Interestingly, given the recent work of Žižek, Groys considers Hegel, whose dialectical method, of course, involves the holding together of seeming opposites, to be not paradoxical, but finally attempting to construct a discourse that is formally-logically consistent). But, again, how to produce this paradox that reveals or, better, actually produces the whole? How to bring about this state in which—as opposed to the Sophists, who secretly choose sides, or the post-structuralists, whose otherness or difference merely repeats the contradictions of the market—opposites are simultaneously true, that is, authentic self-contradiction? In fact, Groys is not always as good on this as he might otherwise be. Perhaps it is his rejection of Hegel that blinds him. (Hegel's notion of "reflexive determination," in which the identity of a thing is given by its standing in for its opposite, for example, would appear to be very useful for Groys' undertaking). Groys' account is in a way clear in its description, but not so strong on its logic. Certainly, as the example above indicates, paradox involves a particular bracketing or suspension along the lines of Descartes' doubt or Husserl's phenomenological reduction, and even a certain finitising or hastening of time, a bringing on of the end. And in a later chapter of *The Communist Postscript*, Groys will speak of this philosophical strategy using the word "metanoia" (2009: 106), a religious term referring to a change or alteration from the object to the context surrounding the object, brought about by adopting a different perspective, say a shift from life to the after-life.

Indeed, considered properly, "metanoia" in Groys' sense is precisely the attempt to reveal the "transcendental" ground for things. As Groys (2009: 108–9) describes it: "Metanoia, understood as the transition from the usual, worldly, natural perspective to an alternative, universal and metaphysical perspective, entailed the abstraction from one's worldly, 'natural' perspective." This is why paradox allows the whole—in the sense of both the object and its context—to be seen for the first time. And it is for this reason that it is only paradox—and not mere contradiction—that involves the question of both a thing and its opposite. That is, how again to produce the authentic philosophical statement, in which we have at once A and not-A? The point is that, no matter how subversive or transgressive, extreme or extravagant we make a statement, we do not necessarily have a paradox (and this is once more Groys' position with regard to both Bataille and the whole post-structuralist tradition that came after him and so much self-proclaimed radical art). All of this is merely different, another opinion for the sake of the market. It is not authentically self-contradictory. We only have true opposites, paradox, self-contradiction, when we attempt to formulate that for which all of these various differences (of opinion, of commodities) stand in. Metanoia is the statement of that absence which all that is present takes the place of. Now, the word for that for which all stands in—even in dialectical materialism—is "spirit," which is ultimately a kind of nothingness. This is why, to recall for a moment an argument from Groys' *The Total Art of Stalinism*, Russian poet Velimir Khlebnikov and artist Kazimir Malevich both sought to overcome ordinary linguistic and artistic forms, invent a new language of communicative universality and use it to remodel the world in its image—and do all of this, moreover, on the basis of a certain "nothing," an "all-negating material infinity, a non-objectivity of the world" that "transcended all beliefs and ideologies" (Groys 1992: 31).

However, as Groys' subsequent criticism of Malevich for dubbing his artistic movement Suprematism reveals, this "nothing" is always something; the artist cannot simply transcend all beliefs and ideologies. Malevich falls back into the trap of thinking that his discourse is non-contradictory. This is the unavoidable risk of speaking of the transcendental, which is why the attempt to do so is always self-contradictory, and why Groys can speak of the *necessary* hiding or covering over of paradox, when this is meant to be rather an outcome of the market. It is to point to the fact that the transcendental is always both transcendent and, insofar as we can think it at all, empirical. Groys puts this in precisely Hegelian terms when he speaks the way that, if there is to be metanoia, there must always be another possible metanoia, in which we ask not merely about the context but about the context of that context, leading back, as Groys (2009: 107) suggests, to the "'earlier perspective at a different level of reflection." It is to begin to think—in what Hegel indeed called "reflexive determination"—not that there is some opposite beyond things for which they stand in, but that things are their own opposites, stand in *for themselves*. (And this would be Groys' response to those "deviationists," a term of Soviet obloquy, who insisted that with regard to dialectical materialism it was not enough to assert the thesis, it was necessary also to deny and negate the opposite of what just had been asserted: "The negation of what has been asserted appears to be a trivial consequence of the first assertion itself. But for dialectical materialism, this second step is logically independent of the first step, and moreover it is this second step that is critical" [Groys 2009: 40–41]. In fact, Groys' argument is that this first step is *its own* denial and negation. Things are already the opposite of their opposite. Or, to employ a Hegelian vocabulary, they are the negation of their negation).

It is for this reason that metanoia leaves us in a radically undecidable position. Dialectical philosophy does not merely propose some new and unrealised transcendental condition for things. Groys (2009: 105) breaks with any Kantian Enlightenment-style infinite striving, which he compares to the "bad infinity" of capitalism. Rather, the radical "anti-utopianism" of the Russian revolution—which is also a form of utopianism—tells us that we are in a world that is post-Enlightenment and post-modern, in which there is no longer any rational approach towards the real. Utopia is at once already here (insofar as art and language always go further than capitalism) and can never be realised (not only because capitalism still persists, but because this utopia could always be the work of the devil). Metanoia operates as a kind of pure doubling of the world, at once irrefutable and undemonstrable, rendering everything at once the same and different. As Groys (2009: 125–6) writes of Soviet Communism: "It is impossible to dismiss the famous claim 'it is done' from the world once and for all simply by referring to factual injustices and shortcomings, for it involved a paradoxical identity of utopia and anti-utopia, hell and paradise, damnation and salvation." And the example Groys uses to explain this performative doubling—very reminiscent of Baudrillard's arguments concerning simulation, which are also a perfect instance of the paradoxical metanoia Groys is advocating—is terrorism. The paradox of terrorism, or the so-called "war on terror" we seem to be involved in, is not only that random accidents can now always be understood as coming about as a result of terrorist acts, but that the fight against terrorism—with its state of constant surveillance and curtailing of civil liberties—would be the very terrorism anti-terrorism fights against (both in the sense that these infringements are what would occur if we were somehow taken over by terrorists and that these infringements, as seen recently in Britain, are actually what produces home-grown terrorists) (see Baudrillard 1983: 31–2).

We might return once more to Groys' argument that French philosophy's resistance against capitalism fails because capitalism is already self-subverting, because it can be not-A just as easily as A. No, we would not oppose capitalism by means of the Other but only by proposing another Reason. It would be the idea that behind capitalism there is always a possible conspiracy, a diabolical subject that plays a game it always wins, insofar as it can profit from seemingly opposed outcomes. But then, as Groys (2009: 24–6) goes on to argue, the aim of the philosophical subject—by which he means the revolutionary subject—is to "appropriate" this diabolical logic by means of a doubling in which *it* cannot lose. However, at the same time it must also be admitted that capitalism would not be diabolical before its appropriation like this. This is why Groys speaks of the "suspicion" that there is not just capitalism but as well a certain conspiracy behind capitalism. This doubling would undoubtedly be a slander, but, as Groys argues, following Kojève, the ultimate responsibility for this slander would be seen to lie not with the one making it but with the one about whom it is made. And this is why Groys speaks of this capitalist diabolical reason as a kind of "obscure object" that cannot be seen because it can only ever be reproduced as "black on black." For precisely the aim of these doubling hypotheses is to bring out this obscure object by introducing a split between it and itself, between the world and its transcendental condition, between black and black. It is an exercise motivated by the belief that there is a subject or reason lurking behind appearances; but this subject would not exist until after the attempt to bring it out by means of this doubling, and indeed this doubling *is* the very subject. The philosophical task begins with a kind of suspicion, and yet it does not want it entirely confirmed, when it would turn into merely another opinion or commodity. (If Groys speaks of a paradox that conceals its paradoxical nature by becoming a commodity, we might equally suggest that a paradox that entirely reveals its paradoxical nature also becomes a commodity. In a way, one paradox is revealed only by another, in what suggests itself as an infinite cascade of paradoxes.)

Following this logic, Groys (2009: 29) suggests that Communism is revolutionary not by opposing capitalism but proposing itself as the diabolical reason behind capitalism. It puts itself forward as an "answer" to the paradoxical nature of capitalism and its commodities, which means as the repressed contradiction behind capitalism. And the great achievement of Soviet philosophy, particularly under Stalin, is the absolute liberation of paradox in this sense. A proper Soviet philosophy would exist, insists Groys, but only insofar as it is able to think its opposite. As he says: "The demand to think and feel globally and with the whole of language was paradoxical insofar as it presupposed that the thought of the Soviet person was both Soviet and anti-Soviet at the same time" (Groys 2009: 70). And the most profound sign of this coming together of Soviet and anti-Soviet thinking is the idea that capitalism is possible only because of Communism, that capitalism becomes visible only from the perspective of Communism. Indeed, this doubling is repeated from both ends, in line with that paradoxical temporality we have previously attempted to outline. We would say that Communism comes *after* capitalism, as the essential linguistic freeing-up of the restricted economy of the circulation of commodities, This would be Groys' argument that in capitalism large-scale social projects are always unfinished because of a lack of funds, that capitalism is a necessarily unfinished project: "The reason why things are finite, why they are present at all, why they have a form, why they are offered to the gaze of the observer as these concrete objects, is because they are under-financed" (94). And, against this, Communism seeks to grasp things from a radically metanoic change of perspective (again, like that of the religious after-life), which at once sees things as complete and opens them up to another entirely different destiny. But perhaps more profoundly—and paradoxically—Communism can also be seen as coming *before* capitalism. This is Groys' idea that the true advent of capitalism in the former Soviet Union is to be understood not as any kind of defeat or surpassing of Communism, but on the contrary as the last act of Communism itself, its *perestroika* or auto-dissolution, as it were. That is, capitalism is possible only because of a prior Communism: the commodity is a forgetting of the paradoxical nature of reason; exchange value is merely the compromise struck between various incommensurable and self-contradictory positions. Again, as Groys explains: "Passing from a project to its context is a necessity for anyone who seeks to grasp the whole. And because the context of Soviet Communism was capitalism, the next step in the realization of Communism had to be the transition from Communism to capitalism. The project of building Communism in a single country is not refuted by this transition, but is instead confirmed and definitively realized" (103–4). If capitalism makes the contradictions of Communism clearer by turning them into commodities, capitalism for its part is able to be explained only because of a certain Communist Reason. As Groys (2009: 123–4) writes of the recent period of post-Soviet privatisation or appropriation of previously Communist resources: "In both cases [Communism and post-Communism], private property is equally subordinate to a *raison d'état* ... The post-Communist situation is distinguished by the fact that it reveals the artificiality of capitalism, in that it presents the emergence of capitalism as a purely political project of social reorganization, and not as the result of a 'natural' process of economic development." In other words, if there is a Communist postscript, it is written by Communism itself. Or, indeed—and this brings us back to the Christian origin of the notion of metanoia—if Communism lives on after its death, it is in a sense only because it is already dead. It lives its life as a kind of after-life, as its own postscript, as it were. It lives—to recall what we began by speaking of here—as a work of art lives on, as a "living corpse" that is able to be revived at any moment.

Communism and the Work of Art

The Communist Postscript is in many regards the logical continuation of Groys' *The Total Art of Stalinism*, originally published in 1988. There, in a now famous thesis, Groys argues that Stalinism is to be understood not as the enemy of, reaction to or censoring of the avant-garde of Mayakovsky and Malevich, but as its most profound continuation. It is Stalin who inherits—and ultimately realises—the avant-garde ambition for the total making-over of society. In a sense—and here we have a premonition of Groys' analysis to come—Stalin represents a more complete "nothing" than even the Suprematism of Malevich, for he adds the figure of the "diabolical" to it. He is the author who is always missing in the avant-garde, the author exactly in the sense of "demiurge" (Groys 1992: 56), who opens what is up to its transcendental conditions. Indeed, the only thing that Groys does not like about Stalinist art at this stage—this is where he differs from his later *Postscript*—is its belief that it had effectively brought history to an end. In a complex formulation, uniting modernism, post-modernism and anti-modernism, Groys (79) writes that we have post-modernism as the anti-modern in the (Stalinist) modernist idea of a totally harmonious society brought about by the halting of history. This is why Groys sees Stalinist art—again, against its common conception and already as an indication of his later taste for paradox—as essentially eclectic, citational and heterogeneous. And it is a post-historicality that Soviet dissident art (for example, Ilya Kabakov and Erik Bulatov), for all of its apparent opposition to Stalinism, would share. But what Communism did not foresee—and how could it in 1988, the year before the fall of the Berlin Wall?—was that history had one more twist in store for it: the turning of it into capitalism, capitalism as the completion of Communism.

We have the same paradoxical Communism in Groys' essay 'The Logic of Equal Aesthetic Rights' from *Art Power*. In this essay, Groys argues for a certain universalising or making-equal of all images. But, read carefully, this universality is not a mere plurality. Again, Groys sees the post-modern plurality of simple difference or transgression as merely standing in for the market. Rather, this universality is to be grasped only through paradox, or this universality must itself be paradoxical. In 'The Logic of Equal Aesthetic Rights,' Groys brilliantly inverts the usually understood relationship between the museum and the mass media, between what we might call elitism and populism. In fact, it is not the mass media or popular taste that opens up the otherwise closed or restricted canon of museum or high art images. On the contrary, it is the museum that challenges the prevailing consensus—the consensus of both the market and the media—as to what is (or can be recognised as) the shocking and different. The paradox of the museum is that a new work can enter it only if it resembles nothing inside if it. But implied in this is something more than mere "opinion." The new work of art is also *about* this newness, *about* this break it makes with other works of art. It might be able to enter the museum only insofar as it is different from all of the other works in it, but it is also a difference that allows us to see all of these other works for the first time, or at least allows us to see them in a new way. In a complex sense—which bears some relation to what we were saying a moment ago about that fleeting moment during which the listeners are under the speaker's spell in Plato—the new work of art attempts to state the conditions of possibility of all of those other works of art already in the museum. The avant-garde, as Groys (2010: 111) says, produces "transcendental images, in the Kantian [but, as we will see, not quite Kantian] sense of the term." Each new image—as new—is the image that all images now stand in for. But this is paradoxical because this new image is at once, therefore, the same as and different from all other images, which—it demonstrates—were also originally like this. It is for this reason that Groys can speak of each new image at once "clarifying and confusing" (116) the others. That is, again—and here Groys renovates the logic of American art critic Harold Rosenberg in his *The Tradition of the New*: Groys is profoundly *modernist* at this point—the image is new only insofar as it reveals all of the others as the same, insofar as it is speaks of what is common to all of them. In fact, as we have seen, this very "wholeness" or "'equality" could not have been seen before this new image. But, it must be emphasised, each new addition has to be able to do this before entering the museum. This is why modernism has constantly to be renewed in order to continue or, to put it otherwise, modernism—in almost a Beckettian sense—is always beginning again from zero. As Groys (2009: 112) writes in *The Communist Postscript*: "Metanoia leads to a renunciation—namely the renunciation of always doing the same thing, of always following the same path, always seeking to ride out further in some bad infinity. Badiou speaks about fidelity to the revolutionary event. But fidelity to revolution is fidelity to infidelity."

Paradoxically, then, each new image aims at the equality of all images by being the single one different from all of them. This image is therefore self-contradictory, not so much in the sense that it is both the same and different (this will be realised at different times: it is always another that speaks of how it is the same) as because it speaks of all images as the same while it regards itself as different. This is undoubtedly the modern image's (for example, Warhol's) complex relationship to capitalism: it at once stands outside of what it speaks of, like the Sophists, hoping to profit from either alternative (the same or different), and it is a critique of the capitalist necessity to have one image different from another. All of this is why in the essay 'The Weak Universalism' Groys speaks—perhaps against his earlier Kantianism—of all new images being at once transcendental and empirical. Again, it would be not simply because they have to be visibly manifested in order to be art, but because, if each new image posits itself as transcendental, it can do so only by rendering all images as empirical. The new arises not merely to replace what has become old and familiar, but to show that what we have previously taken to be new is itself old and familiar. This is why Groys' "taste" prefers not the otherness or difference of post-modernism but the uniformity or regularity of something like the Bauhaus. It is undoubtedly because from the beginning it realises not merely that all other images are equal but also that its own are equal, seen from the point of view of the transcendental condition it introduces. It is why Groys (2008: 29) speaks, for instance, of Duchamp's readymade—one of the great "transcendental" works of art—as introducing not a difference but a "difference beyond difference": it is a difference that allows all other images to be seen as different; the variety of possible images to be universal; the entire range of visual experience to be covered in the images' difference from each other. The avant-garde work of art does not so much repeat a difference, even a critical one, such as race, gender or class, which society already formulates for itself, but invents a transcendental difference, a difference that does not yet exist, which allows us to see all of those other differences, that is, formulate the actually-existing field of art as such in its sameness or comparability.

But all of this must be treated with great caution. Groys in *The Communist Postscript* speaks of the way that there can be any number of philosophical paradoxes because these paradoxes do not affect each other; but it is perhaps also true to say that each new entry to the museum becomes harder and harder because each has to double, that is, reveal the transcendental condition of, all of the others. Put simply, it gets more difficult as time goes on to make a work that at once looks like and does not look like other works of art. It is in this sense that we must understand Groys' point that modern art is not a series of liberations or breakings of taboo, which make art easier, but rather a series of reductions or renunciations, a constant introduction of limits or things that can no longer be done, which make art harder. And this is Groys' point in 'The Weak Universalism': that any proposed universal must constantly be getting weaker, insofar as it has to keep on including all of those previous "weak" universals. It is just this "weakness" that is Groys' unemphatic, almost invisible avant-garde art—it is what connects Malevich's *Black Square*, Duchamp's readymades, Fischli and Weiss's remakes of Duchamp's readymades as fabricated products and the Slovenian collective Irwin's *Corpse of Art* (2003). It is also what explains for Groys the revival of religion and religious images in an age of digitality (and let us not forget that Groys [2008: 29–30] refers to Duchamp's *Fountain* as a "Christ" among things and the art of the readymade as a "Christianity of the artworld"—in part at least because Christ too in his difference from us constituted us all as the same).

Why is it exactly, Groys asks, that religious images are so suited to the era of mechanical reproduction, when this has previously always been associated with the loss of aura? In his essay 'Religion in the Age of Digital Reproduction,' Groys makes the point that what characterises fundamentalism is an adherence not to some inner spiritual truth but to the external form of ritual, by which he means the repeated performance of belief and not belief itself. But Groys then goes on to invert the view that this adherence to the letter is the sign of a "dead" rather than a "living" religion. On the contrary, it is the living religions in their flexibility and adaptation to changing circumstances that are dying today and the dead ones in their observance of outer form and the letter that are flourishing. As Groys writes: "Thus, contemporary religious fundamentalism may be regarded as the most radical product of the European Enlightenment and the materialist [we would add dialectical materialist] view of the world. Religious fundamentalism is religion after the death of the spirit, the loss of spirituality" (Groys 2010: 143). That is, if we can say this, if fundamentalism reduces sprit to the letter, this is only because for it this letter is the spirit. Conventional religions, in seeking to adapt themselves, universalise themselves, propose themselves as different and as responsive to difference, reduce themselves to the status of "opinion," and will always eventually run out of the circumstances in which they apply. They are not truly transcendental, and will die out in wishing to retain some "inner" spirit or content outside the letter or law, no matter how minimal. On the other hand, fundamentalism, in being a kind of nothing, in having no inner content but existing only n its reproduction, will live on forever. And this is indeed like digital reproduction, seemingly the very antithesis of these "primitive," non-Western religions. Again, in one of Groys' startling inversions of common sense, he insists that what characterises digital reproduction is precisely not its unchanging code, the way that unlike analogue it reproduces itself perfectly, but the fact that it is now transmissible across a potentially infinite number of plateaus, in a potentially infinite variety of circumstances. Indeed, that apparently "unchanging" code is never seen as such: it is already reproduced, different from itself, from the very beginning (see Groys 2010: 147–9). And this is, for all of Groys' criticism of it, the deepest truth of Christianity. Again, not only is God's Word not some unchanging core of doctrinal orthodoxy, but—as historically has always been the case—only whatever its listeners take from it. And, more than this—this is what allows it to break with *doxa* and become a true, self-fulfilling prophecy—its proper lesson just *is* this fact. The fundamental content of Christ's teachings is the very scene of instruction or transmission itself. Put simply, the word of God is always different, but it is also *about* this difference, that is, it is always different from itself (and one because of the other). As Groys (2009: 73) says, in an undeniably religious locution: "Only those who are themselves flames can pass through the flames unburnt."

All of this accounts for Groys' interest in the new participatory media—blogging, Facebook, Twitter—in which the participants are the audience. Not only, argues Groys, are such social media indebted to the practices of the neo-avant-garde artists of the 1960s, but they actually come to realise the dreams of such utopians as Joseph Beuys that everyone become an artist (in something of the same way that Stalin came to realise the dreams of the Constructivists). The idea of actually becoming an artist when everybody is already an artist, therefore, is a weak gesture, but it is not altogether nothing. Groys writes at the end of his essay

'The Production of Sincerity' that "when the viewer is involved in the artistic practice from the outset, every piece of criticism uttered becomes self-criticism ... To put it bluntly, it is now better to be a dead artist than a bad artist. Though the artist's decision to relinquish exclusive authorship would seem primarily to be in the interest of empowering the viewer, his sacrifice ultimately benefits the artist by liberating his or her work from the cold eye of the uninvolved viewer's judgement" (Groys 2010: 49). It is, of course, the fundamentally Christian idea of the artist living on through their disciples that is at stake here, with the undoubtedly paradoxical corollary that it is the artist's death that is necessary to allow them to live on. And Groys' own critical writing—pursued primarily today through the internet in such journals as *e-flux*—follows a similar logic. It is transcendental, unsurpassable, indispensable, precisely in its weakness, its unemphaticness, its non-judgmentality, even its self-erasure and self-contradictions. In a radical sense, as Groys admits, it is not even critical, in the sense of negating, excluding or opposing to the world as it is the way it should be. Rather, Groys' discourse attempts simply to double the world, opposing we might say the world only to itself. The world now, after the revealing of its transcendental condition, which is nothing else but more of the world, is at once unchanged and totally transformed. Like the world after Communism. Indeed, as Groys says of the utopian ambitions of Communism, in a description that applies also to his own practice: "The politics of inclusion was pursued by many Russian and Eastern European artists even after the break up of the Communist regime. One might say that it is the extension of the paradise of real Socialism in which everything is accepted that had previously been excluded ... This kind of radicalized utopian inclusivity was often misunderstood as irony, but it is rather a post-historical idyll that sought analogies instead of differences" (Groys 2008: 170). And Groys' point ultimately is that this utopia has already been realised. Groys is not only a Communist art historian, but the world is already Communist in the most profound sense: it includes everything.

In Groys' writing on art, there are only rarely images or examples. This would be because, as we have tried to make clear, his writing is transcendental: it attempts to propose the conditions that make all images the same. (This is why Groys' writing so suits the internet or, at least, so brilliantly adapts itself to the internet: in the essays Groys writes for *e-flux*, for example, it is almost as though the images chosen to illustrate his argument are arbitrary, nothing more than a random sampling of a database on contemporary art. At once no image could illustrate what Groys says about art and any image could be seen to illustrate what he has to say about art.) But one beautiful "image" of what Groys is speaking about is to be found in the essay 'Beyond Diversity' in *Art Power*. It concerns the rebuilding of an exact replica of the Cathedral of Christ in the middle of Moscow in the late 1990s after it had been torn down by Stalin in 1931, with the site remaining empty for many years before being turned into a public swimming pool some time in the 1960s. Groys' obvious point is that in today's post-Soviet society an original ethnic or religious identity is now replayed as ersatz post-modern diversity. But Groys' more subtle point is that between the two copies of the same thing or, indeed, introducing a split between what we might see as the same thing is a certain Communist "void" or "absence." As Groys writes: "The Soviet time manifests itself here as an ecstatic interruption of historical time, as a pure absence, as materialized nothingness, as a void, a blank space. So it seems that if this void disappears, nothing will be changed: the deletion will be deleted, and a copy will become identical with the original" (Groys 2008: 161). And here is the Communist metanoia in a nutshell: a kind of "nothing," as figured by that vacant lot or swimming pool, for which everything that is stands in. It is a nothing that separates what is from itself, turning it into a kind of simulacrum or false copy of itself. So that not only can the pre-Communist only be seen as already Post-Communist, but the post-Communist can only be seen as the harbinger or forerunner of a Communism to come. To attempt to think a post-capitalist scenario is precisely a metanoic gesture of this kind.

References

Abdullah, Hannah and Benzer, Mathias (2011) "… Our Fate as a Living Corpse: An Interview with Boris Groys," *Theory, Culture and Society* 28(2).

Badiou, Alain (2005) *Being and Event*. London: Continuum.

Baudrillard, Jean (1983) *Simulations*. New York: Semiotext(e).

Deleuze, Gilles and Guattari, Félix (1994) *What is Philosophy?* London: Verso.

Groys, Boris (1992) *The Total Art of Stalinism*. Princeton: Princeton University Press.

——— (2008) *Art Power*. Cambridge, Mass.: MIT Press.

——— (2009) *The Communist Postscript*. London: Verso.

——— (2010) *Going Public*. Berlin: Sternberg Press.

Hardt, Michael and Negri, Antonio (2000) *Empire*. Cambridge, Mass: Harvard University Press.

Žižek, Slavoj (2012) *Less than Nothing: Hegel and the Shadow of Dialectical Materialism*. London: Verso.

Index

For Product Safety Concerns and Information please contact our EU
representative GPSR@taylorandfrancis.com Taylor & Francis Verlag GmbH,
Kaufingerstraße 24, 80331 München, Germany

Printed and bound by CPI Group (UK) Ltd, Croydon, CR0 4YY

01/05/2025

01858452-0004